CIVIL WAR WRITING

CONFLICTING WORLDS

New Dimensions of the American Civil War

T. Michael Parrish, Series Editor

CIVIL WAR WRITING

NEW PERSPECTIVES ON
ICONIC TEXTS

Edited by

GARY W. GALLAGHER &
STEPHEN CUSHMAN

LOUISIANA STATE UNIVERSITY PRESS   BATON ROUGE

Published by Louisiana State University Press
Copyright © 2019 by Louisiana State University Press
All rights reserved
Manufactured in the United States of America
First printing

Designer: Barbara Neely Bourgoyne
Typeface: Ingeborg
Printer and binder: Sheridan Books

LIBRARY OF CONGRESS CATALOGING-IN-PUBLICATION DATA
Names: Gallagher, Gary W., editor. | Cushman, Stephen, 1956– editor.
Title: Civil War writing : new perspectives on iconic texts / edited by Gary W. Gallagher and Stephen Cushman.
Description: Baton Rouge : Louisiana State University Press, [2019] | Series: Conflicting worlds : new dimensions of the American Civil War | Includes bibliographical references and index.
Identifiers: LCCN 2018036955| ISBN 978-0-8071-7024-3 (cloth : alk. paper) | ISBN 978-0-8071-7100-4 (pdf) | ISBN 978-0-8071-7101-1 (epub)
Subjects: LCSH: United States—History—Civil War, 1861–1865—Sources. | United States—History—Civil War, 1861–1865—Personal narratives. | United States—History—Civil War, 1861–1865—Literature and the war. | American literature—19th century—History and criticism. | War in literature.
Classification: LCC E464 .C57 2019 | DDC 973.7/8—dc23
LC record available at https://lccn.loc.gov/2018036955

For John L. Nau III, with gratitude on behalf of
students, scholars, and the public for his unstinting support
of Civil War–era studies at the University of Virginia

CONTENTS

CIVIL WAR WRITING

Introduction

STEPHEN CUSHMAN AND GARY W. GALLAGHER

"Writing—the art of communicating thoughts to the mind, through the eye—is the great invention of the world." So Abraham Lincoln told the audience for his "Lecture on Discoveries and Inventions," delivered in Jacksonville, Illinois, on February 11, 1859. The defeat by Stephen A. Douglas just over his shoulder, and the address at Cooper Institute one year away, Lincoln took time between debating the territorial expansion of slavery and running for the presidency in the face of disunion to contemplate the power of writing, so "great, very great in enabling us to converse with the dead, the absent, and the unborn, at all distances of time and of space." Speaking the day before his fiftieth birthday, he could not know how truly and prophetically he spoke, both about his own writing and about writing arising from the war that overshadowed most of the rest of his life.[1]

This volume gathers new essays by scholars who have been asked to focus on significant writing about the Civil War by participants who lived through it, whether as civilians or combatants, southerners or northerners, women or men, blacks or whites. We include examples of iconic writings that influenced many generations of readers and scholars. The word "iconic" has several meanings and connotations. In religious contexts, an icon is an image to which people attribute special value or power. In secular contexts, the word has come to mean something widely recognized or well established, as in an iconic brand name, especially something characterized by particular excellence or distinction. Lincoln's Gettysburg Address would be an example of an iconic work, one with lasting powers that for many readers blur the boundaries between religious and secular. Several of the works discussed in the following pages, such as the memoirs of generals, will be familiar to many, but other works may not. Introducing the unfamiliar to wider acquaintance and rereading the familiar in unfamiliar ways are among the aims of this volume. In all cases the editors have encouraged contributors to attend to what makes these works "great, very great in enabling us to converse with the dead, the absent, and the unborn, at all distances of time and of space." Although the works discussed in these essays have considerable documentary value as supporting evidence for historical and biographical narratives, they also have considerable value as deliberately designed communications of "thoughts to the mind, through the eye." The following essays explore this latter value in various ways, some attending to differences among drafts and editions of particular works, some listening closely to fluctuations in tone or voice, some looking at features of structure and expository strategy, some tracing responses in private correspondence or published reviews.

One assumption behind this collection is that certain easy oppositions or antitheses cannot stand or long endure. Although they do not assume or mean to imply that all of the contributors necessarily share their views, the editors believe that just as Loreta Velasquez's pseudo-memoir *The Woman in Battle* (1876) upsets, or at least shakes the stability of, some conventional pairings (civilian-combatant, southerner-northerner, woman-man) so the works discussed by the following essays challenge two overused distinctions of diminishing worth—the first that of military history versus nonmilitary history, the second that of history versus literature. With respect to the first distinction, the productive conversation about the role of military history in the history of the United States between 1861 and 1865, conducted predominantly by Civil War historians, is fruitfully ongoing.[2]

The second distinction, that between history and literature, has a revealing history of its own, one that could begin with the etymology of *story*, which descends, through *history*, from Greek *histōr* (ἵστωρ), "one who knows" or "wise one." First attested in English in the early thirteenth century, *story* remained synonymous with *history*, a narrative of past events, through the fifteenth. But then, as early as 1500, the two words parted ways, *story* beginning to shade in a different direction, toward that of fiction, according to the fifth definition of the *Oxford English Dictio-*

nary: "A narrative of real, or more usually fictitious events, designed for the entertainment of the hearer or reader; a series of traditional or imaginary incidents forming the matter of such a narrative; a tale." Although the primary meaning of *literature* is a body of writing (from *litterae* or "letters")—so that, for example, Edward Gibbon's *The History of the Decline and Fall of the Roman Empire* (1776–1789) can be said to belong to English literature—the secondary meaning of imaginative or creative writing has come to dominate vernacular usage. For this reason, if one were to take a course in, say, the Bible as literature, one would infer from the qualifying phrase "as literature" an implicit assumption that the question of historical truth value had been set aside or dismissed altogether.

Fast-forwarding from the sixteenth century to the nineteenth, we see the founding of the Modern Language Association in 1883 and the American Historical Association in 1884. The two associations appeared during a prolific decade that brought the reading public two longtime best sellers, Lew Wallace's *Ben-Hur: A Tale of the Christ* (1880) and Edward Bellamy's *Looking Backward: 2000–1887* (1888). It also brought an abundance of Civil War writing, represented here by Joseph T. Wilson's *The Black Phalanx* (1887), but the outpouring included well-known books by U. S. Grant, George B. McClellan, Philip H. Sheridan, Sam Watkins, and Frank Wilkeson; most of the short Civil War pieces by Ambrose Bierce, both fiction and nonfiction; and the first ten years of the massive undertaking by the Government Printing Office, *The War of the Rebellion: A Compilation of the Official Records of the Union and Confederate Armies* (1880–1901). With the appearance of their separate professional associations, the disciplinary estrangement of history and literature into competing academic specializations, now mutually suspicious, now grudgingly respectful, was only a matter of time. Never mind that the Greeks who gave us the word *history* also invoked Clio, a supernatural muse for the inspired creation of stories about the past.

In the first half of the twentieth century a new interdisciplinary hybrid, in departments known as American Studies or American Civilization, combined the approaches of history and literature, and the founding of the American Studies Association in 1950 reflected the alliance. Like many such alliances, this one had, and still has, both advocates and detractors, differences in attitude often coinciding with fluctuating attitudes of literary scholars between 1883 and the present toward the appropriate uses of history in their work and with fluctuating attitudes of historians during the same span toward theoretical models and nomenclature adopted by literary scholars. Whatever one thinks of the alliance in the case of the Civil War, the subtitles of two important early books, both of them acknowledged antecedents of this volume, reflect two sides of a divide. In 1939, Douglas Southall Freeman published *The South to Posterity: An Introduction to the Writing of Confederate History,* and Robert A. Lively followed in 1957 with *Fiction Fights the Civil War: An Unfinished Chapter in the Literary History of the American People.* Civil War history and the literary history of the American people: where does the boundary between them fall? Borrowing the terms of Lincoln's 1859 lecture in Jacksonville, ought we to assume that one side, the historical, has more to do with discovery, whereas the other, the literary, has more to do with invention? Between the publication of Lively's book and the assembling of this volume, other titles have appeared on either side of this disciplinary analogue of Mason and Dixon's line—laid out in the 1760s to settle a border dispute among colonies without reference to the existing geography of slavery, which flanked the surveyors' demarcation on both sides—foremost among them Edmund Wilson's *Patriotic Gore: Studies in the Literature of the American Civil War* (1962), George M. Frederickson's *The Inner Civil War: Northern Intellectuals and the Crisis of the Union* (1965), and Daniel Aaron's *The Unwritten War: American Writers and the Civil War* (1973). Since the last of these books appeared in the wake of the Civil War centennial, the list of titles has grown steadily through and beyond the sesquicentennial, including *A History of American Civil War Literature* (2016), a collection of essays edited by Coleman Hutchison.

Of the contributors to this last-named volume, two are professional historians while the rest are professors in English or American Studies departments or both. The present volume reverses that ratio; here, with one exception, all the contributors are affiliated with college or university departments of history. If the assumptions behind the present volume are sound, this difference should point to enriching complementarity of the kind the editors hope to advance with respect to Civil War writing, not to the competitive territoriality of academic colonies squabbling over borders. It is the firm conviction here that the writing of history does not monopolize discovery, nor does the writing of literature, in the vernacular sense of imaginative or creative work, monopolize invention. Because the root meaning of *invention* is "to come upon" or "find," it should not be difficult to see that the distinction between discovery and invention is yet another flimsy one.

That said, this volume differs from the ambitiously titled *History of American Civil War Literature* by not presuming to offer up a comprehensive history of Civil War writing. Quite the contrary: this is the first volume of an ongoing work-in-progress, which in turn represents a larger institutional undertaking. Because of the generosity of John L. Nau III, a center bearing his name was formed in 2015 at the University of Virginia to further the study of Civil War history. The UVA Nau Center holds annual spring conferences open to the public, hosts speakers for smaller events throughout the year, supports research among graduate and undergraduate students, maintains a website that includes short contributions by many hands, and, with this volume, aims to invite a wider Civil War readership, academic and nonacademic, into its conversations.

The nine essays in this volume assemble recent work by scholars who kindly obliged the editors by setting aside other projects in order to contribute discoveries and inventions to this one. Several scholars not included here are at work on essays that will appear in a subsequent volume, and their contributions will complement this offering, which for no reasons other than individual commitments and calendars includes only one writer from the U.S. high command, William Tecumseh Sherman, and no writer from the ranks of so-called common soldiers, either U.S. or Confederate. In other respects the editors are pleased with the balance of both writers discussed and their respective genres: history, memoir, journal or diary, novel, and a pungent example of literary fraud posing as autobiographical narrative.

A few words need to be said about organization. Among works discussed in this volume, the first to appear was Jubal Anderson Early's *A Memoir of the Last Year of the War of Independence, in the Confederate States of America, Containing an Account of the Operations of His Commands in the Years 1864 and 1865,* published in Toronto by Lovell and Gibson in 1866. Because Early was also the first writer to be born, in 1816, organization by simple chronology would suggest that Kathryn Shively's essay about him should lead off; however, chronology among these works is anything but simple. In Early's case, his subsequent *Autobiographical Sketch and Narrative of the War between the States,* though composed in Canada from 1867 to 1868 and only slightly revised during the remainder of his life, did not appear until

1912, when it was published in Philadelphia by J. B. Lippincott eighteen years after his death. In three other cases, those of Mary Boykin Chesnut, Charlotte Forten Grimké, and Edward Porter Alexander, the gaps between composition and publication are also large, with the most complete editions of their writings appearing in 1981, 1988, and 1989, respectively. Complications mount as, in the case of Chesnut, earlier editions of the diaries had appeared in 1905 and 1949, and an edition of her previously unpublished diaries followed in 1984. The first edition of Grimké's journal appeared in 1953. Alexander, like Early, wrote two books, the first of which, *Military Memoirs of a Confederate: A Critical Narrative,* was published in New York by Scribner's in 1907, three years before his death but eighty-two before the second, his very different *Fighting for the Confederacy: The Personal Recollections of General Edward Porter Alexander.*

In the end, chronological arrangement, whether by birth, composition, or publication, has not guided the arrangement of the essays, which instead have found their order according to an editorial sense of rhythm and equilibrium. First in line is Elizabeth R. Varon's dexterous treatment of Joseph T. Wilson's undervalued book *The Black Phalanx: A History of the Negro Soldiers of the United States in the Wars of 1775–1812, 1861–1865,* published in Hartford, Connecticut, in 1887. Born in Norfolk, Virginia, in 1837, Wilson served in two black regiments, the Second Louisiana Native Guard and the celebrated Fifty-Fourth Massachusetts Infantry, and was wounded in Florida at the battle of Olustee in February 1864. After the war he became a leading public figure in Virginia as a Republican Party stalwart and officeholder, as well as an author of editorials, poems, speeches, and historical works. Drawing on a range of sources, including Wilson's previously unexamined pension file, Varon follows this early historian of black soldiers through his political efforts in Norfolk and Richmond to win black suffrage, through the writings he produced to advance this cause by deepening historical awareness of the contributions of black veterans, and through his frustrating attempts to secure the pension support he believed was due to him. As Varon conclusively demonstrates, *The Black Phalanx,* Wilson's landmark contribution to the emerging genre of race history, took shape against a background of political struggle and activism from which his literary career cannot be separated.

With William C. Davis's essay on Loreta Janeta Velasquez or Velazquez or Velázquez, also known by a legion of aliases, we enter the complex world of nineteenth-century American imposture. It was a world aided by burgeoning news and advertising industries that whetted public appetite for spectacle and celebrity, without which P. T. Barnum could never have flourished and his friend Samuel Clemens, traveling under his own alias as Mark Twain, could never have scored so many satiric successes. According to Davis, Velasquez's contribution to Civil War writing falls under the heading of what many would call "hoax," an eighteenth-century contraction of the *hocus* in *hocus-pocus*. With formidably thorough research, Davis unearths and unmasks many levels of deceptive hocus-pocus, both in Velasquez's public self-presentations as a Confederate soldier and in her book *The Woman in Battle: A Narrative of the Exploits, Adventures, and Travels of Madame Loreta Janeta Velazquez, Otherwise Known as Lieutenant Harry T. Buford, Confederate States Army,* published in 1876 in Richmond and in Hartford. Much more than an instance of revisionary debunking, Davis's lively essay closes by scrutinizing twentieth- and twenty-first-century efforts to interpret Velasquez and her book in the contexts of gender and racial identities.

Stephen Cushman's essay shifts the focus from a dissembling grifter to a pair of the war's leading military figures, Joseph Eggleston Johnston and William Tecumseh Sherman, and their accounts of the surrender proceedings at Durham Station, North Carolina, in late April 1865. In *Narrative of Military Operations, Directed, During the Late War Between the States by Joseph E. Johnston* and *Memoirs of General William T. Sherman,* published in 1874 and 1875 respectively by D. Appleton and Company of New York, the generals wrote about their negotiations for the capitulation of the Confederacy's last large field army. Cushman explores not only the ways in which Sherman's account played off Johnston's, but also how the publisher used the Union hero's book to boost anemic sales of his old opponent's. Primarily interested in scoring points against Jefferson Davis and John Bell Hood in *Narrative of Military Operations,* Johnston treated Sherman with considerable respect, and Sherman returned the favor in *Memoirs.* Cushman goes beyond a close examination of the two men's use of language and literary strategies to consider how their postwar relationship figured in a powerful reconciliationist narrative that thrived by the late nineteenth century.

J. Matthew Gallman turns us to the genre of the popular novel with his engaging discussion of Louisa May Alcott's *Little Women; or, Meg, Jo, Beth and Amy,* originally published in Boston in two parts, the first in 1868, the second in 1869. Certainly the most familiar and widely read of any work treated in this volume—and a staple among more than a century and a half of young female readers—*Little Women* provides the one example of prose fiction discussed here, depending on how one classifies *Woman in Battle*. Having served as a nurse at the Union Hotel Hospital in Georgetown, District of Columbia, to which she was assigned in December 1862, just as the wounded began arriving from the battle of Fredericksburg, Alcott fulfilled the resolve recorded in her journal in April 1861: "I long to be a man; but as I can't fight, I will content myself with working for those who can." Five years after the appearance of *Hospital Sketches* (1863), the short narrative based on her nursing service, Alcott published the first volume of the famous novel Gallman reads as a book about northern domestic life during the war. Attending astutely to the silences of Alcott's invention as well as to its storytelling, he argues that it offers an early example of Civil War memory, a topic he pursues by considering several film versions of *Little Women* as well.[3]

Jubal Anderson Early wrote two memoirs with the dual intention of burnishing his own tarnished reputation and establishing himself as the leading authority on the Confederate military effort in the Eastern Theater. Kathryn Shively's essay reveals the degree to which Early, whose record as a general in Lee's army and as an independent commander in the Shenandoah Valley in 1864 included many high points before culminating in shattering failure, achieved success on both counts. In *A Memoir of the Last Year of the War* (1866), the first book of its kind by any major military figure on either side, and the posthumous *Narrative of the War Between the States* (1912), Early used a detailed evaluation of relative manpower and resources to construct an explanation for Confederate defeat that resonated among former Rebels and enjoyed remarkable longevity. Shively reconstructs the process by which Early sought to establish his credentials as a historian of the war, to create doubt about the validity of Union records and postwar accounts, and to use his presence on many important battlefields to gain additional credibility. The accumulation of detail in his second and much longer narrative, together with a willingness to criticize some former comrades, argues Shively, conveyed a sense of informed and honest analysis that positioned Early among the more important Confederate writers.

Charlotte Forten spent more than eighteen months between late 1862 and mid-1864 in the South Carolina Low Country, where she recorded her thoughts about the experience in five journals. An African American woman with deep ties to abolitionists in Philadelphia and elsewhere, Forten, who was born in 1837, interacted with black refugees—usually called contrabands during the war—and a range of Union officers including Thomas Wentworth Higginson and Robert Gould Shaw, northern missionaries and teachers who had gone south to help freedpeople, and others who found themselves in an area largely abandoned by Confederates. Brenda E. Stevenson, editor of the definitive version of Forten's Civil War journals (1988), illuminates her attitude toward a conflict that initially did not include emancipation as an official goal, her evolving racial identity, her fascination with the Low Country's Gullah/Geechee culture, and her social and romantic life within a biracial community. The journals, not readily available until more than a century and a quarter after their composition, afford readers a revealing glimpse behind the scenes in one of the first areas where large-scale emancipation became a possibility and then a reality.

Sarah E. Gardner's essay introduces South Carolinian Mary Boykin Chesnut, the most famous and perhaps most quoted Confederate diarist. Married to a former U.S. senator who served as an aide to President Jefferson Davis, Chesnut was well situated to comment on prominent individuals and public events. She kept a diary throughout the conflict, which she later edited but left unfinished at her death in 1886. Two versions of the manuscript (which after her postwar revisions was no longer a conventional diary at all) appeared as *A Diary from Dixie* in 1905 and 1949 before historian C. Vann Woodward, in 1981, untangled the history of the "diary" in *Mary Chesnut's Civil War*. Sarah Gardner approaches the author through the analytical lens of what Chesnut read and how that reading shaped the structure of the diary. Moreover, suggests Gardner, only by paying attention to Chesnut's reading can we grasp the interplay between her intellectual imagination and her wartime experiences. No provincial when it came to literary taste, Chesnut generally scorned novels concerned with feminine domestic duties—too much "[p]iety and pie-making" she insisted—and counted William Makepeace Thackeray and Honoré de Balzac among her favorites. What and how Chesnut read, concludes Gardner, helped her navigate immensely trying circumstances and cope with frightful human carnage during the Confederacy's brief history.

Publication in 1903 of John Brown Gordon's *Reminiscences of the Civil War* offered readers a first look at one of the most-cited military accounts produced by the wartime generation. Despite a lack of formal training as an officer, Gordon rose to the rank of major general and ended the conflict as one of Robert E. Lee's most trusted lieutenants. The postwar years brought Gordon high political office from the voters of Georgia and a successful speaking career—two arenas in which he deployed considerable skill in crafting an engaging personal narrative. His *Reminiscences* abound with memorable anecdotes and gripping battle accounts, almost always featuring Gordon playing a leading role as a perceptive soldier whose sound good sense at Gettysburg, the Wilderness, and Cedar Creek ran aground on his superiors' stubbornness or lack of imagination. Many scholars have criticized Gordon's memoirs as self-serving and untrustworthy, concocted late in life when his memory might have failed him. Keith S. Bohannon's essay revisits some of the most controversial elements of the *Reminiscences* and demonstrates that most of Gordon's key passages had wartime and early postwar roots. Far from tailoring his memoirs to suit ideological and commemorative currents of the late nineteenth and early twentieth centuries, Gordon, from the end of the war through his death in January 1904, offered a largely consistent narrative of his activities. That narrative clashed with those of Jubal A. Early, his Confederate superior, and others, contributing to a lively and sometimes openly combative arena of Confederate remembrance.

The volume closes with Gary W. Gallagher's handling of Edward Porter Alexander, whom Douglas Southall Freeman called "certainly one of the ablest of the younger officers of the Confederate Army" (Alexander was born in Georgia in May 1835), adding, "Had he been in command of the guns of the entire Army of Northern Virginia, he would have given the Confederate batteries a better chance in combat." Gallagher's essay compares Alexander's two big books, *Military Memoirs of a Confederate* (1907) and *Fighting for the Confederacy* (1989), showing in much greater detail than Freeman undertook why the author of *The South to Posterity* could have considered *Military Memoirs* "a candid and withal a generous book," as well as one of "the most frequently quoted of Confederate authorities." As for *Fighting for the Confederacy*, which Gallagher reveals to be a unique blend of narrative skill, unsentimental acuity, bracing critique, and racy humor, Freeman could have nothing to say, as this book—quite possibly the best by any high-ranking Confederate officer—was unknown to him. The book came to light only a generation ago, as the result of painstaking archival detective work, reminding us that the body of inventive literature we know as Civil War writing awaits further discovery.[4]

Essays in this volume underscore how participants in the Civil War employed various literary forms to record, describe, and explain aspects and episodes of a conflict that assumed proportions none of them imagined possible at the outset. The nine individuals wrote with different audiences, and purposes, in mind, and as a group achieved an impressive and continuing degree of influence. Another volume in the series, and perhaps two, will extend investigation to the writings of additional figures, among them U. S. Grant, Phoebe Yates Pember, George B. McClellan, Henry Wilson, and James Longstreet. The astonishing body of literary evidence from the war raises high expectations for what future essayists will have to say.

The editors thank the contributors to this volume and Mike Parrish, whose series "Conflicting Worlds: New Dimensions of the American Civil War" is a perfect fit for *Civil War Writing*. They are grateful also to Cecily Zander for preparing the index.

NOTES

1. *The Collected Works of Abraham Lincoln,* ed. Roy P. Basler, 9 vols. (New Brunswick, NJ: Rutgers University Press, 1953–55), 3:360. The lecture delivered in Jacksonville was actually the "Second Lecture on Discoveries and Inventions." An earlier, much shorter draft, which does not include the remarks on writing, appears as "First Lecture on Discoveries and Inventions" in *Collected Works* 2:437–42. Lincoln delivered this earlier version, or something based on it, to the Young Men's Association of Bloomington, Illinois, on April 6, 1858.

2. On the state of military topics within the broader scope of literature devoted to the Civil War, see Gary W. Gallagher and Kathryn Shively, "Coming to Terms with Civil War Military History," *Journal of the Civil War Era* (December 2014): 487–508, and Earl J. Hess, "Where Do We Stand? A Critical Assessment of Civil War Studies in the Sesquicentennial Era," *Civil War History* 60 (December 2014): 371–403.

3. Louisa May Alcott, *The Journals of Louisa May Alcott,* ed. Joel Myerson, Daniel Shealy, and Madeleine B. Stern (Boston: Little, Brown, 1989), 105.

4. Douglas Southall Freeman, *The South to Posterity: An Introduction to the Writing of Confederate History,* introd. by Gary W. Gallagher (1939; rpt., Baton Rouge: Louisiana State University Press, 1998), 177–78.

"Joseph T. Wilson. Of 2d Reg't La. N. G. Vols., also 54th Mass. Vols." The frontispiece for the first edition of *The Black Phalanx* showed its author, in the postwar years, with his Grand Army of the Republic Medal on his jacket. From Joseph T. Wilson, *The Black Phalanx; A History of the Negro Soldiers of the United States in the Wars of 1775–1812, 1861–'65* (Hartford, Conn.: American Publishing Co., 1890).

Joseph T. Wilson's *The Black Phalanx*

African American Patriotism and the Won Cause

ELIZABETH R. VARON

Joseph T. Wilson's 1887 book *The Black Phalanx* was a publishing phenomenon. The most comprehensive study of African American military service of its era, *The Black Phalanx* was highly anticipated, vigorously marketed, and widely hailed. Its author, Joseph T. Wilson of Norfolk, Virginia, was a veteran of not one but two pathbreaking black regiments in the Civil War, and achieved renown in the postwar period as a writer, orator, and activist. Even before *The Black Phalanx* appeared, Wilson was regarded by the African American press as "no doubt the best living authority" on the United States Colored Troops and "one of the few dauntless pioneers who are opening up a way in the vast field of literature." In 1883, the Washington, D.C., *People's Advocate* praised Wilson for gathering "the needful material for a proper history of the colored soldier" and predicted that, once his book was ready, it would "meet with a wide sale"; a second black newspaper, the *Petersburg Lancet,* imagined that "fifty years hence, [when] a cyclopaedia of Negro authors shall be published, a look at the 'W's' will no doubt discover the name of Wilson."[1]

To insure that *The Black Phalanx* met these expectations, Wilson's chosen press, the American Publishing Company of Hartford, Connecticut, undertook a rigorous publicity campaign for the book, to sell it on subscription, by agents, door-to-door—the same way the company sold the books of its star author, Mark Twain. Beginning in 1887, newspapers across the

United States began running American Publishing Company advertisements, recruiting agents to market *The Black Phalanx,* with promises of big profits. "Sells Fast to Whites and Blacks," ran one ad. "All say it is the grandest book ever written," ran another, adding "piles of money to be made selling it for every body wants it." Behind this hyperbole was a record of real success: editor Irvine Garland Penn, an authority on black literary culture, wrote in 1891 that the sales of *The Black Phalanx* "surpass[ed] that of any other work written by an Afro-American." Moreover, this success was enduring: for more than a decade after the initial publication of the book, newspapers such as T. Thomas Fortune's *New York Age* advertised *The Black Phalanx* and even offered copies of it as prizes for long-term subscribers. An 1898 ad in the *Richmond Planet* insisted that "every patriotic colored man, woman, and child" in America should own *The Black Phalanx,* and offered the book at half price to loyal readers of the paper.[2]

Wilson's book earned not only robust sales but also considerable acclaim. Wilson fulfilled a "long felt want" among blacks in treating "fully and truthfully of our forefathers' services to the country and selves, during their three hundred years residence here," the *Cleveland Gazette* noted in an 1888 review. When Wilson died in 1891 his eulogists, even as they praised his long career of political activism, declared the *Black Phalanx* to be his "masterpiece" and the "proudest monument to his memory." In 1900 *The Black Phalanx* was featured at the World's Fair in Paris in an exhibit on black literary achievement. In 1911 it was hailed by Arthur Schomburg and John Edward Bruce, as they organized the Negro Society for Historical Research in New York, as one of the foundational works in the field. In 1944, Carter G. Woodson recalled in the *Negro History Bulletin* that his own historical consciousness had been shaped by the experience of reading *The Black Phalanx* aloud to an illiterate United States Colored Troops (U.S.C.T.) veteran he had befriended when he worked as a coal miner in West Virginia. In short, *The Black Phalanx* was an influential as well as a popular book.[3]

And yet *The Black Phalanx* and its author have, in the modern day, been underappreciated. Among scholars of African American historical writing, Wilson has been overshadowed by his contemporary George Washington Williams, a fellow Civil War veteran turned scholar, who is regarded as the dean of modern black history and a pioneer in the professionalization of the field. It is telling that Williams is the subject of a magisterial biography, by John Hope Franklin, while Wilson has yet to find a biographer.[4]

Historians of the United States Colored Troops and of Civil War memory, for their part, frequently cite *The Black Phalanx,* but they have tended to treat it as a reference work rather than as a piece of scholarship worthy of sustained analysis. Meanwhile, studies of postwar black politics in Wilson's native Virginia acknowledge his political activism but do not connect it to his literary pursuits. Part of the problem lies with the format of *The Black Phalanx.* The book contains long passages of primary-source excerpts, which the reader is left to sift through, often without much guidance from Wilson on where their meaning lies. This format has led some critics, in Wilson's day and in ours, to dismiss the book as a mere compilation.[5]

The Black Phalanx rewards a close reading, one that situates the book in the context of Wilson's prodigious public output of editorials, poems, speeches, and histories, and in the context of his long private struggle to receive disability pension payments for injuries sustained during the war. Wilson was a crusader against the denial of history, and *The Black Phalanx* was the culmination of a more than twenty-year battle he waged over Civil War memory. Wilson's unique experiences during the war, and the politics he practiced in the singular setting of postwar Norfolk, shaped his textual strategies, particularly his emphasis on the themes of black leadership and unity.

Wilson's battle over Civil War memory began in earnest with a fateful decision he made in September of 1864: to return home to his native Virginia. Wilson was born in Norfolk in 1837. Few details of his early life survive, but the records we do have suggest that his mother was a free woman of English and Native American descent and his father was black and enslaved; the 1870 federal census designated Joseph Wilson as "mulatto."[6] In his youth, Wilson was compelled to leave Norfolk, after having revealed to city authorities the identity of a fugitive white penitentiary convict; the information led to the convict's recapture but left Wilson vulnerable to reprisals. He was sent to New Bedford, Massachusetts, where he attended public schools and chose, as did so many young men in that port town, to take to the sea, aboard a whaler bound for the South Pacific.

Wilson was working in Chile, on the Valparaiso and Santiago Railroad, when he received word in 1862 that the Civil War had broken out. He decided to return, as soon as possible, to America. He booked passage to New York, and from there to Union-occupied New Orleans, where he hoped to be reunited with his father, Bristow, who had been sold south years before. In New Orleans, Wilson enlisted as a private in a newly formed black Union regiment, the Second Louisiana Native Guard. After being hospitalized with "chronic diarrhea" and honorably discharged, he returned home to Massachusetts, only to reenlist, this time in the famous Fifty-Fourth Massachusetts Infantry (immortalized in the movie *Glory*). In February of 1864 he was wounded at the battle of Olustee in Florida, and that spring he was again honorably discharged and sent back to Massachusetts. Remarkably, Wilson chose to enter the fray a third time. In September of 1864, after a fourteen-year absence, he returned to Norfolk. That winter he signed on, as a wheelman on a Union dispatch boat, in General Benjamin F. Butler's amphibious expedition from Hampton Roads to capture Fort Fisher near Wilmington, North Carolina, the South's last major Atlantic port. After the failure of that abortive mission, he then signed on with the U.S. secret service, "operating with his squad on the Elizabeth and James rivers, and in front of Richmond with the army of the James." The end of the war found Wilson back in Norfolk, tending a government supply store that provided goods to freedpeople.[7]

Why did Wilson—who had in effect escaped the South three times—choose to return to Virginia? Family ties surely played a role but so too, we can surmise, did Norfolk's distinct position in the southern political landscape. Occupied by the Union army in May of 1862, Norfolk, like the Hampton Roads region more broadly, was a proving ground in which southern blacks could define freedom in the presence of white allies such as Union army personnel and northern missionaries. African Americans in Norfolk were soon able to establish black-led churches and schools and to make use of institutions such as freedmen's savings banks, employment societies, and poor-relief agencies. And they were able to express their aspirations in civic rituals such as the massive parades marking the anniversary of the Emancipation Proclamation. Indeed Norfolk was the setting for what may have been the first attempt by African Americans to vote in the postwar South. On April 4, 1865, in the week before Lee's surrender at Appomattox, a group of Norfolk men, Joseph T. Wilson among them, established the Colored Monitor Union Club, dedicated to obtaining the right of suffrage.

Later that spring, on May 25, they attempted the bold experiment of casting ballots in a local election for state assemblymen, voting for white candidates who supported black suffrage. Officials in one of Norfolk's wards agreed to record their names on disputed ballots. In the end, the votes did not count, but the men had made a point: if their votes had counted, the suffrage candidates would have won.[8]

On June 5, a committee of eight men, Wilson among them, disseminated an address on "Equal Suffrage," insisting that black voting was "a necessity as a protection against the votes of secessionists and disloyal men." Wilson's voice comes through clearly in this address, which, according to Philip S. Foner and George E. Walker, ranks as "one of the most moving documents ever issued by an assembly of southern blacks." The address began by offering a history lesson. "It is a common assertion, by our enemies, that 'this is a white man's country, settled by white men, its government established by white men, and shall therefore be ruled by white men only,'" they noted. But such a view could not stand up to the facts: black labor, they argued, had built the nation, and the blood of black patriots had sanctified it in the Revolutionary War and the Civil War. Wilson and his cadre cast themselves as guardians of Virginia's future: "Give us the suffrage, and you may rely upon us . . . to keep the State forever in the Union."[9]

The need for protection was dramatized the following year, when, on April 16, 1866, Norfolk was the site of the first major race riot of the Reconstruction era. The trouble broke out when angry whites, emboldened by Andrew Johnson's conciliation of former Confederates, disrupted a parade of Africans Americans, who were commemorating the passage that April of the Civil Rights Act of 1866. The whites were particularly incensed that the black marchers were escorted by a group of armed, uniformed U.S.C.T. veterans. Joseph Wilson, who had assumed editorship of the local Unionist newspaper, the *True Southerner,* was slated to preside over the day's main event. He was on the speaker's stand, awaiting the arrival of the processional, when he heard the report of pistol fire and watched the peaceful gathering devolve into violent melee, followed by a wave of vigilante attacks on the black community and a slander campaign by the white press, which cast the black marchers as a drunken, depraved, blood-thirsty mob of armed ex-slaves. Wilson's *True Southerner* refuted these slanders with another history lesson: "These liberated slaves are soldiers just from the war," his April 19 editorial noted archly. "It has been a custom, not only in this, but in every nation, for returned soldiers to attend national celebrations in their arms. . . . Are we to be forbidden to hold national celebrations in our own country, lest we offend the enemy?" Later that year, a white mob ransacked the *True Southerner* offices, forcing the paper to shut down.[10]

These formative events in Wilson's postwar political career established a pattern, which would be repeated over the next two decades, of progress met by reaction. In 1867, Congress's Reconstruction Acts enfranchised the freedmen, and Wilson assumed a prominent political role at the state level as a fixture at Republican Party conventions and events. His was a radical voice. In an electrifying speech at the April 1867 Republican Party State Convention at Richmond's First African Baptist Church, Wilson called for land confiscation and for the impeachment of Andrew Johnson, telling his fellow delegates that if they did not support a "platform of human rights" they were "no better than rebels." In 1869, Virginia's white conservative leaders negotiated a compromise with the Grant administration and Republican Congress whereby they agreed to abide black suffrage in the state's new constitution provided that former Confederates would suffer no penalties of disfranchisement. The state was readmitted to the Union on these terms, and military Reconstruction formally ended; as whites outnumbered blacks in Virginia, the white Conservative Party (as the Democrat-led coalition called itself) soon seized control of the state government from the Republicans. The existence of black-majority wards in places like Richmond and Norfolk meant that some black men continued to be elected to the General Assembly and other political offices, and to win Republican Party patronage appointments, in the early 1870s. Wilson himself served on the Norfolk City Council, and as Internal Revenue Service gauger and customs inspector. He joined prominent white Republicans in stumping for Ulysses S. Grant in the presidential election campaign of 1872 and served as a presidential elector for Rutherford B. Hayes in 1876.[11]

But as Wilson rose up the ranks the specter of violent reprisals continued to haunt him. In 1871 a mob of Conservative Party men attacked the house of white Republican John Dezendorf, one of Wilson's close allies and fellow IRS assessors, calling Dezendorf a "d—m Radical, n— loving son of a bitch." The crowd then set upon Wilson's house, smashing his windows, firing their pistols, and shouting "'where is the n——, we have got one, and we will have another, &c!'" In the midst of such hostility, the opportunities for black men to participate in governing were steadily eroded. Through his writing and oratory, Wilson called for vigilance and resistance. For example, in 1873 he published a letter under the pseudonym "Eskiam" in the Washington, D.C., *New National Era,* pushing for Federal monitoring of elections to prevent the Democrats' "ballot-box stuffing and intimidation of colored voters." And he spoke out boldly in public forums: at an 1875 labor convention in Richmond, Wilson warned blacks not to be "the political serfs of unworthy white leaders," and in the Republican State Convention of that same year he condemned Virginia whites for having "filled up the jails and penitentiary with our race." In 1876, as the last Federal troops were removed from the South, Conservatives in Virginia imposed measures designed to suppress the black vote: a poll tax and a law making petty theft grounds for disfranchisement. Wilson was in the vanguard of those protesting these new measures, but to no avail; as disfranchisement kicked in, the numbers of blacks elected to the General Assembly declined precipitously in the late 1870s.[12]

Many black Virginians took heart from the emergence in 1879 of the Readjuster Party, a reform-minded coalition of Republicans and Democrats that proposed to repudiate part of the antebellum state debt and reduce the rate of interest to be paid on it in order to protect services like public schooling. The new party's head, former Confederate general William Mahone, successfully appealed to black voters, promising to promote education and protect black voting. Wilson, though, regarded the Readjuster movement with suspicion, as he believed it undermined Republican unity and that white Readjusters saw blacks as political pawns. Wilson became a champion of the loyal Republican "straightouts," who tried to offer an alternative to the Funder-Democrats (who opposed repudiation of the debt) and to the Readjusters. As Wilson explained in a testy 1881 public letter to Frederick Douglass, published in various newspapers, the white Readjusters in Norfolk had proven no better than their conservative Democrat predecessors: they imprisoned blacks "without authority of the law, ordered them whipped for trivial offences, [and] sentenced them to the chain gang for no crime." In 1884, with the Readjuster movement in retreat, Democratic majorities in the state legislature appointed new electoral boards for the Commonwealth's cities and counties, giving them license to further suppress black voting. In 1889, only four black men were elected to the Virginia General Assembly. No others would be elected until 1968.[13]

Such was the political atmosphere in which Joseph T. Wilson wrote *The Black Phalanx*, and it is essential context for understanding his narrative choices. *The Black Phalanx* represents the genre of "race history," and in many respects it closely resembles the two other pioneering studies of African Americans in the Civil War written in the nineteenth century: William Wells Brown's *The Negro in the American Rebellion: His Heroism and His Fidelity*, published in 1867, and George Washington Williams's *A History of the Negro Troops in the War of the Rebellion*, published in 1888. Race histories took the distinctive civilizationist discourse of the Victorian era— which emphasized the stages of advancement of Western society—and reworked it, to cast emancipation as a millennial drama. The premise of such histories, to quote the modern-day historian Stephen G. Hall, was that, "if African Americans could prove they were a progressive race, it would be impossible to deny them full entry to the body politic." Wilson's book, like those of Wells Brown and Williams, portrayed history as "an ongoing struggle toward the goal of human freedom." All three books chronicled the desire of blacks to enlist and the opposition they faced in the North; the evolution of the Union's emancipation policy; the heroic comportment of blacks troops at Port Hudson, Fort Wagner, and other storied battles; the discrimination they faced, particularly with regards to pay; the Confederate policy of no quarter and its tragic implications at the Fort Pillow massacre; and the final triumph of Union forces in the Virginia theater. All offered what the scholar Dickson D. Bruce Jr. has called "an ironic conception of American history," by pointing up the irony that America's survival as a nation during the Civil War era had "depended upon a supposedly 'dependent' people." And all struck notes of hope, reassuring their readers, as William Wells Brown put it, that "progress is slow, but sure."[14]

And yet in other ways *The Black Phalanx* stands out because of Wilson's unconventional choices. While Brown found antecedents for black soldiering in the slave rebellions of Denmark Vesey and Nat Turner, and Williams found them in the Haitian revolution, Wilson, by contrast, made no mention either of slave rebellion as a context for black Civil War service or of Vesey, Toussaint, and Turner. Instead Wilson focused, in his two introductory chapters, on black military service in the American Revolution and the War of 1812, emphasizing, as he had in his response to the Norfolk riot some twenty years earlier, that African American soldiers were agents of the state, and of the nation—patriots not insurrectionists. This choice was in no sense naive or provincial. Wilson was very learned in the global history of abolition; indeed, in 1882 he published a book on that subject, titled *Emancipation: Its Course and Progress, from 1491 B.C. to A.D. 1875,* which connected abolition in the United States to emancipation in the West Indies, Russia, Cuba, Brazil, and other societies. Wilson was keenly aware that opponents of emancipation had long invoked dystopian images of the Haitian Revolution in order to associate black freedom with, as he put it, the "crimson flame of carnage and crime." And so he chose to portray American slaves not as rebels but as recruits, who were mobilized by the "steady tramp of the steel-crowned, blue-clad legions." In Wilson's view, there was only one set of rebels in the American Civil War—and they wore the Confederate gray.[15]

This emphasis was essential to establishing Wilson's second major theme in his introductory chapters: the galling ingratitude of whites towards black patriotism. Wilson furnished as his central example the experience of William Wells Brown's own grandfather, Simon Lee, who served in the American army only to be re-enslaved afterwards—"sent back to his master, where he spent the remainder of his life toiling on a tobacco plantation." This was a typical fate for black soldiers in America's early wars, Wilson argued, proof that patriotic service was "no protection against outrage."[16] Wilson signaled to his reader early on, in other words, that he was not going to offer an uplifting tale of the Civil War generation building upon the struggles of past generations. Indeed, Wilson's chapters on the Civil War begin with his assertion that white prejudice grew more virulent in the decades after the Revolution and was at a peak during the Civil War. Over the course of fourteen chapters on the war years, Wilson details the indignities blacks suffered within the Union army and the atrocities perpetrated on them by Confederates. What makes his account distinctly poignant and revealing is that he shares his personal experiences of soldiering, typically in discursive footnotes. In his chapter on U.S.C.T. recruitment, he relates that, when stationed in New Orleans, he was accosted by a mob of white Union soldiers who demanded that he take off his blue uniform and literally tore it from his body when he refused; such attacks on black soldiers, he notes, were frequent. In his chapter on the Department of the Gulf, Wilson shares, again in a footnote, an even more troubling story—of black pickets in his regiment, the Second Louisiana Native Guards, being fired upon one night by fellow Union soldiers, of the white Eighth Vermont Infantry. Black soldiers, Wilson establishes, "suffered much at the hands of their white fellow comrades in arms."[17]

Wilson understandably regarded Confederate mistreatment of blacks to be altogether more shocking—a regime of outrages rather than indignities. He used *The Black Phalanx* to drive home the point that barbarity towards blacks was Confederate policy, promulgated from on high by Jefferson Davis, who sought to bring about a "war of extermination against the negro soldiers." Wilson recounts the April 12, 1864, massacre of surrendered black soldiers at Fort Pillow, Tennessee, in unflinching detail, calling it a "shocking crime of wanton, indiscriminate murder." And he describes the Confederate massacre of retreating and surrendering black troops at the battle of the Crater in Virginia on July 30, 1864, as an inhuman "repetition of the Fort Pillow Massacre." Once again, what sets Wilson's account apart is that this was all deeply personal for him because he bore direct witness to a postwar campaign to cover up these crimes. Reflecting on white commemorations of the war in his native Virginia, Wilson observes that "No battle fought during the war . . . elicited so much comment and glorification among the confederates as that of the crater. It . . . has been the subject of praise by poets and orators upon the confederate side." Wilson furnishes examples, of an orator whose description of the fight "so gladdened the hearts of his audience that they reproduced the [rebel] 'yell,' and yelled themselves hoarse," and of a second oration, in 1876, in which a Confederate veteran claimed fraudulently that the blacks troops at the Crater were "inflamed with drink" and therefore deserved the treatment they got. The preeminent Confederate hero of the Crater was none other than William Mahone, who had been one of Norfolk's leading citizens before the war and would later head the Readjuster Party, the very reform coalition that Wilson rejected. In 1875 and 1876, reunions of Mahone's brigade took place in Norfolk, on the anniversary of the Crater, and Mahone assiduously "used his fame as the 'Hero of the Crater' to advance both his business and political interests."[18]

Wilson's own deep knowledge of the war prevented him from ever trusting Mahone, even after the Readjusters delivered on some of the reforms they promised, such as abolishing the whipping post as a punishment for African Americans. Wilson repeatedly, publicly, characterized Mahone as a master manipulator, who pretended to be "in favor of giving increased rights to the colored population" because it would increase his own power base and ensnare unwary voters. In one 1881 speech, Wilson likened Mahone to "the arch-fiend who when thrown down from Heaven, left the realms of chaos to confound the harmony of earth and wreak his vengeance." Mahone responded by using his patronage powers as a U.S. senator to exact vengeance on Wilson, securing his removal late in 1881 from the U.S. Customs Service.[19]

In *The Black Phalanx,* Wilson countered Mahone's false narratives of the war by setting the record straight. The battle of the Crater, Wilson argued, had been a debacle for the Union because the black soldiers who were initially tasked to lead the assault had been replaced at the last minute with white troops, who charged into the Crater, created by the mine, rather than around it, trapping themselves and the black units who then tried to rescue them. For Wilson, the Crater symbolized not only Confederate barbarity but also the costs to the Union of failing to recognize the capacity of blacks for leadership. Indeed, Wilson's desire to defend and vindicate black leadership rings out in the pages of *The Black Phalanx.* He opens the book by explaining how he was commissioned to write it by members of the Grand Army of the Republic (G.A.R.), the venerable Union veterans' organization in which Wilson had served as the first African American member of the Grand Council of Administration (akin to a board of directors) and earned the title of aide-de-camp to the commander-in-chief, at the rank of colonel. And he features early on in his book a chapter titled "Officers of the Phalanx" that focuses on black officers, not white ones. Wilson knew that black officers, especially commissioned officers at the rank of lieutenant or above, were rare; black regiments were typically under the command of white officers. But he believed that the symbolic importance of black officers, commissioned and noncommissioned, far exceeded their numbers. The illustrations in *The Black Phalanx* feature portraits of U.S.C.T. soldiers who entered the officer ranks during war, such as Major Martin Delaney, Captain P. B. S. Pinchback, and Lieutenant James Monroe Trotter. Especially significant were the leaders of the First, Second, and Third Louisiana Native Guard regiments, for those regiments contained "nearly 90 percent of the total number of black officers who would serve in infantry or artillery units in the war."[20]

The First Louisiana Native Guard had its origins in a local militia unit consisting of members of New Orleans's elite free men of color. Technically this militia had been available for service to the Confederacy—but shortly after the Federal occupation of New Orleans in the spring of 1862, its leaders pledged their allegiance to the Union. In the fall of 1862, the Second and Third regiments, consisting primarily of former slaves, were mustered into Union service. Most of the line officers of these units were African American, and Wilson draws on their stories to illustrate black gallantry. He tells for example the story of Captain Andre Cailloux, an Afro-Creole from New Orleans's distinctive class of *gens de couleur libres,* who led a brave if futile charge against Confederate defenses at Port Hudson, Louisiana. Wilson reminds his readers that the martyred Cailloux became the first African American military hero of the war, his sacrifices celebrated in newspaper articles, poems, and in a massive funeral procession in Union-occupied New Orleans. Cailloux had faced indignities even in death: his decomposing corpse had lain on the Port Hudson battlefield for forty-seven days, until the Confederate fort surrendered in July of 1863—only then could his remains at last be returned home to his native city, and he be given military honors. Wilson lingers on the funeral ceremony: "Flowers were strewn in the greatest profusion, and candles were kept continuously burning" in the hall where Cailloux's body lay in state, draped in an American flag; the officiating priest offered the rites of the Catholic Church, and "called upon all present to offer themselves, as Cailloux had done, martyrs to the cause of justice." Wilson also brings to light the story of Major Francois Ernest Dumas of his own Second Regiment. "A gentleman of fine tact and ability," Dumas was one of only two African Americans (along with Martin Delaney) to hold the rank of major during the war, and he ably led his men in combat at East Pascagoula, Mississippi, in the spring of 1863, the first Civil War engagement featuring black company-grade officers.[21]

Wilson clearly believed that Cailloux and Dumas, with their fine educations, were officer material from the start. But in fairness to those of humble origins Wilson was also careful to point out that men who had "worn the galling chains of slavery" proved, in their own right, to be able and efficient noncommissioned officers. Lamentably, the Louisiana experiment with black officers proved to be short-lived. When General Nathaniel Banks, who regarded black officers as unfit for duty, took over command of the Department of the Gulf, he pressured men such as Dumas, by subjecting them to humiliating examination boards, into resigning. But the black-led Louisiana regiments had nonetheless made their mark. Had the Louisianans failed to display courage, "the colored troops would have been universally condemned" and consigned permanently to noncombat roles.[22]

In Wilson's analysis, the stories of black officers serve to dramatize the ways that the veil of racism occludes the past. Wilson ends his chapter on the officers of the phalanx by raising the issue of racial passing. He notes that "quite a number of mulattoes served in white regiments, some as officers," and he related a personal story. Wilson was lying wounded on the battlefield of Olustee in February of 1864 while he was serving with the Fifty-Fourth Massachusetts, when an officer rode up and passed him his canteen. The officer asked, "Don't you know me?" to which Wilson said, "No." The man identified himself as "Tom Bunting" and said to a shocked Wilson, "We used to play together in our boyhood days in Virginia." The officer then dashed away to his white Massachusetts regiment. "Numerous instances of this kind could be cited," Wilson notes. This story was meant to illustrate that racism and not racial inferiority held blacks back—whites literally could not see the achievements of people of African descent. Wilson reiterates that point in an appendix, "The Black Phalanx at School," in which he avers that illiterate U.S.C.T. soldiers hungered for knowledge, feeling "that if educated, they [too] might be lieutenants and captains."[23]

It must be noted that no modern scholars acknowledge Wilson's focus on black leadership. Instead, recent works repeatedly characterize Wilson's account of black military service as "defensive" in tone, implying that Wilson and his allies were in retreat, in the 1880s, against the surging forces of white supremacy—of disfranchisement, lynching, segregation, Lost Cause mythology, and pseudo-Darwinian theories of black inferiority.[24] But to characterize Wilson's tone as defensive is fundamentally to misunderstand him. Wilson's commemorating of black military leadership dated back to the very moment of Union victory. In May of 1865, he offered the first of his many public tributes to the Louisiana Native Guard regiments, in a speech in Norfolk that was reprinted in the Unionist newspaper there. After crediting his comrades in arms with redeeming the nation from tyranny,

Wilson concluded, "We must ask for equal rights. . . . without this America is dishonored by the whole world." For Wilson to celebrate black leadership in the spring of 1865, when the experiment of black voting had not yet begun, was bold; for him to celebrate black leadership in 1887, at a time when most whites had deemed the experiment in black citizenship a failure, was, arguably, even bolder.[25]

Tellingly, African American readers in Wilson's own day did take note of his focus on leadership. The review of *The Black Phalanx* in the *New York Age*, for example, proudly listed the names of the "colored commissioned officers," men such as Delaney and Pinchback, whose portraits were featured in Wilson's book. The eminent reformer Charlotte Forten Grimké cited Wilson in an 1889 published letter to the editor of the *New York Evangelist*, whom she accused of being misinformed about the Civil War. That periodical had claimed that though black soldiers "were brave enough in the ranks . . . no one had the natural capacity to command." Grimké shot back, "May I ask what authority you have for this statement?" "I would like to refer you to a book entitled 'The Black Phalanx,'" she continued, noting "there were many colored officers who acquitted themselves honorably, and the fact that there were no colored colonels or generals, may readily be accounted for by the strong prejudice" which kept blacks out of the ranks until midway through the war.[26]

Perhaps Wilson's boldest decision was his choice of a title: *The Black Phalanx*. A phalanx was "an ancient Greek military formation of heavy armed infantrymen in close ranks." The word connoted courage, efficiency, and prowess. Scholars of the role of the classics in African American thought have observed that Wilson chose the term both to tap "the prestige of Greece and Rome in Euro-American culture" and to associate African Americans with Greco-Roman heroism. Wilson also chose the term particularly for its connotations of discipline and unity. Quoting Ulysses S. Grant's assessment that the black man was "in discipline a better soldier than the white man," Wilson argued that it took a special kind of self-control for black troops to face a foe that would give them no quarter and yet to refrain from any acts of inhumanity, of vengeance and retaliation, against that foe.[27]

Success for a phalanx "depended on fighting as one united and cohesive unit." It was just such unity that Wilson felt was missing from black politics in the wake of Reconstruction. In the years he researched and wrote *The Black Phalanx*, political divisions and personal rivalries plagued the Republican Party in Virginia. The early 1880s furnished numerous examples of how costly such divisions could be. At a peak moment in the chaos, in August of 1881, the Republican State Convention in Lynchburg fractured, with Wilson's straight-outs splitting with the Readjusters and opting to hold a rump convention. Wilson was elected chairman of that convention, and in his opening speech he "urged the Republicans to stand by their colors, and to surrender to no set of men their principles and their manhood." The convention bickered over whether to nominate its own ticket of candidates for governor and lieutenant governor, and although some delegates nominated Wilson himself for these posts, he could not garner the necessary support. The meeting ended in shambles, with Wilson giving a closing speech expressing his "extreme chagrin and bitter disappointment" at lack of solidarity among the delegates.[28]

Wilson's own position—that Readjusters who were former Confederates and Democrats simply could not be trusted to represent the interests of black Republican voters—received a grim vindication in 1884, when John S. Wise, a Readjuster congressman, gave his infamous "kitchen" testimony to the congressional committee investigating the recent race riot in Danville, Virginia, in 1883. Wise told the committee that he viewed blacks as political constituents but not as social equals—when black legislators had come to his house to consult with him, he claimed, they had gone to the kitchen and sent their messages up to the parlor, and then Wise had met with them in the backyard, rather than permitting them to enter his house. African American politicians in Virginia's General Assembly took great offense, and denied that they had ever visited Wise's kitchen. Wilson himself gave numerous speeches denouncing Wise's remarks.[29]

Divisions among Republicans got so bad in Norfolk that for a time rival factions there held two separate celebrations of the Emancipation Proclamation. Wilson used the occasion of an 1885 speech commemorating emancipation to decry these developments. The enemies of equality were united, he proclaimed, in their determination to keep black men down; whites had made a "science" of "injustice and wrong." In the face of such a reality, blacks could not afford to divide their votes, to defer to white leaders, or to choose any but the very best men—"men of learning and moral worth"—to lead them. "Freedom is not individual privileges but the right to organize," Wilson insisted, adding, in a military metaphor, "Let us see to it in the future that we stand united and feel the touch of the elbow." The freedom "won by the blood of our fathers and brothers," he concluded, could only be preserved by "the united effort of ourselves."[30]

In proposing that blacks must close ranks in peacetime as they had during the war, Wilson appropriated elements of the "regenerative militarism" that was such a strong feature of late-nineteenth-century culture—its "celebration of blood sacrifice in combat" and of the efficiency of armies as a model for social organization. As T. J. Jackson Lears and others have shown, militarism could be adapted to various ideological agendas, from the bellicose imperialism of Teddy Roosevelt to the utopian reforms of Edward Bellamy. In Wilson's case, militarism tapped a current in abolitionist culture that cast the leaders of the freedom struggle as "moral gladiators," wielding the weapons of oratory and of the written word. Wilson's emphasis on the phalanx as the metaphor for political unity also reflected his own theory of history, as the long struggle of democracy against aristocracy. "History proves beyond a doubt," he wrote in his 1882 book, *Emancipation,* "that the advancing spirit of freedom has always been met by a relentless war waged by the oppressors of mankind." In such a universe, the forces of freedom could never break ranks or let their guard down.[31]

Even as he crafted his account of black heroism for the reading public, Wilson waged a prolonged campaign to claim the pension support he believed was due him. Beginning in 1862, Union veterans could receive monthly payments from the federal government if they could prove to the Pension Bureau that their wartime service had caused a disability rendering them unable to subsist through "manual labor." Proving such a disability was a daunting task. Applicants had to furnish documentation of their military records and disabilities, including affidavits from their commanders and fellow soldiers, and the results of examinations by government-designated doctors, to the Pension Bureau for evaluation. Until 1890, the prevailing standard of proof required that applicants demonstrate that their disabilities resulted from wartime military service; after liberalization of the pension laws in 1890, pensions "became a general disability benefit. Almost any serious impairment, whether it was service-related or not, would qualify a veteran for a pension," as the historians Larry M. Logue and Peter Blanck have put it. They explain, too, that while the pension system was in principle race-neutral, in practice it was grossly discriminatory, with African Americans receiving "more outright rejections and smaller pension awards" than whites, because of "biased pension examiners and documentation rules that were more difficult for black veterans than white veterans to satisfy." Factors that disadvantaged black claimants included the higher difficulty of proving disability from disease than from combat wounds.[32]

In the very years Wilson achieved prominence within the G.A.R. that organization was flexing its muscle as a force in partisan politics, lobbying for the liberalization of the pension laws. G.A.R. membership grew from 45,000 in 1879 to 397,974 in 1889, as pension law reform became a signature issue of the national Republican Party, which denounced Democratic President Grover Cleveland's vetoing of reform legislation and curtailment of pension approvals during the years 1885 to 1889. The return to power of the Republicans secured passage of the 1890 reform and witnessed "an immediate increase in pension approvals," including for blacks, although they still lagged behind whites in approval rates.[33]

While Wilson's education and literacy, his political experience and connections, were potential assets in his personal quest for pension payments, they did not guarantee success. That Wilson had been grievously wounded in action was not in doubt. His May 1864 "Certificate of Disability for Discharge," filed in Boston, cited his "inability to stand erect in consequence of Gun Shot wound in Abdomen received at Olustee Feb 20 1864," and designated him as "not fit for the Veterans Reserve Corps" and "totally disabled." (The battle of Olustee, part of an ill-conceived Union effort to penetrate Florida, was a tactical defeat for the North in which "the 54th Massachusetts executed a controlled retreat under heavy fire that allowed the rest of the Northern forces to escape.") Letters Wilson sent to Union authorities in November 1864 and February 1865 from Norfolk began his twenty-five-year struggle for proper compensation. Noting that he had not received back pay and his bounty payment for his service in the Fifty-Fourth, Wilson explained in November that he was sick and in great need of his wages, with a "heavy doctors Bill" upon him. "You will do me a great favor by remiting the amount due me," Wilson wrote, striking notes of formality and deference, adding, with understatement, "I am not able to get about at Present." Three months later, indignation had crept into his language: "It is but hard after serving my country faithfully now that I have become a cripple that I should want for lifes necessity."[34]

In November of 1866, Wilson applied for an "Invalid Pension," arguing that the effects of the Olustee gunshot wound had compelled him to "give up his regular avocation as a whaleman" and rendered him unable to "perform manual labor." Wilson was scraping by, he noted, through the assistance of his friends and "by attending to such writings as he is able to perform"—but such was not "sufficient to support him and his family" of fifteen dependent females (including his grandmother, widowed mother, and sisters). A few months later Wilson testified that he had tried in vain to locate officers or surgeons who could corroborate his account of his wounding. The Pension Bureau decided in March of 1867, based on a surgeon's recent examination of Wilson, to award Wilson a pension of two dollars a month, ruling him one-fourth disabled (a rating of fully disabled would have fixed the monthly rate at eight dollars a month); Wilson's payments were retroactive to November 1866, when he first filed his claim.[35]

Wilson knew his rights and asserted them. In November of 1868, citing a recently enacted change in the pensions laws, Wilson successfully appealed to have his monthly payments made retroactive to his discharge date in 1864, and in November of 1874 he succeeded in having his payments increased to four dollars, based on a surgeon's determination that the disability resulting from his Olustee gunshot wound had been "rated to [sic] low" back in 1866. But starting in 1879, as Wilson reapplied for his pension under the new "Arrears Act," which allowed veterans to seek additional retroactive payments, he hit a wall of rejection: the Pension Bureau was unwilling to accept Wilson's claim that a back injury, incurred in the war, had eclipsed the old gunshot wound as a source of impairment and should be rated as a pensionable injury. The surgeons' exams to which Wilson repeatedly subjected himself over the course of the 1880s charted his descent into excruciating pain, traceable to a puncture wound near his spinal column, sustained at Olustee, when a tree limb fell on Wilson's back. Wilson noted that he received "but little attention" to that wound at Beaufort Hospital, South Carolina, where he was evacuated, as the Minié ball wound to his abdomen necessitated his lying on his injured back for the duration of his time in the hospital. A surgeon examining Wilson in 1882 recommended that his pension be increased from four to six dollars a month on the grounds that his back injury and scarring from a shell injury to his knee each entitled him to an extra two dollars. But this recommendation was rejected because of Wilson's alleged "inability to furnish evidence that said disabilities originated in the service and line of duty."[36]

In the 1880s, as he prepared and then publicized *The Black Phalanx,* Wilson kept submitting requests for a pension increase only to have them turned down, despite examining surgeons' reports that he suffered not only from the wartime abdomen, back, and knee injuries but also from kidney, liver, and heart disease, all of which left him unable to "sit or stand in any position without pain." Again and again the Pension Bureau ruled that there was insufficient evidence of a pensionable "increase of disability" from the back injury over time.[37]

Interspersed with the physicians' affidavits in Wilson's pension application file are testimonials from Wilson's wartime comrades-in-arms and postwar friends and associates, who attempted to persuade the Pension Bureau that Wilson was not only a credible claimant but also a man of distinction. In 1888, Reverend Henry A. Monroe, recently appointed pastor of St. Mark's AME Church in New York City, furnished an affidavit in support of Wilson's bid for a pension increase. Monroe, who grew up in New Bedford, had been a drummer boy in Company C of the Fifty-Fourth Massachusetts, having joined up at age thirteen only to find himself beating out battle instructions during the famous Fort Wagner assault six months after enlisting. After the war, Monroe worked as a teacher for the Freedman's Bureau, as a newspaper publisher, and as a customs inspector for the Port of Baltimore. Monroe in his 1888 affidavit related that he had known Wilson since boyhood, and that he had been present at Olustee to bear witness to Wilson's agonies there. He found Wilson in the woods "three or four miles from the battle field, entirely exhausted and suffering from wounds received in said battle of Olustee and also from the falling of a tree limb upon him at the same time and place." Monroe dressed Wilson's wounds as best he could and helped him "to Sanderson station, and seated him on a log by a fire, to await proper medical attention." "I did not see the said Joseph T. Wilson after that night until 1882, at Baltimore, Maryland, while I was attending the Grand Army Encampment" of the G.A.R. there, Monroe observed.[38]

A second boyhood acquaintance from New Bedford vouched for Wilson in 1888: W. D. Kelly, formerly a corporal in Company C, now residing in Leavenworth, Kansas. Kelly was near Wilson during Olustee and saw him wounded in the abdomen and back; "from appearance I thought it impossible for him to live," Kelly revealed. The next morning, Kelly found Wilson "lying among the wounded" at "Barbour Station," ten miles from the battlefield. Kelly did not see Wilson again until 1876, at the unveiling in Washington, D.C., of the Freedmen's Memorial (also known as the Emancipation Memorial or Lincoln Statue), which was funded primarily by contributions from ex-slaves; the unveiling featured a stirring speech of tribute to the late president by Frederick Douglass. Kelly was incredulous that Wilson had survived the gut shot at Olustee. "I had him go home with me that night," Kelly related, "that I might see the scar on the abdomen."[39]

The following year, Wilson added to his roster of character-witnesses fellow Virginians such as William F. Galt, a Norfolk saloonkeeper whose affidavit identified Wilson as the organizer and former commander of the local Grand Army Post and described him as severely hampered by his back injury. "While he was inspector of customs I worked under his direction," Galt explained, "and knew that he was unable to put down the beam of the scales in weighing salt without injury to his back." A second Norfolk friend, the hotel owner and caterer Thomas F. Paige, who served with Wilson in Norfolk's City Council in the early 1870s, explained that he had "frequently assisted [Wilson] in putting braces and plasters on his back," and that on a recent visit to Wilson's home in Richmond, he found his old friend had deteriorated to such a point that he was "confined in his room and unable to walk any distance." The Reverend John H. Riddick, formerly of St. Johns AME Church in Norfolk, also spoke of Wilson's seeking relief from back pain with braces and plasters and an "electric belt." While Wilson had been employed "in various government offices and in editing and publishing newspapers and books," Riddick explained, he was too disabled to perform manual labor or indeed to even lift a pail of water.[40]

The most revealing and remarkable affidavit in Wilson's pension file came in 1890 from John Mitchell Jr. of Richmond, a former slave and postwar journalistic prodigy who was appointed editor of the influential black newspaper the *Richmond Planet* in 1884 at the age of twenty-one, and became a major crusader against lynching and segregation. Clearly Mitchell had found in Wilson a mentor; Mitchell saw Wilson "frequently—almost every week" and admired him as a "man of good character and excellent habits." But clearly too Wilson had entered a phase of acute physical decline. "He is in fact a badly broken up man with injuries wounds and diseases" which were "permanent," Mitchell lamented.[41]

While Wilson did not explicitly address the issue of disabilities or pensions in *The Black Phalanx,* the book's themes—the right of black soldiers to recognition and respect for their patriotic sacrifices, and the moral superiority of the Won Cause to the Lost Cause—went right to the heart of his pension struggle and the struggles of his fellow U.S.C.T. veterans. Just as he made the case that blacks had shown remarkable wartime forbearance in the face of white cruelty, so too did Wilson argue that blacks had shown both discipline and generosity in marshaling their meager resources to sustain the memory of the Union war. The closing chapter of *The Black Phalanx,* titled "Benevolence and Frugality," credited black veterans with founding a path-breaking school, the Lincoln Institute in Missouri, with their charitable contributions, and credited them too with having bankrolled the Freedmen's Memorial (Lincoln statue) in Washington, D.C. How could the nation fail to support such men in turn?[42]

Just as Wilson's close comrades vouched for him in their pension testimonials, he vouched for them in *The Black Phalanx,* praising Corporal W. D. Kelly for having led a successful wartime protest at Morris Island, South Carolina, against local "negro barbers" who refused to shave and cut the hair of black troops, and reprinting the Reverend Henry A. Monroe's poem on the battle of Boykin's Mill, South Carolina (the Fifty-Fourth's last engagement, and "a fitting seal," in Wilson's words, "of the negro to his new covenant with freedom and his country"). As Barbara A. Gannon has observed, "comradeship was not merely about the need for organized political action; instead, it was a complex synergy between the memory of wartime misery and the reality of postwar anguish." Thus *The Black Phalanx* most closely echoes Wilson's pension file in the book's passages on Olustee, for in those passages not only heroism and solidarity but also indelible physical and mental trauma are on display. Wilson describes the scenes he lived through as history not memory—the phalanx is "they" not "we" in his account. But he cannot keep the past at a safe distance. He conjures the "intense anxiety" the night before the battle; the Confederate rifle pits, artillery, sharpshooters, earthworks, cavalry, and "impassable swamp" that confronted the Federals; the "torrent of rebel bullets" that poured volley after volley "into the very faces" of the outnumbered Union men; the frightful carnage as men entered the "very jaws of death . . . slaughtered by the enemy at will."

Wilson conjures too the "sickening and sad" scene the next morning, at Barber's station, where the Fifty-Fourth had fallen back: "The wounded lay everywhere, upon the ground, huddled around the embers of fagot fires, groaning and uttering cries of distress. The surgeons were busy relieving, as best they could, the more dangerously wounded. The foot-sore and hungry soldiers sought out their bleeding and injured comrades and placed them upon railroad flats. . . . [T]he mangled and mutilated forms of about three hundred soldiers were dragged forward mile after mile."

In no other portion of *The Black Phalanx* do so many desperate descriptors crowd the text: the men are shattered, scattered, stampeded, slaughtered, mowed down, maimed, mangled, and routed. But the battle was their crucible and courage and solidarity their saving grace. Wilson ends his account of Olustee with a tribute to the white and black Union troops there who had risen above "distinction based upon color" and had "fought together" and "endured its horrors together." The tribute doubled as a rebuke to those Americans who had already forgotten these sacrifices and who would not give the saviors of the Union their due.[43]

On September 25, 1891, less than a year after John Mitchell Jr. had described him as "badly broken up," Joseph T. Wilson died of heart disease, while visiting Norfolk from Richmond, to deliver a lecture at a church there. His widow, Elizabeth, submitted a "Declaration for Widow's Pension" in October, reminding the authorities that Wilson's multiple requests for an increase in his payments were still pending at the time of his death. Joseph T. Wilson "was wounded and contracted disease in the service and line of duty, which finally killed him," Elizabeth noted with pathos. Mitchell stepped forward to plead her case, explaining that she was in dire financial circumstances, with no regular work or business save for "odd jobs of light work" and no real or personal property save for dower rights in a modest house and lot Wilson owned on Brook Avenue in Richmond. The critical success of *The Black Phalanx* had not translated into financial security. In February of 1892, Elizabeth Wilson was awarded payments of twelve dollars a month and belated acknowledgment that her husband's back injury, as well as his abdomen wound and failing organs, were traceable to his wartime service and entitled his family to a greater measure of support.[44]

Wilson was buried in the cemetery of the Soldiers' Home near Fort Monroe, with military honors, in a ceremony attended by an "immense throng of battle-scarred veterans (mostly white)." Obituaries described him as a man of refinement who "carefully cultivated his mind with the best literature of the world," and as an "agitator" who showed "bulldog tenacity" in addressing "questions of great concern to the race."[45]

What then should we make of Wilson's life? His literary career was inseparable from his political activism. Wilson was in many respects a transitional figure: a bridge between the early black historians such as William Wells Brown and modern pioneers such as Carter G. Woodson; a bridge between Frederick Douglass's antislavery activism and W. E. B. Du Bois's promotion of the talented tenth (a concept Wilson would have heartily endorsed); and a bridge between the emancipationist mode of Civil War commemoration, with its emphasis on abolition as the great achievement of the war, and the Union Cause tradition, with its emphasis on the saving of the nation.

It was a source of deep disappointment to Wilson that his intellectual achievement did not translate into greater political authority. In his last years, Wilson received many touching tributes from his admirers. Among them is a June 1890 article in Mitchell's *Richmond Planet* titled "A Lesson in Patriotism." It urged readers to go see a stirring painting, by a Richmonder named John Walker, on exhibition at a bookstore in the city. The painting depicted African American children heading from a distant schoolhouse to a Memorial Day celebration, and being greeted there by a "Colored soldier in uniform with the initials of the Grand Army of the Republic on his cap and the badges of that powerful organization on his breast." The soldier "points to a grave on which he has placed the choicest flowers," and "as the children gather around him with open mouthed astonishment and awe he relates the story of the war . . . and impresses upon them the necessity of revering the memory of those who died." After describing the painting, the author of the article closes by noting that "the soldier is an admirable likeness of Col. Joseph T. Wilson, one of the survivors of the famous 54th Regiment, and author of the 'Black Phalanx.'"[46]

Unfortunately for Wilson, this tribute came in the midst of a new wave of indignities and outrages. The white press in Richmond, covering an 1890

"Colored People's Convention" in the city chaired by Wilson, sneeringly put his G.A.R. title of colonel in quotation marks. That year Wilson had already undertaken a sobering mission to Washington, D.C., on behalf of Virginia's blacks, to protest the deterioration of their political status: he was part of a five-man delegation that testified before the House committee on the election of the president and vice-president that widespread election fraud in the last presidential race had disfranchised tens of thousands of black voters. Invoking the Fourteenth Amendment, they asked that the representation of the South be reduced to the extent that suffrage was suppressed. Their appeals fell on deaf ears.[47]

The disjuncture between achievement and reward is the theme of what is perhaps Wilson's most moving piece of writing: his poem, published in the 1881 volume *Voice of a New Race*, titled "The Negro Statesman." The poem tells the story of a humble freedman who has a stirring vision—the dream that he appears on the Senate floor to argue on behalf of Charles Sumner's Civil Rights Bill, an anti-segregation measure that was debated for years before finally passing in 1875. Wilson writes of this character,

> He dreamed the nation's forum he'd won
> To tell the marvelous tale of his race,
> Upon the Senate floor he stood;
> A thousand waiting ears were opened
> To catch his matchless eloquence.

In the speech that follows, the protagonist traces out in microcosm the very themes of solidarity and patriotism that would animate *The Black Phalanx*:

> Because I am black, the color of the skin
> May enhance the opinion, where prejudice has root,
> That I am lured by individualism,
> To contend for equal rights.
> But sirs, I speak not for myself alone,
> But for thousands of those who me have sent
> Do I plead here for equal public rights
> For which your fathers and our fathers
> In the Revolutionary strife did fight. . . .

. . . War necessity made the Negro free
You agree his manhood with yours the country from
            dissolution helped to save.
Equal in patriotism even with the bravest brave.
        Equal now in the law,
He seeks to be raised with those whose lives
        And fortunes he helped to save.

In the poem's final verses the speaker, his fantasy dispelled, crashes to earth, finding himself alone in his gloomy cabin, a storm pattering on the roof, the darkness pierced by flashes of lightning. In conjuring this character's "brooding mingled vision of hope, ambition and despair," Joseph T. Wilson described himself.[48]

NOTES

1. *People's Advocate* (Washington, D.C.) as qtd. in *Washington* (D.C.) *Bee,* July 14, 1883; *Washington Bee,* September 8, 1883; *Petersburg Lancet,* August 4, 1883. On the press's anticipation of the publication of *Black Phalanx,* see also *New York Freeman,* January 24, 1885, and August 14, 1886.

2. For the "Sells Fast" ad see, for example, *Forest Republican* (Tionesta, Pa.), November 9, 1887; *Essex County Herald* (Guildhall, Vt.), November 4, 1887; *Middleburgh* (Pa.) *Post,* January 12, 1888; *Cacoctin* (Md.) *Clarion,* May 16, 1889. For the "All Say" ad see *The Comet* (Johnston City, Tenn.), November 22, 1888, and *The Appeal* (Saint Paul, Minn.), October 3, 1891. For the Penn quotation, see Irvine Garland Penn, *The Afro-American Press and Its Editors* (Springfield, Mass.: Willey & Co., 1891), 179. For the book as a prize and "special offer," see *New York Age,* August 3, 1889; *Southwestern Christian Advocate* (New Orleans), November 4, 1897; *Richmond Planet,* July 23, 1898.

3. *Cleveland Gazette,* February 18, 1888; *New York Age,* March 10, 1888; *A.M.E. Church Review* (January 1890): [385]; W. T. Andrews and J. W. Cromwell, *In Memoriam. Tally R. Holmes, of South Carolina, and Col. Joseph T. Wilson, of Virginia. Eulogies Delivered by W. T. Andrews and J. W. Cromwell* (Washington, D.C.: Howard University Print, 1891), 11; *New York Age,* October 10, 1891; *Richmond Planet,* October 3, 1891; *Los Angeles Times,* February 13, 1900; *Lexington Standard,* October 21, 1911; C. G. Woodson, "My Recollections of Veterans of the Civil War," in *Negro History Bulletin* (February 1, 1944): 115–16.

4. W. Fitzhugh Brundage, *The Southern Past: A Clash of Race and Memory* (Cambridge, Mass.: Harvard University Press, 2008), 90–100; Laurie F. Maffly-Kipp, *Setting Down the Sacred Past: African-American Race Histories* (Cambridge, Mass.: Harvard University Press, 2010), 212; Stephen G. Hall, *A Faithful Account of the Race: African American Historical Writing in Nineteenth-Century America* (Chapel Hill: University of North Carolina Press.

2009), 155; Lisa A. Long, *Rehabilitating Bodies: Health, History, and the American Civil* War (Philadelphia: University of Pennsylvania Press, 2004), 236–37; John Hope Franklin, *George Washington Williams* (Chicago: University of Chicago Press, 1985). 130–35, 307.

5. For books on the U.S.C.T. that mention Wilson, see for example Dudley Taylor Cornish, *The Sable Arm: Black Troops in the Union Army, 1861–1865* (1956; rpt., Lawrence: University Press of Kansas, 1987); James M. McPherson, *The Negro's Civil War: How American Blacks Felt and Acted during the War for the Union* (New York: Pantheon, 1965); Noah Andre Trudeau, *Like Men of War: Black Troops in the Civil War 1862–1865* (New York: Little, Brown, 1998); John David Smith, ed., *Black Soldiers in Blue: African American Troops in the Civil War Era* (Chapel Hill: University of North Carolina Press, 2002); Donald R. Shaffer, *After the Glory: The Struggles of Black Civil War Veterans* (Lawrence: University Press of Kansas, 2004); John A. Casey Jr., *New Men: Reconstructing the Image of the Veteran in Late Nineteenth Century American Literature and Culture* (New York: Fordham University Press, 2015). On memory, see David W. Blight, *Race and Reunion: The Civil War in American Memory* (Cambridge, Mass.: Harvard University Press, 2001), and Barbara Gannon, *The Won Cause: Black and White Comradeship in the Grand Army of the Republic* (Chapel Hill: University of North Carolina Press, 2011). For negative critical reception of the *Black Phalanx*, see Franklin, *George Washington Williams*, 131–32, and Shaffer, *After the Glory*, 183–84. For books on black politics in Virginia that mention Wilson, see Cassandra L. Newby-Alexander, *An African American History of the Civil War in Hampton Roads* (Charleston, S.C.: The History Press, 2010); Thomas C. Parramore et al., *Norfolk: The First Four Centuries* (Charlottesville: University Press of Virginia, 1994); Peter Rachleff, *Black Labor in Richmond, 1865–1890* (Urbana: University of Illinois Press, 1989).

6. *New York Freeman*, January 24, 1885; 1870 U.S. Federal Census, Norfolk Ward 2, Norfolk, Virginia, accessed through Ancestry.com; 1880 U.S. Federal Census, Norfolk, accessed through Ancestry.com.

7. Certificate of Disability for Discharge, September 30, 1862, Joseph T. Wilson Pension File (hereafter cited as JWP), RG 15, National Archives, Washington, D.C. (repository hereafter cited as NA); *New York Freeman*, January 24, 1885; *Richmond Daily Dispatch*, August 20, 1875; Andrews and Cromwell, *In Memoriam*, 8. In his speech at the 1867 Republican State Convention in Richmond, Wilson himself revealed that he had been "'driven' from his mother when only nine years old for having made such disclosures as led to the recapture of a penitentiary convict—a *white man*," according to the transcription in the *Richmond Daily Dispatch*, April 19, 1867. Wartime sources furnishing details of Wilson's participation in the Fort Fisher expedition and his secret-service work have not come to light, and he does not reference either in his pension application.

8. Brent Tarter, "African Americans and Politics in Virginia (1865–1902)," Encyclopedia Virginia, www.encyclopediavirginia.org/African_Americans_and_Politics_in_Virginia_1865-1902.

9. Philip S. Foner and George E. Walker, *Proceedings of the Black National and State Conventions, 1865–1900* (Philadelphia: Temple University Press, 1986), 1:81–85.

10. John Hammond Moore, "The Norfolk Riot: 16 April 1866," *Virginia Magazine of History and Biography* 90 (April 1982): 156–61; *True Southerner*, April 19, 1866; *Riot at Norfolk*:

Letter from the Secretary of War (Washington, D.C.: GPO, 1867), in Albert and Shirley Small Special Collections Library, University of Virginia, Charlottesville (repository hereafter cited as UVA).

11. *Richmond Daily Dispatch,* April 19, 1867; Andrews and Cromwell, *In Memoriam,* 8–11; Penn, *Afro-American Press,* 176–77; Michael Hucles, "Many Voices, Similar Concerns: Traditional Methods of African-American Political Activity in Norfolk, Virginia, 1865–1875," *Virginia Magazine of History and Biography* 100 (October 1992): 560–61.

12. *New National Era* (Washington, D.C.), August 28, 1873; *Richmond Daily Dispatch,* August 20, 1875; Rachleff, *Black Labor in Richmond,* 78; *Norfolk Daily State Journal,* November 27, 1871; Pippa Holloway, "'A Chicken-Stealer Shall Lose His Vote': Disfranchisement for Larceny in the South, 1874–1890," *Journal of Southern History* 75 (November 2009): 956–57.

13. *Richmond Dispatch,* July 22, 1881; Tarter, "African Americans and Politics."

14. William Wells Brown, *The Negro in the American Rebellion: His Heroism and His Fidelity* (Boston: Lee and Shephard, 1867); George Washington Williams, *A History of the Negro Troops in the War of the Rebellion* (New York: Harper and Brothers, 1888); Maffly-Kipp, *Setting Down the Sacred Past,* 211; Dickson D. Bruce Jr., "The Ironic Conception of American History: The Early Black Historians, 1881–1915," *Journal of Negro History* 69 (Spring 1984): 57.

15. Joseph T. Wilson, *Emancipation: Its Course and Progress, from 1491 B.C. to A.D. 1875* (Hampton, Va.: Normal School Steam Power Press Print, 1882), 139–41.

16. Wilson, *Black Phalanx,* 49–50, 68, 88.

17. Ibid., 93–95, 132, 199, 207, 211.

18. Ibid., 316, 349, 418, 420–21. On Mahone and Confederate commemoration of the battle of the Crater, see Kevin M. Levin, *Remembering the Battle of the Crater: War as Murder* (Lexington: University Press of Kentucky, 2012), 42–51.

19. *Lynchburg Virginian,* August 11, 12, 1881; *People's Advocate,* November 19, 1881.

20. Wilson, *Black Phalanx,* 167, 173, 176–77, 181; *Proceedings of the First to Tenth Meetings, 1866–1876, of the National Encampment Grand Army of the Republic* (Philadelphia: Samuel P. Town, 1877), 144; Nathan W. Daniels, *Thank God My Regiment Is an African One: The Civil War Diary of Colonel Nathan W. Daniels,* ed. C. P. Weaver (Baton Rouge: Louisiana State University Press, 1998), xvi.

21. Wilson, *Black Phalanx,* 176, 208, 211–14; Daniels, *Thank God My Regiment Is an African One,* 15, 40–42, 168.

22. Wilson, *Black Phalanx,* 528.

23. Ibid., 179–80, 200, 397, 503.

24. For characterizations of Wilson as defensive, see Shaffer, *After the Glory,* 183; Casey, *New Men,* 160; and Levin, *Remembering the Battle of the Crater,* 84.

25. *True Southerner,* December 28, 1865. See also "Andre Cailloux" in Joseph T. Wilson, *Voice of a New Race: Original Selections of Poems, with a Trilogy and Oration* (Hampton, Va.: Normal School Steam Press, 1882).

26. *New York Age,* March 10, 1888; Charlotte F. Grimké, "Colored People in New England," *New York Evangelist,* October 24, 1889.

27. Barry Strauss, "The Black Phalanx: African-Americans and the Classics after the Civil War," *Arion* 12 (Winter 2005): 40–45; Wilson, *Black Phalanx,* 397, 420–21 (quotations).

28. *Lynchburg Virginian,* August 11, 1881; *Richmond Whig,* August 12, 118.

29. *Staunton Spectator,* March 4, 1884, *New York Times,* February 28, 1884, Rachleff, *Black Labor in Richmond,* 109; (Richmond) *State,* September 25, 1891.

30. Joseph T. Wilson, *Twenty Two Years of Freedom* (Norfolk: Thomas F. Paige, 1885), 10, 54–59, 61–62.

31. Margaret Malamud, "'A Kind of Moral Gladiatorship': Abolitionist Use of the Classics," *Arion* 23 (Fall 2015): 57–90; Wilson, *Emancipation, 49.* On regenerative militarism, see Jackson Lears, *Rebirth of a Nation: The Making of Modern America, 1877–1920* (New York: Harper Perennial, 2010), 2, 31, 204.

32. Larry M. Logue and Peter Blanck, "'Benefit of the Doubt': African-American Civil War Veterans and Pensions," *Journal of Interdisciplinary History* 38 (Winter 2008): 379–82.

33. Heywood T. Sanders, "'Paying for the 'Bloody Shirt': The Politics of Civil War Pensions," in Barry S. Rundquist, ed., *Political Benefits: Empirical Studies of American Public Programs* (Lexington, Mass.: D. C. Heath, 1980), 139–40, 146–49; Sven E. Wilson, "Prejudice & Policy: Racial Discrimination in the Union Army Disability Pension System, 1865–1906," *American Journal of Public Health* 100 (April 2010): 56–65.

34. Certificate of Disability for Discharge, May 2, 1864, Wilson to Major Clark, November 22, 1864, and February 15, 1865, Wilson Compiled Service Record, NA (accessed through Fold3); Barbara A. Gannon, "African American Soldiers," Essential Civil War Curriculum, www.essentialcivilwarcurriculum.com/african-american-soldiers.html.

35. Wilson Declaration for Invalid Pension, November 14, 1866; Wilson affidavit, November 14, 1866; Examining Surgeon's Certificate, February 25, 1867, JWP.

36. Examining Surgeon's Certificate, December 23, 1874, Compiled Service Record; Wilson "Hospital Statement," Richmond, ca. 1883; Examining Surgeon's Certificate, November 15, 1882; Increase in Invalid Pension Request (rejection), November 2, 1883, JWP.

37. Physician's Affidavits, January 2 and April 15, 1889; June 3, 1891. Surgeon's Certificates, August 25, 1886; December 12, 1888. Increase in Invalid Pension Request (rejection), September 10, 1888. All in JWP.

38. Henry A. Monroe, General Affidavit, September 19, 1888. In his initial 1866 application, Wilson tapped as witnesses Norfolk–based veterans of the Thirty-Fifth U.S.C.T. (formerly First North Carolina) Noah Lamb and Morris Phillip, who were engaged at Olustee and saw Wilson during the retreat "bleeding at the stomach" (Lamb and Phillips testimony, November 14. 1866, JWP).

39. William D. Kelly, General Affidavit, September 28, 1888, JWP.

40. William F. Galt, General Affidavit, June 26, 1889; Thomas F. Paige, General Affidavit, June 27, 1889; John H. Riddick Affidavit, August 28, 1889, all in JWP; *Chataigne's City Directory of Norfolk* (Norfolk, Va.: J H Chataigne, 1889), 244, 384; Hucles, "Many Voices," 561.

41. John Mitchell Jr. Affidavit, December 4, 1890, JWP. On Mitchell, see Ann Field Alexander, *Race Man: The Rise and Fall of the "Fighting Editor" John Mitchell Jr.* (Charlottesville: University of Virginia Press, 2002).

42. Wilson, *Black Phalanx,* 508–12.

43. Ibid., 129, 267–73, 278–79.

44. Elizabeth H. Wilson, Declaration for Widow's Pension, October 1, 1891; Wilson Invalid Pension approval, February 9, 1892, JWP.

45. *New York Age,* October 10, 1891; *Los Angeles Times,* October 22, 1891; Andrews and Cromwell, *In Memoriam,* 11–12.

46. *Richmond Planet,* June 28, 1890.

47. *Richmond Dispatch,* April 15, 1890; *New York Times, Philadelphia Inquirer,* and *Macon Telegraph,* January 26, 1890.

48. Wilson, "The Negro Statesman," in *Voice of a New Race,* 14–22.

"Madam Velasquez in Female Attire." Frontispiece for the 1876 edition of
The Woman in Battle. From C. J. Worthington, ed., *The Woman in Battle: A
Narrative of the Exploits, Adventures, and Travels of Madame Loreta Janeta
Velasquez, otherwise Known as Lieutenant Harry T. Buford, Confederate
States Army* (Richmond, Va.: Dustin, Gilman & Co., 1876).

The Soldier Who Never Was

Loreta Velasquez and The Woman in Battle

WILLIAM C. DAVIS

In 1961 historian Daniel Boorstin published *The Image: A Guide to Pseudo-events in America.* In it he defined a celebrity as "a person who is known for his well-knownness." As he saw it, the revolution in journalism and other forms of communication, particularly television, had for the first-time separated fame from greatness, and that in turn had hastened the decay of fame into mere notoriety. British journalist Malcolm Muggeridge later gave the phenomenon a name still used today. In 1967 he wrote that "In the past if someone was famous or notorious, it was for something—as a writer or an actor or a criminal; for some talent or distinction or abomination." But "today one is famous for being famous."

Critic Neal Gabler recently refined the definition of celebrity to distinguish those who gain recognition for doing virtually nothing of significance. He dubbed this the "Zsa Zsa Factor" in honor of Zsa Zsa Gabor, further defining that kind of celebrity as "human entertainment," by which he meant a person who provided entertainment solely by being alive. All agreed that celebrity is fame and public attention in the media. There have always been celebrities. Earlier generations mobbed composer and pianist Franz Liszt, aviator Charles Lindberg, and chess master Paul Morphy.

The true modern media celebrity is a different kind of animal, a creation that capitalizes on our ever more trivialized popular culture. Amy Argetsinger asserted in the *Washington Post* in 2009 that such characters first appeared in the dawn of television thanks to that medium's ability to make seemingly anyone famous overnight. In fact, this is not at all a new phenomenon. This kind of celebrity really dates to around 1880 when mass monthly magazines like *Harper's, McClure's,* and *Scribner's* had their heyday. Detecting a growing public interest in celebrities—stage actors in particular—this new press fed and encouraged that appetite.

Yet there was one person, one woman, who was decades ahead of everyone else. She may not have been the first of her kind in the modern sense of the term, but almost certainly she made herself the Confederacy's one and only self-created "media celebrity." If any Americans today know her at all, it is as Loreta Janeta Velasquez, the Cuban-born southern heroine who masqueraded as Lieutenant Harry T. Buford of the "Independent Scouts," to fight for the Confederacy on battlefields from Virginia to Mississippi. She detailed it all in her startling 1876 book *The Woman in Battle,* which is still in print today.

There she told the story of her aristocratic origins in a Spanish family in Cuba, her childhood move to New Orleans, her privileged upbringing and private tutoring, and her secret yearnings to experience the adventurous life then reserved only for men. Indeed, from an early age she occasionally tried on her brother's clothing and daydreamed of performing heroic feats of arms. When a young woman she defied her family and married an army officer, following him to the West in the "Mormon Expedition" of 1857, and then saw him resign his commission in 1861 to take a commission in the Confederate forces from Louisiana. At the same time, she determined to outfit herself in a man's uniform and accompany him to the front leading her own company, which she raised in Arkansas. But no sooner did she get her company to her husband's posting at Pensacola than he was killed accidentally, and she left for Richmond to fight with the army in Virginia.

As Lieutenant Harry T. Buford, she saw dramatic action at Blackburn's Ford and the First Battle of Bull Run in July 1861, then at Ball's Bluff that fall, after which for the first time she decided to cross the lines as a spy, once more in female attire. She went to Washington, learned secret plans for an attack on New Orleans, and of course had an audience with President Lincoln. Then she was off for Confederate lines in Kentucky, soon afterward being engaged at Fort Donelson, and then Shiloh, after which she had an opportunity to assassinate General Ulysses S. Grant but thought better of it. Then she went to New Orleans in time to be present when the

Federals occupied the city. She began spying again, meanwhile smuggling drugs into the city for Confederate sympathizers, until she ran afoul of General Benjamin F. "Beast" Butler, the Union commander of the occupied city, who sent her to prison for defying him. Once released, she crossed into Mississippi and went to Jackson, carrying messages for Confederate commanders there in the summer of 1863, appearing in uniform as needed and as herself when useful. She then went to Richmond as Buford but attracted suspicion and was arrested at first, but soon employed in the Confederate Secret Service to carry important dispatches to Mississippi. On her way west she stopped in Atlanta and was admitted to an army hospital with a high fever, and there she met the convalescing Captain Thomas DeCaulp of the Third Arkansas Cavalry. She was still posing as Buford, but soon love blossomed, she revealed herself to him, and they were married.

All too soon, DeCaulp was back in the field and suffered a relapse that led to his death that fall. In her grief, Velasquez returned once more to spying, and crossed the lines into Union-held Memphis. For much of the rest of the war she operated as a spy in the North, particularly in Washington, where she penetrated the inner counsels of the Federal secret service. Then she infiltrated the U.S. Arsenal at Indianapolis, helped organize a planned prison break at the Johnson's Island camp for Confederate prisoners of war, and began blockade running, once more getting contraband goods into the Confederacy. At the same time, she masterminded the counterfeiting of millions of dollars' worth of U.S. Treasury notes, traveled back and forth across the North and next to England to help finance the Rebel cause. When the Confederate surrender came, she left the country for Venezuela, married the handsome Major Wasson, who soon died of fever, and returned to the United States to start her life again in the West. She went to the mining camps of Utah and Nevada, lived among the Mormons, married a prospector she never named in her book, then in 1872 abandoned him to return to the East. She had gotten as far as the Pecos River in Texas in December 1873 when she decided her narrative was long enough and brought it to a close.

From the day of its appearance in print in the summer of 1876, *The Woman in Battle* has been itself an embattled book, questioned and condemned by critics—some of them former Confederates, and warmly embraced by others whose needs it served. If her story sounded too good to be true—and it did to many even in her own time—that is because it is.

In fact, almost everything in her book is a fiction, written as she frankly admitted at the time, because she needed to make money. Even the name on the title page is an invention. We have no idea what her real name was at birth, though her given name *may have been* Lauretta or some variant. Her unknown parents were certainly not called Velasquez, a surname she invented for herself in 1875. They might have been named Williams, but we will likely never know. Prior to becoming Velasquez, Lauretta claimed a number of other names and parentages—Clark, Williams, Roche or Roach, and Clapp being just the ones we know. She did not decide to become Cuban until the 1870s, too, and before then gave her birthplace as Louisiana, Texas, Mississippi, Barbados, New Providence, and elsewhere. Her nativities, like her many names, were each just a stage in a continually evolving narrative she began to create publicly in the fall of 1861 and continued to hone and manipulate for years even after her book's appearance.

We know nothing trustworthy of her life prior to 1860 when she was living in New Orleans under the name Ann Williams, nineteen years of age, working as a prostitute in a brothel on Dryades Street run by a notorious local madam named Clara Fisher.[1] However, from what is genuinely known of her life we can infer some assumptions about her on the eve of war. She was ambitious. She knew how to charm and use people, particularly men, to further her own aims. She hungered for fame and notoriety. She had some desire to be a writer. She was a facile liar, though a careless one, and routinely contradicted her past fabrications with her newer ones. For her lying seems to have been more than just means toward ends. No lie was too big for her to tell, and when one of her stories was publicly exposed as falsehood, she either just brazened it out by repeating her story more emphatically, or brought out a set of new inventions to explain away the old ones. She genuinely appears to have enjoyed lying for its own sake, and often lied when she had nothing to gain.

The score or more of her surviving letters testify to her moderate literacy with a pen. Her crude penmanship and command of spelling, grammar, and syntax were on a par with that to be expected from the public-school education available to lower- and working-class females of her generation, but they vociferously gainsay her book's claims of privileged private tutoring under a governess and an exclusive New Orleans finishing school. There is no question that she could read well. That is likely what attracted her to the one and only public "medium" of the time, the newspaper press, first as a reader, but at some point, with the thought of writing for it herself. Once the war started she saw in the New Orleans papers that soldiers going to the front wrote letters back to editors that were published. She also must have seen the frequent accounts of young heroines trying to pose as soldiers, and the compliments they got for their patriotism. If only she could do that she could satisfy multiple urges—become a writer, earn some money, and achieve notoriety. The problem was that war journalism was exclusively a male realm.

One fact is evident from the outset. She never intended to be a real soldier, or to pass for a man. She either made or bought some semblance of a Confederate officer's uniform, but she did not wear it in public in New Orleans at first. She was well known there for her profession and occasional encounters with the police, and the less notoriety about that the better. But in September 1861 she boarded a train to Memphis to begin the journey to Virginia to make her "debut." In that month, Memphis authorities arrested a mysterious woman dressed in a Confederate officer's uniform on suspicion of being a spy. She gave no name, but told the local press that her husband had been a captain killed at First Bull Run, that thereafter his company elected her to take his place, and now she was en route to join her command.

Everything about the story bore hallmarks of Lauretta's later modus. Far from concealing her gender, this woman's uniform was a prop to *gain* attention. She *wanted* to be identified as a woman, and immediately after her release she apparently took her story to a local editor. She wanted notoriety. Moreover, her story was complete fiction. No captain from Louisiana was killed in the battle, but to be safe she gave no details like a name or regiment that could be checked. Moreover, a person traveling by train from Louisiana to Virginia would not pass through Memphis. Within days, papers in Nashville, New Orleans, Richmond, Alabama, and North Carolina, among others, republished her story. Soon it crossed the lines into the North, appearing in Wisconsin, Indiana, Ohio, and elsewhere, so great was the interest in such a novelty.[2]

There was a valuable lesson to be learned, if Lauretta did not already know it. Every newspaper on the continent participated in editorial exchanges with other papers in their region, or across the country. Depending on the speed of the railroads, a story in a Memphis newspaper could appear in a Richmond paper in just two or three days. The telegraph could cut that time to just hours, though sending lengthy news articles by the wires was cumbersome and done only for the most important scoops. Nevertheless, technology now meant that there was no longer such a thing as a "local" story.

If the Memphis woman was not Lauretta, *she* unquestionably made "*his*" debut in Lynchburg, Virginia, on the evening of September 24 when people saw an officer step off the eastbound train and walk across the street to the Piedmont House. He signed the hotel register as "Lt. Buford," the first known usage of Lauretta's alias. That done, "he" went back outside and paraded the streets and sidewalks of the city in what witnesses believed to be a deliberate effort to attract notice. The mayor ordered his arrest on suspicion of being a spy, and police quickly brought "Buford" before a magistrate, where Lauretta admitted her charade and gave her name as Mary Ann Keith of Memphis. As her story unfolded, however, it revealed beyond doubt that she was Ann Williams—Lauretta.

She said she had been twice married, first to a man now in the Yankee army, and then to a Confederate soldier from whom she was separated. She said nothing now of being the widow of the fictional dead captain, the first example of how quickly her lies could evolve, often for no apparent reason. She said now that her real reason for impersonating an officer was that she felt "determined to fight the battles of her country, and thought such disguise more likely to enable her to accomplish her object."[3] She was sent to Richmond for investigation, still in her uniform, but on arrival managed to talk her way free and then called at the War Department. She boldly demanded a passport back to west Tennessee, where she now said she was on active service under General Leonidas Polk. No one saw through her disguise, and she actually got the pass but almost gave herself away on leaving the office when, instead of saluting, she curtsied.[4]

The notoriety came instantly and was practically universal. All of the Richmond papers carried items on Keith/Buford, and within a week editorial exchanges saw her story in print in Staunton, Virginia; Raleigh, North Carolina; Memphis; and Nashville, and then it jumped the battle lines to an even larger readership in Washington, Baltimore, Philadelphia, Boston, Cincinnati, Louisville, and Milwaukee. Before the end of October, it was being read in San Francisco. Thus was celebrity born. In an instant, her tale became the most widely circulated story of any Confederate woman thus far in the war. Having done absolutely nothing in fact, she was becoming famous just for being famous, and the media made her so. And still no one knew her real name.

Lauretta and Lieutenant Buford disappeared for a time for reasons unknown, though one New Orleans journalist who seemed to know a good bit about her reported that she had married a wealthy Arkansas planter and gone home with him until he discovered her past and sent her packing back to the city.[5] She suddenly appeared again on April 23, 1862, dressed as Buford, and surrendered herself at the mayor's office, though for what infraction no one seems to have known. She was interviewed by the provost martial and told him her name was Mrs. M. M. Arnold of Arkansas, and now she said that the reason for her disguise was that she wanted to write a history of the war and believed that posing as a soldier would gain her access to the material she needed. She told of her trip to Lynchburg and arrest there, added some time serving with the army in Virginia, and then claimed to have been back west in time to fight at Shiloh earlier that month. She turned herself in, she said, out of fear that her masquerade might get her in trouble, a transparently false explanation given that no one was forcing her to dress as a man, and the absence of any notice of her doing so in New Orleans suggests that she only put on her uniform in order to turn herself in. Any reader of the city's press knew that reporters covered the mayor's court. By turning herself in she would inevitably get the attention of the press.[6]

Released the next day, she stayed in her uniform, and people saw her as Buford dashing about the city streets on horseback to attract more attention. Now the city press began to connect her with Mary Ann Keith of the Lynchburg episode, but Lauretta's timing was bad, for within hours New Orleans fell to the Federals. At once the local press had more important things for its columns, and editorial exchange with other southern papers was cut off indefinitely. She spent the next seven months in the city living as Mrs. Arnold, though some knew her as Buford and by other aliases, and apparently, she was forced back to her old trade to work in a house run by "the notorious Nelly Bremer."[7] When she made the papers again that fall it was for stealing jewelry from a couple who gave her a room in their home after she told a touching story of being a Union woman cut off from home and friends in the North. Calling herself Lauretta J. Clark, she had formed a liaison with a Federal soldier in the Thirteenth Connecticut Infantry, though her goal seems to have been less romance and more to get access to rations and money, and a hiding place in his tent. Sentenced to six months in prison for larceny, she was released in May 1863, and immediately deported along with other undesirables being shipped to Confederate lines in southern Mississippi.[8] It might seem to be a low ebb, but she was about to rocket to front pages for the next three months. The summer of Harry Buford had begun.

During those months in prison, Lauretta had time to consider what to do next and to evolve her creation, Buford. On her release, she had a revised version ready, and seems to have chosen a course of action to make herself a household name in the Confederacy. She made her way to Jackson, Mississippi, and there on June 4 or 5 called on editor Robert Purdom of Jackson's *Mississippian* to give him what she called a "true account of her remarkable career" as Lieutenant Buford. She did not wait for the press to come to her. She went to the press, which she would do for the rest of her life. Perhaps using wiles developed in her earlier occupation, she charmed Purdom into believing everything she said.

Now her name was Lauretta J. Williams. When the war broke out she was living in Arkansas, married to a man of northern birth devoted to the Union, who afterwards joined the Yankee army. Outraged at her husband's betrayal of her and the South, she vowed to "offer her life upon the altar of her country" and became a soldier herself, donned a Confederate uniform, and assumed the name Buford, now giving him the first name Harry, and implied that "he" was an officer. Buford then went to Texas to raise a company of infantry that she led in the fight at Leesburg or Ball's Bluff on October 21, as well as in other skirmishes, but when authorities attached her company to the Fifth Texas Infantry its surgeon discovered her sex and forced her to return to Arkansas. Continuing to spin her story, Lauretta said she remained in Arkansas until shortly before Shiloh, thus covering the period November 1861 to February 1862 that she left blank in her earlier accounts. After fighting at Shiloh, she went to New Orleans, where she fell ill and was still unwell when the Yankees occupied the city. She told Purdom nothing to link her with the Arnold/Williams who turned herself in to the mayor on April 23.

Once recovered, she said she escaped the occupied city and went to the Louisiana coast, acting as a courier for Confederate sympathizers, and running drugs and uniform cloth through the Union naval blockade of the coast. The Federals arrested her and took her before General Benjamin F.

"Beast" Butler. She defiantly told him that she "gloried in being a rebel," refused to take an oath of allegiance, and proudly declared that she "had fought side by side with Southern men for Southern rights" and would do so again. Butler denounced her as "the most incorrigible she-rebel he had ever met with," and sent her to a "dungeon" to languish "on bread and water," after which the Federals put her in prison as "a dangerous enemy." Thus, she turned those embarrassing six months in prison for larceny into martyrdom to Butler's wrath. When Butler's successor, Major General Nathaniel P. Banks, assumed command in New Orleans, he kept her in confinement until May 17, when he sent her away with other registered enemies.

In offering her story to his readers on June 6, Purdom called her "a lady whose adventures place her in the ranks of the Mollie Pitchers of the present revolution." He saw in her "little of the characteristic weakness of the sex, either in body or mind," but rather "her whole soul was enlisted in the struggle for independence." Lauretta apparently made her story more convincing by socializing with Purdom, for three years later he said he "knew her well during Confederate times," hinting at more than just an interview, especially when he added that he found her "good looking and in speech and manner a perfect lady.[9] This was her first lengthy interview given to the press, the fullest and most detailed to date. It contained foundational elements of the story she told for the rest of her life, though that story constantly evolved. She estimated the press brilliantly. Through editorial exchange it soon ran in newspapers all across the Confederacy, one version headlined "Adventures of a Young Lady in the Army," and the other titled "Career of a Female Volunteer."[10] Probably a quarter-million or more Confederates either read her story or got it by word of mouth. It gained even more circulation in 1864 when Felix G. DeFontaine published his popular *Marginalia; or, Gleanings from an Army Note-book,* a compilation of newspaper articles in which he included an edited variant.[11] Her story even prompted a surge of other stories of female soldiers in the Confederate press, and soon it was appearing in Yankee papers as well.

Now Lauretta managed to sustain public notice on a scale much larger than before. She decided to parlay her past publicity and the more fully realized story she had now into becoming the first woman in American history to become a commissioned officer by getting from President Jefferson Davis a genuine commission for Lieutenant Buford. Such a distinction would create even more notoriety, and something she could manipulate to provide more secure support. Only she knew if she really expected to get a commission to perform active service. Somehow, she acquired gray fabric and shiny brass buttons and made something approximating military pantaloons, and perhaps a short uniform-style jacket. Lauretta left Jackson as soon as she finished her "uniform," and traveled to Mobile, arriving on or before June 16. The *Mississippian* interview had appeared in the local press three days earlier, so the city was primed when she donned her gray suit and paraded its streets just as she had in Lynchburg in 1861, identifying herself as Lieutenant Buford, yet virtually announcing that she was not a man, but the famed Lauretta Williams. For the rest of the summer she deliberately called attention to herself, proof enough that discovery was always her goal.

From Mobile, she wrote to the War Department in Richmond seeking a commission for her alias, "H. T. Buford."[12] Soon she returned to Jackson, perhaps to inspire more press coverage in the *Mississippian,* but she left behind troubling questions in Mobile. A woman dressed as a man aroused suspicion, and impersonating an officer was a serious matter. Obvious though she made it that she was neither a man nor an officer, the local provost marshal issued an order for her arrest shortly after she left Mobile, and meanwhile notified Richmond.

Unaware of the brewing trouble, Lauretta displayed herself and her new uniform back on Jackson's streets on June 24. Within hours a local man described her on the sidewalks walking with "a very perceptible strut, and a trifle of a swagger." He called her "a *rare bird,*" adding that she was "a well made, but not pretty, Confederate lieutenant, of the *genus femina.*" Though her story was certainly romantic, he did not approve her imposture. "We admire angels in calico, but we never could see the charm of dressing up 'the last and best gift of heaven' in pantaloons," he wrote, "though the trowsers were of nice Confederate gray, with brass buttons thrown in." "It may be a splendid opportunity for showing a well turned ankle, but 'while it makes the unthinking laugh, it cannot but make the judicious grieve.'" It was a spectacle, he said, meriting tears more than laughter.[13]

The next day the War Department received her application, which immediately aroused suspicion, and a clerk docketed her letter with the notation "alias H. T. Buford Lt. C.S.A." Within hours a telegram sped west ordering her arrest and transport to Richmond for investigation. Thus, when she returned to Mobile hoping for a response to her application, the provost arrested her and sent her to Virginia, still in her uniform, which attracted attention whenever she and her guard changed trains en route. In Richmond on the morning of July 1, her guard took her immediately to provost martial general Brigadier General John H. Winder.

The *Mississippian* story appeared in the city papers a dozen days earlier so editors—and Winder's office—ought to have known her as Laura J. Williams, but on her arrival now the *Enquirer* misidentified her as Alice Williams. The rest of the capital press copied the *Enquirer*'s mistake, and Lauretta apparently did nothing to correct them. Given her appetite for publicity, she may have allowed the erroneous Alice to stand when she saw how much press coverage she got. Her focus always was on immediate publicity.

Confronting Winder now, she adopted what someone in the War Office regarded as "an independent air," warning him that, if he tried to press charges against her, she would "claim foreign protection" as a British subject (which she certainly was not). Nevertheless, Winder concluded that "there was something wrong about her" and ordered her sent to Castle Thunder, the city's prison for suspected disloyal citizens, spies, and political prisoners. Learning of her arrest, the *Enquirer* speculated that she was "not of the build to be frightened easily by either gun or goblin." The next day newspaper coverage really commenced, rather unsympathetically at first when the *Enquirer* observed that she was "not quite as pretty as the romance of her case might admit."[14] Referring to her Purdom interview, the *Examiner* recalled that "recently a glowing account of a female, in Confederate uniform, went the rounds of the Southern press," and sarcastically commented that "she was a second Joan of Arc, and had done, and was to do more remarkable things."[15] Still, so far as anyone knew, no specific charges faced her other than posing as a man and officer. Within days Confederates read of "a female Lieutenant" in the capital.

During her fortnight at Castle Thunder, Lauretta alternately charmed and bullied the inmates and the superintendents. One recalled in 1879 that she wore her uniform constantly, probably having no other clothes with her when arrested, and though generally good-natured, she often became indignant at her treatment. Jailors allowed her to roam in the prison and employed her in its office when they needed letters written. They also let her walk outside occasionally under guard, and characteristically she soon demanded that she be allowed to go out on her own since no charges were as yet filed against her.

When Winder found nothing warranting further incarceration, he ordered Lauretta's release on July 10. Meanwhile one or two reporters got some brief details from her to flesh out the *Mississippian* profile, as Lauretta continued to hone her story. Forgetting or discarding her earlier claims to have been born Clark or Williams, she now for the first time named her father as Major J. B. Roche, a nonexistent wealthy Mississippi planter. She boasted that she had an annual income of $20,000 before the war, but that for the past two years she spent most of that buying medicine for the Confederate government, or following the army in her own ambulance loaded with medicines, bandages, and a slave, tending the wounded. Thus, she made herself a Florence Nightingale, a guise she would return to again. Meanwhile, based on rumor, the press, or Lauretta's own claims, one reporter declared that "she has been known to lend a helping hand with the musket at several battles in which she participated."[16] Still she said nothing about First Bull Run and only implied presence at Shiloh. And still she wore her uniform.

Back at Castle Thunder a rumor soon circulated that Lauretta became so popular that someone offered her an appointment as a clerk, and even that she may have accepted. "She longs for the wars, however," noted one journalist.[17] Sometime during the five days following her release, Lauretta called at the War Department to see Adjutant General Samuel Cooper, perhaps to inquire about her application for a commission—on which no action was ever taken—or to offer her services as Mrs. Williams or Harry Buford alike. She certainly prevailed on Cooper to give her a pass and some money for rail travel. The government brought her to Richmond for no good reason, and she could rightfully demand that it return her at its expense at least as far as Atlanta. She may have gotten his permission to write occasionally with any pertinent observations made as she traveled, but he did not in any way employ her. Cooper could expect little of use, but for her part such letters should at least generate letters of thanks in return, documents she could display as evidence of her connections and intimacy with high-ranking Confederates. She understood instinctively that the most mundane note from someone in authority could be parlayed into a document lending legitimacy to almost any claim.

Armed with Cooper's pass, she boarded a train on July 16 to start for Atlanta. Behind her she left charmed newsmen entirely taken in by her story. "It is hardly probable that this brave but eccentric woman will be kept out of the fights in Mississippi," wrote one.[18] Vicksburg had fallen to Grant on July 4, and the Federals were threatening Jackson once more. Noting on her departure that "she is brave, but eccentric, and certainly has an ambition to distinguish herself in the sphere allotted to man," another paper agreed that, "if she is allowed the opportunity, she will doubtless take a hand in the fight at Jackson."[19] Most fulsome of all was the *Enquirer,* which touted the valuable service of "the distinguished female lieutenant" as both nurse and soldier, and concluded that "she appears to be all her published history represents her to be—a woman of heroic character, fearing no danger, dreading no trial, shunning no duty that her self-chosen fortune may send her." The writer wished her a long life "to enjoy her fame." The *Enquirer* gave her a new sobriquet that other papers copied, and which she immediately adopted herself. Hereafter she would be "the female Lieutenant."[20] Hearing that she was in Richmond, prominent visitors, foreign diplomats, and important military officers sought audiences to hear her story. When she left for Atlanta, more senior officers called on her when they learned she was on their train. She had succeeded brilliantly. She had actually *done nothing.* She had made herself famous for being famous. More than a century before Neal Gabler identified the "Zsa Zsa Factor," the "Female Lieutenant" inaugurated the "Lauretta Factor."

The press continued to cover her movements after she left Richmond. When she changed trains on July 18 in Columbia, South Carolina, a local editor commented of "this far-famed female soldier" that "she has already been in the service a great while, and is represented to be a woman of heroic character, fearing no danger and shrinking from no undertaking."[21] Many of her new embellishments to her story got into the papers, no doubt through her own agency, and soon the fame of "the female Lieutenant" spread through the Confederacy. Articles from the Richmond papers found their way into journals elsewhere in Virginia, in South Carolina and Georgia, and probably as far away as Alabama and Tennessee.

In fact, she did a small service for the Confederacy now, though clearly unsolicited and entirely unofficial. When she reached Atlanta on the evening of July 19, she wrote a brief letter to General Cooper to give him "my oppinion of the war." It is clear in her letter that she had no official mission as an agent of the War Department, and she actually closed it with an apology for sending unsolicited information. "I take this liberty of adressing you and hope you will not think me bold by so doing," she told Cooper. "Boldness in woman I deprecate," she continued, while "the want of it in Man att the present crisis of times I deplore." In closing she spoke of herself as "the female Lieutenant whoes whole soul is Enlisted in her countrys cause," and signed it "Mrs. Laurretta J. Williams Alias Lieut H. T. Buford."[22]

There in Atlanta, her life was about to take a sudden, and bizarre, new turn. She met and on September 5, 1863, married Captain Thomas C. De-Caulp. He was the perfect match for her, since his name was not DeCaulp, and he already had a wife and child in Arkansas.[23] The marriage, too, got her publicity, but not the kind she wanted. "We know nothing of the character of these parties," an Augusta editor opined about ten days after the marriage. "The matter is invested with an air of romance that may be captivating to the young and thoughtless, and mischievous in its influence, and we therefore allude to it to express regret that any Southern woman, however ardent her patriotism and pure her purposes, should so far discard the delicacy of her sex, and all regard for a public sense of decorum as to enter the army as a soldier."[24] Lauretta was learning the lesson facing all celebrities, that glory is fleeting and the press can turn on you overnight.

That was Lauretta's final press coverage in the Confederacy, appropriately enough because now she said farewell to Lieutenant Buford. Despite her notoriety, not one Confederate official had taken her seriously. Many in the press doubted her claims, and now criticism tarnished even the notice of her wedding. Her Confederate loyalty—like her later attachments to men, causes, and even children—was driven more by self-interest than conviction. Years later she lauded southerners who held out to the last in 1865, but her dedication now was nothing if not elastic. In October, DeCaulp deserted to become a galvanized Yankee in a Wisconsin regiment, with at least her agreement if not her active encouragement, and she followed him North, where first she worked in an Indianapolis ammunition plant making cartridges to be fired at Confederates, and offering to sell the Federals supposedly vital secret information on the Confederacy in return for giving her husband a promotion. That was only the beginning of new adventures that she also later lied about and embellished, but her days as Lieutenant Harry T. Buford were over, days she soon recalled as her "former glory."

The rest of her verifiable wartime career is equally at odds with her claims in *The Woman in Battle,* and equally fantastic. Early in 1864 she appeared in Detroit, claiming to have married a young Union soldier while DeCaulp was still very much alive. After briefly posing as "Mrs. Major Gates," a Union widow supposedly commissioned by Lincoln, she spent early 1864 living with DeCaulp at Milwaukee and Fort Snelling, Minnesota Territory, before she simply left him in June 1864. She went to New York, became a life insurance salesperson, went to Nashville hoping to do business with soldiers, but was arrested that summer when authorities confused her with another woman suspected of being a spy. On her release in August she rejoined DeCaulp, who was now seriously ill, and then she just disappeared. She emerged only once during the rest of the war, in a December 1864 announcement that she must herself have placed in the Richmond press, announcing that she was being sought for a fabulous inheritance left by her entirely fictional "father" Roach, now a commodore.[25] As her later life showed, it was a setup preparatory to a financial scam.

She really did go to Venezuela after the war, originally intending it as part of an emigration swindle that collapsed. She married John Wasson of Missouri so that she could go with him instead; then they parted company soon after arrival. She did go to the West, where she met and married miner Edward Hardy Bonner, whom she systematically cleaned out every time he made a fresh strike, then abandoned him first for a man who took her to San Francisco for a time, then for good when she left the hotel they were running in New Mexico to travel east via Texas. Along the way, she became involved with a stagecoach driver, Andrew J. Bobo, and wed him in February 1874 while she was still married to Bonner. Within months she left Bobo, too, continued her return to the East, and in 1875 recast herself as Madame Velasquez, announcing that she was preparing her breathtaking memoir for publication, and for a time claiming publicly that it was to be written for her by none other than the celebrated Mark Twain (who repeatedly denied ever knowing or hearing of her).

Her life after 1876 was a continuation on the same theme. There would be another marriage without benefit of divorce from either of her two living husbands, making her a double-bigamist. There would be an immigration scam in North Carolina that fell through, a fictitious import-export business, a failed boarding house operation, a years-long incredible railroad investment scam for a fictitious line connecting the Southwest with the

Pacific coast of Mexico, and more. Along with it there came little success and more than one abrupt departure from a hotel with a bill unpaid. Toward the end there would be dementia and finally death in an asylum in 1923. Nothing in her career after the war offers any justification for taking anything she said about her life, at any time in her life, as anything other than lies. Until 2016, none of this was known. Her story just stopped abruptly not long after publication of her book, a fact that itself has helped in its way to allow and even encourage readers to take her at something like face value. Even then, however, there were questions almost from the beginning.

The first printing of *The Woman in Battle* appeared in the late spring of 1876, and reviews soon followed. Publicity Lauretta attracted during an 1874 tour to boost advance subscription sales had primed press and readers readily to receive the book. One of the first reviews, in the *Atlanta Daily Constitution,* was hardly glowing, saying only that "it is rather a readable book."[26] From that humble beginning, more notices followed, first in Georgia, and then off and on for the next two years all across the South, and to some extent in the North as well. A few of the reviewers positively gushed with praise. Others merely glowed. Her story of unreconstructed heroism and making fools of the Yankees appealed to former Confederates still anxious to salvage pride from defeat. At the opposite end of the spectrum, while no one forthrightly accused the book of being a fiction, still there were those North and South alike who genteelly hinted that it was a bit too good to be true.

Remembering the wartime newspaper stories about Lieutenant Harry Buford, one reviewer complained that "much of the book is tame," though "female readers will be pleased with it."[27] *The Woman in Battle* "is a volume of romantic interest," said another, "written in that fascinating style that never fails to enlist the deepest interest." Still, he believed that a reader "can with difficulty persuade himself that the story is real, and not a wild creation of fantasy."[28] Reviewers in North Carolina were kinder. "It has been promised to the public a long time and has come at last," declared one, calling it "an autobiography of a most adventurous woman. . . . the reader of a few pages will not willingly lay it down."[29] Another Tar Heel reviewer called it "a pleasant and animated personal narrative that thrills the reader," adding that after Lauretta won reputation as "Lieut. Harry Bufford" her "name alone is sufficient to arrest the attention."[30]

Only at the end of 1876 did she get her first real rave. "Madame Velasquez can wield the pen as well as the sword," said the *Raleigh Observer*. "Her finesse, singleness of purpose, heroism and patriotism can best be admired among all the intelligent people North and South," found the reviewer. "It is no wishy-washy, sensational tale, but real matters-of-fact alone, told in an able and eloquent manner, in simple, pure, chaste and elegant language." He went on to declare that "in her rare elements of character are concentrated, quickness of perception, love of glory and country, true courage and chivalry, love of danger and the finesse necessary to self-preservation." Madame Velasquez was a "truly remarkable woman."[31] Another Raleigh paper pronounced it "one of the most remarkable books of the age."[32]

By that time, Lauretta also had her first potentially damaging review written by someone knowledgeable and careful enough to analyze her book's claims. The soon to be enormously influential *Southern Historical Society Papers* began publication that same year and quickly assumed authority as the journal of record for all things Confederate. In its October 1876 issue, editor John William Jones was surgically dismissive without ever actually accusing her of falsehood. *The Woman in Battle* was interesting, he said, but "how far it can be received as *history,* is altogether another question." How was it possible for Buford to be in the thick of the action at Blackburn's Ford near Manassas on July 18, 1861, and yet wake up the next morning forty miles to the east with a reinforcement on its way to Manassas? Jones asked how Buford could "be at so many battles fought by the different armies in different sections of the country—or how he managed to accomplish various other physical impossibilities." Jones's restrained condemnation did not dismiss the book as an outright humbug, but he concluded with the anodyne comment that "we can only say that it is a very *readable* book, and would serve well to while away a winter's evening."[33]

He was not the last to spot the essential weaknesses of *The Woman in Battle*. The narrative strained credulity until it snapped. A poor notice in the *Southern Historical Society Papers,* even one as genteel as Jones's, risked compromising sales. Lauretta protested to Jones that "your notice is unfair and unjust to me and I would ask you to reconsider the matter." She avoided addressing any of his specific criticisms, and instead offered to show him a file of alleged "testimonials" from prominent former Confederates that would attest to the truth of her claims.[34] It was a technique she began to employ during the war, and continued until near the close of her life. She wrote letters on topics of no consequence to generals and presidents, and when out of politeness they sent brief replies of no significance to anything, she kept them in a file to produce as evidence of her high connections and the implied "endorsement" of prominent leaders. Jones chose not to pursue the matter, and that ended the business of the *Southern Historical Society Papers.*

Meanwhile the encomiums continued. In New Orleans, the *Daily Picayune* called her account the "romantic—we might say most romantic—career of a most remarkable woman."[35] Still, the adjective used more often than any other to describe her book was "romance," which carried with it an implication of fiction as much as history. Few reviewers were more restrained than the Galveston writer who said simply that it was well printed and bound, the illustrations good, and that it might "be attractive to lovers of that particular style of literature." A Chicago editor wrote only that it was "a remarkably interesting romance," and in Washington, D.C., one paper simply dismissed it as "curious."[36] A Texas reviewer reminded readers that the wartime stories about her were "often absurdly exaggerated," and that "some have refused to believe there was such a person." Averring that "there is the most abundant testimony of a kind that cannot be disputed, to the effect that she did succeed in disguising herself as a man," he concluded that all had to admire "her courage in undertaking the perilous adventures she passed through."[37] Perhaps more careless than insightful, a Kansas reviewer dismissed the book as "a novel."[38]

There was someone much more influential who entertained the same opinion of *The Woman in Battle,* and he represented a real potential danger to Lauretta. Former Lieutenant General Jubal A. Early, then living in a Lynchburg, Virginia, hotel, was a founder and president of the Southern Historical Society, and already a self-appointed arbiter of right and wrong in Confederate history. His endorsement could boost sales and overcome Jones's criticisms, just as his condemnation could seriously damage any book's future prospects. Early had seen her book some months before in New Orleans and looked into its contents. Later discussing it with a visitor in Lynchburg, he told his guest that Velasquez could not be what she pretended to be. With a copy of the book in hand he pointed out what he termed its "inconsistencies, absurdities, and impossibilities." He doubted it was even written by a woman, or for that matter by anyone with real

Confederate service. Forthrightly, he condemned it as the work of "a mere pretender."[39]

Lauretta learned of Early's strictures and sent him a pleading letter on May 18, 1878, protesting that her "high sense of honor" forced her to protest his "endeavoring to injure me and my Book owing to some incorrect dates." Then she tried to divert him as she had tried to do earlier with Jones's. "I had to gather my information from my own personal observation of the movements of our army," she told him, adding that he being a general and she a mere "lieutenant," naturally the two would not "see such a gigantic struggle from the same stand point." If Early's comments became public they would hazard sales of her book. She was living close to poverty, she pleaded. Worse, her health was failing, most likely an attempt to appeal to Early's sympathy, since she would live another forty-five years. She had a son to raise and educate, or so she claimed, pleading that "my whole souls devotion is the education of him who is to live after I have passed away," and that "I have had trials enough to have driven almost any proud spirited woman to madness, or to commit suicide." Undaunted, "I have struggled and born my lot with the hope of prosperity before me, casting the buffeting of my inferiors beneath my feet." She begged Early for "justice to my *child*," for "I live for him and him alone."[40]

She decided to confront Early face-to-face. Without warning, she appeared at his hotel and asked him to meet her in the parlor. Their interview was brief and unsatisfactory. Early came away from it more convinced than ever that her book was a fiction. Having spent some time in both Mexico and Cuba, he also concluded that she was not Hispanic. Certainly, he heard no Spanish accent (out of her scores of press interviews only two mentioned an accent, and one of those noted that it came and went), and he concluded that "her appearance and voice are both those of an American, and have no resemblance to those of a Spanish lady of genteel aspirations." Reflecting her book's depictions of Confederate officers as drunken braggarts, and southern women as silly flirts throwing themselves into the arms of the nearest male, he further concluded that "Madame Velasquez is no true type of a Southern woman."[41]

Early was uninterested in her file of "testimonials" from prominent Confederates, and remained unconvinced. Still, contrary to her fears, he unintentionally did her a favor by forbearing to make his conclusions about her public.[42] In any case, after almost two years in print, *The Woman in Battle* now attracted less attention. There is no way to determine how many copies sold, though sales may not have met her expectation.[43] Over the next two decades, Lauretta reissued her book in 1890 and 1894, both times under different titles.[44] She claimed to be working on a revised edition in June 1912 just two months before she was committed to the Government Hospital for the Insane in Washington, better known as St. Elizabeths.[45]

Long before that time, Lauretta's celebrity as Lieutenant Harry T. Buford had faded, and in the 1880s she began occasionally omitting any mention of her manufactured Confederate career in interviews with the press, whose attention she then and thereafter cultivated to advance her mercurial Cuban nationalist efforts, and subsequently a series of increasingly ambitious—and unsuccessful—confidence schemes. But if people no longer knew or hailed her as "The Female Lieutenant," still the memory of her story remained alive. Indeed, the farther away from the war years the nation moved, the more the caveats of her 1876 reviewers were forgotten.

Evidence of that forgetting came in 1893 with the appearance of Ménie Muriel Dowie's *Women Adventurers: The Lives of Madame Velazquez, Hannah Snell, Mary Ann Talbot, and Mrs. Christian Davies.* Along with extended excerpts from her subjects' published narratives, Dowie added her own comments. "It is difficult to take them quite seriously, these ladies of the saber," she wrote. "They are to me something of a classic jest: their day is done, their histories forgotten, their devotion dead, and they have left us no genuine descendants." Without going into any circumstantial detail, she also questioned their authenticity. "It is well, too, that we have little means of investigating their exploits," she declared, and "well for their reputations and for our history that we can't find the truth of such minor points."

Yet she found Lauretta to be a different sort of creature from the others. "Amongst these the American soldier Loreta Velazquez cannot be counted," Dowie went on. "She stands upon a different—a more serious platform, for she is of our own day, and plenty of men now living must have known her as Lieutenant Harry Buford." Dowie accepted *The Woman in Battle* completely. "Throughout her history upon every page" she went on, "there is an air of truthfulness which comes—dare I confess?—with very great refreshment to a connoisseur of the elaborated adventures of the average adventurer": "Madame Velazquez was before everything a practical, single-minded woman. . . . She lived her life; she did not dream it, think it, hope for it, or regret her inability to experience it. She had the gift of actualizing her ambitions. Such a character as hers must always rouse one's admiration, especially when one is left to read of it. It is doings that look well on paper."[46] In reviewing the book, the *New York Times* agreed, declaring that Lauretta's narrative "has to be treated with more respect" for "there is reason to believe that there is some foundation of truth in it."[47] Harry Buford's myth gained a small degree of new life, and a renewed—and un-informed—veneer of authenticity.

The timing was perfect, if accidental, for three years after publication of Dowie's book stories began to appear in the American press telling of Cuban women fighting as partisans and soldiers in the latest rebellion against Spain. Inevitably that development stimulated news features of women who went into battle in earlier times, resurrecting old recollections of "The Female Lieutenant." Editors remembered Harry Buford. The *New York Age-Herald* looked back to Lauretta and her story as an example of a woman of courage, declaring that "this is by no means a fictitious romance."[48] When the Cuban revolt ultimately propelled the United States into a war with Spain, at least one writer trotted out Lauretta as an example of an American woman of action, relying without question on her story for her article "Women as Soldiers."[49]

That summertime war was too brief to generate much more, but memories of Lauretta's story as told in her book lingered on into the new century, while time calcified it as fact rather than fancy. World War I had scarcely begun before American newspapers began reminding readers of the women who had gone into battle over the centuries, and in particular "Loretta Velasquez, who wore a lieutenant's shoulder straps in the Confederate army."[50] Thereafter a book or essay about women at war occasionally retold a brief bit of her story, particularly as the world approached another conflict in 1939.[51] In March 1941, a newspaper article on Greek women fighting the Italians and Chinese women resisting the Japanese mentioned her as one of two examples from the Civil War.[52] That August, with America still four months away from war, she got brief mention in an essay about women fighting Germany and Japan titled "When Women Go to War," though it dismissed her memoir as "rather boastful," and concluded that "little is known of her military career."[53] By June 1942, with millions of women engaged in war efforts around the globe, the past seemed irrelevant. Perhaps her last wartime press appearance was on June 4 when an obscure newspaper mentioned her book and cited her as a woman warrior of yore.[54]

Peacetime relegated her almost to pulp fantasy, the most bizarre being the claim in July 1946 that when her war began she lived in Cuba disguised as "a beautiful boy" with her American army officer husband, whom she left for a vagrant Welshman named John Rowlands, who turned out to be Sir Henry Morton Stanley, with whom she enlisted in the Confederate army.[55] A few years later she inevitably made her debut on the printed stage where virtually all celebrities appeared, the newspaper Sunday supplement magazine. In June 1950, a slightly fictionalized one-page distillation of *The Woman in Battle* appeared in the *American Weekly,* titled "The Girl in Gray." A sultry illustration of a blondish beauty with a darkly handsome mustached man dominated, while to the side a bosomy Lauretta in full uniform astride her white charger held the Confederate battle flag aloft as she led soldiers to battle. Lauretta herself could have written the headline: "Three Times the Beautiful Loreta Velasquez Lost a Husband at the Hands of Death, but Her Love of Adventure Always Sustained Her."[56]

Interest in—and acceptance of—her story burgeoned with the Civil War Centennial commencing in 1961, and it always came straight from the pages of her book without question. For two years, a two-sentence filler ran in dozens of newspapers, saying that "Loreta J. Velazques" was a noted Confederate spy who wore a special brace to make her appear masculine.[57] She gained modestly enhanced authenticity in 1961 when Jacob Mogelever published a biography of Lafayette C. Baker that was itself almost as fictional as *The Woman in Battle.* Not only accepting her book without cavil, Mogelever went on to invent scenes and dialog for her, all the while referring to her as "the slim Cuban girl," "the Cuban adventuress," or "the dark-eyed Cuban charmer, a woman to tempt any man with the lure of her sex." No one, he declared, "could resist this Latin beauty, with her flashing dark eyes, provocative lips, and slender figure."[58] Mogelever went even beyond Lauretta herself in making her out to be a *femme fatale.*

At almost the same time, a subtle shift emerged in June 1961 when a Washington Sunday supplement published Ruth Dean's "Women in the Civil War," covering Sarah Edmonds, Emma Brownell, and Loreta Velazquez. For perhaps the first time a modern journalist cast a skeptical eye at the claims of "the Female Lieutenant." Dean concluded that "Mme. Velazquez' account of her military adventures is also a lively one but somehow doesn't seem to ring true," adding that "the reader gets the impression she was more of a spectator than a participant." Finding Lauretta's book less believable than Edmonds's, Dean added that *The Woman in Battle* was one that "historians pretty much discount."[59] Seventeen years later, continuing that skepticism, another columnist writing on "Antebellum Amazons" rhetorically asked "if the book describing the adventures of Madame Velasquez of New Orleans be true."[60]

Dean was right that at last Lauretta and her book were in the hands of historians, and now all those earlier doubts about her reliability became serious academic questions. In 1940 in her groundbreaking *Foreigners in the Confederacy,* Ella Lonn declared of the Civil War memoirs of women "none was stranger" than Lauretta's, though she did not appraise its content.[61] Fifteen years later Katherine Jones published an extended excerpt from *The Woman in Battle* in her *Heroines of Dixie,* but prefaced it by noting that research in New Orleans newspapers was challenging some of Lauretta's claims.[62] Then in 1966 Mary Elizabeth Massey aimed at Lauretta head on. "It seems impossible that any one woman could have done all she claimed," Massey charged, and concluded that this "questionable" book was "the most fantastic of all accounts which claimed to be factual" and nothing more than "sensational exaggerations."[63]

Sylvia D. Hoffert penned the first extended scholarly examination of Lauretta and her book in 1978 and went well beyond Massey. Highlighting the generalities and lack of specifics in names and dates in the book, Hoffert focused on Lauretta's claim to have served in Company B of the Twenty-First Louisiana, and went to the official documents to check facts. There was no record of any such enlistment. That and numerous other factual errors led Hoffert to the conclusion that *The Woman in Battle* was "bizarre" and revealed a high degree of literary opportunism.[64]

But *The Woman in Battle* was not discredited just yet. In 1993 amateur historian Richard Hall went into considerable depth investigating the book in his *Patriots in Disguise: Women Warriors of the Civil War.* To his credit, he made a commendable effort to be objective, but ultimately it was clear that he wanted to find in favor of authenticity. He rationalized the failure of many of the author's schemes as detailed in her book into confirmation of authenticity, reasoning that a writer creating a fictional account would have her efforts ending in success rather than failure. "On balance," he wrote, "this tends to support the interpretation that she was trying to give an honest account of her experiences, rather than consciously trying to deceive anyone for some ulterior motive." What Hall failed to appreciate is that a charlatan creating a fictional narrative had to have bold ventures end unsuccessfully; otherwise, claiming successes would highlight outcomes that would susceptible to verification. Among other arguments in favor of her book, he cited James D. Horan's assertion that Federal agent Felix Stidger met with Lauretta in St. Louis in the "summer of 1863." In fact, Horan's statement is a mix of his own imagination and flawed readings of Lauretta's and Stidger's memoirs.[65] Hall also praised the accuracy of her battle descriptions as circumstantial evidence of authenticity, failing to take into account that there were abundant popular histories in print when she wrote from which anyone could draw sufficient narrative detail to write a superficially convincing "eyewitness participant" account.

Nevertheless, and to his credit, Hall kept asking questions. He granted the possibility that the gross errors in chronology and dates in *The Woman in Battle* might be the result of "concocting fiction for personal gain." He leapt on the glaring discrepancies between her account of Captain Thomas C. DeCaulp and what his official record disclosed. Hall even allowed that several of Jubal Early's devastating criticisms of her narrative seemed irrefutable. He also highlighted the fact that Lauretta's claims of Spanish ancestry and Cuban nativity rested solely on her own claims and could not be otherwise confirmed.

"Velasquez mixed fiction with fact in some unknown but significant proportions," Hall concluded, but went on to say that "we know it is not entirely a work of fiction." He did not deny the "major discrepancies" in her narrative, nor the fact that "serious questions remain unanswered." Nevertheless, he took it as established that "she did serve in male uniform as 'Lieutenant Buford.'"[66] That conclusion is now unsupportable. The crucial word is "serve." She did unquestionably don a uniform on three known occasions while traveling on trains and on arriving in cities like New Orleans, Lynchburg, and Jackson. However, that fact emphatically fails to translate into her "serving" in action on the battlefield, or being a regularly enlisted member of the Confederate armed forces in *any* capacity, or even just traveling with the army in the field as a noncombatant.

In 1999 historian Elizabeth D. Leonard found that "it is a fantastic tale in many ways, but there is evidence as well that the narrative's elements . . . are rooted in real experience," while at the same time acknowledging that almost nothing in the book could be authenticated.[67] Leonard believed that Lauretta was indeed Buford, and that her "wartime movements, activities, and use of aliases" matched those appearing in her book. Most of that is true. There is no question that Lauretta was the person known in 1861–63 as Harry Buford, and her actual wartime travels 1861–63 do loosely agree with those depicted in her book, though from September 1863 onward her claimed itinerary bears little relation to what is today known of her established movements and activities. However, Leonard went beyond the evidence when she concluded that Lauretta "served in a number of battles, and became a spy and a smuggler." There was, and remains, not one piece of official or eyewitness *contemporary* evidence to establish that she ever saw action, operated as a spy or smuggler, or even spent time with a Confederate combat force in the field. Leonard took *The Woman in Battle* at face value, and while she acknowledged Lauretta's financial motivation in writing it, she did not come to grips with it as a narrative designed to titillate readers and sell copies, or as a work that was part of a large postwar literary genre of sensationalized, exaggerated, and sometimes wholly fictional memoirs.[68]

Part of the problem, even for historians, is that Lauretta offers so much. Only one other book-length memoir of a woman who claimed to have served as a soldier was ever published, and that author, Sarah Edmonds, was genuinely a soldier, even though she fictionalized some of her own narrative as part of that same genre. Thus, Edmonds's book is unique, which leaves scholars interested in working on the very genuine topic of women combatants in the war in a difficult spot. The result has been an almost irresistible wish somehow to rationalize *The Woman in Battle* into something "authentic" enough to allow it to be used, thereby doubling the women-warriors research base.

In 2002, in their generally excellent *They Fought Like Demons: Women Soldiers in the American Civil War,* DeAnne Blanton and Lauren M. Cook were the first to assert that Velasquez might have been a *nom-de-plume* used for her book and not her actual name, as indeed it was not. They also seconded Hall in questioning her Spanish blood and Cuban nativity.[69] Otherwise, however, they echoed Leonard. "The veracity of much of her narrative is corroborated in Civil War–era newspapers, the testimony of fellow Confederates, and government documents," they wrote, and again that it is "largely corroborated by contemporary sources."[70] Such is not the case. The newspapers corroborate only that Lauretta told them her story, and that other newspapers repeated them. They substantiate *some* of her September 1861–July 1863 travels to Lynchburg, Richmond, New Orleans, Jackson, Mobile, and Atlanta, but nothing in them corroborates any claim that she was an enlisted or commissioned Confederate soldier, or that she ever set foot on any battlefield even as a noncombatant. The newspapers' only source for their stories was Lauretta herself.

As for the "testimony of fellow Confederates," there is none. The testimony Lauretta produced was written a decade after the war, often revealing that she was the source for what obliging men wrote for her. With the exception of one questionable attester, all they confirmed was that she was the same person who claimed to be Harry Buford in 1861–63. Not one affidavit attested to her serving as a regular or irregular soldier with any army, on any battlefield, at any time. The government documents corroborate only the unquestioned fact that in 1862–63 she sometimes appeared in Confederate cities in a uniform and called herself Harry Buford. Those documents contain no claim by her to have served in the army as a soldier or combatant, a claim that officials in the Confederate War Department easily could have confirmed or gainsaid.

The subject of women who served as combatant soldiers in the Civil War is a fascinating one, too often muddied by unsubstantiated hyperbolic claims that hundreds—even thousands—of women did so. Such assertions trivialize the formidable obstacles faced by the few women who actually succeeded, as illustrated by the contemporary press accounts of hundreds of women discovered in the attempt, or who revealed themselves. We can never know how many actually stood in the ranks as regularly enlisted soldiers and engaged in combat, especially since the most successful ones—like successful spies—kept their mouths shut at the time, and for societal reasons may not have spoken of it after the war. Whatever the number, it will be small, more likely at most a few dozen rather than hundreds, and again because of the myriad official, environmental, and personal hazards of discovery. That scarcity makes any source all the more important and explains the rush to gloss over questions of Lauretta's authenticity in order to employ her narrative, thereby unintentionally focusing a harsh light on the paucity of genuine evidence to support the great majority of claimants.

Discredited though it may be today among historians, *The Woman in Battle* still meets a welcoming audience among other social sciences. In his 1997 *Women Warriors: A History,* cultural anthropologist David E. Jones devoted a third of his Civil War discussion to Lauretta's battle accounts. Ignoring entirely the issue of authenticity, he concluded that hers was "the most complete account" of a woman warrior in the Civil War, one entitling her to eminence in the world's "pantheon of historic woman warriors."[71]

Meanwhile Lauretta was on the verge of stepping into other pantheons once unimagined—literature, economics, and gender studies. New inter-related approaches designated "postmodernism" and "poststructuralism" emerged in literary theory and soon jumped into linguistics, anthropology, and sociology, where emphasis shifted from "facts" as historians knew them to an assumption that no text is "authentic," but rather any text can have multiple interpretations of equal validity. Having many meanings, any narrative is thus self-contradictory, hence compromising the concept of "fact" itself. "There are no truths," one critic averred, "only interpreta-tions."[72] If one is not fettered by concern over the conflicts and falsehoods in *The Woman in Battle,* it can be made to wear any clothes in which schol-ars choose to drape it. Lauretta's claims of Hispanic origin give her a seat at the table with other ethnic and racial underdogs. Her youthful poverty and stridently unfeminine behavior at times bring class into the discussion. Posing as a man, even if she fooled no one, raises gender issues, and opens the door to speculations about her sexuality, while her claim to have been a soldier in the field brought her to the attention of those studying the "woman warrior."

Julie Wheelwright in 1989 accepted *The Woman in Battle* at face value for her book *Amazons and Military Maids: Women Who Dressed as Men in the Pursuit of Life, Liberty and Happiness,* implying that modern audiences ought to believe Lauretta's story without concerns over authenticity be-cause readers in Lauretta's own time did so.[73] English and American literary studies professor Jesse Alemán addressed the authenticity issue in his 1994 essay "Crossing the Mason-Dixon Line in Drag: The Narrative of Loreta Ja-neta Velasquez, Cuban Woman and Confederate Soldier." There he testified that he was "less concerned with finding an historical Velazquez" than he was in exploring how her book challenged definitions of what it meant to be male or female, Cuban or Confederate.[74] He regarded separating truth from fiction in Lauretta's book as irrelevant. Only what she wrote mattered.

The areas of her story that attracted the most interest were her sexuality and her alleged Cuban birth. While only three instances of Lauretta posing as Buford are independently documented—Lynchburg/Richmond in fall 1861, New Orleans in April 1862, and Jackson/Mobile/Richmond in summer 1863, in all of which she actively called attention to herself as a female—Alemán portrayed her as primarily a cross-dresser and transvestite, concluding that she was a "protolesbian," thereby inaugurating a small industry in interpreting her life through her writing.[75] Even though Thomas DeCaulp was the only one of her multiple husbands to see Lauretta as Buford, Alemán maintained that when she married him and others she brought southern masculinity "to a homoerotic crisis."[76]

Dismissing the question of authenticity in *The Woman in Battle,* Alemán maintained that her cross-dressing made authentication impossible. "Gender, race, and nation are sartorial performances that dislodge stable identity markers," he wrote, "wreaking havoc, as they did for Jubal Early, on ideologies, national institutions, and literary histories that demand readable signs of subjectivity."[77] Her Cubanness drew from him equally challenging conclusions, as he argued that historians had ignored it because of their single-minded focus on the authenticity of her Buford incarnation.[78] He was himself unaware that she did not "become" Cuban until 1874, and did not "become" Velasquez until a year later.[79]

Others soon followed. Elizabeth Young echoed Alemán in declaring that calling *The Woman in Battle* fictional was a "a point of departure for literary analysis" and not "a cause for historical censure." Factual truths could be drawn from the book as a "picaresque novel," and particularly from the "cross-dressing plot" that occupied a fraction of its pages. Following Alemán's path, Young concluded that it was evidence of Lauretta's repressed protolesbianism.[80] Occasionally Young veered into the bizarre, as when Lauretta used the phrase "Attack on the Federal Rear" as a chapter subheading, Young declared it to be "a strand of imagery that constructs Southern military aggression as anal penetration."[81] It is quite possible, and even probable, that Lauretta had nothing to do with selecting chapter subheadings, a task then universally done by publishers.

In 2003, Alemán provided an introduction for a paperback reprint of *The Woman in Battle* that remains the most thoughtful essay from this new school to date. Lauretta, he said, dwelled "somewhere between history and story," and "even a seemingly inauthentic author can nonetheless produce an authentic cultural text that embodies and enacts the prevailing beliefs and anxieties of its historical context."[82] Fictional or not, her book offered human truths. He reaffirmed that the central matter in her book was cross-dressing.[83] "Instead of a fixed state of being, identity in *The Woman in Battle* is a series of performances that render authenticity an impossibility," he argued, yet somehow it gave an "accurate picture of the Civil War's gender crises."[84] The book offered "an ideologically authentic cultural text that reflects—through cross-dressing—the gender and national crises the Civil War generated." Transvestism was "an authentic symptom of the Civil War."[85]

Moreover, he added that "her transnational transvestism keeps Velazquez on the move between national boundaries and gender categories to the point that her only authenticity is as a symbolic, historical embodiment of a pro-slavery Cuban Confederate with no place in the Americas." Our knowledge now that she lived in the North as a Gilded Age con artist for many more years than she ever did in the South, that she almost certainly was not Cuban, and that her wartime loyalty to the Confederacy ended in an offer to sell military information to the Union, atomizes Alemán's definition of her authenticity. The allegorical "truth" in the book, he argued, was that "gender, race, and nation are simple matters of clothing that, when cross-dressed, challenge the ideologies of authenticity that determine the battle lines between masculinity and femininity, black and white, North and South, autobiography and fiction, and ultimately, self and Other."[86] One must wonder what happens to "authenticity" when motives are attributed to a writer that she never actually entertained. Lauretta was open and frank in admitting that she just wanted to make some money, and her career as a confidence artist demonstrated that she knew enough of human nature and nineteenth-century prudery to realize that the spicier her suggested sexual encounters, the better the potential sales.[87]

In 1997 Coleman Hutchison, a distinguished specialist on Civil War literature, set aside the lure of sex to read into Velasquez's descriptions of her wartime and postwar travels evidence that her "awareness of a world outside of the United and Confederate States helps to disrupt the insularity of Civil War narrative convention and to tell the belated story of a Confederacy in and of the world."[88] Hers was "a restless text, one that moves dexterously and recurrently across lines of nation and region," hence her book "elegantly 'embodies and enacts' the international dimensions of the American Civil War." Hutchison argued that *The Woman in Battle* forced readers to the realization that the war escaped the bounds of North and South and disrupted "the insularity of Civil War narrative convention."[89] At the same time humanities and English scholar Caroline Levander asserted that Lauretta's alleged travels reinforced "her desire to imagine an independent Cuba aligned with an independent South," as Cuba and the Confederacy cherished "a colonial fantasy of white privilege through black slave labor."[90]

In 2008, Matthew Teorey, a specialist on postmodern narrative techniques, tried to assemble all the strands of Lauretta's story under one umbrella. He accepted *The Woman in Battle* as essentially genuine, admitting that "Velazquez did add a little embellishment." Still Teorey believed that the book "revealed the true, brutal nature of warfare," and called it a "patriotic, honest, and realistic" account of her "four years of military service" (by her own account she spent less than two years with the army). Buying into Lauretta's new transgender identity, he went on to declare her "quintessentially American," imbued with the United States' "promise of personal freedom and socio-economic opportunities," an idea at odds with her willingness to leave America for Venezuela in 1866, and that her "socio-economic" endeavors were all confidence schemes. Adeptly encapsulating the approach of all of Lauretta's new students, Teorey concluded that her narrative was important "regardless of whether or not these experiences actually happened or not."[91]

Then in 2010 Hutchison returned to her, concluding that the "signal achievement of the narrative" was "to situate the American Civil War in a truly international context."[92] In fact, Lauretta's multiple postwar interests in developing Nicaragua, Mexico, Cuba, and in seeing North, Central, and South America united under a single commercial umbrella, certainly did speak to an internationalist outlook on trade at least, though most of that came years after the appearance of *The Woman in Battle*. As for Lauretta's account of her postwar wanderings, Hutchison thought her narrative of her western travels "inadvertently burlesques Confederate remasculiniza-tion."[93] All roads lead to gender.

Filmmakers had to be drawn to the story. In 2007, the Arts and Enter-tainment Network's *Full Metal Corset: Secret Soldiers of the Civil War* dealt with Lauretta, but only by adopting her story without question. Infinitely better was 2013's *Rebel: Loreta Velazquez, Secret Soldier of the American Civil War.* Still uncritically buying *The Woman in Battle* narratively as au-thentic, at least it explored worthwhile subthemes such as the status of His-panic women in the Old South and the motivation of the unknown number of women who did serve in the armies, not to mention how that motivation imperiled contemporary definitions of womanhood. Unfortunately the film ignored its own consultants' strong caveats about Lauretta's book, at the same time implying its corroboration by contemporary 1861–63 newspaper articles, unaware of their inaccuracies and that all were based on what Lauretta herself told the press. Meanwhile its conclusion suggesting that contemporary white male southern leaders tried to write Lauretta and her story out of Civil War history is a nonsensical fiction implicitly suggesting that *The Woman in Battle* was so authentic and so threatening that self-appointed guardians of Confederate history kept it from the public.

The Woman in Battle is unquestionably an unusual memoir, even if over-whelmingly fictional. As Hutchison wrote, "because of her careful manip-ulation of narrative sequence, it is as though Velasquez and her readers are together in time."[94] Certainly it falls well outside the mold of the "Lost Cause" literature of the postwar generation. Far from idealizing the Con-federacy, Velasquez found fault with the behavior and morals of Confed-erate men and women, and the value of most southern institutions except for slavery.[95] Accepting her as an authentic memoirist offering trenchant commentary on her times is virtually impossible, however, given that she almost never actually witnessed what she claimed to have seen, was rarely where she claimed to have been, and so muddied her genuine recollections with inventions and obfuscations as to make her observations practically worthless. Alemán was right when he called the book "sensationalist, se-cessionist, and suspicious," as well as "seemingly impossible," averring with probably more understatement than he realized that it is "undeniably part pulp fiction." Still he and others have concluded that it contains enough details to make it a "legitimate Civil War narrative."[96]

It is not. In the final analysis, the conclusion is unavoidable that *The Woman in Battle* has no merit whatever as a work of history or autobiography. With the exception of a *roughly* genuine representation of her postwar years 1866–74—hopelessly confused in chronology and intentionally selective to omit inconveniences like a swindled and abandoned husband in Utah—this is not the life that Lauretta Williams lived, either before or during the war. Rather, it is a story consciously invented, honed, altered and amended in the press for fifteen years before she codified it in her book, and then largely abandoned as she continued changing and rewriting her story for another quarter-century. Certainly, bits of it are superficially true. She did dress as a soldier, she did call herself Harry Buford, and she did *claim* during the war to have been a soldier serving in action. But claims are a far cry from proof, of which there is none.

Moreover, when her book is viewed in the overall context of her prewar life in the stews of New Orleans, her wartime petty theft and larceny, and a postwar career of more than fifty years of bigamies, deceits, petty swindles, confidence scams, and almost grotesque lies, the conclusion is inescapable that accepting any statement from her, at any time in her long life, and *solely on her own testimony,* abandons wisdom for folly. As one of her own swindle victims admitted fifty years after Harry Buford first appeared in Lynchburg, "she seems to be able to persuade her fellow humans to almost anything—until her absolutely appalling deceptions are found out." "I have never met her equal."[97]

Yet, almost perversely, *The Woman in Battle* may be defined justly as iconic. It continues to have relevance, even if based on a fiction. Lauretta created a legend that has become spiritual fact. Succeeding generations found and still find significance in her story. In every war she is resurrected as a woman warrior, spiritual progenitor of the women in uniform who risk all on the battlefields of freedom. Whenever that resurrection happens, every time her story appears in another anthology, every time *The Woman in Battle* is quoted for statements offered as fact, Lauretta is in command through the myth she consciously created. Now that she has jumped the boundaries of history into other and more esoteric fields of inquiry and debate, her story has only taken on more relevance, even if misunderstood and ultimately misguided. Even allowing that her book may be fictive, these new constructs "work" because no rules bind them if a fictional *The Woman in Battle* has historical significance. Those appraising the book for cultural significance are forced to make the same claim because approaching the book on any other basis sets everyone on a collision course with its over-whelming fictionalization.[98] The late filmmaker John Ford is often quoted as saying that, "when the legend becomes fact, print the legend." Lauretta's book is iconic today in large part because, despite our better judgment, we still prefer to "print the legend."

NOTES

1. U.S. Census, Orleans Parish, Louisiana, 1860.

2. *Memphis Avalanche,* September 12, 1861, qtd. in *New Orleans Daily True Delta,* September 14, 1861.

3. *Lynchburg Republican,* September 26, 1861, qtd. in *Richmond Daily Dispatch,* September 27, 1861.

4. John B. Jones, *A Rebel War Clerk's Diary at the Confederate States Capital,* 2 vols. (Philadelphia: J. B. Lippincott, 1866), 1:94 (entry for November 20, 1861). The dates in Jones's diary do not match the September dates of the actual events, but Jones heavily edited his diary before publication, and dating errors are common.

5. *New Orleans Daily True Delta,* November 2, 1862.

6. Ibid., April 24, 1862.

7. *New Orleans Bee,* October 31, 1862.

8. Ibid.; *New Orleans Daily True Delta,* October 30, 31, 1862; *New Orleans Daily Picayune,* November 2, 1862.

9. *Jackson Mississippian,* June 6, 1863, qtd. in *Montgomery Weekly Advertiser,* June 7, 1863.

10. *Natchez Daily Courier,* June 13, 1863; *Mobile Register & Advertiser,* June 13, 1863.

11. Felix G. DeFontaine, *Marginalia; or, Gleanings from an Army Note-book* (Columbia, S.C.: F. G. DeFontaine & Co., 1864), 65–66.

12. Her letter itself does not survive, but it is extracted in Adjutant and Inspector General's Office, Record Group 109, Register of Letters Received, April–July 1863, M–Z, chap. 1, vol. 56, file 1145 W 1863, National Archives, Washington, D.C. (repository hereafter cited as NA).

13. Letter from Jackson, June 24, 1863, *Memphis Daily Appeal,* June 29, 1863.

14. *Richmond Enquirer,* July 2, 1863.

15. *Richmond Daily Richmond Examiner,* July 2, 1863.

16. Ibid., July 11, 1862.

17. *Richmond Enquirer,* July 15, 1863.

18. *Richmond Daily Dispatch,* July 16, 1863.

19. *Richmond Sentinel,* July 16, 1863.

20. *Richmond Enquirer,* July 18, 1863.

21. *Abbeville* (S.C.) *Press,* July 24, 1863.

22. Lauretta J. Williams to Samuel Cooper, July 20, 1863, Letters Received by Confederate Adjutant-General, July–October 1863, Record Group 109, M474, roll 88, frame 0101, file W1310, NA.

23. For more on the intriguing story of DeCaulp, see William C. Davis, *Inventing Loreta Velasquez: Confederate Soldier Impersonator, Media Celebrity, and Con Artist* (Carbondale: Southern Illinois University Press, 2016).

24. *Augusta* (Ga.) *Daily Constitutionalist,* September 16, 1863.

25. *Richmond Enquirer,* December 22, 1864.

26. *Atlanta Daily Constitution,* July 19, 1876.

27. *Columbus* (Ga.) *Daily Enquirer,* September 7, 1876.

28. *Americus* (Ga.) *Weekly Sumter Republican,* September 15, 1876.

29. *Tarborough* (N.C.) *Southerner,* September 29, 1876.

30. *Wadesboro* (N.C.) *Pee Dee Herald,* October 4, 1876.

31. *Raleigh Observer,* December 20, 1876.

32. *Raleigh News,* January 7, 1877.

33. "Book Notices," *Southern Historical Society Papers* 2 (October 1876): 208.

34. Madame L. J. Velasquez to J. William Jones, October 27, November 12, 1876, Southern Historical Society Collection Correspondence Files, Museum of the Confederacy, Richmond, Va.

35. *New Orleans Daily Picayune,* April 17, 1877.

36. *Galveston Daily News,* September 23, 1876; *New Orleans Daily Picayune,* April 17, 1877; *Baltimore Sun,* May 5, 1877; *Chicago Daily Inter Ocean,* April 6, 1877; *Washington Evening Star,* January 26, 1878.

37. *Dallas Weekly Herald,* September 21, 1878.

38. *Holton* (Kans.) *Recorder,* August 23, 1877.

39. Jubal A. Early to William F. Slemons, May 22, 1878, Tucker Family Papers, Southern Historical Collection, University of North Carolina, Chapel Hill (repository hereafter cited as SHC). It is unclear from Early's letter how much time passed between his meeting the unnamed caller and Lauretta's appearance at his hotel.

40. L. J. Velasquez to Early, May 18, 1878, SHC. This letter is Early's *verbatim* copy of her letter, the original of which does not survive.

41. Early to Slemons, May 22, 1878, SHC.

42. Velasquez to Early, May 18, 1878, SHC.

43. A recent look at the Antiquarian Book Exchange website Abebooks.com revealed copies of the 1876 first edition for sale at prices up to $500. By comparison, copies of the first edition of Lafayette Baker's 1867 *History of the United States Secret Service,* a book of equally sensational claims and slightly lurid overtones, sell for approximately one-quarter that price. A tentative interpolation of that suggests a greater degree of rarity for *The Woman in Battle* based on fewer first-edition survivals, which in turn could indicate fewer copies originally printed and sold, but such a rationalization should not be pushed too far.

44. *Story of the Civil War; or, the Exploits, Adventures and Travels of Mrs. L. J. Velasquez (Lieutenant H. T. Buford, C.S.A.)* (New York: Worthington & Co., 1890); *The Story of the Civil War* (New York: H. W. Hagemann, 1894).

45. *Washington Times,* June 4, 1912.

46. Ménie Muriel Dowie, ed., *Women Adventurers. The Lives of Madame Velazquez, Hannah Snell, Mary Ann Talbot, and Mrs. Christian Davies* (London: T. Fisher Unwin, 1893), x–xi, xix, 51.

47. *New York Times,* June 19, 1893.

48. *New York Age-Herald,* April 12, 1896.

49. Mrs. T. Woods Hopely, "Women as Soldiers," *Harrisburg Telegraph,* August 16, 1898.

50. *Springfield* (Mass.) *Daily News,* December 9, 1914.

51. As for instance, Perrin F. Shaw Jr., "A Lady in Gray Fighting for the Confederacy," *Richmond Times-Dispatch Magazine,* May 21, 1939, which is based solely on *The Woman in Battle.*

52. "Women as Warriors," *Mexia* (Tex.) *Weekly Herald,* March 14, 1941.

53. Andreas Dorpalen, "When Women Go to War," *San Bernardino Daily Sun,* August 10, 1941.

54. *Kannapolis* (N.C.) *Daily Independent,* June 4, 1942.

55. Henry W. Shoemaker, "This Morning's Comment," *Altoona Tribune,* July 15, 1946.

56. Stewart Kelsey, "The Girl in Gray," *American Weekly,* June 18, 1950, 21; *Cleveland Plain Dealer,* June 18, 1950.

57. See for example, *Paris* (Tex.) *News,* August 14, 1958.

58. Jacob H. Mogelever, *Death to Traitors: The Story of General Lafayette C. Baker, Lincoln's Forgotten Secret Service Chief* (New York: Doubleday, 1961), 196–201.

59. Ruth Dean, "Women in the Civil War," *Washington Evening Star,* June 4, 1961. The only other 1961–65 newspaper account found was in the *Deming* (N.M.) *Highlight,* April 18, 1963.

60. Fred Brooks, "Antebellum Amazons," *Baton Rouge State Times Advocate,* January 8, 1978.

61. Ella Lonn, *Foreigners in the Confederacy* (Chapel Hill: University of North Carolina Press, 1940), 380–82.

62. Katherine Jones, *Heroines of Dixie: Confederate Women Tell their Story of the War* (Indianapolis: Bobbs-Merrill, 1955), 290–98.

63. Mary Elizabeth Massey, *Bonnet Brigades* (New York: Alfred A. Knopf, 1966), 82, 195, 310.

64. Sylvia D. Hoffert, "Madame Loreta Velasquez: Heroine or Hoaxer?" *Civil War Times Illustrated* 17 (June 1978): 29–31.

65. Richard Hall, *Patriots in Disguise: Women Warriors of the Civil War* (New York: Marlowe & Co., 1994), 107–53, 189n, 190n, 191n, 192n, 193–94n.

66. Ibid., 208–11.

67. Elizabeth D. Leonard, *All the Daring of the Soldier: Women of the Civil War Armies* (New York: W. W. Norton, 1999), 252.

68. Ibid., 260–61.

69. Ibid., 181, 232n3. DeAnne Blanton and Lauren M. Cook, in *They Fought Like Demons: Women Soldiers in the American Civil War* (Baton Rouge: Louisiana State University Press, 2002), spell the name Velazquez, as do others.

70. Blanton and Cook, *They Fought Like Demons,* 2, 178.

71. David E. Jones, *Women Warriors, A History* (Washington, D.C.: Brassey's, 1997), 233–37.

72. Daniel C. Dennett, "Let's Start With a Respect for Truth," edge.org/conversation/dennett-on-wieseltier-v-pinker-in-the-new-republic.

73. Julie Wheelwright, *Amazons and Military Maids: Women Who Dressed as Men in the Pursuit of Life, Liberty and Happiness* (London: Pandora, 1989), 140.

74. Jesse Alemán, "Crossing the Mason-Dixon Line in Drag: The Narrative of Loreta Janeta Velasquez, Cuban Woman and Confederate Soldier," in Jon Smith and Deborah Cohn, eds., *Look Away: The U.S. South in New World Studies* (Durham, N.C.: Duke University Press, 1994), 125n5.

75. Ibid., 113.

76. Ibid., 116.

77. Ibid., 122.

78. Ibid., 112.

79. Ibid., 120.

80. Ibid., 193.

81. Ibid., 173, 181–82.

82. Jesse Alemán, "Authenticity, Autobiography, and Identity: *The Woman in Battle* as a Civil War Narrative," introd. to Loreta Janeta Velazquez, *The Woman in Battle* (rpt., Madison: University of Wisconsin Press, 2003), xix.

83. Ibid..

84. Ibid., xxii.

85. Ibid., xxvi–xxvii.

86. Ibid., xxxvi–xxxvii.

87. She was used in classroom studies on social psychology for her flaunting of social norms. See for instance Kenneth S. Bordens and Kristin Sommer, *Instructor's Manual/Test Bank to Accompany Social Psychology,* 2nd ed. (Mahwah, N.J.: Lawrence Erlbaum Associates, 2002), 27–29.

88. Coleman Hutchison, "On the Move Again: Tracking the Exploits, Adventures, and Travels of Madame Loreta Janeta Velazquez," *Comparative American Studies* 5 (December 2007): 423.

89. Ibid., 425–26.

90. Caroline Levander, "Confederate Cuba," in Sandhya Shukla and Heidi Tinsman, eds., *Imagining Our Americas: Toward a Transnational Frame* (Durham, N.C.: Duke University Press, 2007), 94.

91. Matthew Teorey, "Unmasking the Gentleman Soldier in the Memoirs of Two Cross-dressing Female US Civil War Soldiers," *War, Literature and the Arts: An International Journal of the Humanities* 20 (November 2008): 74–78, 80–81, 84, 87, 89n.

92. Coleman Hutchison, *Apples & Ashes: Literature, Nationalism, and the Confederate States of America* (Athens: University of Georgia Press, 2010), 200.

93. Hutchison, "On the Move Again," 192.

94. Hutchison, *Apples & Ashes,* 183.

95. Ibid., 178, 183.

96. Alemán, "Authenticity, Autobiography, and Identity," v, xii, xv.

97. *Philadelphia Times,* December 10, 1901.

98. Alemán, "Crossing the Mason-Dixon Line," 126n4, declares that "Blanton and Cook have established the historical veracity of most of the events in the narrative." That contention is now unsupportable.

"W. T. Sherman Maj. Gen. U.S. Army." Joseph E. Johnston included
this engraving of William Tecumseh Sherman in *Narrative of Military
Operations*. Sherman did not return the favor in his memoirs. From
Joseph E. Johnston, *Narrative of Military Operations, Directed, During
the Late War Between the States, by Joseph E. Johnston, General, C.S.A.*
(New York: D. Appleton and Co., 1874).

Surrender According to Johnston and Sherman

STEPHEN CUSHMAN

The history of the word *surrender,* when traced back through Middle English, Old French, and Latin, discloses two meanings. One is to *give up,* and the other is to *give back* or *give over* or *deliver* something. What distinguishes *surrender* from any of its familiar synonyms, formal or colloquial—yield, submit, capitulate, concede, cry uncle, throw in the towel—is that, when used in a military context, it implies two steps or stages: first, the verbal or written acknowledgment of defeat and, second, the action of delivering or giving something over. For the much storied and studied surrender by Robert E. Lee to Ulysses S. Grant at Appomattox Court House, Virginia, for example, the two steps or stages took place on April 9 and April 12, 1865, and the sesquicentennial anniversaries of these dates recalled to popular attention, in various media, the familiar and mythologized outlines of each. For the first, which was also Palm Sunday, there are the details of Grant in his "rough garb" with "a soldier's blouse for a coat," as he recollected in his *Personal Memoirs* (1885–86), meeting Lee in his elegant dress uniform in the parlor of Wilmer McLean's house and offering him magnanimous terms. For the second, four years to the day after the firing on Fort Sumter, details often come from United States General Joshua Lawrence Chamberlain's many accounts of his reconciliatory salute to the soldiers led by Confederate General John B. Gordon into the village for the formal ceremony of handing over their arms, equipment, and flags.[1]

What about the second major surrender, that of Confederate General Joseph E. Johnston to United States General William T. Sherman, at the farmhouse of James and Nancy Bennett, on the road between Hillsborough and Durham Station, North Carolina? There were several smaller, later surrenders, too, the last of them that of the *C.S.S. Shenandoah* by Captain James Waddell to a captain of the British Royal Navy in Liverpool on November 6, 1865. But the negotiations initiated by Johnston—in a letter written April 13, 1865, and received by Sherman the next day, which was also Good Friday and the same day John Wilkes Booth shot Abraham Lincoln in Ford's Theater—led to the largest surrender of the war. Totals for the number of men paroled first at Appomattox and then, three weeks later, at Greensboro, North Carolina, vary from source to source, but *The War of the Rebellion: A Compilation of the Official Records of the Union and Confederate Armies* (1880–1901) gives them as 28,231 and 39,012, respectively. Even if we take for paroles at Greensboro the lower total of 36,817 officially reported by United States General John M. Schofield, commander of the Department of North Carolina, in fact the terms signed by Johnston and Sherman also disbanded Confederate units in South Carolina, Georgia, and Florida, adding another 52,453 soldiers paroled, as reported by United States General James. H. Wilson, commander of the Cavalry Corps of the Military Division of the Mississippi, and bringing the total to 89,270.[2]

Why do most of us hear and know so much less about this surrender, the largest of the war? In *Battle Cry of Freedom: The Civil War Era* (1988) James McPherson includes nothing about either the negotiations between Johnston and Sherman, eventually concluded on April 26, or the surrender of Confederate arms in Greensboro during the first days of May. In the third volume of his massive trilogy *The Civil War: A Narrative* (1958–74), Shelby Foote narrates the April negotiations between the two generals in the Bennett farmhouse, but as soon as he concludes them, he turns to the capture and death of Booth and never returns to the surrender at Greensboro. In *Joseph E. Johnston: A Civil War Biography* (1992), Craig L. Symonds moves in nine lines from the conclusive meeting between the generals on April 26 to Johnston's farewell to his army six days later, giving no details of the surrender proceedings in Greensboro. Those who want further details of the latter must turn to more recent books, such as Mark L. Bradley's *This Astounding Close: The Road to Bennett Place* (2000) or Robert M. Dunkerly's *The Confederate Surrender at Greensboro: The Final Days of the Army of Tennessee, April 1865* (2013) and *To the Bitter End: Appomattox, Bennett Place, and the Surrenders of the Confederacy* (2015). Meanwhile, there is nothing like Appomattox Court House National Historical Park to visit in Greensboro; there is only a small monument to the Army of Tennessee, a short obelisk erected in May 1985 near the location of the wartime rail depot. On it one can read Johnston's General Orders № 22, his farewell address to the army, issued on May 2, 1865, the same date as his own parole and the paroles of his staff.[3]

Why the disparity in memories of the two surrenders? Some may say it reflects the Virginia-centric historiography of the war, and there may be partial truth to this claim, but it cannot be the whole truth. Virginia-centrism has not produced similar acoustic shadows in the cases of Shiloh, Chickamauga, and Sherman's March to the Sea, for example, and, for that matter, Johnston was a Virginian, too. Others may say that, whereas Appomattox offers the pathos, dignity, and catharsis of Aristotelian tragedy, all neatly contained in one small, picturesque place during a handful of days, the surrender in North Carolina was too scattered, protracted, confused, and messy to offer the stuff of clean closure and marketable narrative. Again, there may be partial truth here, but, again, it cannot satisfy fully. The battle of the Wilderness was also scattered, confused, and messy, as well as inconclusive, and yet it has been studied carefully by many fine historians.

Johnston's negotiations with Sherman at the Bennett farmhouse and the subsequent surrender at Greensboro were controversial and belated in ways that events at Appomattox were not. For one thing, Abraham Lincoln was assassinated between the two surrenders, and the assassination disrupted everything. In a letter dated May 5, 1865, Sherman confessed as much to Schofield, whom he had left in charge of North Carolina: "I feel deeply the embarrassment that is sure to result from the indefinite action of our Government. It seems to fail us utterly at this crisis."[4] Had Booth's plot been foiled, the Lincoln plot would have continued; Lincoln almost certainly would have treated Sherman more diplomatically than did his successor, Andrew Johnson, and his secretary of war, Edwin M. Stanton, when the redheaded general exceeded his military authority in initial negotiations with Johnston; and the surrender at Greensboro might have taken another form, one characterized by a bit more of the myth-making pomp and circumstance associated with Appomattox.

For another thing, once the controversial negotiations between Johnston and Sherman concluded, attention immediately shifted elsewhere. With the departure of Lincoln's funeral train from Washington on April 21 and his burial at Springfield on May 4, many northern eyes were not focused on North Carolina at all during this time. In the same letter to Schofield, Sherman described the minds of U.S. government authorities as "so absorbed with the horrid deformities of a few assassins & southern Politicians that they overlook the wants and necessities of the great masses." At the same time, many southern eyes were turning grimly toward the urgent challenges of those same wants and necessities. Most of the U.S. soldiers who had ended their war in North Carolina in late April were being marched to Washington for the Grand Review held there in late May; most Confederate soldiers were on their ways home, between seven and eight thousand of them having deserted, according to Johnston, in the interval between announcement of the surrender and the subsequent delivery of their arms. Whether northern or southern, these soldiers and their families likely had no more thoughts for the clean-up crews in Greensboro than participants in weddings or funerals do for those who close up after them.[5]

Last of all there is the matter of history-writing, which is like many other things in at least one way: it can take it a while to mature. It has taken the historiography of World War II some time to focus popular attention on the often overlooked war in Italy, as, for example, volume 2 of Rick Atkinson's Liberation Trilogy (2002–13) has helped to do; so too it is taking Civil War historiography a while to pay closer attention to events mostly overlooked during its first century and a half.[6] The largest surrender of the war is among these, and one way to begin to remember it a little more fully is to compare the published accounts of the two principals, Johnston and Sherman.

The surrender at Appomattox may eclipse the later and larger surrender in part because it starred the two legendary generals-in-chief and because it conveniently obeyed the neoclassical dramatic unities of time and place, generating in one place on two days such fictions as "the story of the famous apple tree," dismissed by Grant in his *Personal Memoirs*.[7] But in the literary history of the Civil War, or rather the literary-military history of Civil War memory, the surrender at Appomattox has one colossal liability: Lee did not write and publish his memoirs, so we have no public narration by him of the second week of April 1865. The great memoir melee of the late nineteenth and early twentieth centuries gave us narratives by Lee's counterpart, Grant, and by fellow Confederates Jubal A. Early, Richard Taylor, Jefferson Davis, John Bell Hood, James Longstreet, John B. Gordon, and Edward Porter Alexander, among others. But we cannot hear from Lee himself, at least not in memoir form. Two weeks after the surrender at Appomattox, he gave Thomas M. Cook of the *New York Herald* his only formal postwar interview—the interview resulted in a paraphrase by Cook, not a word-for-word transcript—and in February 1866 he appeared in Washington to give testimony before the Joint Congressional Committee on Reconstruction. Otherwise, we must rely on Lee's private letters and statements to others, later reported by them.[8]

By contrast the North Carolina surrender found its way into two big books, each of the principals authoring his own. First, in 1874, came Johnston's, with an original title page reading, rather drily, *Narrative of Military Operations, / Directed, / During the Late War Between the States / By / Joseph E. Johnston, / General, C.S.A.* The next year came Sherman's *Memoirs of General William T. Sherman,* a second edition of which, with new first and last chapters, appeared in 1886. Lee and Grant at Appomattox may have captured most of the limelight in popular imagination of Civil War closure, but the relations between Johnston's and Sherman's books, as well as between the men who wrote them, tell a significant story of their own, one with no counterpart at Appomattox.

To begin with, the two books were published by the same New York publisher, D. Appleton and Company, located at 549–551 Broadway in 1874. Representing a partnership formed by the sons of Daniel Appleton, who published his first book in 1831 and died in 1849, this famous house published a long list of prestigious titles that included the first American edition of Lewis Carroll's *Alice's Adventures in Wonderland* (1865), Joel Chandler Harris's *Uncle Remus* (1880), Stephen Crane's *The Red Badge of Courage* (1895), and works by Noah Webster, James Fenimore Cooper, William Cullen Bryant, Charles Darwin, Florence Nightingale, Benjamin Disraeli, Herbert Spencer, Thomas Huxley, Hamlin Garland, and Edith Wharton.[9]

Two points arise here. First, publication of Johnston's and Sherman's books by the same prominent publisher gives us a vivid image of commercial pragmatism during postwar reconstruction and reconciliation. The rest of us are free to debate the political and social complexities and nuances of reconstruction and reconciliation, but the Appleton brothers had their eyes on the marketplace, and obviously they believed that the public differences and self-justifications of Civil War generals were good business for them, however much they might complicate public remembrance and reconciliation. In 1879, five years after Johnston's book appeared and four years after Sherman's, Appleton and Company followed with Confederate General Richard Taylor's memoir, *Destruction and Reconstruction: Personal Experiences of the Late War*. In 1893, two years after Johnston's death, the company published in its Great Commanders series *General Johnston*, a biography by Virginian Robert M. Hughes—the biography of Johnston preceded those of Lee, Grant, and Sherman in the same series—and in 1913 it brought out Thomas F. Dixon's *The Southerner: A Romance of the Real Lincoln,* this title by the author of the Ku Klux Klan trilogy (1902–7) confirming that once again the complexities of reconciliation were not necessarily opposed to, and might even enhance, the economics of publishing.

Second, the evidence suggests that in the eyes of the Appleton brothers, or their subordinates, Johnston's and Sherman's books were connected from the start. As it turns out, someone at Appleton and Company overestimated the appeal of Johnston's book, which sprang from the author's desire to settle scores with other Confederates, especially Jefferson Davis, and not with Sherman, his wartime opponent. Johnston's *Narrative* sold poorly and was a financial disappointment for Appleton.[10] To boost sales of the troubled volume, which served up too much of its author's resentment of Davis, whose two-volume *The Rise and Fall of the Confederate Government* Appleton published in 1881, and not enough of anything resembling Sherman's more artful, readable prose, the publishers resorted to a singular and telling strategy: on the first page following the end of volume one in the first edition of Sherman's far more successful *Memoirs,* which sold ten thousand copies the month it was published, they printed a "Letter from General Sherman" as part of a full-page advertisement for Johnston's book.[11] Headed and dated "Headquarters Army of the United States / Washington, D.C., October 31, 1873" and addressed to "Messrs. D. Appleton & Co., / 549 Broadway, New York," Sherman's endorsement read this way:

> DEAR SIRS: I have your favor of the 30th, repeating what you said to me in person yesterday, that you have for publication the manuscript of General Johnston's "Narrative of the Military Operations directed by him during the late War between the States."
>
> Without the least hesitation I advise its immediate publication, for I believe it will have a most extensive sale at the North, as well as the South, and even in Europe.

General Johnston is most favorably known to the military world, and is regarded by many as the most skillful general on the Southern side. He is also ready with his pen, and whatever he records will receive the closest attention by students of the art of war on this continent, and will enter largely into the future Military History of the Civil War.

With great respect, your obedient servant,

W. T. Sherman, General

An intriguing document for many reasons, Sherman's letter now appears a hybrid of a perfunctory reader's report, dashed off by someone who appears not to have read the manuscript, and a retroactive blurb, marshaled belatedly by the publisher more than a year after the appearance of the book it describes. Appleton could have printed Sherman's letter the previous year at the back of Johnston's book, after all, but instead the advertisements placed there are for Appleton's "International Scientific Series"; a translation from the French of Professor Deschanel's *Natural Philosophy: An Elementary Treatise*; textbooks on botany, arithmetic, geography, and U.S. history; *The Popular Science Monthly*; a recent title on ovarian tumors; and many novels now consigned to oblivion, among them *Doctor Vandyke* by Lost Cause apostle John Esten Cooke, "a well-conceived story of colonial life in Virginia," according to the *Charleston News*.

By late October 1873, Sherman was already writing his own memoirs, and although he had no formal contract with Appleton at this point, his endorsement of Johnston's *Narrative* could not help but enhance his connection with the people who two years later would bring out his own book. During late 1871 and most of 1872 Sherman had traveled extensively throughout Europe, Egypt, and Turkey, his travels no doubt accounting in part for the assurance with which he prophesied good sales for Johnston abroad. Promoted to general after Grant's first election to the presidency, and now Grant's successor as commanding general of the army, Sherman framed his letter to suggest that he met in person with Messrs. D. Appleton and Company in New York on October 29, 1873, a Wednesday, and then traveled back to Washington in time to locate his imprimatur at "Headquarters Army of the United States" two days later. In fact, however, he merely may have written out his letter on a piece of official stationery he happened to have with him in New York. As for the face-to-face meeting with Appleton in New York, it is certainly possible that the only item on the agenda was the manuscript of Johnston's *Narrative,* but the commanding general of the army was a busy man, who could have corresponded about that manuscript by letter. Perhaps he was discussing the prospects for his own manuscript, and the request for an endorsement of Johnston's was a secondary transaction.

Whatever the truth, it is clear that Sherman composed the second volume of his *Memoirs,* and subsequently revised the whole, with Johnston's *Narrative* before him. At the end of his chapter titled "Atlanta Campaign— Nashville and Chattanooga to Kennesaw," which opens volume 2, Sherman referred to Johnston's book as "just published (March 27, 1874)," not quite five months after his letter to Appleton, and then took issue with Johnston, who was "greatly in error, in his estimates on page 357, in stating our loss, as compared with his, at six or ten to one."[12] As at so many moments in his *Memoirs,* Sherman's meticulously logistical and rhetorically forensic sides emerge clearly here, as he converted to statistical tables the figures usually given by Johnston in complete sentences and then scrupulously referred to the latter by page number to make his case in the manner of a lawyer or professor, both of which he had been before the war.

Despite the corrective tone Sherman adopted here, elsewhere in his *Memoirs* he treated Johnston very well. In fact, he treated him so well that one does not have to be a cynic to wonder about his motives. The October 1873 letter to Messrs. Appleton and Company contained a sentence that foreshadowed what was to come in the *Memoirs:* "General Johnston is most favorably known to the military world, and is regarded by many as the most skillful general on the Southern side." So much for the popular estimation of Robert E. Lee, whom this sentence demoted by omitting altogether. Although Sherman and Johnston served in the regular army together for thirteen years, they did not meet until April 17, 1865, at the Bennett farmhouse. As Sherman put it in his lengthy official report, dated May 9, 1865, "At noon of the day appointed I met General Johnston for the first time in my life, although we had been interchanging shots constantly since May, 1863."[13] Sherman was thinking of interchanging shots in Mississippi during the Vicksburg and Jackson campaigns, but actually he and Johnston had faced each other at First Manassas–Bull Run as well. Unlike Grant and Lee, Sherman and Johnston squared off at various points throughout the war. As a result, Johnston would have been a frequent subject of Sherman's *Memoirs,* even if Sherman had not been consulting Johnston's narrative while composing his own. With Johnston's book also before him, the Confederate leader's presence in Sherman's *Memoirs* became all the more interesting.

All his life Sherman loved attending plays and reading novels, and if his own book had been either one instead, we might have credited him with managing the entrances and exits of Johnston with particular deftness. After a passing assessment of "the reports of the opposing commanders, McDowell and Johnston," on July 21, 1861, as "fair and correct," Sherman brought Johnston back on stage in his Vicksburg chapter, this time with additional commentary that echoed the sentence in the letter to Appleton: "Even then the ability of General Johnston was recognized, and General Grant told me that he was about the only general on that side whom he feared." Again, no mention of Lee. One could argue that in context Sherman understood Grant was referring only to "that side" of the Vicksburg campaign, not of the entire war, so Lee would have had no relevance. But the stronger argument would seem to be that Sherman was working throughout his *Memoirs* to cast Johnston in superlative terms not so much for Johnston's benefit as for his own. If he were successful in his elevation of Johnston to the preeminent place among Confederate generals, the surrender negotiations at the Bennett farmhouse could no longer be viewed as mere postscripts or sideshows to Appomattox.[14]

When Sherman's *Memoirs* introduce Johnston for the final time, now in North Carolina in March 1865, Jefferson Davis having relieved John Bell Hood and returned the Army of Tennessee to Johnston in February, they bestow on him a distinguishing epithet: "I then knew that my special antagonist, General Jos. E. Johnston, was back, with part of his old army; that he would not be misled by feints and false reports, and would somehow compel me to exercise more caution that I had hitherto done."[15] "[M]y special antagonist": it is an apt and accurate phrase, one that describes the relationship between the two soldiers, as well as between the two authors they became. At least twice in his *Memoirs* Sherman turned aside from his narrative present to tell stories that established the tone of this special antagonism, one that distinguishes the relationship of Sherman and Johnston from that of Grant and Lee.

The first digression appears in the opening chapter of volume 2, which narrates the Atlanta campaign through Kennesaw Mountain. In his narrative, Sherman had brought his readers up to the events of May 19 and 20, 1864, when Johnston ordered an attack from his position at Cassville,

Georgia, but then went on the defensive and crossed the Etowah River. Confessing that he "could not then imagine why [Johnston] had declined battle," Sherman added that he "did not learn the real reason till after the war was over."[16]

In the next sentence, which opens a new paragraph, Sherman's narrative suddenly flashes forward to the autumn of 1865: "Taking a steamer for Cairo, I found as fellow-passengers Generals Johnston and Frank Blair [commander of Sherman's XVII Corps]. We were, of course, on the most friendly terms, and on our way up we talked over our battles again, played cards, and questioned each other as to particular parts of our mutual conduct in the game of war." Whether or not the card-playing reminisces included drinking bourbon, as had the surrender negotiations in the Bennett farmhouse the previous spring, one can find nothing comparable in Grant's narration of his relationship with Lee in his *Personal Memoirs*. More to the point, it is nearly impossible even to imagine something comparable between the two principals at Appomattox, and contemporary descriptions of their very brief meeting at the White House on May 1, 1869, reinforce this impossibility, representing that meeting as simple, dignified, and restrained.[17]

As for Sherman and Johnston playing cards en route to Cairo, what is most remarkable is not what Sherman learned and subsequently narrated about tensions between Johnston and his subordinates, Hood and Leonidas Polk (the flash-forward includes Sherman's later conversation with Hood, at the St. Charles Hotel in New Orleans in the spring of 1870, during which Hood gave Sherman a different version of events as Cassville, the difference "very natural," according to Sherman, as "subsequent events estranged these two officers"); what is most remarkable is the narrative bravado of Sherman's "of course" in the statement that he and Johnston "were, of course, on the most friendly terms." Of course? The "most friendly" terms? The meeting on the steamer to Cairo, the fourth one in their lives, was their first since they concluded negotiations at the Bennett farmhouse on April 26, 1865, and although they would go on to become quite close, their families exchanging dinner invitations when both had houses in Washington, D.C., this closeness had to grow throughout the 1870s, culminating in the latter part of the decade.[18] No reader of Johnston's *Narrative* could take such superlative friendliness so confidently for granted on the basis of his book alone, and no reader of Sherman's *Memoirs* up to this point would necessarily do so either, although signs of Sherman's high estimation of

Johnston are readily available. In a small but characteristically skillful touch, Sherman's "of course" does not remind his reader of anything already said or confirm anything inevitably known; it provides new information about his subsequent relationship with Johnston under the guise of treating the reader as an informed insider.

The second digression, which appears in the fifth chapter of volume 2, "Atlanta and After—Pursuit of Hood," is not as long as the first, but it has a distinct flavor of its own, as it describes Johnston's inquiring of Sherman after the war the name of his chief railroad-engineer. Johnston's curiosity was not merely idle, as he worked with railroads throughout his life. An army topographic engineer assigned to survey a possible route through Texas before the war, and briefly the president of a railroad company after it, Johnston wound up as U.S. railroad commissioner in the first administration of Grover Cleveland. Upon learning that Sherman's chief railroad engineer was "Colonel W. W. Wright, a civilian," Johnston expressed his surprise and admiration before turning to an anecdote obviously relished by Sherman in the retelling. Johnston's anecdote revealed that, about the time one of Sherman's trains was reaching him at Big Shanty on tracks recently repaired by his men, Confederates were reporting to Johnston at Marietta that the break they had made in those tracks, near Tilton Station, would take Sherman's people another two weeks to repair.[19]

Johnston would not have seen these most friendly representations of his special antagonism with Sherman until he read them in his antagonist's *Memoirs,* and he may have been gratified by what he read or somewhat surprised or wryly amused by Sherman's typically unguarded warmbloodedness. But Sherman would have read what Johnston had written of him by the time he was writing. What did he find when he looked in the mirror of Johnston's *Narrative*? If he was hoping to find himself complimented, as he would go on to compliment Johnston, Sherman would have had a long wait and a long time to call upon the patience for which he was never famous. Twenty-nine times in Johnston's narrative Sherman's name comes and goes with perfunctory matter-of-factness before the narrative begins to inch toward greater intimacy in a section of the eleventh chapter, when Johnston gave his reasons for leaving Dalton, Georgia: "I supposed, from General Sherman's great superiority of numbers, that he intended to decide the contest by a battle." At this point, when Johnston finally ventured into his opponent's thinking, with his narrative nearly three-quarters finished, the movement into Sherman's psyche was neither deep nor color-ful. But, having subsisted on such a meager narrative diet up to this point, Sherman would have found himself thrown his first nourishing crumb on the next page. There Johnston commented on the high quality of U.S. soldiers and added, with reference to Sherman, "It was not to be supposed that such troops, under a sagacious and resolute leader, and covered by intrenchments [sic], were to be beaten by greatly inferior numbers." True, it is faint praise; to be "sagacious and resolute" is not quite the same thing as being the most skillful and feared soldier on his side, and Sherman's resolute sagacity gets somewhat discounted by the mention of his covering entrenchments and Johnston's inferior numbers. But as Johnston moved toward the denouement he became more liberal with praise, although he tended to direct that praise toward Sherman's soldiers and thus only indi-rectly toward their leader.[20]

In his account of his first meeting with Sherman, at the Bennett farm-house on April 17, 1865, Johnston once again hinted at a deeper portrait of his antagonist. Narrating in the muted register of indirect discourse, he briefly recounted Sherman's showing him news of Lincoln's assassination, noting, "I told General Sherman that, in my opinion, the event was the greatest possible calamity to the South." He then summarized his desire for an armistice to give "the civil authorities" an opportunity to negotiate; Sherman's objection that the United States did not recognize the existence of a Southern Confederacy or its civil authorities; Sherman's counteroffer of the same terms that Grant offered Lee; and his, Johnston's, countering response that "we might do more than he proposed" and "arrange the terms of a permanent peace," citing as precedent Napoleon's belief that "the civic crown earned by preserving the life of one citizen confers truer glory than the highest achievement merely military."[21]

In light of subsequent events, in which Sherman was publicly chastised and humiliated for exceeding his "merely military" authority, it is easy to see this moment in Johnston's *Narrative* as the temptation scene in which Johnston plays Satan to Sherman's Eve. If Sherman had stuck to the merely military, he would have saved himself, and many others, much distress. But there is no suggestion by Johnston that he thought of himself as luring Sherman into difficulty, and in the pages that followed he did not describe or take any responsibility for the controversy he helped create for Sher-man. It is not hard to imagine that Sherman, reading Johnston's account in 1874, would have felt vindicated by it, since it showed the controversial suggestion that the U.S. government recognize existing governments in the Confederate states originated with Johnston, not with him. Instead of any hint of controversy, what Johnston's narrative of the first meeting does give is one suggestive glimpse into Sherman's interior: "General Sherman replied, with heightened color, that he appreciated such a sentiment, and that to put an end to further devastation and bloodshed, and restore the Union, and with it the prosperity of the country, were to him objects of ambition."[22]

Johnston's understated phrase "with heightened color" has the ring of truth about it, as it describes succinctly the flushed face Sherman showed to the world on many occasions, both in war and in peace. No doubt, negotiations with him at the Bennett farmhouse included many moments of Sherman's heightened coloring and provided a sharp contrast with the unbroken dignity of negotiations between Grant and Lee in Wilmer McLean's parlor. Sherman's heightened coloring is not remarkable; what is remarkable is that throughout his account of the surrender negotiations Johnston represented himself as both coolly rational and in control, while he was advancing initiatives that put Sherman on the defensive.

When Sherman came to write his version of the negotiations, he made no reference to the specifics of Johnston's account, which he summarized as "quite accurate and correct," but he reciprocated in kind, fully turning the tables and casting himself as the coolly shrewd one, whose skillful management of the situation put Johnston on the defensive and got an emotional rise out of him. Having described his arrangement of a private interview with his adversary at the Bennett farmhouse, Sherman continued in a new paragraph: "As soon as we were alone together I showed him the dispatch announcing Mr. Lincoln's assassination, and watched him closely." The four-word phrase "and watched him closely" moved Sherman's observation of Johnston closer to that of a detective or a psychotherapist, someone whose study of his subject was particularly keen and charged. In the draft of Sherman's manuscript in the Library of Congress, the first version of Johnston's reaction read this way: "The perspiration came out on his forehead, and he did not attempt to conceal his distress." The detail of Johnston's anxious sweating at noon on an April day in North Carolina was a small but compelling one, but Sherman was not yet content with it. His manuscript shows that he chose to insert over a caret mark after "out" the prepositional phrase, which appeared in the published version, "in large drops": "The perspiration come out in large drops on his forehead." In a work of eight hundred pages, this one prepositional phrase would be easy for a reader to miss. But it certainly suggested that at this extraordinary moment Johnston was in the grip of intense feelings and not at all as cool as his own narrative suggested.[23]

Small as Sherman's detail of Johnston sweating large drops may seem, it was large enough to prompt a published response from Johnston once he had read Sherman's *Memoirs*. In an article titled "My Negotiations with General Sherman," published in the *North American Review* in 1886, the same year the second edition of Sherman's *Memoirs* appeared, Johnston objected to Sherman's depiction of him in the Bennett farmhouse: "From his account of this interview, it is evident that General Sherman's memory confounds, I think, occurrences in Raleigh with those in Mr. Bennett's house. The idea that the Confederates should be suspected of such a crime [the assassination of Lincoln] never entered my mind, and the amount of sensibility ascribed to me is unnatural; nor is General Sherman capable of the rudeness of speaking to me in such terms of my President as he attributes to himself."[24]

Johnston protested a little too much in rejecting the very idea that the outspoken Sherman could possibly be capable of rudeness to Davis, Johnston's own very public grudge against his president often veering in that direction. But this quibble aside, Johnston's statement that "the amount of sensibility" ascribed to him by Sherman "is unnatural" again has the ring of truth to it. Any reader of Sherman's *Memoirs* can easily imagine its author both coloring and sweating large drops at various points in his career, but few readers of Johnston's temperate prose could imagine the same of him. Johnston's rejection of Sherman's description not only asserts his own coolness; it reads like a fastidious critic's judgment against what he sees as sensational overwriting, a fault of which Johnston himself could never be accused. But if Sherman overstepped here, perhaps projecting his own heightened sensibility onto his special antagonist, this moment in his *Memoirs* had a long foreground. In 1868, seven years before the publication of his book, Sherman narrated the same moment for his friend John W. Draper, a founder of the New York University School of Medicine and author of the three-volume *History of the American Civil War* (1867–70). Draper's papers include Sherman's earlier version of the moment at the Bennett farmhouse: "The perspiration came in heavy blots on his high forehead as he was reading [the dispatch about Lincoln's assassination], and he made many ejaculations, such as 'Great God!' 'Terrible!' &c.&c. . . . He declaimed against it in terms harsher than I did, and I believed him sincere. I still believe he was sincere."[25]

Johnston's reaction was even more dramatic in this version, and if he could have seen it, he would have been even more displeased than he was with the toned-down version eventually published in Sherman's *Memoirs*. Admittedly, Sherman may have been absolutely truthful in his recounting of Johnston's reaction. It is perfectly possible that in the privacy of the Bennett farmhouse, with both generals' staff officers waiting in the yard, in contrast to well-populated surrender scenes in the McLean parlor at Appomattox, Johnston may have dropped both his guard and his mask in reacting quite naturally to the shocking news of the first assassination of a United States president. One can only imagine what Lee and Grant might have said to one another if they, too, had been left alone for a few minutes. But they were not and, after the private moment in the Bennett farmhouse, neither were Sherman and Johnston.

What is at stake here is public perception of a private moment between the special antagonists, one with no counterpart at Appomattox. Different points of view will see the same situation differently, and Sherman may have seen Johnston as agitated by news of the assassination, while Johnston was seeing himself as relatively calm under the circumstances. More important, at least to these two soldiers and authors, was the narrative staging of the moment in their respective books. On one level, quite understandably, each man wanted to look composed and self-possessed, especially in the face of all the public criticism and controversy each one encountered, both during the war and after. Military surrender was one thing, but surrender to what Johnston called an unnatural amount of sensibility would have been another thing altogether, one that violated codes of masculinity and conduct becoming to an officer. In his official report of May 9, 1865, Sherman showed clearly that, in the rhetoric of a military report, he, too, subscribed to these codes, as he described his first interview with Johnston as "frank and soldier-like." No signs of distress, no great drops of perspiration, no agitated ejaculations marked by un-soldierlike exclamation points. These would have to wait for his memoirs.

But on another level something else may have been going on, particularly on Sherman's end. When one reads the two books side by side, it is difficult to avoid the conjecture that Sherman's representation of their special antagonism was an attempt to invent the friendship it purported to describe. In other words, upon reading Johnston's rather constrained version of the relationship, Sherman may have been moved, consciously or unconsciously, to extend himself toward Johnston and in doing so attempt to move the relationship up a notch. Sherman's feelings for Johnston appeared in the official records as early as April 23, 1865, when he wrote to his enemy during the tense, unsettled, six-day interval between the signing of their first agreement on Tuesday, April 18, and Monday, April 24, when Grant visited Sherman with the news that the terms of the agreement were rejected and the truce must end immediately. During this fretful interval, also without counterpart at Appomattox, the two opposing generals had to work hard to maintain the status quo and keep their respective lines from changing, in violation of the truce agreement. In particular, Sherman had to rein in his cavalry commander, James. H. Wilson, whom he had described to Johnston, in a letter written April 20, the same day Wilson occupied Macon, Georgia, as "impetuous and rapid." Having added, in a letter written to Johnston the next day, that Wilson "seems to have his blood up and will be hard to hold," Sherman returned to the subject of checking his cavalry commander again on April 23, by which date Wilson also had occupied Talladega, Alabama. But this time Sherman added something extra for his special antagonist: "Indeed, I have almost exceeded the bounds of prudence in checking him without the means of direct communication, and only did so on my absolute faith in your personal character."[26]

"[M]y absolute faith in your personal character": it is an extraordinary declaration for one human being to make to another, let alone a combatant to his adversary in the midst of especially fraught surrender negotiations. This was not a tactical declaration made during the calmly reflective aftermath of civilian memoir-writing; it was made in the heat of the moment, and it was pure Sherman, a signature mixture of abiding commitment to an ethos of moral integrity and a trusting, impulsive guilelessness that many might consider imprudent indeed under the circumstances. One has only to recall Sherman's heated correspondence with Hood about the treatment of the civilians of Atlanta to realize that there was nothing formulaic or perfunctory about his declaration of faith in Johnston's character; Sherman did not make such statements lightly. In fact, readers of his *Memoirs* will find them rare, with Grant the prominent exception eliciting from Sherman such direct second-person expressions of respect and admiration.

Sherman often exceeded the bounds of prudence, especially when it came to talking and writing, but to his credit he often knew it, and if his lack of prudent restraint frequently caused him problems, most spectacularly and painfully in his negotiations toward the rejected first agreement with Johnston, it also produced results with lasting benefits that spread beyond their postwar friendship. Sherman's side of the correspondence with Johnston during the six-day interval between their first agreement and news of its rejection by Washington reads like nothing else in the paper trail left by either the surrender at Appomattox or the one in North Carolina. In his letter of April 21, for example, the same in which he referred to Wilson as having his blood up and being hard to hold, Sherman included the kind of visionary meditation that would have infuriated anyone, such as Stanton, who wanted him to stick to the merely military: "I believe, if the South would simply and publicly declare what we all feel, that slavery is dead, that you would inaugurate an era of peace and prosperity that would soon erase the ravages of the past four years of war." Turning to the subject of the labor force available in freed men and women, Sherman slipped into an informal tone more appropriate to subsequent dinner conversations of the late 1870s: "Negroes would remain in the South and afford you abundance of cheap labor which otherwise will be driven away, and it will save the country the senseless discussions which have kept us all in hot water for fifty years." Then, in the next sentence, Sherman's prudence made a token attempt to check him, producing results that testify, with sad irony, to his naïveté: "Although strictly speaking this is no subject of a military convention, yet I am honestly convinced that our simple declaration of a result will be accepted as good law everywhere." A final sentence only compounded the irony: "Of course I have not a single word from Washington on this or any other point of our agreement, but I know the effect of such a step by us will be universally accepted."[27]

The official records do not contain any direct response by Johnston to Sherman's dizzying dilation into personal opinions about the proper course of reconstruction, a dilation well beyond the bounds of a military convention, but clearly Sherman's letters, and the actions they announced, had a profound effect on him. On April 23, Sherman addressed an unofficial letter, accompanying a "bundle of papers" with the latest news about the assassins and their victims, to both Johnston and Confederate General William J. Hardee, a letter that included his views on the negative effects the assassination would have on the South, as well as the bald statement, "I am thus frank with you and have asserted as much to the War Department." Sherman's next long letter to Johnston came on April 27, after three short, terse ones of April 23–24, in which he conveyed the arrival of the reply from Washington, the rejection of their first agreement, and his demand for Johnston's surrender on the same terms offered to Lee "pure and simply." On April 27, with the final agreement of April 26 now signed and behind them, Sherman sent Johnston copies of his Field Orders Nos. 65 and 66, empowering Schofield to carry out the surrender terms, along with an offer of "ten days' rations for 25,000 men." This magnanimous gesture might well have been enough to stir Johnston's gratitude, but for good measure Sherman threw in another memorable example of his unguarded frankness: "Now that the war is over, I am as willing to risk my person and reputation as heretofore to heal the wounds made by the past war, and I think my feeling is shared by the whole army."[28]

In reading over Sherman's often effusive side of the correspondence, one may be tempted to ascribe to him a certain amount of strategic calculation, as though he knowingly weighed everything he wrote to Johnston with fully prescient anticipation of the eventual publication of their correspondence by the Government Printing Office. But although Sherman had learned the hard way, beginning as early as his service in Kentucky in 1862, that he was a public figure whose statements were subject to critical scrutiny by a national audience, a full reading of his letters and his *Memoirs* leads to the conclusion that his intelligence, which was both quick and deep, did not necessarily include this kind of calculation. In contrast with Lincoln, who had an unusual capacity to see a given situation from multiple points of view, Sherman tended to see things from his own perspective, credit others with seeing the world as clearly as he did, and then wince in bewildered and indignant astonishment when it turned out otherwise. In the negotiations with Johnston at the Bennett farmhouse, he encountered someone who did see many things as he did, or so he believed, and the correspondence that accompanied and followed those negotiations reflected Sherman's immediate, instinctive trust in what he took to be a congruence of visions, not his shrewdly far-sighted performance before the audience of posterity.

The proof that Sherman's instincts were sound, at least about Johnston, if not at all about Washington, came the next day in Johnston's answer of April 28. For a dutiful reader of Johnston's *Narrative,* and his side of the official correspondence with Sherman, the moving mixture of professional utterance with private feeling makes his response stand out: "The enlarged patriotism manifested in these papers reconciles me to what I had previously regarded as the misfortune of my life—that of having had you to encounter in the field. The enlightened and humane policy you have adopted will certainly be successful. It is fortunate for the people of North Carolina that your views are to be carried out by one so capable of appreciating them. I hope that you are as well represented in the other departments of your command; if so, an early and complete pacification in it may be expected." Having demonstrated in this well-crafted blending of complex and simple sentences the ready pen with which Sherman credited him in the letter to the Appletons, Johnston "very gladly" accepted Sherman's "generous offer" of food for his troops and then went on to confirm the like-mindedness of the special antagonists: "The disposition you express to heal the wounds made by the past war has been evident to me in all our interviews. You are right that similar feelings are entertained by the mass of the army. I am sure that all the leading men in it will exert their influence for that object."[29]

As it turned out, Johnston was no better than Sherman at seeing the end of the war from points of view radically different from his own. Among the leading men of the Confederate army who did not entertain similar feelings, Jubal Early and Nathan Bedford Forrest immediately come to mind as counterexamples. But his April 28 letter to Sherman marked the written beginning of their friendship and anticipated the public performance of that friendship, along with the mythologizing of it that culminated, and continues to this day, in the public narration of Johnston's presence at Sherman's funeral services in New York on February 19, 1891.

Front-page coverage of the funeral procession in the *New York Times* the next day (Sherman would be buried in St. Louis on February 21) helped set the dominant tone, beginning with a rhythmic catalog of warriors that echoed English translations of Homeric epic: "Then came the pallbearers. An added sense of melancholy confronted the sightseer as the veterans came into view: the brave Schofield; Howard, who gave an arm to the cause while commanding Sherman's right wing; Braine, whose shells crashed against Forts Fisher and Anderson; Greer, who fought beside Porter at Vicksburg; Sickles, Dodge, and Corse; Swayne, Woodford, Wright, and Moore, brave men and true—these did the last honors beside the bier of their lamented chieftain." Then, after this long and resonant sentence, came the dramatic turn with all its rolling, sonorous parallelism: "There was another face among them—that of Johnston, the same Joseph E. Johnston who threw himself and his army before Sherman in the march to the sea—the same Johnston, who in April, 1865, surrendered to the soldier whose corpse he was following in sorrow." The heightened language was certainly compelling, even if some of the facts were wrong, Johnston having been relieved of command four months before Sherman began his march to the sea.[30]

Serving as an honorary pallbearer was nothing new to Johnston at this point. Six years earlier, in 1885, he had performed the same service at the funerals of Grant and his old friend George B. McClellan. But the coverage of his presence at Sherman's funeral set it apart. The myth-making began with obituaries printed after Johnston died in Washington, D.C., four weeks later on March 21, 1891. On this occasion the *New York Times* stated that "The General had been suffering for the past three weeks with an affection of the heart, aggravated by a cold he caught soon after Gen. Sherman's funeral in New-York." The same sentence appeared in the *Chicago Sunday Tribune,* and the *Washington Post* also mentioned Johnston's cold, "supposed to have been contracted while he was in attendance on the Sherman obsequies." The *Los Angeles Times* did not mention the cold or Sherman's funeral, but the subheading of its obituary echoed the emerging tenor: "The Confederate General Who Became Sherman's Friend." Two weeks later *Harper's Weekly* drove the point home with a rhetorical flourish: "The day of the funeral pageant was cold and raw, and the ex-Confederate soldier suffered so far from the exposure that he died of it, and so gave up his life in showing this last respect to the memory of the man whose forces he had once tried to cut to pieces."[31]

With the appearance of Robert M. Hughes's biography of Johnston two years later, the causal link between Johnston's service as a pallbearer for Sherman and his own death was firmly established: "Though unusually feeble at the time, Johnston attended the obsequies; and the bad weather which prevailed gave him a cold, which greatly enfeebled him." Although the nineteenth century believed that cold weather could cause colds, a belief embedded in the continuing use of "cold" to mean "a viral infection characterized by inflammation of the mucous membranes of the respiratory passages and accompanying fever, chills, coughing, and sneezing" (*American*

Heritage Dictionary), the present does not concur. In the words of the *Merck Manual of Medical Information,* "Becoming chilled doesn't by itself cause colds or increase a person's susceptibility to infection by a respiratory virus. A person's general health or eating habits don't seem to make any difference either." What is noteworthy here is not that the present thinks differently from the past about the common cold; what is noteworthy is that despite its different thinking the present continues to repeat the discredited causality in the case of Johnston at Sherman's funeral, as in, for example, Craig L. Symonds's biography of Johnston (1992) or Edward G. Longacre's *Worthy Opponents* (2006). The myth is too attractive and compelling to discard.[32]

Making the myth more attractive and more compelling was Oliver Otis Howard's account of Sherman's funeral in his two-volume *Autobiography,* published in 1907. There Howard put words into Johnston's mouth, words that do not appear in the original newspaper coverage or in Hughes's biography but that nevertheless continue to be repeated as frequently as any quotable lines associated with Civil War memory. Howard's full account went this way: "The weather was exceedingly cold. Some one said to General Joseph E. Johnston, one of the bearers: 'General, put on your hat, you will take cold.' Johnston answered: 'If I were in his place and he standing here in mine he would not put on his hat.'" Howard then went on to moralize Johnston's utterance in case anyone had missed the point: "Thus delicately he signified his deep regard for Sherman. In fact, these two, after their campaign was over, behaved always toward each other as brothers."[33]

Here was the myth of reconciliation much of the country wanted and needed. It took the familiar image of "the brothers' war" or of "brother against brother"—referring literally to families divided by the war, especially in the Border States and Upper South, as well as figuratively to fellow citizens pitted against each other in civil war—and extended it. Strangers to each other in the regular army, Johnston and Sherman were not antebellum brothers sadly divided by the war; it was the war itself that made them brothers. In their case the war was not the occasion for tragic fratricide; it was the agent of their postwar fraternity. Magnanimous and dignified as Lee and Grant had been at Appomattox, they could offer the popular imagination nothing comparable.

Those who have repeated and continue to repeat what Johnston supposedly said at Sherman's funeral either quote and cite Howard's 1907 version of the famous statement made sixteen years later—if not others who quote and cite Howard—or a slightly varied version that appeared a quarter-century after Howard's in Lloyd Lewis's biography *Sherman: Fighting Prophet* (1932). Because of the citation conventions Lewis adopted in his endnotes, his source for Johnston's famous reply is not clear; he simply cited "newspapers of the time," which did not contain it. In his version of the funeral, however, Lewis introduced another perspective, that of Sherman's son-in-law, Alexander Montgomery Thackara, from whom Lewis did receive a statement, according to his endnotes, although he did not make clear whether Thackara's statement was the source for Johnston's words.[34] At any rate, Lewis's version of the famous moment went like this:

> The day was raw and cold. Bareheaded stood the honorary pallbearers. One was seen by Thackara to bend toward the oldest of the group, a man who had celebrated his eighty-second birthday twelve days earlier. He said:
> "General, please put on your hat; you might get sick."
> Joe Johnston turned. "If I were in his place and he were standing here in mine, he would not put on his hat." From this last meeting with Sherman, Johnston would not retreat. In his breast as he went home were the seeds of the pneumonia that killed him ten days later.[35]

Although he had a flare for readable narrative, the calendar does not seem to have been Lewis's specialty, Johnston having turned eighty-four sixteen days earlier, not eighty-two twelve days earlier, and dying thirty days later, not ten, and although Thackara would seem from internal evidence to be his source here, Lewis's bibliography did include Howard's *Autobiography,* even if the relevant endnote did not. Perhaps Lewis got his version from Howard; perhaps he got it from Thackara, who had gotten it from Howard. Either way, what is telling is that Lewis's slight variant introduced into Howard's version, along with a comma, a second "were" that bolstered even further Johnston's suspiciously metrical reply, one that, broken into lines of verse, suggests an iambic sound shape, alternating stressed and unstressed syllables: "If *I* were *in* his *place* / and *he* were *stand*ing *here* in *mine,* / *he* would *not* put *on* his *hat.*"

The response Howard attributed to Johnston came ready-made for admission into the public imagination. Did an eighty-four-year-old man standing bare-headed in cold, raw weather, with the seeds of pneumonia in his lungs and with no record in print of any previous tendency toward metrical composition, suddenly erupt spontaneously into such resonant elegance? It is not very likely. But it is believable that Johnston said something similar, and simpler, and if Howard's recollection burnished the response a decade and a half later, one should not attribute to him any motives less than honorable. Howard, too, was a writer with a ready pen, one who turned to writing in the 1870s because he "was forced to do something to earn money over and beyond my pay."[36] But unlike some writers he did not direct his ready pen toward promoting postwar images of fraternal reconciliation intended to reassure only the white populations of the formerly opposed sections, images that ignored or suppressed the concurrent realities of life for many black people. Commissioner of the Freedmen's Bureau, as well as founding president of Howard University, the so-called Christian General was anything but indifferent to the racial dimensions of reconciliation. If the words he transmitted from Johnston's mouth to the reading public were somewhat new and improved—there is no statement in his *Autobiography* that he was necessarily the first recipient of Johnston's words, so they may have come to him already second-hand—that improvement certainly did not reflect any self-serving motive on his part or any devious scheme to harmonize some people while excluding others.

Whatever size the grain of salt should be to acknowledge the inevitable vicissitudes of oral transmission and later recollection, Howard's account of Johnston at Sherman's funeral in February 1891 finally completed the surrender in North Carolina that began nearly twenty-six years before. Whereas the requisite two parts of the Appomattox surrender occurred within days of one another and did so with a fictive, mythic potential subsequently fulfilled by the writings and speeches of Joshua Lawrence Chamberlain and John B. Gordon, the second part of the North Carolina surrender, the one that involved delivering or handing over, did not come into its fully fictive, mythic force until, in the words of *Harper's Weekly,* Johnston "gave up his life in showing this last respect to the memory of the man whose forces he had once tried to cut to pieces." The soldiers remaining in the Army of Tennessee may have sporadically handed over their arms, without pageantry or fanfare, to the small body of United States soldiers detailed to receive them near the railroad depot in Greensboro during late April and early May 1865, but the ceremonial and richly symbolic handing over occurred when the public began to imagine, with the help of various writers, both anonymous and named, that Johnston self-sacrificingly handed over his life to Sherman's memory, thereby effecting a closure, in the eyes of warriors and civilians, that approached, if not reached, the sublime.

NOTES

1. "Surrender," *The American Heritage Dictionary of the English Language,* ed. William Morris (Boston: American Heritage Publishing Co., 1969), 1295; Ulysses S. Grant, *Personal Memoirs of Ulysses S. Grant,* 2 vols. (New York: Charles L. Webster, 1885–86), 2:489. For the development of Joshua Lawrence Chamberlain's accounts of the surrender ceremony at Appomattox, see Stephen Cushman, *Belligerent Muse: Five Northern Writers and How They Shaped Our Understanding of the Civil War* (Chapel Hill: University of North Carolina Press, 2014), 147–63.

2. See U. S. War Department, *The War of the Rebellion: A Compilation of the Official Records of the Union and Confederate Armies,* 128 vols. (Washington: Government Printing Office, 1880–1901), ser. 1, vol. 46, pt. 1:1277–79, for "Tabular statement of officers and men of the Confederate Army paroled at Appomattox Court-House" (28,231 total), and ser. 1, vol. 47, pt. 1:1066, for "Tabular statement of officers and men of the Confederate Army paroled at Greensborough, N.C., and other points, in accordance with the military convention of April 26, 1865" (39,012 total; compilation hereafter cited as *OR*; all references are to series 1). For totals reported by Schofield and Wilson, see William T. Sherman, *Memoirs of General William T. Sherman,* 2 vols. (New York: D. Appleton and Co., 1875), 2:370.

3. Craig L. Symonds, *Joseph E. Johnston: A Civil War Biography* (New York: W. W. Norton, 1992), 357; Mark L. Bradley, *This Astounding Close: The Road to Bennett Place* (Chapel Hill: University of North Carolina Press, 2000); Robert M. Dunkerly, *The Confederate Surrender at Greensboro: The Final Days of the Army of Tennessee, April 1865* (Jefferson, N.C.: McFarland, 2013); and Dunkerly, *To the Bitter End: Appomattox, Bennett Place, and the Surrenders of the Confederacy* (El Dorado Hills, Calif.: Savas Beatie, 2015). For Johnston's General Orders No. 22, see *OR* 47(1): 1061; for paroles of Johnston and his staff, see *OR* 47(3): 379–80.

4. William T. Sherman to John M. Schofield, May 5, 1865, *Sherman's Civil War: Selected Correspondence of William T. Sherman, 1861–1865,* ed. Brooks D. Simpson and Jean V. Berlin (Chapel Hill: University of North Carolina Press, 1999), 887.

5. For Johnston's remarks about desertions from his army, see Joseph E. Johnston, *Narrative of Military Operations, Directed, During the Late War between the States, by Joseph E. Johnston, General C.S.A.* (New York: D. Appleton and Co., 1874), 410: "It was very commonly believed among the soldiers that there was to be a surrender, by which they would be prisoners of war, to which they were very averse. This apprehension caused a great number of desertions between the 19th and 24th of April—not less than four thousand in the infantry and artillery, and almost as many from the cavalry; many of them rode off artillery horses, and mules belonging to the baggage-trains."

6. The three volumes of Rick Atkinson's trilogy are *An Army at Dawn: The War in North Africa: 1942–43* (New York: Henry Holt and Co., 2002); *The Day of Battle: The War in Sicily and Italy, 1943–44* (New York: Henry Holt and Co., 2007); and *The Guns at Last Light: The War in Europe, 1944–1945* (New York: Henry Holt and Co., 2013).

7. Grant, *Personal Memoirs* 2:488.

8. Thomas M. Cook, "The Rebellion: Views of General Robert E. Lee," *New York Herald,* April 29, 1865, 5. "Mr. Thomas M. Cook's Despatch" was dated April 24, 1865. This issue of the *New York Herald* should not be confused with that of the *New York Weekly Herald* published the same day, which contained extensive coverage of "Obsequies to Abraham Lincoln," including the funeral procession in New York, as well as coverage of Sherman's negotiations with Johnston in North Carolina and the rejection of their agreement by Andrew Johnson and his cabinet. For transcriptions of three postwar "conversations" with Lee, see Gary W. Gallagher, ed., *Lee: The Soldier* (Lincoln: University of Nebraska Press, 1996), 3–34.

9. For background on D. Appleton and Company, see Grant Overton, *Portrait of a Publisher and the First Hundred Years of the House of Appleton* (New York: D. Appleton and Co., 1925); D. Appleton-Century Company, *The House of Appleton-Century* (New York: D. Appleton-Century Co., 1936); and Gerald R. Wolfe, *The House of Appleton: The History of a Publishing House and Its Relationship to the Cultural, Social, and Political Events That Helped Shape the Destiny of New York City* (Metuchen, N.J.: Scarecrow Press, 1981). See especially Wolfe's chapter, "New Pastures and the Civil War Memoirs" (145–64).

10. See Symonds, *Joseph E. Johnston,* 364. Compare Douglas Southall Freeman's assessment in *The South to Posterity: An Introduction to the Writing of Confederate History* (1939; rpt. with introd. by Gary W. Gallagher, Baton Rouge: Louisiana State University Press, 1998), 72: "[Joseph E. Johnston's] *Narrative of Military Operations,* published in 1874, was written vigorously and unsparingly and, of course, was read with high interest; but it cannot be said to have increased his reputation as a soldier. His grievance against President Davis, whom he accused of overslaughing him [passing him over], was too manifest for objective or even for effective presentation of his defence." No doubt many read Johnston with high interest, especially those who expected to find themselves in his narrative, but their interest did not translate into high sales.

11. For sales of Sherman's book, see William Tecumseh Sherman, *Memoirs of General W. T. Sherman,* ed. Charles Royster (New York: Library of America, 1990), 1112. In *Portrait of a Publisher,* Overton called Sherman's book "an enormous success" and a "gigantic success" (20, 64). He did not mention Johnston's book at all.

12. Sherman, *Memoirs* 2:47, 49.

13. *OR* 47(1): 32. See also Sherman, *Memoirs* 2:348.

14. Sherman, *Memoirs* 1:181, 328.

15. Ibid., 2:299.

16. For the conversations with Johnston and, subsequently, Hood, see Sherman, *Memoirs* 2:39–41.

17. See Douglas Southall Freeman, *R. E. Lee: A Biography,* 4 vols. (New York: Charles Scribner's Sons, 1934–35), 4:520–21.

18. See Edward G. Longacre, *Worthy Opponents: William T. Sherman and Joseph E. Johnston: Antagonists in War—Friends in Peace* (Nashville, Tenn.: Rutledge Hill Press, 2006), 319–22.

19. Sherman, *Memoirs* 2:151–52.

20. Johnston, *Narrative,* 317, 318, 329, 344, 358.

21. Ibid., 402–3.

22. Johnston, *Narrative,* 403. For Sherman's official account of his dealings with Johnston, see his long report of May 9, 1865, which is vintage Sherman and a tour de force,

including such memorable formulations as "To push an army whose commander had so frankly and honestly confessed his inability to cope with me were cowardly and unworthy the brave men I led"; "As for myself I know my motives, and challenge the instance during the past four years where an armed and defiant foe stood before me that I did not go in for a fight, and I would blush for shame if I had ever insulted or struck a fallen foe"; and "I have my opinions on the questions involved, and I will stand by the memorandum; but this forms no part of a military report." This last sentence provides a textbook example of the rhetoric of paralipsis, or making an assertion by announcing that one is withholding the assertion. Sherman's report is in *OR* 47(1): 32–35. One familiar way of explaining Sherman's over-stepping of his military authority is to say that he was simply trying to do what he thought Lincoln wanted him to do after the final meeting of the two men on the *River Queen* at City Point, Virginia, on Monday and Tuesday, March 27 and 28, 1865. But Sherman's inclination to follow victory with magnanimity and generosity outside his jurisdiction had already emerged in his treatment of the citizens of Jackson, Mississippi, after Johnston evacuated the city in July 1863. In the first of two letters he wrote to Grant from Jackson on July 21, 1863, he asked permission to "promise mayor and committee of citizens, say, 200 barrels of flour and 100 barrels of salt pork, if they will send for it to Big Black Bridge and give me pledges that it shall be devoted to pure charity?" In the second he sought authorization to establish trade with local civilians: "Would I be justified in making a distinct proposition to the people that if Johnston or President Davis will agree that no Confederate soldiers or guerrillas will operate west of Pearl River, we will establish at Big Black River railroad bridge a kind of trading depot, where the people of Mississippi may exchange their cotton, corn, and produce for provisions, clothing, and family supplies?" In the next paragraph, despite an initial disclaimer about his detachment from politics, Sherman went on to offer Grant his opinion on the larger strategy of reconstructing Mississippi: "I profess to know nothing of polities, but I think we have here an admirable wedge which may be encouraged without committing the President or War Department. If prominent men in Mississippi admit the fact of being subdued, it will have a powerful effect all over the South." Grant's reply, which does not appear in the *OR,* apparently checked his friend's eagerness and brought him back to his merely military authority. Sherman's next letter, written on July 22, 1863, acknowledged as much: "All right about trade. I will not promise or do anything except to relieve the immedi-ate wants of suffering humanity." This correspondence shows that Sherman's conversations with Lincoln on the *River Queen,* or his understanding of them, merely confirmed tendencies he already exhibited. See *OR* 24(2): 530–31. The most recent narrative of the surrender ne-gotiations between Johnston and Sherman appears in James Lee McDonough's biography *William Tecumseh Sherman: In the Service of My Country: A Life* (New York: Norton, 2016), 625–36. McDonough's account of the surrender negotiations, while admirably readable, adds no new information, and it contains nothing about the Greensboro phase of the sur-render, having left North Carolina with Sherman after the final meeting with Johnston. Subsequently, McDonough includes nothing about Johnston at Sherman's funeral. See also Robert L. O'Connell's *Fierce Patriot: The Tangled Lives of William Tecumseh Sherman* (New York: Random House, 2014), 181–83. In reconstructing the surrender negotiations, O'Connell adopts a vernacular mode to cast Sherman as the unwitting dupe of Johnston, "another cagey strategist" (181), and John Breckinridge, "the wily former U.S. vice president and currently Confederate secretary of war." Describing the first agreement between Sherman and Johnston as "a sweetheart of a deal" for people from the South, O'Connell offers this formulation: "Earlier, Sherman was described as tipsy on himself; this document reflects serious inebriation" (182). O'Connell does not mention the Greensboro phase of the surrender.

23. Sherman, *Memoirs* 2:349; William T. Sherman Papers, Library of Congress, Washington, D.C., box 105 or reel 49. For further discussion of Sherman's description of his first meeting with Johnston, see Cushman, *Belligerent Muse,* 105–6, 111.

24. Joseph E. Johnston, "My Negotiations with General Sherman," *North American Review* 143 (August 1886): 189.

25. Qtd. by Stanley P. Hirshson in *The White Tecumseh: A Biography of General William T. Sherman* (New York: John Wiley and Sons, 1997), 304–5.

26. *OR* 47(3): 257, 265, 286. Johnston and Sherman had exchanged letters not quite two years earlier, in July 1863 during the second campaign against Jackson, Mississippi. After complaints from Confederate Major General John C. Breckinridge that the unburied bodies of United States soldiers in front of his position at Jackson were becoming "offensive" in the oppressive heat and causing sickness among his men, Johnston wrote Sherman to ask for a truce during which Confederate burial parties could do their work. Sherman thanked Johnston and granted the truce, albeit a brief one. The two short letters from Johnston and one from Sherman are respectful, but quite understandably they do not yet show the mutual admiration of the April 1865 correspondence (*OR* 24[2]: 538–39; [3]: 1002–3).

27. *OR* 47(3): 266.

28. Ibid., 287, 293, 294, 320.

29. Ibid., 336–37.

30. "On the Way to His Rest: New-York's Sad Farewell to the Great Soldier," *New York Times,* February 20, 189, 1.

31. Symonds, *Joseph E. Johnston,* 380; "Gen. Joe Johnston Dead: One of the Last of the Confederate Leaders," *New York Times,* March 22, 1891, 1; "Gen. Joseph E. Johnston is Dead," *Chicago Sunday Tribune,* March 22, 1891, 2; "Gen. Jos. E. Johnston: Death of the Brave Old Leader of the Late Confederacy," *Washington Post,* March 22, 1891, 1; "Joseph E. Johnston: The Confederate General Who Became Sherman's Friend, *Los Angeles Times,* March 22, 1891, 1; "General Joseph E. Johnston," *Harper's Weekly,* April 4, 1891, 252.

32. Robert M. Hughes, *General Johnston* (New York: D. Appleton, 1893), 288; "Cold," *American Heritage Dictionary,* 260; "Common Cold," *The Merck Manual of Medical Information* (Whitehouse Station, N.J.: Merck Research Laboratories, 1997), 913; Symonds, *Joseph E. Johnston,* 380–81; Longacre, *Worthy Opponents,* 322. Symonds cites Gilbert E. Govan and James W. Livingood, *A Different Valor: The Story of General Joseph E. Johnston, C.S.A.* (Indianapolis: Bobbs-Merrill, 1956), 397, and Longacre cites Symonds, among others.

33. Oliver Otis Howard, *Autobiography of Oliver Otis Howard,* 2 vols. (New York: Baker and Taylor, 1907), 2:553–54.

34. Lloyd Lewis, *Sherman: Fighting Prophet* (1932; rpt., New York: Harcourt, Brace, 1958), 669n.

35. Ibid., 652.

36. Howard, *Autobiography* 2:473.

Frontispiece for the first edition of *Little Women*. From *Little Women or, Meg, Jo, Beth and Amy* (Boston: Roberts Brothers, 1868).

Little Women

Louisa May Alcott's Novel of the Home Front

J. MATTHEW GALLMAN

"'Christmas won't be Christmas without any presents,' grumbled Jo, lying on the rug."[1] So begins one of the most beloved novels in American literature. It is hardly "I sing of arms, and of a man," or even "Call me Ishmael," but generations of readers—especially those who encountered Louisa May Alcott's *Little Women* as young women themselves—will immediately recognize Jo March's frustrated complaint. The feisty Jo was fifteen years old, the second oldest of four March sisters. In the next sentence older sister Meg considers her dingy dress and sighs "'It's so dreadful to be poor!'" The March sisters were heroines young readers could embrace. They were fundamentally good souls who loved each other, and yet they were not the idealized young women who would grow tiresome in their perfection. Nor were they the stuff of heavy-handed prescription, where terrible misdeeds by misguided characters would lead the young reader to didactic morals about proper behavior and the price of ill-considered missteps. The four were appealing because they were distinct personalities, and all were essentially believable to their readers. They have their adventures and misfortunes, and Alcott crams a good bit of drama into the novel's forty-seven chapters, but this is not a book filled with heroines saved from runaway carriages or innocent girls fighting off the overtures of unscrupulous rakes. It is about a family living life in and around a small New England town, not unlike Alcott's own Concord, Massachusetts.

Alcott did not follow convention by setting her book in an indeterminate moment, untouched by events beyond the isolated world of her young characters. *Little Women* begins just before Christmas in 1861, eight months after the outbreak of the American Civil War. In that first moment Jo and Meg are whining about simple material things, but in a few paragraphs the reader learns that their father is off at war with the Union army. It is, by the author's explicit design, a book about life in the North during the American Civil War.

There is much to unpack about that simple observation. Louisa May Alcott, as a young woman, lived through the four years of Civil War, and in a brief stint as a Union nurse she saw her share of the war's devastating impact on young men and their families. And Alcott, as a budding author, had already written about the war on several occasions prior to publishing *Little Women*. Now, writing three years after Appomattox, Alcott set out to create a book for young readers. She selected a setting close to home, with characters drawn from her own life, and she began her narrative seven years earlier, as the war was underway. For the novelist, then, *Little Women* is perhaps an early statement of historic memory about the Civil War. But that memory is refracted through the lens of her intended audience. She wrote for young readers, and she hoped to attract an enthusiastic audience. What would she say about the war itself, and what would she omit?

For 150 years *Little Women* has been an iconic literary statement about the northern home front. And for over half the life of the novel each new generation of readers has had its own cinematic version of *Little Women*. Alcott may have invented the Marches, but many others have reinvented both the characters and their wartime context to suit new viewers. Both the book and its ongoing memory tell us something about the place of the Civil War in American culture.

Little Women in Wartime: Part I, 1868

Although we commonly think of *Little Women* as a single novel, it was originally published separately in two parts. Part I appeared in print in 1868, and Part II—which Alcott only began drafting after the first book had reached the public—arrived on bookdealers' shelves the following year.[2] Before long, publishers took to publishing the two parts together in a single volume, and it is fair to see them as two parts of the same novel, as opposed to a novel and a sequel. In fact, in 1871 Alcott returned to her subjects with a true sequel, *Little Men,* and then again in 1886 with *Jo's Boys.* But for readers interested in how Alcott treated the Civil War, and perhaps how her readers thought about the war and its immediate aftermath, the two parts are quite distinct.

In the novel's first pages, the March girls are preparing for what promises to be a modest Christmas. After the eldest sisters complain about their sad plight, Amy—the youngest—makes the point even more dramatically, declaring that it is not "'fair for some girls to have plenty of pretty things, and other girls have nothing at all.'" It is left to Beth—the most sensitive of the four—to remind them that they have "'got Father and Mother and each other.'" But Jo, with characteristic bluntness, points out that "'We haven't got Father, and shall not have him for a long time.'" Thus, Alcott has set the stage very quickly, moving from young women complaining about a Christmas without presents to those same girls shifting their thoughts to the far bigger concern: their father is not there.

Gradually the reader discovers that Mr. March has gone off to war, leaving his "little women" at home with Mrs. March and Hannah, their dutiful housekeeper. The thought of a frugal Christmas has come from Mrs. March, who explained to her girls that it would be wrong for them to be enjoying an opulent holiday while soldiers were suffering in the army. The March girls seem to accept the general idea, but at first they are less sold on the notion that they should go entirely without gifts. Soon, though, they gravitate towards the less selfish conclusion that they should focus on getting gifts for their ever-generous "Marmee" while accepting some personal sacrifices.

This discussion of Christmas presents (both the giving and the receiving), which no doubt immediately absorbed young readers, is disrupted by a much grander event: a long letter from their absent father. Mr. March is too old to be a regular soldier but has volunteered as a chaplain. The girls and their mother talk about the sacrifices their father is making, although their comments focus on the physical discomforts of the soldier's life: poor food, drinking out of a tin cup, sleeping on the ground, and so forth. There is no sense that they are worried about battles or physical danger. Moreover, unlike the loved ones of Union soldiers who had enlisted for three years, the March girls assume that their father will be home in a matter of months "unless," as Marmee explains, "he is sick." While all agree that

Father is sacrificing for a worthy cause, it is the tomboyish Jo who declares that she wishes that she were a drummer, or perhaps a nurse. Jo likes the idea of being with her Father, but she seems more drawn to the promise of adventure.

As the March women gather to hear Marmee read Mr. March's letter, Alcott makes an unusual decision. She shifts her authorial voice to that of the historian, telling her young readers that "Very few letters were written in those hard times that were not touching, especially those which fathers sent home." Shifting back to her narrator's role, Alcott reports that this letter omitted talk of dangers faced, hardships endured, or homesickness overcome. This was, instead, a "hopeful letter, full of lively descriptions of camp life, marches, and military news.'" It left the girls missing their father, but not particularly worried for his safety.[3]

The first chapter of *Little Women* does quite a bit of work in the novel's structure. It establishes the core personality of each sister, Mrs. March's almost sainted role at the center of their lives, and the important absence of Mr. March. And, in that single sentence about soldiers' letters, Alcott reminds her readers that this is a work of fiction set in a specific moment in the immediate past, and that this fictional family experienced something that a huge number of real wartime families shared: the absence of a loved one. The twenty-three chapters in Part I span almost precisely one year, ending as Christmas approaches in 1862. Mr. March does not appear in person until the twenty-second chapter.

A huge number of Civil War families—in both the Union and the Confederacy—faced the challenges of separation, and in many cases the injury or death of loved ones. Most families in the North could rely on fairly regular mail delivery from the military camps, but that did not insulate them from a multitude of fears about wounds, disease, capture, or other calamities. Unlike Mr. March, most Union soldiers were relatively young, unmarried, men, but their absence still had an important impact on the daily lives of families back home. For the wives and children of married soldiers, the challenges were more dramatic, as those left behind had to navigate a new world without a major breadwinner as well as a father and spouse. Mr. March was not a typical Union soldier in that he was an older man who had signed on as a chaplain. Still, for the duration of Part I, the March family is without the man of the house.

Although overall the northern economy fared well during the Civil War, many military families faced serious financial difficulties. The March girls saw themselves as poor (and presumably their young readers would have accepted that description), but in fact their decline in economic status was not a product of the war or their father's absence. Instead, we learn—in a fairly murky description—that the March family had come upon hard times after Mr. March lost property, "trying to help an unfortunate friend."[4] It would appear that the family finances suffered during the economic downturn of the late 1850s rather than during the war. And, although their material deprivations in the novel are real to the girls who had been accustomed to more wealth, the family still lived in a comfortable home and enjoyed a dedicated housekeeper.

Between December and the following November, Mr. March is a fairly distant presence in the girls' lives, or at least in their fictional adventures. The letter from camp in the first chapter establishes that the girls miss their father, and that they love to receive his letters. But once Alcott introduces that fact she does not make it a point of reminding her reader of the joys that letters from Mr. March no doubt continued to bring. In fact, the absent patriarch rarely comes up in conversation at all. Early in the novel Jo visits her neighbor Laurence, who is ill at home. In this crucial conversation, which becomes the starting point to a lasting friendship, Jo shares many things about her life and family, including her sisters' "hopes and fears for father."[5] Several chapters later, Jo and her youngest sister, Amy, have a horrible falling out, and Amy tosses the book that the aspiring author was writing into the fire. Jo is inconsolable, declaring that she was planning to have the finished book "before father got home." Later in the same chapter Jo has a long talk with her mother, and they discuss how they both miss Mr. March's soothing temperament, particularly when tempers are flaring.[6] When Jo publishes a short story in the local paper, one of the sisters declares, "'What will father say?'"[7]

Apart from these occasional passing remarks, Mr. March barely appears in his daughters' conversation. The individual chapters concern dramas, large and small, involving the girls and their devoted neighbor Laurie. But after that first introduction, Alcott rarely reminds her readers of what it was really like to have a father off at war. In a sense, for much of the novel Mr. March plays a role much like that of a beloved Victorian father, who is admired from a distance, while the four girls turn to their mother for guidance on their social roles and on life's challenges. The younger reader would have been forgiven if she occasionally forgot that Mr. March was not merely in some office rather than off at war.

For most of the novel, men in uniform are curiously absent, even for a tale set in a fairly remote northern town. The exception is in an early chapter, when we do see a brief discussion of flesh-and-blood soldiers, but only as described by Mrs. March. The chapter—which Alcott called "Burdens"—begins early in the new year, with the sisters feeling a little crabby about their reduced economic circumstances and bickering about silly things. Meg and Jo both had taken jobs, Meg as a governess and Jo as the companion to their wealthy aunt. Beth, who was too shy for school, studied at home, while Amy—the youngest and a budding artist—attended school. Late in the day, Beth shares what she describes as an amusing story about her trip to the fish market earlier in the day. While she was buying oysters, Beth saw a poor woman enter the shop and ask the fish dealer for some scraps to feed her children. The fisherman was in the process of kicking her out of his store when the Marches' wealthy neighbor Mr. Laurence "'hooked up a big fish with the crooked end of his cane and held it out to her,'" telling her to take it home and cook it for her family. Beth tells the story for laughs, describing how funny the woman looked leaving the shop with the giant fish in her arms.

The girls then turn to Mrs. March, asking her to contribute an amusing story from her day, which she had spent at the Soldiers' Aid. Mrs. March describes her time spent cutting flannel for soldiers' coats, and she tells her girls how she found herself worrying about what their life would be like if father did not return. She tells the girls about an elderly man who dropped into the store, interrupting her thoughts. This man, she learned, had sent four sons to the army: two had been killed, one was a prisoner of war, and the fourth was sick in a Washington hospital. Mrs. March, shaken out of her own personal reveries, tells the man how much she respects his family's patriotic sacrifices. He responds: "'Not a mite more than I ought, ma'am. I'd go myself, if I was any use; as I ain't, I give my boys, and give 'em free.'" In sharing the story with her girls, Mrs. March makes the point that they have only "given one man," while this other family had sacrificed far more to the cause. The chapter ends with Marmee telling her daughters another story, really a parable based on their own lives, about girls who learned to count their blessings rather than complaining about silly things.[8]

"Burdens" works at multiple levels. In its most simple sense, the chapter gives the girls—and their readers—a clear moral in the contrast between their simple discomforts and the true sacrifices made by the father of four soldiers. Meanwhile, the girls do not seem to recognize, and Marmee does not underscore, how their lot in life was so much better than the poor woman who had been begging for food at the fish market. Surely Alcott intended readers to note the relationship between Mr. Laurence's impulsive act of generosity in the fish story and Mrs. March's regular work at the Soldiers' Aid. Both adults acted to ease the burdens of others. The chapter is also a rare window into Mrs. March's own wartime thoughts and feelings, as she shares just a bit about her real fears for her husband and her daughters' father. Finally, "Burdens" is distinctive in that it includes explicit talk about patriotic sacrifice. Such ideas almost never appear in *Little Women,* presumably because almost everything in the novel is seen through the eyes of the young girls.

Apart from "Burdens," the first half of Part I makes almost no direct reference to the Civil War raging at a distance. And, perhaps because Alcott focuses on the wartime lives of young women, there is little talk of children playing war or admiring men in uniform.[9] The closest thing to an exception is in July of 1862, when young Laurence invites the girls to come visit him and a group of new friends for an afternoon picnic. They enjoy a fun getaway at "Camp Laurence," playing games and bantering in an unfamiliar place. Although for most of the afternoon there is no talk of the war, Alcott has Laurie use military terms to describe their day. When the girls arrive, Laurie greets them by explaining that "'Brooke is commander in chief, I am commissary general, the other fellows are staff officers, and you, ladies, are company.'" As the chapter progresses, Alcott maintains the titles "commander in chief" and "commissary general" in describing Mr. Brooke and Laurie. When the teens throw themselves into an energetic game of croquet, Alcott describes the contests as a series of "skirmishes." On this sunny day, in a playful space created by the girls' male friend, the reader sees the young male character using martial language, far removed from the realities of war.

But later in the day, after the group has sprawled on the grass, sharing fantasy tales of knights and ladies and pirate captains and princesses, the tone shifts. The chapter closes with Meg, the eldest sister, talking with John Brooke, Laurie's tutor. Brooke explains that Laurie will soon be going off to college, and then "'I shall turn soldier. I am needed.'" Meg declares that she is "'glad of that!'" adding that she assumes that "'every young man would want to go, though it is hard for the mothers and sisters who stay at home.'" Brooke, in a moment of self-pity, tells her that he has no family and nobody would really care if he went. Meg insists that of course Laurie and his grandfather would miss him, adding that "'we should all be very sorry to have any harm happen to you.'" At these words, Brooke cheers up, and presumably the perceptive reader recognizes that a romance is in their future. Over the next many chapters, Brooke's role in the novel expands, and his relationship with Meg blossoms, yet there is no further mention of his impending enlistment and their eventual separation.

The Civil War finally intervenes in the lives of the March family in November, when a telegram arrives announcing that Mr. March is terribly sick in a Washington, D.C., hospital. The family leaps into action. Marmee plans to rush to his side, and Mr. Brooke offers to travel as her escort. In a scene that calls to mind the opening pages of Alcott's *Hospital Sketches,* Jo cuts her hair, selling her long locks to help fund Marmee's journey.[10] After many months of living a home-front life where the war barely intervened, the harsher realities of warfare had reached the March home.

With Marmee away, the girls are left at home under Hannah's supervision. In a reverse of the opening chapter, each sister sends Mr. March a letter revealing her own personality while sharing a concern for their father's welfare. And, like his martial conversation at "Camp Laurence," young Laurie adopts the vernacular of the soldier, suggesting a boy playing at wartime things even in such a moment.[11] In these chapters Alcott presents a variation on the traditional home-front narrative. Yes, their father is sick and in a military hospital, forcing his family into an experience they shared with tens of thousands of northern families. But, for the four Marsh girls, the greatest feeling of wartime separation comes with their mother's absence.

Marmee is an idealized mother figure who regular shaped the daily lives of her girls, and her absence proves crucial. For most of the year she had provided her quartet of girls with wisdom and guidance, periodically nudging them towards good behavior when they strayed towards selfishness or vanity or some such sin. On several occasions she had had detailed chats with individual daughters as they wrestled with life's problems. Mrs. March is also a virtuous and engaged citizen in her larger community, providing her girls—and readers—with a model to admire and emulate. Alcott makes these points with a light hand. Mrs. March volunteers at the Soldiers' Aid, but she does not bring any of her daughters with her. In fact the girls are never involved in patriotic voluntarism, unlike a huge portion of real wartime children in the North. Alcott is equally attentive to the broader social strains that may or may not have been the product of war. Even while the March girls periodically bemoan their poverty, Mrs. March attempts to remind them that others are far worse off.

During the novel's first Christmas, Mrs. March encouraged the girls to take their festive breakfast to the Hummels, a truly poor German immigrant family who lived nearby.[12] Not long afterwards, when Jo visits Mr. Laurence next door, she reports that her mother has arranged for "richer friends" to aid the Hummels.[13] But Mrs. March, following a long tradition of Christian charity, had continued to look in on the poor family in Mr. March's absence. With their Marmee gone, the girls' character was put to the test in a vital chapter. Although the sisters felt that they were working hard and suffering through the "self denial" of a life with both parents away, Alcott notes that all but Beth were drifting off course: Jo was happily reading while nursing a cold; Amy had set aside her homework in favor of mud pies; and Meg—who had sewing to complete—was more interested in rereading letters from Mr. Brooke.

In a crucial scene, Beth asks her sisters to go and see poor Mrs. Hummel, as their mother had instructed. Beth had been going to visit the Hummels regularly, but she was worried because the Hummel baby was sick and she did not know what to do. Beth also tells her sisters that her head aches and she is tired and hopes that one of her sisters will go in her place. The sisters promise that one of them will run out to visit the indigent German family, but all get distracted with their own pursuits. After waiting for an hour or so, the ailing Beth gets off the couch and sneaks out to see the Hummel baby without anyone noticing. She returns hours later with the sad news that the baby had died of fever while sitting on Beth's lap.

This moment of childish self-absorption by the sisters produces the great crisis in Part I. Beth, who is particularly generous and shy, and also quite frail, falls deathly ill with scarlet fever. Her older sisters, and especially

Jo, are burdened with remorse, realizing that they had selfishly let their younger sibling stand in for their absent mother. Amy, who has never had the illness, is sent off to live with their wealthy aunt, effectively shunted aside for her own health. Two things seem clear. They all desperately wish that their mother were there to care for Beth and take control of the situation, and they agree that they cannot tell her because she is still needed with their father. As Beth remains in bed under a doctor's care, they receive word that Mr. March has taken a turn for the worse, requiring Marmee to remain away longer than expected. For a time it seems that Beth's life hangs in the balance, until finally Hannah and the doctor agree that Mrs. March must be called home from Washington. But Laurie has already made that call and telegraphed the matriarch about Beth's condition.

In early December, Beth's fever breaks, Marmee returns home, and the plot turns in different directions. It turns out that John Brooke has grown quite smitten with Meg, opening up an emerging love story—with multiple dashes of confusion and tension—that no doubt thrilled Alcott's readers. Here, as with Marmee's absence, the plot uses the war to produce separations, but in atypical ways. The relationship between John and Meg develops in their letters while she is separated from John, but unlike innumerable wartime novels and short stories, and countless real wartime relationships, John Brooke is not a soldier away at war. Although he is of military age, the separation between the two is created by his gallant decision to travel as a civilian to Washington, accompanying Mrs. March. This was a wartime separation created by masculine chivalry, but with no real sense of patriotic sacrifice or risk-taking.

With both Beth and Father safely on the mend, the children return to their lives with little thought of the war or of life's dangers. When Laurie gets in trouble with both his grandfather and Mrs. March after playing a cruel joke on Meg, the boy fantasizes with Jo about running away. He suggests venturing to Washington, where he can visit with John Brooke. The idea seems appealing because, as he explains, "'it is gay there.'" For a moment Jo—the ever adventurous tomboy—seems drawn to the crazy idea, as "thoughts of her father blended temptingly with the novel charms of camps and hospitals, liberty and fun."[14] Alcott, who had seen the harsh truths of life in a Washington military hospital, has her characters imagining such institutions as sites of liberty and grand amusement far removed from their grim truths.

Part I of *Little Women* ends a year after it began, with a Christmas of reunion. A year earlier, in the novel's first line, Jo had complained that "'Christmas won't be Christmas without any presents.'" As the next Christmas approaches, a recuperating Beth sighs contentedly, announcing that "'I'm so full of happiness, that, if Father was only here, I couldn't hold one drop more.'"[15] As if on cue, Mr. March and John Brooke arrive. All rush to hug the family patriarch, and John impulsively kisses Meg, "entirely by mistake."[16] The two men in their world have returned safely, but without the familiar reminders of warfare that so often accompanied such reunions. In the final chapter, Alcott ties up the crucial drama as John proposes to Meg, who accepts his offer against her wealthy aunt's wishes (and despite Jo's private fears that she is losing her sister). Part I ends in the midst of the Civil War with no mention of the conversation John and Meg had had about his hopes of enlisting in the Union army.

Marmee's War

Part I of *Little Women* spans roughly a year of the American Civil War. A decade after the conflict the poet Walt Whitman would declare that "the real war will never get in the books." Whitman, who had devoted long hours ministering to wounded men in military hospitals, had in mind the sort of "real war" that was far removed from glorious charges, bold rhetoric, and heroic battlefield deaths. Alcott's wartime novel not only omitted the "real war," it also largely ignored the imagined one. Although its author had witnessed some of the Civil War's true horrors in her brief stint in a D.C. hospital, readers who read *Little Women* in search of rich evidence of the Civil War—either real or fanciful—are likely to be disappointed. It is true that the war drives the plot in important ways: Mr. March is away at war for most of Part I, and Mrs. March's absence tending to her ill husband produces the crucial crisis when Beth falls ill in her absence. But month in and month out the war is largely absent. Characters do not pore over newspapers or debate political or military events, men in uniform do not drop in for tea, nobody worries about conscription, and the March children only rarely express concerns about their father's safety. Instead, Laurie very occasionally engages in silly military talk, and in one conversation Mr. Brooke mentions that he might enlist at some point in the future.

One obvious response to this relative absence of war talk is that Alcott was portraying life in a northern community far from the seat of military conflict. And, in truth, residents of their New England town could easily have lived a life free of fear and material hardship. A home-front novel set in a Union state far removed from the fighting might reasonably be free of the sort of suffering that characters in a book set in the Border States or the Confederacy would have had to endure. In the North, the economy generally did well, and a large percentage of able-bodied men, even those of military age, stayed home. Social events continued, shortages were rare, and people of the economic class of the Marches lived fairly comfortable lives.

But that argument tells only part of the story. The mass of evidence from letters, diaries, and wartime publications describes a world of northerners—both women and men—who were perpetually aware of the Civil War and deeply concerned about how it was unfolding. Ordinary civilians who had no history of paying much attention to events beyond their own community began following news of military campaigns and political developments with new fervor. Those with loved ones at the front lived for the latest letters. Yes, they also worked, shopped, gossiped, danced, and drank, but the war remained in their consciousness even when its immediate impact seemed far away. Alcott set her novel during the Civil War, and yet she made less use of the war's challenges and tragedies to drive her narrative than one might find in the real diaries and letters of wartime northerners.[17]

The real war did not get in this book (much) because it was written both to children and about children. The four March girls and their neighbor Laurie are at the center of the story and the focus for the novel's many episodes, both prescriptive and amusing. Even when the various adults in *Little Women* appear in crucial conversations, their words and actions are usually presented as they would be heard by and absorbed by the young characters. Time and again the March girls stumble over their natural tendencies towards self-absorption, only to be guided towards greater empathy and social conscience by Marmee. The realities of warfare were far away, and no doubt Mrs. March was anxious to shield her daughters from the war's harshest truths, even as Alcott sought to appeal to her young readers by telling them lighter tales about the March sisters.

But hidden in the pages of Part I is another narrative. Even though Jo and her sisters might have been happily oblivious to the larger dramas swirling around them in the midst of Civil War, readers could—if they looked hard enough—see glimmers of a different home-front story. In the very first chapter, Marmee comes home with a special treat, a letter from their absent father. It includes "lively descriptions" of life in the army and nothing of dangers or hardships, and it concludes with an uplifting message to the girls. But Mrs. March has already read her husband's letter, and we have no way of knowing what messages Mr. March had included for her eyes only. Soldiers' letters commonly included inserts directed towards particular correspondents, knowing that their letters would be passed through many hands. The young readers, like the March girls, learn of the letter Marmee wishes them to hear. We can easily imagine that Mr. March shared other truths with his wife.

For the next many months there is no mention of letters from the absent patriarch, although surely they were arriving on a regular basis. No doubt the portion the girls saw was, like this first letter, full of bright news and no despair. But for Mrs. March—like thousands of wartime spouses—letters from camp became a vital source of emotional contact. A few chapters later Marmee is busily writing a letter that she is desperate to get out in the morning mail. The girls, and thus the reader, know nothing about this letter (and presumably young readers thought little of it), but surely Marmee was writing to Mr. March.[18] Many months later, in November, Mrs. March returns home and asks "her usual question, 'Any letter from Father, girls?'" The question seems mundane, and none of the girls answers, but it reminds us that their mother was likely asking her "usual question" every day. On this occasion Marmee was worried enough to ask Laurie to go to the office in search of mail because a letter was overdue and "Father is as regular as the sun." The wartime mails were so reliable that home-front families commonly became worried if more than a few days passed without a new letter from a loved one in uniform. Marmee had reason to worry because she had not heard from her "regular" husband. Young readers would have missed that nuance, but surely not their mothers. Before Laurie can leave on his errand a telegram arrives at the door, which Marmee immediately snatches from Hannah's hands.[19] Here is when we discover that Mr. March is ill in Washington, and Mrs. March must go to his side. But before we learn the disturbing news we have a small window into the life of wartime separation that Mrs. March lived, waiting for the next letter and, when faced with a telegram instead, "snatching" the envelope, knowing full well what sort of news it might contain.

Another side to this world of wartime separation recurs throughout Part I, as—on repeated occasions—Marmee has long individual chats with each of her daughters. On the one hand, these conversations leave us with a window into her maternal role, raising young girls to a life of Christian duty and responsibility. And they illustrate the mother that the girls adore. But those conversations hint at how Marmee was also filling in for their father and feeling that absence. On several occasions she assures a daughter that she will ask their father's advice on some point, or she reminds them of how good he is at helping them work through their problems. After Marmee tells the girl about the gentleman she met at the Soldiers' Aid, Meg praises her for turning her story into the sort of sermon "Father used to tell us."[20] Although the girls are largely focused on their mother's parenting, Mrs. March clearly is missing her partner in all their minor crises. As she explains to Jo, "Your father never loses patience, never doubts or complains." That is a useful lesson for the impetuous Jo, but perhaps to the solitary parent as well.[21] Alcott no doubt meant for her young readers to wrestle with the life lessons that the March sisters faced, but the narrative left ample hints at the challenges—and fundamental loneliness—that the single parent endured.

There are other hints of a world of adults beyond the contemplation of the March girls, and their young readers. While Marmee is still in town, she visits the poor Hummels regularly, filling a charitable role that her minister husband had established. But it is not until she leaves for Washington that the girls are expected to step into that void and appear to be fully aware of what she had been doing all along. And in a single chapter we learn of her work at the Soldiers' Aid, although that was another regular stop on her weekly schedule. Even with her husband away, Marmee continues to be a charitable and patriotic citizen, living that life largely outside her daughters' vision. When Beth grows ill, the girls are terribly worried, but Alcott—in one of her occasional moments where she shifts her authorial voice—explains that the poor girl was "much sicker than anyone but Hannah and the doctor suspected."[22] Alcott's tale captures the life of northern children during wartime, often happily oblivious to the true horrors wrought by the Civil War. But occasionally Alcott reminded her more astute readers that adults experienced a very different war, even in the quiet safety of New England towns.

Louisa May Alcott, the Civil War, and *Little Women*

By the eve of the Civil War, Louisa May Alcott had already taken the first steps towards her dream of becoming an independent writer. That war would prove crucial to her development as a highly successful author.

In September 1859, Concord hosted a large military encampment. The twenty-six-year-old noted in her journal that "The town [is] full of soldiers, with military fuss and feathers." Sounding very much like her eventual alter ego, Jo March, she added, "I like a camp, and long for a war, to see how it all seems. I can't fight, but I can nurse."[23] As the secession crisis mounted, Alcott and her family were firm abolitionists, living in an intellectual orbit populated by some of the strongest voices of the day. In November 1860 the local John Brown Association invited her to write a poem for the cause. The result, she concluded, was "not good." "I'm a better patriot than poet, and couldn't say what I felt," she admitted.[24] The following April, when political tensions devolved into armed conflict, Alcott wrote that "I long to be a man; but as I can't fight, I will content myself with working for those who can."[25] Even more so than Jo March, the young Louisa May Alcott seemed drawn to excitement.

During the first years of the war, Alcott continued to write short pieces for publication while making regular comments in her journals about political meetings, voluntary activities, and occasional war news. In November 1862, Alcott—anxious for "new experiences"—offered her services as a military nurse. The following month the thirty-year-old received an invitation to work at the Union Hospital in Georgetown.[26] Alcott spent about six intense weeks on duty in that small military hospital, sending regular letters home to her family, capturing the life she lived and the tales of the women and men she worked with and the men she nursed. The adventure did not last long. Alcott soon grew deathly ill, and in January 1863 returned to Concord, where she gradually recovered after weeks of delirium. By the time she came home Alcott had produced the core of a hugely important book about hospital life during the Civil War. *Commonwealth,* a Boston newspaper, published her lively letters as a series of popular "sketches." James Redpath, a family friend and one of the nation's leading publishers, issued these *Hospital Sketches*—only modestly edited—as a small volume later that year.[27]

In *Hospital Sketches,* Alcott certainly came much closer to capturing the "real war"—or at least attempting to—than she would in *Little Women.* Written as slightly fictionalized autobiography, Alcott's account of hospital life combines humor and irony with large doses of harsh reality, as she told her northern readers about endurance and death in a military hospital. During these professionally fecund years, Alcott returned to serious wartime themes on several other occasions, including her short story "My Contraband; or, The Brothers," which she published in the *Atlantic Monthly.* Here Alcott wrestled with the war's racial complexities. As her central character—a nurse—confronts Bob, a recently freed biracial slave, he contemplates killing a deathly ill Confederate officer. The nurse learns that the contraband and the rebel soldier are in fact half-brothers, and in their previous life the soldier—and master—had ravished Bob's wife.[28] Alcott had been quite willing to tackle complex moral issues in her early prose.

Although *Hospital Sketches* and Alcott's other wartime writings engaged with themes that would be absent in *Little Women,* it is certainly possible to see aspects of Tribulation Periwinkle—her alter ego in the hospital novella—in the younger Jo March. Jo, like Tribulation, is anxious for something to do during the war, and she is drawn to the bustle and excitement of a military hospital. And Jo, again like Tribulation, cuts off her hair in a moment of transformation. Finally, neither Jo nor Tribulation reveals a powerful patriotic or political side, unlike her creator. But Jo's very occasional thoughts about the war, and her one dream of escaping to Washington, D.C., in search of adventure, only parallel the life of Tribulation up to that moment when the older woman actually sets out for her real adventure. Jo March of the war years remains essentially untouched by the national crisis.

Several years after the war, publisher Thomas Nile suggested that Alcott might consider a "*girls'* story" for her next project. Nile's savvy suggestion spoke to an emerging market for literature aimed at adolescents, and particularly young women. Alcott immediately threw herself into the project, although she privately admitted that "I don't enjoy this sort of thing." The following month the energetic author had fired off a dozen chapters to Nile, who found the result "*dull.*" But Alcott pressed on, convinced that "simple books are very much needed for girls."[29] In mid-July 1868 she submitted a completed 402-page manuscript, drawing heavily on her own childhood experiences with her sisters. It was an astonishing burst of productivity.

Eight years later, when Alcott reviewed her journal, and considered her frenetic writing pace, she concluded that it was "Too much for one young woman. No wonder she broke down." Just over a month later the proofs of the book arrived.[30]

By the end of October, Alcott was pleased to report that *Little Women* was selling very well, and Mr. Niles had suggested a second volume.[31] It was a heady time. Nearly overnight Alcott had become a best-selling children's author. By the first of November she had returned to the intertwined lives of the March girls with a new fervor. As she waded into Part II, Alcott's subjects were older, and she wrote with her newfound audience in mind. "Began the second part of 'Little Women,'" she wrote on November 1, 1868. "I can do a chapter a day, and in a month I mean to be done. A little success is so inspiring that I now find my 'Marches' sober, nice people, and as I can launch into the future, my fancy has more play. Girls write to ask who the little women marry, as if that was the only end and aim of a woman's life. I won't marry Jo to Laurie to please any one."[32]

Two months later Alcott was pleased to report that *Little Women* was receiving strong reviews, and she submitted the "sequel" on New Year's Day.[33] Later that year she enthusiastically reported that *Hospital Sketches* had been reissued and sold 2,000 copies in one week, reflecting her growing celebrity.[34] In 1869 Alcott's publisher printed 15,000 copies of Part I and 18,000 of Part II.[35] Even in those first months, *Little Women* had established Alcott as a major author. That year and the following year, Brooklyn's Mercantile Library reported that the two volumes of *Little Women* were among the library's most popular volumes.[36]

Part II: *Little Women* in a Changing World

Alcott plowed into Part II only months after Part I had hit the bookstores. But she already had a clear sense of her relationship with her readers, and she drafted Part II after those young enthusiasts had bonded with the March girls. In fact, when she brought Part I to a close, Alcott teased her readers by announcing that the curtain had fallen on the lives of the four sisters, and "Whether it ever rises again, depends upon the reception given the first act of the domestic drama called LITTLE WOMEN."[37]

Part I had spanned an active year in the lives of the March family in the midst of the Civil War. Family togetherness and family separation drove much of the story. For most of the book Mr. March had been away at war, and Marmee gone for the crucial weeks when Beth fell ill. As the final chapter ended at the close of 1862, a smitten John Brooke has asked for Meg's hand, and she has accepted his proposal. As she sat down to write Part II, Alcott had all sorts of options for her continuing plot. After all, the war was still raging at the end of Part I, John had declared his intention of enlisting in the Union Army, and even young Laurie might have donned a uniform had Alcott chosen. But instead Alcott opted to nearly ignore the Civil War as she moved on to her Part II.

Instead of picking up precisely where she had left it off, Part II begins three years after the close of Part I. Alcott explained this decision, or at least suggested an explanation, in the initial paragraph: "let me premise that if any of the elders think there is too much 'lovering' in the story, as I fear they may (I'm not afraid the young folks will make that objection), I can only say with Mr. March, 'What can you expect when I have four gay girls in the house, and a dashing young neighbor over the way?'" In this brief passage Alcott acknowledged that she wrote for two audiences: the "young folks" who would be desperate for romance, and "the elders" who might have other ideas. But she also knew that the former would drive sales. And if she was going to entice her young readers with stories of romance, marriage, and motherhood, it would be best to have those four gay girls grown up just a bit.[38]

Other authors might have milked John's military service for long chapters of pathos and patriotism. Home-front novels written during or soon after the war commonly featured soldiers who were captured, or reported dead in the press, only to return home to their loved ones many months later in time to sweep admiring young women off their feet. Alcott, no fan of the literary cliché, opted to dispense with John's military career in a few short sentences. "John Brooke," she explained at the outset of Part II, "did his duty manfully for a year, got wounded, was sent home, and not allowed to return. He received no stars or bars, but he deserved them, for he cheerfully risked all he had, and life and love are very precious when both are in full bloom. Perfectly resigned to his discharge, he devoted himself to getting well, preparing for business, and earning a home for Meg." And so she covered John's entire military career in less than a paragraph, before moving on to the serious business of wedding plans.[39]

In a broader historical sense, writing only a few years after the Civil War, Alcott declined to engage with any of the large national questions about reunion, reconciliation, or reconstruction in Part II. No returning soldiers appear in the narrative, even on the periphery of the plot. We see no hint of the popular figure of the wounded veteran with an empty sleeve or pants leg. As with Part I, the only postwar glimpses of the Civil War soldier are seen through the actions of the March parents, and then only in very brief passages. We learn that Mrs. March became so absorbed with preparing for Meg's wedding that she neglected "the hospitals and homes still full of wounded 'boys' and soldiers' widows" that had been partly the focus of her "missionary visits."[40] When the happy day finally arrived, Mr. March—a strident teetotaler—insisted that the wine purchased for the wedding reception should instead go to the local Soldiers' Home.[41] Perhaps Alcott was making an ironic point here about veterans and the nation's collective memory. Essentially, as the family turns its focus to a peacetime wedding, Mrs. March neglects her visits to wounded soldiers, and Mr. March sends them wine that he personally would not consume. The only other reference to the larger political world beyond the lives of the individual characters occurs in an amusing passage where Meg is trying to demonstrate greater interest in John's life. The dutiful young wife invites her husband to read her "something about the election," which they then discuss. He counters by asking her about bonnets. The exchange reveals nothing about politics or the outside world, but it does suggest a nineteenth-century model for harmony between newlyweds.[42]

True to her promise in the first paragraph, Alcott treats readers of the second part of the novel to much "lovering" and more than a little emotional hardship. By the time the book closes, Meg, Amy, and Jo have all married, and the frail Beth—like Alcott's own sister Elizabeth—has died young. For the historian of gender and of prescriptive literature, there is much to dissect in these romantic tales. Meg's marriage to John becomes the occasion for a frank examination of married life. Good to her promise, Alcott resisted any pressure to marry Jo to Laurie, even when he declares his love. Instead, Amy—the youngest sister—marries Laurie, but only after both partners overcome their frivolous ways and transform into serious adults. Jo eventually accepts the proposal of Friedrich Bhaer, the scholarly German immigrant she befriends in a New York boarding house. Although separated by age, the pair are true kindred spirits. The novel closes when

Jo is thirty, and she and Friedrich have set up a home for young boys in an old mansion Jo has inherited from Aunt March. All three romances and marriages provided young readers with much to chew on, as do various misunderstandings that produce ample personal drama.

Amidst these various plot lines, much of Part II concerns Jo's efforts to find her voice as a budding author. Here, too, Alcott is inviting her readers to wrestle with complex issues from a gender perspective. Whereas her sisters seem much more focused on finding a perfect partner, Jo concentrates on finding her literary voice, and along the way her partner finds her. If Part I is thick with life lessons about personal responsibility and combating minor character flaws, Part II guides young female readers through various challenges that await their dealings with the opposite sex.

Like Part I, the second half of *Little Women* unfolds in distinct episodes, often involving only one or two of the main characters. One episode, which extends over two chapters, is particularly revealing. The events surrounding the Chester family and their gala fair for the relief of freedpeople provide Alcott with an opportunity to comment on voluntarism and hypocrisy during the Civil War era. Aunt Carrol, a wealthy relative, wants the girls to learn how to navigate polite society. Jo resists these efforts, and she wants nothing to do with the snooty girls of the community, including the particularly annoying May Chester. Her younger sister Amy is more drawn to polite society and embarrassed whenever Jo grows too brusque. Things become complicated when the elitist Chesters announce their fund-raising fair.

The Chesters invite the Alcott girls to tend tables at the fair. Amy loves the idea, announcing that she has nothing but her time to donate, so she is happy to give that. Jo declares that she "hate[s] to be patronized" and wants nothing of it, although her younger sister reminds her that the fair is "for the freedmen as well as the Chesters" and thus worthy of their time. Jo insists—apparently without intended irony—that the Chesters make her feel "like a slave" and she prefers her independence.[43] The fair itself becomes a complex drama involving the fundamentally evil May Chester and poor Amy, who is anxious to please and fit in and is also a much more gifted artist. At first Amy's display attracts more attention than May's work, so Mrs. Chester has them switch tables so that her daughter is selling Amy's art and Amy is stuck with May's less popular flowers. Laurie saves the day when he arrives with a group of his college chums, who are directed to buy up all of Amy's flowers. Amy, ever magnanimous, has the boys buy up May's table as well. The fair is deemed a great success, and May Chester treats Amy with uncharacteristic graciousness.[44] Alcott calls the chapter about the fair "Consequences." In the chapter's final pages, Aunt Carrol invites the more polite Amy—and not the older Jo—to go on a grand tour of Europe with her.

This drama about the Chesters' fair allows Alcott to comment on class tensions, social pretensions, and the silly squabbles that divide young girls. But the specific backdrop is also of interest. This was a fair to aid recently freed slaves, but the particulars of the cause are barely mentioned. The very brief reference to freedpeople in preparation for the fair is the only occasion in the entire novel when slavery or emancipation is mentioned at all. The fair is very similar to small-town fund-raising fairs staged by abolitionists before the Civil War, or the many sanitary fairs and similar fund-raisers that dotted the wartime calendar. Alcott—who no doubt knew those events well—appears to be suggesting a philanthropic world where the cause itself is little more than a thin veneer over social events that conferred status on white elites, and especially on elite women.

The Chesters' fair serves as a subject of ridicule, and also as the vehicle that sends Amy to Europe and leaves Jo fending for herself at home. But, while the fair lacks any redeeming value, Alcott provided her young Civil War–era readers with ample models for a different sort of philanthropy, grounded in sensitivity to social conditions and quiet sacrifice. In Part I, Marmee—filling a charitable void left by her minister husband—regularly visited the poor Hummel family. Marmee also volunteered with the local Soldiers' Aid, performing valuable work without fanfare. For much of their youth and young adulthood, Laurie and Amy are self-absorbed and frivolous, until they fall in love while both are in Europe. Once they are married and back in town the two share a deep conversation about their ideals and future goals. Both agree that in the future they will try to find ways to help young men and women of the sort who are not "out and out beggars" but still in need of assistance. Laurie reflects on his journey abroad, where he had met many young men who were struggling to survive, having fallen from better circumstances. "I must say," he explains, "I like to serve a decayed gentleman better than a blarneying beggar."[45] Alcott seemed to be suggesting an alternative way to think about philanthropy that would move beyond institutions for the abject poor and think about the needs of others who have fallen upon hard times.

In the book's final chapters Professor Bhaer comes to visit Jo, both to present her with a copy of her newly published book and—he hopes—to seek her hand in marriage. Friedrich worries that he has no wealth to bring to a marriage, but Jo reassures him that she is "'glad you are poor'" and happily accepts his proposal.[46] Alcott devotes the book's final chapter to following the couple's life for several more years, ending when Jo is thirty (or fifteen years after the story began). Aunt March has died and left her sprawling mansion to Jo. Jo enlists Friedrich to turn the house into a school for young boys. She hopes to provide an education to poor "raga-muffins" who otherwise would have no such opportunity, but she proposes a business model where they would accept the occasional tuition-paying rich child in order to pay the bills. At the story's conclusion, their school is thriving and doing great good for the community. They have even accepted a "merry little quadroon" as a student, defying the warnings of those who feared this act of integration would ruin their school.[47] Here again Alcott's characters pose a distinctive vision for postwar philanthropy that seems to challenge conventional attitudes towards the poor.

Little Women closes at Marmee's sixtieth birthday celebration. Jo and Friedrich have been married for five years, and their school is thriving. Meg has had twins who are growing up nicely. Amy and Laurie are happy parents. Marmee is surrounded by her children and grandchildren. Beth, always frail, died years ago, but the other sisters have each found a distinctive form of marital bliss and a true purpose to their lives.

Little Women was in many senses a timeless tale of sisters growing up together, each navigating her own path through life. If Part I offered guidance on growing into maturity, Part II provided all sorts of models for finding happiness in adulthood. But although the messages might have been timeless Alcott grounded her novel in various historic realities. The first half of the book is about the Civil War home front, even if that bloody conflict often recedes into the background. Beyond that national conflict, and the personal strains that came with it, Alcott reminds her readers of other crucial themes that were shaping mid-nineteenth-century America. The Hummel family represents the enduring importance of poverty, even in prosperous New England, and reminds readers of the significance of immigrants as part of the larger society. When Jo ventures to New York City in Part II she enters a foreign world, both as a resident of an urban boarding house and as a straight-laced New Englander in a society of exotic immigrants. Alcott does not turn Jo into a wide-eyed tourist, wandering the streets of the massive metropolis. In fact, her encounters with urban America do not stray beyond the boardinghouse. Instead, Jo remains in the comfortable confines of her new home, but there she meets various foreigners and falls in love with a German refugee. Meanwhile, Amy and Laurie expand their horizons by touring Europe. Alcott does not use their travels as an opportunity to explore cultural differences, but the fact that they left home to see the world seems to have shaped their characters in valuable ways. And, as the book comes to a close, Jo, Amy, and Laurie all seem committed to social activism, allowing Alcott to offer her thoughts about how society might help the needy. In the midst of a book written to appeal to young girls, with plenty of romance, Alcott manages to sneak in passages that appear to be speaking to the likes of social reformers such as Charles Loring Brace and Josephine Shaw Lowell, rather than to young teenage readers who were her intended audience. As in Part I, it is as if Alcott felt compelled to insert messages into her novel even while her young readers wanted to read about tales of "lovering."

Movies and Memory

Perhaps the enduring appeal of *Little Women* comes from the fact that Louisa May Alcott's story of the March sisters captured themes that transcended a particular place and time. Generations of new readers, and particularly young girls, could find something timeless in Alcott's stories. *Little Women* certainly captured a large audience in those first few years, and it continued to attract readers for generations to come.

Alcott's story of the four March sisters also inspired an impressive array of theatrical interpretations. Two silent films—one American and one British—appeared during World War I. *Little Women* has been the subject of three major feature films, produced in 1933, 1949, and 1994. All three featured impressive ensemble casts, and each attracted large audiences. The novel was also the subject of at least two two-part television movies, one produced in the Westinghouse Studio One series in 1950; the second— starring major television stars Meredith Baxter Birney and Susan Dey— appeared in 1978. The BBC produced multipart versions televised in 1950, 1958, and 1970. Two different animated versions appeared in Japan during the 1980s. *Little Women* has also been the subject of a Broadway musical and an opera.[48] In 2005, the novelist Geraldine Brooks published *March,* a creative imagining of Mr. March's own wartime life.[49]

It is striking how much of Alcott's vision, and even words, appear in each new version.[50] But *Little Women* is a long novel, and even entirely faithful adaptations had to eliminate more than they included. A close reading of several of these adaptations suggests ways in which each generation created a new version of *Little Women.*

The American Civil War is generally more present in the movies than in the novel. The 1933 version begins with a scene of soldiers marching and immediately moves to Marmee working at the local branch of the U.S. Christian Commission. The actual scene (which Alcott placed in "the rooms" of the local Soldiers' Aid Society rather than the USCC) occurs later in the novel, and we only hear about it through the story Marmee tells the girls in "Burdens." By starting the movie with Marmee's conversation with the older man who had sent four sons to war, the viewer is not only reminded of the greater sacrifices endured during the conflict, but we also begin the story seeing events through Mrs. March's eyes, whereas the book begins with Jo and her sisters, barely aware of the Civil War.

The filmmakers employed other devices to remind viewers that the first half of the story unfolded during wartime. Early in the novel the older sisters dress up to attend a fashionable dance. Each movie includes this crucial scene, and all feature men in uniform at the dance. This detail makes perfect sense for a wartime ball, but Alcott does not include it in the book. The 1994 version adds a brief moment as the story moves from Part I to Part II, showing a stream of Union soldiers walking home along a dirt road. Nothing at all like this scene of returning veterans, which is very reminiscent of the bedraggled Confederate troops walking home between the two parts of "Gone With the Wind," appears in the book. In the television movie, Jo's voiceovers make several references to the war as a patriotic conflict and a war for emancipation, giving the main character a more ardently patriotic appearance than Alcott envisioned. In one entirely original scene, Marmee reads about military events in a local newspaper, offering her sympathy for "poor Mr. Lincoln." In these ways, twentieth-century moviemakers reminded their viewers that this was a drama set during wartime, and the Marches were true patriots.

Even where the films are explicitly true to Alcott's narrative, the significance of the war seems elevated by what they choose to include and what is omitted from the long book. The directors of the three feature films all took pains to create the iconic tableau with Marmee reading Father's letter, surrounded by her four daughters. (The 1978 television movie curiously omits that scene in favor of one where Marmee is writing to her husband.) All include some version of the arrival of the fateful telegram from Washington, followed by Mrs. March's hurried departure. And Mr. March's joyous return the following Christmas provides another iconic moment of a uniformed soldier returning home. These scenes are all drawn from the text, but even if they were faithfully rendered (and they generally were), the significance of the absent father is enhanced in the truncated film versions simply because so many other episodes spanning the first twenty-three chapters are omitted. Some of the filmmakers also took minor liberties with Mr. March's infirmity. The telegram Marmee reads in the novel informs her that "Your husband is very ill. Come at once."[51] But in the 1994 version, Mr. March returns with his arm in a sling, suggesting that he had been heroically wounded in action rather than felled by illness.

Laurie, the precocious neighbor, and his tutor, John Brooke, present the filmmakers with a minor conundrum. Laurie is just about to turn sixteen when the book begins near the close of 1861. Certainly many young men of his age would have enlisted in the Union army by the end of the war, but Alcott's character never speaks of enlisting, even though in his youthful way he does play around with the language of the soldier.[52] John is substantially older and surely of military age. In the novel he tells Meg that he will eventually enlist, but that conversation does not occur until halfway through Part I when he has already appeared as an able-bodied civilian in many chapters. At the start of Part II we learn that he did indeed serve for a year before getting wounded and being sent home. John's status as a future volunteer and then as a wounded veteran only appears in two short passages in the novel, and Laurie neither volunteers nor chafes at the fact that he has not. Neither man's experience is out of the norm for northern men during the conflict, and home-front novels written during the war commonly included male characters who were not soldiers and seemed unbothered by that fact. But the filmmakers apparently expected more of their male characters.

The 1933 version is fairly true to Alcott's plot, but John's conversation with Meg—where he reveals his plans to enlist—occurs at the initial dance, rather than after the two have known each other for months. In the 1949 production, filmed shortly after the end of World War II, the filmmakers took greater liberties with their male leads. Laurie—played by Peter Lawford—has an exciting backstory. Prior to arriving to live with his grandfather, the boy had run away from school, enlisted in the Union army, and been wounded.[53] And in this postwar version, John Brooke is already in the Union army when the story begins and appears throughout the movie in a full Union infantry uniform, which pleases Jo very much. In the 1994 version Eric Stoltz, playing John Brooke, attends his wedding with Meg in full uniform, even though the war had been over for quite some time. The 1978 made-for-television movie, starring Susan Dey as Jo, abandons Alcott's narrative framework altogether. Halfway through the first installment of this two-part drama a voiceover from Jo explains that two years had passed, Lincoln had elevated General Ulysses S. Grant to command of the Union military, and father was still in the army.[54] Soon afterwards, John Brooke appears in uniform, recovering from a wound in his arm, and begins wooing Meg. These various strategies in the cinematic version all underscore that Brooke either was—or would soon be—a Union soldier, rather than merely an able-bodied tutor.

As already noted, *Little Women* is two fairly distinct books that would be published and read as a single volume. When Part I begins, the March girls are quite young, ranging in age from twelve (Amy) to sixteen (Meg). The Civil War takes their father from them for most of that year, and their mother for several crucial weeks, but Alcott's young March girls were not very concerned with the war that raged at such a distance. They have suffered financial hardship, but not because of the war. Even the separation from their father is atypical: he enlists as a military clergyman. When Part II begins, the girls are three years older, and they mature rapidly through the book's final chapters. In their postwar dramas the sisters respond to new challenges in their personal lives, but as young adults they also demonstrate more awareness of their larger world.

The film versions of *Little Women* smooth out some distinctions between the two parts. Certainly the transition from naive children to young adults is hard to portray with a single ensemble cast. In fact, the actresses who played Jo ranged in age from twenty-three (Winona Ryder) to thirty-two (June Allyson) when their movies were released.[55] None manages to present a realistic fifteen-year-old Josephine March; all appear more at home as budding authors and as partners to Frederich Bhaer. In the novel the reader feels the weight of the war as experienced by Marmee more so than by her girls, but those glimpses into Mrs. March's worries are rare and subtle. On film, the Civil War became more apparent, establishing *Little Women* as an iconic story of the home front. The moviemakers accomplished this change by maintaining all the scenes where Mr. March appeared—in fact or through letters—while omitting many of the minor scenes involving the March girls. And they took liberties with Alcott's narrative when they portrayed the other male characters, commonly putting John Brooke into uniform. In so doing, they made the timeless story suit the assumptions of subsequent generations. A film set in the Civil War home front must surely include handsome men in blue uniforms and occasional bursts of patriotic rhetoric. But, at its core, *Little Women* remained a story about four young girls and their sainted mother, navigating life in the midst of a distant war, and then growing into womanhood in the postwar decades.

NOTES

1. Louisa May Alcott, *Little Women* (1868; Signet Classic, 2012), chap. 1, p. 7. All citations, unless otherwise noted, will be to the Signet Classic edition, hereafter cited as *LW.*

2. In England, Part II originally appeared under the title *Little Wives.* The two volumes were not regularly published together until the 1880s.

3. *LW,* chap. 1.

4. *LW,* chap. 4.

5. *LW,* chap. 5.

6. *LW,* chap. 8.

7. *LW,* chap. 14.

8. All in *LW,* chap. 4.

9. Although Jo is a tomboy, whose amateur theatricals often involve bloody swordfights, Alcott does not present her as interested in the real military conflict.

10. *LW,* chap. 15.

11. *LW,* chap. 16.

12. *LW,* chap. 2, pp. 20–21.

13. *LW,* chap. 5, p. 59.

14. *LW,* chap. 21, pp. 217–18.

15. *LW,* chap. 22, p. 224.

16. *LW,* chap. 22, p. 225.

17. Novels and short stories published during the Civil War and set in the home front invariably made more use of military themes than did *Little Women.* For one discussion of this war culture, see J. Matthew Gallman, *Defining Duty in the Civil War: Personal Choice, Popular Culture, and the Union Home Front* (Chapel Hill: University of North Carolina Press, 2015).

18. *LW,* chap. 4 (two mentions).

19. *LW,* chap. 15.

20. *LW,* chap. 4.

21. *LW,* chap. 8.

22. *LW,* chap. 18.

23. Years later, when Alcott reread and annotated her journals, she noted that here she had been "prophetic again" (*The Journals of Louisa May Alcott,* ed. Joel Myerson, Daniel Shealy, and Madeline B. Stern [Boston: Little, Brown, 1989], entry for September 1859, p. 95 [hereafter cited as *Journals*]). For Alcott's journals, see also *Louisa May Alcott: Her Life, Letters, and Journals,* ed. Ednah D. Cheney (Boston: Roberts Brothers, 1890).

24. *Journals,* 100–101 (November and December 1860).

25. Ibid., 105 (April 1861).

26. Ibid., 110–11 (November and December 1862).

27. Ibid., 113–20 (January–September 1863), 123n18–19. Louisa May Alcott, *Hospital Sketches* (Boston: James Redpath, 1863). For a modern edition with an excellent introduction by Alice Fahs, see Alcott, *Hospital Sketches* (Boston: Bedford/St. Martins, 2003).

28. *Journals,* 119 (August 1863), 124n31; *Atlantic Monthly* 12 (November 1863): 584–95. For this short story and other Alcott writings on race and slavery, see Sarah Elbert, ed., *Louisa May Alcott On Race, Sex, and Slavery* (Boston: Northeastern University Press, 1997).

29. *Journals,* 165–66 (May–June 1868).

30. Ibid., 166 (July 15, 1868); 1876 notation from Alcott beside her July 15, 1868, entry; August 1868. Nile suggested the idea some time in May, and by August the book was completed and the proofs had already been produced.

31. *Journals,* 167 (October 30, 1868).

32. Ibid., 167 (November 1, 1868).

33. Ibid., 171 (January 1869).

34. Ibid., 172.

35. Ibid., 173n10.

36. "What People Read," *Philadelphia Evening Telegraph,* October 14, 1870.

37. *LW,* chap. 23, final sentence.

38. *LW,* chap. 24.

39. *LW,* chap. 25.

40. *LW,* chap. 24, p. 244.

41. *LW,* chap. 25, pp. 258–59.

42. *LW,* chap. 38, pp. 405–6.

43. *LW,* chap. 29, pp. 305–6.

44. *LW,* chap. 30.

45. *LW,* chap. 44, p. 467.

46. *LW,* chap. 47, p. 487.

47. *LW,* chap. 47, p. 494.

48. Much of this information comes from Wikipedia and is not presented as a complete list. The Broadway musical played in Gainesville, Florida, as this essay was being written in 2016.

49. Geraldine Brooks, *March* (New York: Viking, 2005).

50. I am not in the position to make any systematic assessment, but my impression is that the *Little Women* movies are generally closer to the original texts than most movies based on books.

51. *LW,* chap. 15.

52. The first part of the novel only spans a year of the war before skipping ahead four years into the postwar years. So, Laurie might have wrestled with thoughts of enlistment in his later teens.

53. Lawford was twenty-six when the movie was released, and he certainly does not look like a fifteen-year-old in the early scenes. This discrepancy might explain why he is given this history.

54. In fact, Part I only spanned twelve months. It is not really clear why this version made that change.

55. They were a bit younger when filmed. The 1994 version included two actresses to play Amy, as a young girl and then as a young woman.

"General Jubal Anderson Early." This photograph, the frontispiece
for the first edition of Early's posthumously published memoir, was
taken more than two decades after he completed work on the text for the
book in the late 1860s. From Jubal A. Early, *Lieutenant General Jubal
Anderson Early, C.S.A.: Autobiographical Sketch and Narrative of the
War Between the States* (Philadelphia: J. B. Lippincott, 1912).

"Duty to My Country and Myself"

The Jubal A. Early Memoirs

KATHRYN SHIVELY

Confederate General Jubal A. Early's prudent management of his personal narrative from 1865 to Robert E. Lee's death in 1870 achieved two improbable victories for a man contemporaries and historians often dismissed as impetuous.[1] Early's memoirs both rehabilitated his tarnished military reputation and positioned him as the premier historical authority on the Army of Northern Virginia. Southern and northern newspapers alike acknowledged his proficiency as a military historian, and by 1869 former Confederate General D. H. Hill proclaimed Early "nearer to the hearts of the Southern people than any other man."[2]

Early composed his first memoir, *A Memoir of the Last Year of the War for Independence* (hereafter the *Memoir*), before any other general from either side, in late December 1865 to March 1866, after a "rough ride" and circuitous sea voyage out of the fallen Confederacy deposited him in Mexico.[3] By July 1866, Early arrived in Canada, where he spent the majority of his self-exile, and began the process of publishing this recollection of the Overland and Shenandoah Valley campaigns.[4] The short timeline from experience to publication distinguished the *Memoir* as exceptionally fresh and, he hoped, exceptionally convincing. Early thought it critical to advance his argument quickly—that he had lost the Shenandoah Valley because of inferior manpower rather than tactical error—to reverse his disgrace before it permanently blackened his military record. He thought it especially important to burnish his reputation in the immediate aftermath of Confederate defeat, when angry and despairing southern whites sought targets for blame. Dyspeptic and often at odds with social norms, Early could expect little generosity from his critics; consequently, he set out to manage public opinion with remarkable energy for a man suffering from arthritis, poverty, and grief. The memoir additionally magnified Early's self-justification into a thesis of overall Confederate defeat, again from inferior manpower and materiel, which became central to the ex-Confederate memory of the Civil War. Though Lee first proposed the argument in his farewell address to the Army of Northern Virginia, the profound influence of Early's memoir demands that it been seen as one of the central texts of the Lost Cause.[5]

To solidify his status as chief historian for the Army of Northern Virginia, Early produced a second, complete *Narrative of the War Between the States* (hereafter the *Narrative*) in Canada between 1867 and 1868 before returning to Virginia in 1869. The earlier memoir composed the last portion of the new work. Early only slightly revised the *Narrative* in his last decades of life as he came across missing military reports, and he provided for its posthumous release.[6] His niece, Ruth H. Early, published the tome in 1912, eighteen years after her uncle died, true to the original save the omission of a handful of provocative footnotes that had appeared in the *Memoir*.[7] The fact that Lee himself encouraged Early's work and never published his own recollections reinforced Early's claim to influence. Moreover, Lee's moderating influence significantly constrained Early's tone in these two works, which enhanced their popular reception, in contrast to his later, more controversial writings.[8] The *Narrative*'s posthumous publication brought Early's historical career full circle to its origins in Canada and solidified his legacy as a careful, trustworthy scholar.

What Early accomplished in such short order and with such skill should captivate and trouble the modern historian. While primarily serving his personal interests, Early managed to attain the highest standards of historical scholarship for his era. He established such a convincing argument for Confederate defeat that we have scarcely displaced it from the public consciousness even today.[9] We must contend with Early's memoirs, because they have proven among the most influential in American collective memory. By exposing Early's process we also gain valuable insights into how historical authority was constructed in postwar America.[10]

This essay will explore how Early built his case for authority both with his writings and with his personal conduct during the period in which he wrote his two memoirs. Nineteenth-century readers, especially critics and consumers of history, were well informed; they increasingly craved quality and truth.[11] Being mere eyewitness to events, though important, was insufficient qualification for expertise when millions of potential authors could invoke that rubric. To construct convincing reminiscences Early, a lawyer by trade, first applied his legal skills, marshaling primary sources and numbers to produce ironclad arguments. Second, as a West Pointer and veteran of the Seminole and Mexican wars, and as one of the few generals whom Lee elevated to independent command, Early staked a convincing claim to military expertise. Even Early admitted the difficulty of analyzing chaotic battlefield events as they unfolded, and he positioned himself as the rare officer who could interpret such minutiae for a public audience. Third, as a member of Lee's favored circle, Early could appraise the Army of Northern Virginia with unusual intimacy. Finally, a textual authority had to be possessed of pure rather than selfish motives. Here Early was at pains to avoid hypocrisy. Yet time and again he detailed how Union generals and politicians obfuscated wartime events to advance their reputations, while he proudly owned even those actions that rendered him likely to hang for treason. The glue that bound these rhetorical approaches was an uncharacteristically pragmatic tone, which, with Lee's encouragement, rarely strayed into the acrimony for which Early was renowned. Likewise did his tone avoid an air of special pleading so common to the latter-day memoirists of his cohort.[12] Early's textual approaches drew on an emerging trend among histories of the era, some of which emphasized impartiality, an elastic concept that embraced unbiased presentation of facts, an "unprejudiced . . . assessment of historical testimony," thereby resulting in a "judgment about which side was 'right.'"[13]

Because character and authority were concomitant in Victorian America, Early could not advance his textual case without concurrently restoring his public reputation.[14] This did not mean that Early dispensed wholesale with his prickly personality, but he did soften some contours in the public eye with the help of friends. He actively sought to rehabilitate key strained relationships, specifically those with his soldiers and Valley residents, and fashioned himself a martyr for the Confederate cause when his people's need for catharsis was most acute.

Understanding Early's memoir project requires a brief retelling of the failures he sought most urgently to explain. The 1864 Shenandoah Valley campaign began well for Early and ended with a series of reputation-shattering blows. In June 1864, Lee demonstrated considerable confidence in Early by promoting him to lieutenant general and dispatching him on independent command with the Second Corps of the Army of Northern Virginia, temporarily christened the Army of the Valley, to drive Union soldiers from the Shenandoah, menace Washington, and relieve pressure on the Richmond-Petersburg front. Early defeated Union Maj. Gen. David Hunter on June 17–18 at Lynchburg, before proceeding down the Shenandoah to clear it of Federals, temporarily checking the U.S. hard-war policy on civilian property in the area. Early continued to fulfill Gen. Robert E. Lee's instructions to the letter by crossing the Potomac to threaten Maryland, where he defeated a small Federal force at the Monocacy on July 9, and then shelled the U.S. capital on July 11 and 12, before withdrawing to the Valley.

When Maj. Gen. Philip H. Sheridan supplanted Hunter, Early's fortunes changed. In September 1864 Sheridan whipped Early at Third Winchester and Fisher's Hill, embarrassments that Early blamed, not without some basis, on his "shameful" cavalry.[15] Sheridan thought the dual defeats so sound that he was completely unprepared for the Confederate counter-blow at Cedar Creek on October 19. In a testament to impressive planning, Early routed approximately two-thirds of the Federal army before his men paused to plunder the enemy camps and surrendered the initiative. Exhausted and too long deprived of material needs, the men could not be reformed in time to meet Sheridan's counterattack. What could have been Early's greatest triumph fizzled to defeat.[16] In an address to his troops published widely in southern and northern newspapers, Early berated his men for the failure, declining to acknowledge his inability to salvage the "fatal halt."[17] "Soldiers of the Army of the Valley," the general charged, "I have the mortification of announcing to you that, by your . . . mistake, a serious disaster occurred." Worse still, he challenged their masculinity and devotion to cause: "Arouse yourself . . . to a sense of your manhood and appreciation of the sacred cause in which you are engaged."[18]

That Early deflected all blame at the time sealed his fall from grace after Cedar Creek. Publically, some of Early's troops fought back against ridicule. "I cannot admit that the general commanding an army is irresponsible for the plundering and straggling of his men in battle," insisted one Rebel cavalryman in the *Richmond Sentinel.* "He can stop it, *if he will,* and if he don't know how to do it, he is unfit for his position." Others privately bristled: "I have noticed that . . . the [Valley] infantry are all the time straggling. . . . I don't think we will be able to do anything here til some other General is here to take command, who will enforce some discipline." Lee stripped Early of most of his troops, leaving a much-diminished Army of the Valley to face a final defeat at Waynesboro on March 2, 1865. To compound Early's woes, Sheridan had fulfilled his commander's mandate to "do . . . damage to railroads and crops" and "carry off stock of all descriptions, and negroes." The destruction of civilian property encouraged Valley civilians to join in stinging disparagement of Early. Shenandoah resident Sarah Ann Fife remarked, "Oh! how are the mighty fallen! Gen. Early . . . used to be a very great man."[19]

And yet Lee, who had always been very fond of his lieutenant, viewed Early's situation with striking sympathy. On March 28, 1865, to John C. Breckinridge, the current secretary of war and former corps commander under Early in the Valley, Lee called Early "an officer of great intelligence, good judgment, and undoubted bravery. Yet the reverse of his last campaign and his recent defeat at Waynesborough, have materially shaken the confidence of the troops and people." Lee's letter relieving Early of command on March 30 was just as tactful: "I have reluctantly arrived at the conclusion that you cannot command the united and willing co-operation" of the soldiers and the public, "which is so essential to success." But Lee retained "confidence" in Early's "ability, zeal, and devotion to cause." Thus, Early, a veteran of First Manassas and nearly all the major battles of the Army of Northern Virginia, missed Lee's surrender at Appomattox. Instead he lay ill with "chills and fever" in his hometown of Rocky Mount, Virginia, before embarking for Texas, the Caribbean, and Mexico to escape the collapse of the Confederacy.[20]

In Mexico, Early made drafting a vindication of his recent calamity his first priority. A commitment to accuracy required speed, as he worked chiefly from memory. Prior to publication of *The War of the Rebellion: A Compilation of the Official Records of the Union and Confederate Armies* (widely known as the *Official Records* or *OR*), which commenced in 1880 and continued for more than two decades, obtaining campaign details was a desultory endeavor that depended on one's personal relationships with eyewitnesses; as an itinerant, Early's options were limited.[21] Nevertheless, it appears Early either came equipped with or acquired the diary of his aide Lt. William W. Old, the "copious notes" of chief topographical engineer Capt. Jedediah Hotchkiss, and a bevy of annual reports published by the U.S. government printing office.[22] To offset this dearth of primary materials, at least by Early's standards, he emphasized to several former subordinates his "very retentive," "very tenacious" memory, commenting in one instance, "you know I always knew what was going on in my command."[23] Early aimed to emphasize both memory and omniscience, which together underscored his credibility.[24]

Although he determined to rush the account to press, Early's journey from Mexico back to the Caribbean and finally to Canada delayed publication. Upon reflection, it suited him to "render [the manuscript] more perfect." He did so by sending it to Lee and numerous officers who served in the relevant 1864–65 campaigns.[25] These correspondents, in turn, provided Early with additional sources and critical feedback. For instance, in a letter exchange with his former chief of artillery Col. Thomas H. Carter, Early confirmed the whereabouts of cannons at Winchester and Cedar Creek, attesting to his desire to "give the credit to the right party and make no mistakes." Early then used his colleagues' responses to correct errors in his manuscript. As evidenced by correspondence with John C. Breckinridge, Early proved willing, after he had printed copies of the manuscript at his own expense, to alter even trifling minutiae to achieve accuracy.[26] This development of a "scholarly community" was not unique to Early and his cohort; throughout the nineteenth century select historians also embraced the practice. The best soldier personal narratives of the era also engaged in peer review, as detailed by historians Peter C. Luebke and Ann Fabian.[27]

For his second memoir, which included an autobiographical sketch and spanned the entire war, Early had to dig deeper in the annals of his memory. Thus he directed considerable effort toward obtaining eyewitness accounts and verification from fellow officers. While some of his compatriots ventured to pleasanter locales, Early chose to remain in Canada—where the cold produced a marked deterioration in his arthritis—and sought to solicit primary documents.[28] Much of the burden of providing reliable accounts fell to his brother, Capt. Samuel H. Early, who had served on Early's staff and apparently housed the bulk of the general's personal wartime documents in Lexington, Virginia, where he resided. Unsurprisingly, Early also relied on his former adjutant general, Maj. John W. Daniel, who tracked down resources on Second Manassas, Sharpsburg, First and Second Fredericksburg, and various other engagements. As before, Early also wrote to Lee and even delayed finishing the manuscript while he waited for his mentor's report on Gettysburg.[29] Early's considerable efforts to reconstruct accurate details from primary sources distinguished his account from many memoirists who followed.[30] It is, however, important to note that modern historiography has often underemphasized the "small but significant group of historical writers" who by the 1820s employed citations and primary sources as standards to achieve "the ideal of impartial truth."[31] To this lineage Early could lay claim.

Early relished the fact that his meticulous work contrasted with that of his adversaries in the North. With remarkable agility, Early called upon Union reports from Congress and the War Department to indict his foes. For example, in a footnote that Ruth Early chose to omit from the posthumous *Narrative* but which beamed brazenly from the *Memoir*, Early needled Ulysses S. Grant for lying. In Grant's 1865 annual report, one of Early's chief targets in the *Memoir*, Grant claimed that Early's cavalry, after burning Chambersburg, Pennsylvania, in 1864, was "met and defeated by General Kelly"; in fact, Early corrected, John McCausland's horsemen were routed by William W. Averell. "This shows how loose Grant is as to his facts," Early jeered. Yet the vitriol reserved for Secretary of War Edwin M. Stanton, a mere civilian, dwarfed that used against Grant. In a footnote, also omitted by Early's circumspect niece, Early derided Stanton's "keenness of strategic acumen which is altogether unparalleled" when Stanton claimed that "desperate fighting or marching . . . forced the rebel army back . . . and carried the Army of the Potomac to the south side of the James River" during the 1864 Overland campaign. Early countered, "Whether it was the desperate fighting or the desperate marching which did all this . . . it was a wonderful achievement, especially [considering] that the Army of the Potomac might have been carried [there] by transports."[32]

In Early's opinion, whenever U.S. government officials dipped their pens, drivel followed. Early charged that the Joint Committee on the Conduct of the War "gave a most preposterous account of 'Rebel atrocities' committed upon the [Union] dead and wounded" after the battle of First Manassas. Relying on his "personal knowledge" and "authentic official reports," Early condemned the committee's report as "false, and the Federal surgeons, left with the wounded, could bear testimony to their falsehood."[33] Examined together, these instances make it seem as though Early was quite the terrier after rats, but it is important to remember that he confined these statements to the footnotes without detracting from his larger points.

When Early did compliment his foes on accuracy, it was generally to reveal them in their least flattering moments of honesty. For example, in the *Narrative*, Early quoted Maj. Gen. George B. McClellan's analysis of why the Yankees declined to pursue after the battle of Sharpsburg: "Virginia lost, Washington menaced, Maryland invaded," bemoaned McClellan. "One [more] battle lost, and . . . Lee's army might then have marched . . . on Washington, Baltimore, Philadelphia, or New York."[34] Much to Early's satisfaction, the nominal Federal victory at Antietam was therefore undercut by Confederate psychological victory. Early also included snippets from Union correspondence in August 1862, evidence that, he claimed, "exhibits the bewilderment of the Federal authorities under the hallucination which McClellan himself continued to labor in regard to the strength of General Lee's forces."[35] Thus did Early excel at using Federal sources to make his enemy appear incompetent, foolish, and even unmanly. As historian Ann Fabian points out, the trick of writing one's narrative was to maintain control, because the very process of reading surrendered power to another. Early exercised skillful "masculine" authority over his opponents.[36]

Early also managed to present himself as possessed of pure rather than selfish motives, in contrast to his foes. While Union military leaders appeared boastful and prevaricating, Early took pains to remind his readers that he had acted according to conscience and would not shrink from the consequences of his actions. Most prominent was Early's account of the burning of Chambersburg on July 30, 1864, after the town refused to pay ransom. Early insisted that, though he was not physically present for the razing, "I, alone, am responsible, as the officers engaged in it were simply executing my orders, and had no discretion left them." Though his niece omitted the additional statement, Early proudly included in his first memoir, "I am perfectly satisfied with my conduct on this occasion, and see no reason to regret it."[37] Indeed, Early spent several pages justifying his decision to ransom or burn Federal towns in Pennsylvania and Maryland. "A number of towns in the South, as well as private country houses, had been burned by Federal troops," he explained. "We had stood this mode of warfare long enough, and . . . it was time to open the eyes of the people of the North to its enormity." As a result he hoped northerners would urge on "their government the adoption of a different policy."[38] In Early's assessment, his approach was pragmatic. Though he plainly owned his ransom-or-raze strategy, his other writings from his self-exile do betray fear that he would be imprisoned or hanged if he returned to the United States. Though he kept this concern mainly confined to private letters with Sam, his very public newspaper duel in 1866 with Sheridan over numbers in the Shenandoah Valley complained, "If I were to set any foot [in the U.S.] I would . . . [be] arrested and consigned to a military prison."[39]

Early applied his high standards of truth and purity to friends and acquaintances in addition to enemies. In a revealing exchange with Capt. John Esten Cooke, who held Early in high esteem, he quibbled over a footnote from Cooke's *Hammer and Rapier* (1870). Notably, Cooke's text is usually categorized as fiction, though it might be more accurately termed a mix of memoir, history, and fiction; in any case, it by no means aimed for the unimpeachable accuracy Early sought. The offending footnote read, "Many officers of high character, persistently declare that the troops [at Cedar Creek] were ordered to halt, by Gen. Early. The writer was not present" to confirm. Early accused Cooke on several grounds. First, Cooke had written the book too far after events to be accurate, though the book came out in 1870. Second, Cooke's facts were inaccurate; Early had never ordered a halt and demanded that Cooke reveal his sources on the matter. In response Cooke appeared perplexed and hurt. In fact the piece was written in 1866–67 and had previously appeared in the *Old Guard* magazine. Cooke had meant no harm to Early's reputation and promised to strike the passage. "You requested [that I] give you the names of those from whom the report was derived," Cooke demurred, but he had based the note on rumor: "I only remember that in the winter of 1864, when I was with the army at Petersburg, the report was prevalent and was repeated upon many occasions." He attributed the gossip to "the excited condition of the public mind and the army in the latter months of 1864 and the often angry discussions."[40] At least for future publications Cooke would have a reliable source of information, for Early had furnished the contrite staff officer with a copy of his 1866 memoir.

In addition to Early's concern for basing his accounts on verified sources, he also favored presenting numbers, especially numbers in tables, as unassailable facts. This habit began in Mexico and was applied in both memoirs to compelling effect. Early's 1866 newspaper exchange with archenemy Sheridan over "strengths and casualties of the forces in the Shenandoah campaign" was the first sign of this strategy, which, historian Gary W. Gallagher explains, "cast [Early's] own performance in a better light and sustained the honor of hopelessly outnumbered Confederates." More compelling to Early's case for authority is that "Early's numbers were more accurate."[41] Their factual superiority helped eclipse their nature as self-serving. The newspaper duel devolved into a savage tone in which Sheridan called Early "worse than [a] coward," and Early rebutted that Sheridan was "no gentleman" and "as a military commander, he was a mere pretender." Lee responded to Early about the matter, assuring him that emphasis on numbers rather than character attacks was the more convincing rhetorical strategy.[42]

Though both memoirs exhibited many examples of Early effectively marshaling numbers, two will suffice as illustration. His numbers always served the purpose of demonstrating the superiority of Federal manpower. The *Memoir* was accompanied by an appendix titled "Statistics showing the relative strength of the two sections during the war." It employed the 1860 U.S. Census along with quoted figures from Secretary of War Stanton, which demonstrated beyond a doubt that Confederates were grossly outnumbered by Federals. The second memoir likewise used Federal reports and tables to highlight the pitiful overestimation of Rebel forces by Union generals. On the topic of Sharpsburg, Early deemed laughable McClellan's assessment of the Army of the Potomac at 87,164 men in comparison to the Army of Northern Virginia at 97,445. The figures were based on a report made by Maj. Gen. Nathaniel P. Banks, and "It is well known that Banks always saw things with very largely magnifying glasses when 'Stonewall' Jackson was about." Moreover, Early recalled McClellan's previous estimates of his own force as over 220,000, plus new recruits and reinforcements. "Now the question very naturally arises, as to what had become of all that immense force," Early pondered.[43] That the Rebel forces were usually smaller was true (McClellan outnumbered Lee by more than two to one at Antietam); what Early failed to emphasize was that more factored into military victory and defeat than sheer manpower. Still numbers convey an air of unimpeachability. Because they undergirded Early's argument about his own loss and Confederate defeat, their impact on restoring his reputation and cementing Lost Cause hegemony should not be underestimated.

Compared to the numerous memoirists who would follow in his foot-
steps, Early also excelled at providing exceptionally detailed accounts of
events, which confirmed his personal presence and bolstered his historical authority. Scholar Stephen Cushman explains that "the convention of
personal presence" has "classical antecedents"; "autobiography and history
often had much in common."[44] Early's memoirs frequently call to mind
the meticulous nature of nineteenth-century military reports, which, in
part, aimed to justify to one's superior that orders had been followed to the
best of one's abilities despite turbulent, unfolding circumstances. In such
reports officers particularly had to labor for credibility when they lost.
Early, much practiced in this genre of writing, demonstrated a true gift for
campaign history and justification of his command decisions.

Though Early's talent is evident in numerous passages in both memoirs,
the *Narrative*'s description of the battle of Fredericksburg, when he acted
as brigade commander under Stonewall Jackson, will serve as example.
Early opened his account with a reminder of his physical presence in the
Fredericksburg locale, consuming three full pages with intricate descriptions of roads, rivers, and topography. As in any good military report, Early
detailed his orders from his commanding officer, Jackson, on December 12,
1862, to move to Hamilton's Crossing, "which I did by marching nearly all
night." Upon arrival he found the enemy obscured by "a thick wood" and
"heavy fog," "entirely excluded from our view." It is difficult not to be impressed with the fatigue and anxiety of Early's position, when all of a sudden, at noon on December 13, Early met with conflicting orders to action.
Just moments after a Jackson staff officer told Early to hold his troops in
"readiness," up galloped Reuben L. Walker's artillery with the news that
James J. Archer's brigade "had been penetrated by heavy columns of the
enemy . . . and would inevitably be captured unless there was instant relief." Early discarded his previous instructions from Jackson in order to
meet this "serious emergency" and proceeded blind into ground he was
"entirely unacquainted with." Early was met with chaos; the enemy column
had "turned Archer's left and Lane's right." As Early funneled in troops,
he was forced to make quick, independent decisions, while responding to
incoming communications. In he sent Robert F. Hoke only to be interrupted
with the message that Archer had fully given way; Early shifted Hoke in
an oblique movement to support Archer. "Just as Hoke started," Jackson's
message intervened to advance the whole division, and Early obeyed as

best he could. When he finally had the opportunity to ride to the front, he "discovered that Hoke had got too far" into enemy artillery range, which Early corrected, before sending for reinforcements.[45] The successful repulse of the Federals ended just as the brutal assaults on Marye's Heights began.

Early also demonstrated an aptitude for discrediting other's experiences, while reinforcing his own reliability as narrator. In his longer memoir he recounted that "Some officers . . . sometimes fail to preserve that clearness of judgment and calmness of the nerves which is so necessary . . . to see things as they really are during an engagement." This, he claimed, is what led to "so many conflicting reports of the same matters." As an example from the battle of First Manassas, he wrote of a captain who hallucinated about Union Maj. Gen. Irvin McDowell on a white horse. The vision was "produced by a derangement of the nervous system" from "loss of sleep and great anxiety of mind." It fell to the captain's superiors to realize the error. "It requires very great experience and a very discriminating judgment," such as that possessed by Early, "to enable a commanding general to sift the truth out of the great mass of exaggerated reports made to him." Because Early had many times successfully relied on "his own personal inspection," so, too, might the reader take confidence in him.[46]

The fact that he was part of Lee's inner circle also helped Early's case for textual authority a great deal. Frequent reminders of his intimate acquaintance with the revered general confirmed Early's elite status, and indeed his position in Lee's esteem was rare. As Gallagher explains, Early, Lee's "Bad Old Man," was one of two generals on whom Lee bestowed a nickname, along with "Old War Horse" James Longstreet, and Lee entrusted Early with difficult assignments second only to those of Stonewall Jackson.[47] To provide one example of intimacy during the Overland campaign, Early revealed, "I happen to know that General Lee always had the greatest anxiety to strike at Grant."[48] Therein lies insight not only into Lee's private aspirations, but also his feelings. Moreover, Early's friends helped to promote his status as Lee's confidant, and a compliment bestowed by someone other than oneself smacked of greater legitimacy.[49] On January 2, 1866, Charles W. Button, editor of the *Lynchburg Daily Virginian,* expressed his desire to vindicate Early as "an act of justice to an old friend" by reproducing for the public Lee's gentle letter removing Early from command in March 1865. Button characterized Early in near religious terms as a man who never complained about the painful judgments rendered against him and who patiently waited for time to restore his rightful reputation.[50] One might note that, rather than surrendering control of his narrative to time, Early, in fact, published Lee's letter in an appendix to his first memoir.

Yet Early hardly exaggerated his ties with Lee, especially in regard to his memoirs. The two men corresponded, sharing reports and reflections frequently before Lee's death. One of Early's first tasks when he reached Canada was hand-copying his Valley manuscript for Lee, which engaged so much of his time that he temporarily lost touch with nearly everyone except his brother Sam.[51] As Robert K. Krick underscores, Early's 1866 account was the only memoir that Lee read in draft and offered comments on, conferring on it his special approval.[52] In addition Lee consulted with Early regarding his own pet project, entreating "the world to understand the odds against which we fought," which dovetailed nicely with Early's aim to accomplish the same with regard to his Shenandoah campaign.[53] For Early, the two projects merged into one holy ambition. Just as Early sought reports from Lee, his superior coveted Early's documents, for "The destruction, or loss of all returns of the army embarrasses me very much," explained Lee in March 1866.[54]

It is also evident from correspondence that Lee provided counsel to Early regarding the tone of his publications, urging the use of dispassionate facts over disparagement.[55] This tone did much to solidify Early's emerging status as a sympathetic martyr for the Confederate cause and a reliable historian.[56] In this vein Lee urged his friend of the memoir draft, "I would recommend . . . that while giving facts which you think necessary for your own vindication . . . you omit all epithets or remarks calculated to excite bitterness or animosity between different sections of the Country."[57] Early did not wholly succeed in heeding Lee's advice, but he did significantly curtail his usual acerbity, confining it primarily to the footnotes. Lee also noticeably followed Early's newspaper disputes, providing praise or mild rebukes when Early strayed into character attacks.[58] In private correspondence, Early's desire to honor his mentor's advice strained against his natural disposition. For example, Early wrote to newspaper editor and author Edward Pollard, refusing to endorse Pollard's inclusion of a sketch of him in his new book titled *Lee and His Lieutenants*. In the letter, Early struck through a passage parroting Lee's desire that he avoid controversy because harmony was necessary.[59] It simply did not ring genuine. Early's personal struggles with tone aside, Lee's high standards encouraged a pragmatism in Early's memoirs while also suggesting Lee's endorsement. If Lee had authenticated Early's memoirs, who dared challenge them?

Early's written project would have yielded less acclaim if he had not put considerable work into concurrently rehabilitating his personal reputation, which was imperiled at the end of the war. In addition to his defeat in the Shenandoah, Early's many faults, including maintaining an illiterate, white mistress with whom he fathered four children, were not exactly secret.[60] Some of the public descriptions of Early's character flaws were more blithesome, offering humorous tales of the general's irreligion, profanity, and petulance. Mid-nineteenth-century readers were more accepting of such flaws than one might presume; they often "condemned . . . didactic tendencies to whitewash flaws and make subjects into cookie-cutter models of specific virtues."[61] Still, these accounts of himself, which he read time and again in Canada, did wear on Early despite their substantial basis in truth. Early's friend Lt. Col. George Taylor Denison of the British army related one such instance from Canada. To Denison, Early pointed out an article, which related an anecdote from the 1864 Shenandoah Valley campaign. It recounted a rare occasion on which Early attended church with his staff. The sermon depicted the end times and the final resurrection of the dead. In order to electrify the congregants the reverend repeatedly goaded, "What would be your feelings on that day?" Early muttered in response to a staff officer, "I would conscript every d——d one of them." When Denison inquired as to the truth of the story, Early laughed and replied: "I'm afraid it is Colonel, but what right had that fellow to go and tell it to the papers, that is enough to destroy a man's reputation for piety. The preacher kept on asking how I would feel, I wanted men that last winter very badly, and it was a very natural thought."[62]

While the account captured one facet of Early's personality, friends and family knew in private he was far warmer. At many points in his exile Early wrote to take a special interest in the fortunes of his nieces and nephews. He expressed deep affection and concern for his siblings and aging father.[63] Those who met Early in Canada were impressed by his countenance. "I have been quite astonished to find how much I like 'Old Jubal,' and how quick and pleasant he can be," wrote one such visitor, Ida Mason.[64] Early could also be remarkably charitable. Though destitute himself he scrounged fifty dollars in gold to help a Confederate widow whom he encountered in a desperate state. A war refugee, she had recently lost two children to illness with a third baby sick, and her pocket had been picked during travels in New York.[65] Early felt keenly the unbalanced nature of the public's perception of him, and when he refused to endorse his inclusion in Edward Pollard's biography, he plainly revealed his fear of being misunderstood: "During my life I have often associated with men who thought they knew me, but who in fact had very little appreciation of my true character; I would not therefore expect it to be understood by one who is an entire stranger."[66] Fundamentally, Early's reputation contrasted with that of Lee, who was esteemed as pious and temperate. Early's image demanded aggressive management.

The autobiographical sketch included in the *Narrative* sought to counteract some of the more cartoonish images rampant in the newspapers. Again Ann Fabian's work is informative; nineteenth-century readers had the power to right the wrongs an author had suffered by reading and believing.[67] As a general, Early presented himself as a disciplinarian, far from the kind of commander who would suffer rampant plundering and straggling, as the accusations surrounding Cedar Creek suggested. When discussing his Mexican War service he narrated his evolution in his soldiers' perspectives from being viewed as "strict" and "harsh" to celebrated as "the most popular officer in the regiment." Early then answered public indictments of his personality with humility: "I was never blessed with popular or captivating manners, and the consequence was that I was often misjudged and thought to be haughty and disdainful in my temperament." Yet "those who knew me best, liked me best." He even sought to correct some of the physical descriptions in papers, which always emphasized his arthritic "stoop." "[T]here have been some descriptions of my person attempted, in which I have failed to recognize the slightest resemblance," he chided, before going on to provide a more flattering portrait of a man of "170 pounds," possessing hair as "straight as an Indian's" with "smooth and moderate eyebrows." He sought compassion for his defect; the famous stoop was the "result of rheumatism contracted in Mexico," and when he was "bent up, it has been very often the result of actual pain to which I have been very much subjected for the last nineteen years." Finally, he took care with his dress, contrary to one writer's description comparing Early to a "stage-driver." He assured, "I have always been one of the most particular men about the cut and fit of my clothes," but during the war he was too often in the field to meet his own standards.[68] In short, Early portrayed himself as a sympathetic, attractive gentleman and a respectable general.

Beyond Early's written defense of his maligned personality and appearance, his suffering in self-exile procured for him a claim to morality in Victorian culture that he otherwise lacked. It also reinforced his claim to elite status. Frances Clarke has stressed the importance of "humble self-sacrifice in a virtuous cause" as evidence of genteel manliness.[69] Through prolonged misery and poverty Early positioned himself as a martyr to the Confederate cause. Repeatedly in correspondence with his brother Sam, Early manifested anxiety for his country, embarrassment about his need to borrow money, and physical agony from his rheumatism. By mid-1867, the letters became so pitiful they are difficult to read. In May he described himself as "so much crippled up that I move about with difficulty, and am more bent than I have ever been." In July his mood had taken a turn for the morose: "Perhaps it might be better to . . . be killed off by the climate, so that there might be an end to my troubles in this world." By August his unease over borrowing Sam's money had mounted to the point of "greatest mortification and grief." And in October he felt "as if I were taking from you the means of educating your children, and in that way doing a great injustice to them."[70]

Though Sam saw the true depths of Early's sorrow, the general's martyrdom was by no means a private affair. Visitors to Canada noticed and spread news of his pain. After seeing Early hobble about on his cane, Elizabeth A. F. Harris lamented, "How indignant it makes me, when I think of the conduct of our enemies & their desire to humiliate our noble heroes by forcing them to leave their native land."[71] Supportive newspaper editors also presented Early's case for martyrdom to the masses, concentrating on his exile as the pinnacle of self-sacrifice. Button of the *Daily Virginian* framed it in baldly religious terms: "General Early has made a sacrifice of self . . . for the crucifixion of his love. He remains in exile, while some of those who reviled him for his opposition to secession have been duly pardoned."[72] Though Early was more difficult to cram into the pious mold of Lee or Jackson, his miserable exile was the closest he came to righteousness in the public's eye.

Cleverly, Early set his exile in contrast to where his heart truly resided—the Shenandoah Valley and, more generally, his ruined country—both of which were lost causes he had labored valiantly to defend. Symbolically, the three merged—Early, the Valley, the Confederacy—into a holy triad that became difficult to disentangle.[73] If one loved the Shenandoah and the Confederacy, how could one be against Jubal Early? In praising Winchester as a place "peculiarly sacred," second only to that of his birthplace and mother's grave, Early demonstrated the depth of his commitment to the Valley. Indeed, "I have many cherished recollections connected with the Valley of the Shenandoah, from one end to the other, and I trust that peace and prosperity may soon return to bless the inhabitants of that beautiful Valley, as well as of all our now desolated country." He likened his current wanderings, dislocated from the land he loved, to a pilgrimage of self-sacrifice. "It is sad, sad indeed to be an exile from my country, and still sadder to mourn the loss of the most just and most sacred cause for which man ever fought." But, he added, "there is some comfort in knowing that the struggle which developed so much heroism on the part of our soldiers and so many virtues in our women has not been all in vain."[74]

As indicated by this quotation, to aid in his rehabilitation Early extended his focus beyond himself to the people most hurt by his military loss in the Shenandoah—his former soldiers and Valley residents, especially women. Early tempered his criticism regarding his cavalry's failings, emphasizing that their defeat by General Averell on August 7, 1864, was because of a severe manpower deficiency and "had a very damaging effect upon my cavalry for the rest of the campaign." Also diminished was his scolding tone toward the plundering troops at Cedar Creek. Early defanged his past castigation: "I read a sharp lecture to my troops . . . but I have never attributed the result to a want of courage on their part." He dedicated the *Memoir* in part to "the brave soldiers who fought under me," echoing Lee's 1865 farewell speech to the Army of Northern Virginia: "I believe that the world has never produced a body of men superior, in courage, in patriotism, and endurance, to the private soldiers of the Confederate armies." Likewise did his second memoir frequently emphasize the "admirable" conduct of his troops under circumstances of extreme material deprivation. Thus did Early take another important cue from Lee's farewell address by shifting responsibility for the loss of the Valley from his soldiers to the prevailing state of inferior manpower and materiel. Regarding Cedar Creek, Early addressed directly those who might ask why he attacked with so small a force in comparison to the enemy: "I can only say we had been fighting large odds during the whole war." Yet it should be noted that, even with the softening of his tone, Early was not Lee. He concluded, "[I] still think I would have [won the day], if my directions had been strictly complied with, and my troops had awaited my orders to retire."[75]

Early also concentrated on rebuilding relationships with the public, especially residents of the Valley. In his first memoir he declared the public interest above his own, offering magnanimous sympathy to those who had vilified him in the past. Even before Lee removed him in March 1865, explained Early, he had stated "my willingness to be relieved from command . . . for the public interests." And to those "countrymen who judged me harshly, I have not a word of reproach. When there was so much at stake, it was not unnatural" to pass "severe judgments on those commanders who met with reverses."[76]

But the main focus of his outreach was on the women of the Shenandoah Valley. The *Memoir* framed his more controversial policies regarding northern towns as acts of vindication on behalf of these women. In a footnote he declared, "I had often seen delicate ladies, who had been plundered, insulted, and rendered desolate by the acts of our most atrocious enemies." He linked his ransom-and-raze strategy to manly honor: "There was a mute appeal to every manly sentiment of my bosom for retribution." He heaped epithets of "heroic courage" on the Valley's Confederate women, believing the ordeal in the Valley fell with the "most crushing effect . . . upon them." In the newspapers he also credited Shenandoah ladies with standing by his reputation and the truth when others had forsaken him. To the Ladies' Memorial Association of Winchester he wrote, "When many of my countrymen . . . judged me harshly, the ladies of [Winchester], who knew the tremendous odds with which I had to contend, attached no blame to me." Moreover, he praised their recent efforts to reinter the Confederate dead: "I know that many of those [buried by the ladies] fell while fighting under my command—among them being a number of valued personal friends—and this sad and touching tribute to their memories affected me very deeply."[77] He also lauded the Ladies' Memorial Association of Mount Jackson for their self-sacrifice in caring for the wounded during the war and burying the dead after the war. The affection was mutual, as the ladies, in turn, elected Early as honorary member.[78] As witnesses from the period recounted, reflecting on the actions of the Ladies' Memorial Associations brought tears to

the general's eyes.[79] He was genuinely affected by their work, but his growing connection with them also served his greater purpose of redemption.

Early's ability to tap into the work of the memorial associations reinforced his selfless claim to bolstering the reputation of the Confederacy
rather than his own. As William A. Blair points out, "White southerners had
to accept the sacrifice of nearly one-quarter of their seventeen-to-fifty-year-
old men, many of whose bodies lay in unmarked graves far from home."
Ex-Confederates had to curtail their public ceremonies in conformity with
U.S. law. While the U.S. government created beautiful, orderly military cem-
eteries throughout the South, they reinterred only Federal bodies. This policy confirmed for Confederates that they would be treated as "second-class
citizens within the new nation."[80] Caroline E. Janney affirms that white
southerners were well aware that it was Ladies' Memorial Associations
who "established Confederate cities of the dead," thereby "keeping alive
a sense of white southern solidarity."[81] Early understood that by paying
public homage to these women and their project he was reinforcing claims
to righteousness and authority. He and the ladies shared the same purpose
of constructing a positive Confederate historical narrative in the face of
northern neglect.

The manner in which Early chose to print, publish, distribute, and donate the proceeds of his first memoir helped restore his reputation and
establish his historical influence.[82] In this process the Ladies' Memorial
Associations, again, figured prominently. Early chose to print the first thousand copies of the *Memoir* at his own expense, paying roughly nineteen
cents per copy, and for distribution to friends and acquaintances. He did so
in part to solicit reactions about the veracity of his account, but many other
motivations prompted his initial choices. While seeking foreign publishers
to spread his message abroad, he sent some of his first imprints to friends
living in England and France to distribute them on his behalf. For example,
he sent Breckinridge fifty-four copies to give away in Paris and twenty to
James M. Mason, former Confederate diplomat, in London. Early, Breckinridge, and Mason previously had forged close ties while living together
in exile in Canada. In addition, Early sent copies of the *Memoirs* as tokens
to various widows of Rebels who had been slain in the 1864 Valley campaign, perhaps as a subtle reminder that he was not responsible for their
deaths. For example, Early sent a copy to Mrs. E. C. Wing of Kentucky out

of respect for her deceased husband. In return she prayed for Early's safety and welfare in exile and hoped he would soon return to his native land.[83]

Early also wished to reward those loyal to the Confederate cause, as evidenced by his venom when a memoir recipient disappointed him. Believing a certain Sam Swann of Kanawha, West Virginia, had remained faithful to the cause, Early favored him with a copy, but after reviewing a subsequent letter from Swann to a local newspaper, "the cloven foot was shown very clearly." Indeed Early was "so much disgusted at the renegadism and the truckling spirit shown by the letter, that I thought of . . . requesting him to hand over the book I had sent him to some Confederate who had not apostatized"; however, "on reflection I thought he was too contemptible even for that notice." Privately to Sam, Early complained that as word spread about his memoir he received many requests for books without postage paid.[84]

Beyond the private copies, Early planned to relinquish printing rights and donate all financial proceeds to the Ladies' Memorial Associations, particularly those of the Shenandoah Valley and Richmond. Supporting the Valley ladies once again helped compensate for his military loss, while supporting those of Richmond, the former capital of the Confederacy, symbolized Early's devotion to his former nation. At first he hoped to reserve the exclusive right to publish to Ladies' Memorial Associations, but these groups proved slower to respond than private parties. Early began to accept outside solicitations to print as long as the principal revenue was still donated to the ladies. Once again Lynchburg-based newspaper editor Charles Button rushed to the aid of his friend, offering to print an inexpensive edition without maps. Along with the *Memoir*, Button offered discounted subscriptions to the *Daily Virginian*. In early 1867 Early received a request from A. R. Wright, formerly of William Mahone's brigade, to print several thousand copies. To Early's satisfaction Wright offered to pay all expenses and to give Early half the profit, to be passed along to the Ladies' Memorial Associations.[85] Just as Early's public praise of the ladies advanced his greater purposes of redemption and authority, so also did his sacrificial donation of all proceeds to their project of honoring the Confederate dead. The act of donation itself was important; the most truthful, or best believed, personal accounts of the era were by authors who could not profit from their books, since financial gain was self-serving. For this reason, convict confessionals, written on the eve of execution, appealed enormously to readers of the era.[86]

The fact that Early earned not a penny from the *Memoir* resulted in painful financial hardship. It should be recalled that in exile Early was utterly reliant on charity from his family, mainly Sam, and this dependency brought him to the brink of despair.[87] Early was also subjected to the embarrassment of relying on frequent handouts from strangers.[88] His shame and suffering were real, and yet they conferred on Early a seeming purity of motives. He appeared a man who would spread the truth whatever the cost. Button picked up on this narrative, characterizing Early as a true "patriot," who sought neither vindication nor profit. The importance of Early's accomplishment here should not be missed. It is remarkable that any person, even a friend, could conceive of Early's Valley memoir as anything other than justification for his defeat. Prior to publication even Lee had acknowledged "vindication" as Early's central aim in writing the account.[89] That Button published this sentiment means Early's calculation paid off. He may have suffered in temporary poverty, but donating the revenue of his book to the ladies remade him as a selfless public figure, regardless of what the book contained.

Critical reception of the book was strikingly positive in both northern and southern newspapers, attesting to the success of Early's efforts. A *New York Times* special correspondent explained that reading the account changed his negative perception of Early, which he believed most northerners shared. "I had always thought of the doughty rebel—as I suppose most persons at the North have—in a rather ludicrous and contemptuous light, as the bad old boy of apple-jack memory, mighty with the whisky bottle but mediocre with the sword." In other words, this was precisely the reputation Early hoped to change. The reporter was pleasantly impressed not only by Early's actual character, but also by the quality of his military scholarship. "The memoir is excellently written," he mused, "though occasionally he falls in the Ercles vein, and now and then goes beyond the modesty of a soldier." That is not to say that every northern newspaper could tolerate the defense of secession contained in the *Memoir*'s introduction. One *New York Times* review was titled, "Jubal A. Early: His Memoir of the Last Year of the War—Sentiments of one who can Neither Forget nor Learn Anything."[90]

Southern newspapers and periodicals lavished praise on Early and his memoir in late 1866 and early 1867. The *Richmond Times* declared that Early's statue should stand next to those of Lee and Jackson at the state capitol. The *Richmond Whig* printed a letter, from "Kittoola" of Pulaski

County, advocating Early for governor of Virginia. Kittoola styled herself as "one of the ladies of the State, and an admirer of General Jubal A. Early," requesting that "good ladies . . . appeal to their husbands, fathers, brothers and sons with one voice to elect [Early] to that position, and relive him of the humiliating condition of an exile in a land of strangers to preside over his native state." The *Whig* editorialized that "a note is struck which it will not surprise us to see taken up and echoed throughout the state." The *Old Guard* magazine wrote feelingly of Early's journey from humiliation to redemption. For "reverses" in the Valley "Old Jubal had to suffer," it lamented. "The press and the people . . . condemned him . . . unmercifully." But now that "General Early has prepared a history of his last campaign, with great care and minuteness," it would "dispel the clouds which now hang over his military reputation." The *Old Guard* further remarked on Early's hidden "tender feelings" and kindness, and the significance of his exile: "Jubal A. Early, unrelenting and unsurrendered, wandered, sulkily and secretly, from that ancient commonwealth which he loved more than his life."[91] The article touched all the major aspects of Early's desired redemption, absolving him of blame for Valley defeat, vindicating his maligned personality, and heaping laurels on his martyrdom.

The fact that Early did not publish his second narrative of the war in his lifetime benefited his reputation and his legacy.[92] While writing the longer memoir, he explained to his friend John Daniel that he did not wish the newspapers to get wind of the account and annoy him with false reports.[93] He thus betrayed concern with public reception even before completing the project. His choice to postpone publication until after his death solidified his case for avoiding the appearance of special pleading. Indeed, Early had an example in his mentor; Lee never completed memoirs, leaving the elevation of his reputation strictly to others. On Lee's death his celebrity was virtually unmatched.

After Lee's death, Early demonstrated less and less restraint in his public battles over Confederate history. This did not earn him universal acclaim or love. In fact, Robert Stiles, an influential memoirist of the postwar era, described the prevailing view of the historian Early as one of fear: "No man ever took up his pen to write a line about the great conflict without the fear of Jubal Early before his eyes." That Early held back the *Narrative,* which had been written in the more moderate tone of the period of his exile, worked greatly to his benefit. When published it secured the kind of legacy of which Lee would have been proud. Though Early would no longer be alive to manage his narrative and that of the Confederacy, the second memoir passed down his most important arguments to posterity in the same exceptionally convincing manner as the first.[94]

Much of the critical reaction to the *Narrative* likely would have pleased Early. *The Bookman: A Review of Books and Life,* based in New York, summarized the book's accomplishments in 1913. "That a man who was graduated from West Point and had served in the Seminole and Mexican Wars was well equipped to write as an expert of the Civil War . . . would have been conceded by all," the review began, and Early would have applauded the deference to his military expertise. But what would have particularly charmed Early was the reviewer's acknowledgment that the general could "write the story of that war in a calm spirit, for the most part undisfigured by passion and uncolored by prejudice. . . . It stamps General Early as a rare and notable soul." The *South Atlantic Quarterly*'s assessment of the *Narrative* likewise declared Early as "singularly free from a controversial spirit, his dominant purpose always being to give a straightforward accounts of events and occasionally to explain why more was not accomplished." Charles W. Ramsdell, writing in the *Southwestern Historical Quarterly,* concurred that Early's "tone is calm and judicial. . . . It is in fact hardly necessary to show that he fought against tremendous odds both of men and resources."[95] Thus did Early's central thesis about his and the Confederacy's defeat prevail. Finally, Early's calculation to withhold publication of his second memoir until after his death, when it could bring him no financial gains, paid a high return just as it had with the first. A man who reaped no material rewards from his work commanded authority.

From 1865 to 1870 Jubal Early achieved stunning success in rehabilitating his public image and establishing himself as the major force with which to be reckoned on military history of the Army of Northern Virginia. Robert Stiles perceptively summarized Early's stewardship of wartime "memories" as "Early's religion; his mission [was] to vindicate the truth of history." Early wrote as much to Lee in 1868: "The most that is left to us is the history of our struggle, and I think that ought to be accurately written. We lost nearly everything but honour, and that should be religiously guarded." Early may have lost the Shenandoah Valley and, by extension, his country the war, but he won control of the resulting historical narrative by meticulous, even grueling, effort. In 1913, nearly two decades after his death, a reviewer praised the *Narrative* as "an utterance that is as clear and down-right and blunt as Cæsar's. . . . This book is a great achievement for any man and a distinct contribution to history."[96] It has taken historians a century and a half to appreciate the power of Early's works.

NOTES

The author would like to thank Gary W. Gallagher and Stephen Cushman for inviting me to participate in this collection. Additionally, I extend deep gratitude to Dr. Gallagher for passing on to me his personal collection of Jubal A. Early documents, and special thanks to Peter C. Luebke for editorial suggestions and to William C. Davis for supplying copies of items in his private collection.

1. The title of this essay is taken from the following quotation: "Under a solemn sense of duty to my unhappy country, and to the brave soldiers who fought under me, as well as to myself, the following pages have been written" (Jubal A. Early, *A Memoir of the Last Year of the War for Independence in the Confederate States of America* [1866; rpt. with introd. by Gary W. Gallagher, Columbia: University of South Carolina Press, 2001], xxi). Former staff officer G. Campbell Brown commented on Early's prudent tone in a letter to Jedediah Hotchkiss, former chief topographical engineer of the Confederate Second Corps: "Have you seen Early's new [memoir]? It is published in Canada—very shrewdly written. He comes as near to giving you a fair showing as to the Cedar Creek affair as his nature will allow" (Brown to Hotchkiss, January 15, 1867, Hotchkiss Papers, DLC reel 49, Albert and Shirley Small Special Collections Library, University of Virginia, Charlottesville [repository here-after cited as UVA]). See also Early's modern biographers Millard K. Bushong, *Jubal Early: Robert E. Lee's Bad Old Man* (Boyce, Va.: Carr Publishing, 1955); Charles C. Osborne, *Jubal: The Life and Times of General Jubal A. Early, CSA, Defender of the Lost Cause* (Chapel Hill, N. C.: Algonquin Books, 1992); and Benjamin Franklin Cooling III, *Jubal Early: Robert E. Lee's Bad Old Man* (Lanham, Md.: Rowman & Littlefield, 2014).

2. D. H. Hill to Jubal A. Early (in citing correspondence hereafter shortened to JAE), May 12, 1869, Mss. vol. 5, item 839–40, Jubal Anderson Early Papers, Library of Congress, Washington, D.C. (hereafter cited as Early Papers, LC).

3. JAE to Thomas L. Rosser, May 20, 1866, in "New Light on General Jubal A. Early after Appomattox," William D. Hoyt Jr., ed., *Journal of Southern History* 9 (February 1943): 113.

4. Gallagher, "Introduction," in Early, *Memoir*, xiii.

5. Lee explained, in his General Order № 9, dated April 10, 1865: "After four years of ar-duous service, marked by unsurpassed courage and fortitude, the Army of Northern Virginia has been forced to yield to overwhelming numbers and resource" (General R. E. Lee's Fare-well Address, April 10, 1865, Library of Congress, www.loc.gov/item/2003677965/ [accessed February 01, 2017]).

6. A letter from Early's chief topographical engineer in the Valley, Jedediah Hotchkiss, related, "Gen Early showed me these MSS shortly after he had completed them & said he had provided for their publication after his death" (Hotchkiss letter, January 4, 1898, in "Copies

of Letters from Gen. J. A. Early's Correspondence and his Diary kept while escaping from the states to Canada," Jones Memorial Library, Lynchburg, Va. [hereafter cited as Early Copies, JML]).

7. The long period between writing and publication has provoked some confusion about the extent to which Early revised the manuscript after his exile. See, for example, the book review by Charles W. Ramsdell in *Southwestern Historical Quarterly* 17 (July 1913): 95. I concur with Gary W. Gallagher's assessment that Early composed the majority of the text in Canada. See Gallagher, "Introduction," in Jubal A. Early, *Lieutenant General Jubal Anderson Early, C.S.A.: Autobiographical Sketch and Narrative of the War Between the States* (1912; rpt., New York: De Capo Press, 1991), xxvi–xxviii. Two pieces of evidence support this claim. First, Early confirmed with his brother, Sam, that he would complete the memoir by October 1868 (JAE to Sam, September 6, 1868, Scrapbook, Early Papers, LC). Second, the *Autobiographical Sketch and Narrative* is notably free of the James Longstreet controversy, which consumed Early's writings, especially on Second Manassas and Gettysburg, after Lee's death in 1870. See also Gallagher, "Scapegoat in Victory: James Longstreet and the Battle of Second Manassas," in Gallagher, *Lee and His Generals in War and Memory* (Baton Rouge: Louisiana State University Press, 1998), 139–40.

8. For examples of Early's controversial writings from the 1870s to his death in 1894, see *Three Days at Gettysburg: Essays on Confederate and Union Leadership,* ed. Gary W. Gallagher (Kent, Ohio: Kent State University Press, 1999), and Gallagher, *Lee and His Generals,* 68.

9. For Early's significant influence on the Lost Cause, see Gaines M. Foster, *Ghosts of the Confederacy: Defeat, the Lost Cause, and the Emergence of the New South* (New York: Oxford University Press, 1987); Thomas L. Connelly, *The Marble Man: Robert E. Lee and His Image in American Society* (New York: Knopf, 1977); Connelly and Barbara L. Bellows, *God and General Longstreet: The Lost Cause and the Southern Mind* (Baton Rouge: Louisiana State University Press, 1982); Gallagher, *Lee and His Generals*; Gallagher, *Jubal A. Early, the Lost Cause, and Civil War History: A Persistent Legacy* (Milwaukee, Wis.: Marquette University Press, 1995); Gallagher and Alan T. Nolan, eds., *The Myth of the Lost Cause and Civil War History* (Bloomington: Indiana University Press, 2000); David W. Blight, *Race and Reunion: The Civil War in American Memory* (Cambridge, Mass.: Harvard University Press, 2001); Alice Fahs and Joan Waugh, *The Memory of the Civil War in American Culture* (Chapel Hill: University of North Carolina Press, 2004); William A. Blair, *Cities of the Dead: Contesting the Memory of the Civil War in the South, 1865–1914* (Chapel Hill: University of North Carolina Press, 2004); W. Fitzhugh Brundage, *The Southern Past: A Clash of Race and Memory* (Cambridge, Mass.: Harvard University Press, 2005); and Caroline E. Janney, *Remembering the Civil War: Reunion and the Limits of Reconciliation* (Chapel Hill: University of North Carolina Press, 2013).

10. For scholarship on nineteenth-century histories, personal narratives, and memoirs and their various claims to authority, see Scott E. Casper, *Constructing American Lives: Biography and Culture in Nineteenth-Century America* (Chapel Hill: University of North Carolina Press, 1999); Stephen Cushman, *Bloody Promenade: Reflections on a Civil War Battle* (Charlottesville: University of Virginia Press, 1999); Ann Fabian, *The Unvarnished Truth: Personal Narratives in Nineteenth-Century America* (Berkeley: University of California Press, 2000); and Eileen Ka-May Cheng, *The Plain and Noble Garb of Truth: Nationalism and Impartiality in American Historical Writing, 1784–1860* (Athens: University of Georgia Press, 2008).

11. Casper, *Constructing American Lives,* 5; Cheng, *Plain and Noble,* 8.

12. Early's adjutant general and friend John Warwick Daniel perceptively noted the difference in the tone of Early's memoirs compared to his usual writings and those by fellow memoirists: "Early accredited by some with being a bitter man, wrote in the best possible temper with respect to all his comrades in arms. Each of the others, both Longstreet and Gordon, wrote in a different mood . . . assailing . . . any who had criticized his military record" and "going beyond the range of an the impartial historian" (Daniel, "Introductory Chapter [Notes and Pages of a Rough Draft]," n.d., John Warwick Daniel Papers, 1816–1936, Mss. 158, box 25, UVA).

13. Cheng, *Plain and Noble,* 9–10.

14. Casper, *Constructing American Lives,* 6.

15. To Lee, Early explained on September 25, 1864: "The enemy's immense superiority in cavalry and the inefficiency of the greater part of mine has been the cause of all my disasters. In the affair at Fishers Hill the cavalry gave way, but it was flanked. This could have been remedied if the troops had remained steady, but a panic seized them at the idea of being flanked, and without being defeated they broke, many of them fleeing shamefully" (U.S. War Department, *The War of the Rebellion: A Compilation of the Official Records of the Union and Confederate Armies,* 128 vols. [Washington: Government Printing Office, 1880–1901], ser. 1, vol. 43, pt. 1:558 [hereafter cited as *OR;* all references are to series 1]). Robert K. Krick incisively argues that Early had good reason to blame his cavalry in "'The Cause of All My Disasters': Jubal A. Early and the Undisciplined Valley Cavalry," in Gary W. Gallagher, ed., *Struggle for the Shenandoah: Essays on the 1864 Valley Campaign* (Kent, Ohio: Kent State University Press, 1991), 77–106.

16. For a succinct account of Early's Valley campaign, see Gallagher, "Introduction," in *Struggle for the Shenandoah,* 1–18.

17. In his memoirs, Early's subordinate John B. Gordon termed his commander's error a "fatal halt" (Gordon, *Reminiscences of the Civil War* [New York: Charles Scribner's Sons, 1904], 241–42). For an informative look at Early's and Gordon's accounts of what occurred at Cedar Creek, see Keith S. Bohannon, "'The Fatal Halt' versus 'Bad Conduct': John B. Gordon, Jubal A. Early, and the Battle of Cedar Creek," in Gary W. Gallagher, ed., *The Shenandoah Valley Campaign of 1864* (Chapel Hill: University of North Carolina Press, 2009), 56–84.

18. "Early's Address to his Army, October, 22, 1864," *New York Times,* October 30, 1864. The newspaper extracted the address "from our files of Richmond, Charleston and Mobile papers."

19. Gray Jacket, "The Cavalry," *Richmond Sentinel,* November 1, 1864; Raleigh W. Downman letter, Fourth Virginia Cavalry, October 20–21, 1864, Raleigh W. Downman Letters, Section 10, Virginia Historical Society, Richmond (repository hereafter cited as VHS); *OR* 43(1): 917; Sarah Ann Graves Strickler Fife Diary (March 7, 1865, entry, p. 46), Diary of Sarah Ann Graves Strickler Fife, 1861–1902, UVA.

20. *OR* 49(2): 1166; Early, *Memoir,* 139; N. W. West (a soldier under Stephen D. Ramseur) to JAE, May 25, 1883, Early Copies, JML.

21. On the publication of the *OR,* see "Civil War: Official Records of the Union and Confederate Armies," Archives Library Information Center, National Archives, Washington, D.C.,

www.archives.gov/research/alic/reference/military/civil-war-armies-records.html (accessed February 1, 2017).

22. Early, *Memoir,* xi. The first two sources are recorded in the memoir's preface; the other references can be found by tracing quotations contained in Early's uncited footnotes. For example, cross-referencing Early's footnotes on pp. 33–34 leads one to U. S. Grant, *Report of Lieutenant General U.S. Grant, of the Armies of the United States, 1864–65* (Washington: Government Printing Office, 1865,) 1, 7; and Edwin M. Stanton, Annual Report of the Secretary of War," in *Annual Message of the President of the United States and Accompanying Documents to the Two Houses of Congress at the Commencement of the First Session of the Thirty-ninth Congress* (Washington: Government Printing Office, 1866), 6.

23. JAE to Thomas L. Rosser, May 20, 1866, in Hoyt, ed., "New Light on General Jubal A. Early after Appomattox," p. 113; and JAE to Thomas H. Carter, December 13, 1866, typescript by Robert E. L. Krick, Lee Family Papers 1732–1892, VHS.

24. See Cushman, *Bloody Promenade,* 169–70.

25. Some of the officers Early mentioned as recipients were former chief of artillery Thomas H. Carter; Lt. Cols. Carter Moore Braxton, William Nelson, and John Floyd King of the artillery; Maj. Moses Green Peyton, who had served on both Ramseur's and Grimes's staffs; Maj. Gens. Bryan Grimes, John Brown Gordon, and Henry Heth; and Brig. Gen. Armistead Lindsay Long (JAE to Carter, December 13, 1866, Lee Family Papers 1732–1892, VHS).

26. JAE to Carter, December 13, 1866, Lee Family Papers, 1732–1892, VHS; John C. Breckinridge to JAE, August, 5, 1866, Mss. vol. 4, item 733, Early Papers, LC; and JAE to Breckinridge, March 24, 1867, personal collection of William C. Davis (hereafter cited as Davis Collection).

27. For regimental histories, see Peter C. Luebke, "Shattering the Slave Power: Northern Soldiers Interpret Their Civil War," PhD diss., University of Virginia, 2014, 181–82, and "'To Transmit and Perpetuate the Fruits of This Victory': Union Regimental Histories, 1865–1866, and the Meaning of the Great Rebellion," MA thesis, University of Virginia, 2007, 7, 18. For prisoner of war narratives, see Fabian, *Unvarnished Truth,* 122–24.

28. As Early put it to his brother, Sam, "I am so much crippled up that I move about with difficulty, and am more bent than I have ever been" (JAE to Sam, May 4, 1867, Early Family Papers, Mss1EA765b 35–36, VHS).

29. JAE to Sam, May 30, June 13, August 8, 1866; February 7, June 4, 1868, Scrapbook, Early Papers, LC. JAE to John W. Daniel, February 17, 1867, John Warwick Daniel Papers, Rubenstein Library, Duke University, Durham, N.C. (repository hereafter cited as DU).

30. For example, Gordon's memoir, replete with special pleading, took full credit for the brilliant plan at Cedar Creek and none for its failure (Gordon, *Reminiscences,* 335). Historian Gary W. Gallagher also discusses Gordon's evident "egocentrism" and "willingness to play fast and loose with the truth" in his memoir (Gallagher, *Lee and His Generals,* 166). As historian Peter C. Luebke notes, however, the soldiers who authored regimental histories relied on the same process of acquiring primary sources and vetting accounts with colleagues that Early employed, especially in the years 1865–66 when Early was writing ("Shattering the Slave Power," 178, 181–82).

31. Cheng, *Plain and Noble,* 2.

32. Grant, *Report,* 15; Early, *Memoir,* 75, 34.

33. Early, *Autobiographical Sketch and Narrative,* 30.

34. Ibid., 161. McClellan's report first appeared as "Report of General George B. McClellan" in *Letter of the Secretary of War, Transmitting Report on the Organization of the Army of the Potomac and its Campaigns in Virginia and Maryland Under the Command of George B. McClellan* (Washington: Government Printing Office, 1864), 211.

35. Early, *Autobiographical Sketch and Narrative,* 104.

36. Fabian, *Unvarnished Truth,* 4, 7.

37. Early, *Memoir,* 74.

38. Ibid., 71–72. For information on the United States' "hard war" policy toward southern civilians, see Mark Grimsley, *The Hard Hand of War: Union Military Policy toward Southern Civilians, 1861–1865 1995* (New York: Cambridge University Press, 1995).

39. JAE to Sam, December 27, 1868, and two letters dated September 6, 1868, Scrapbook, Early Papers, LC; "Letter from Gen. Early (City of Mexico)," *Vindicator* (Staunton, Va.), March 16, 1866.

40. John E. Cooke, *Hammer and Rapier* (1870; rpt., New York: G. W. Dillingham, 1898), 280; John E. Cooke to JAE, March 30, 1872, Early Copies, JML.

41. Gallagher, "Jubal A. Early, The Lost Cause, and Civil War History," in Gallagher and Nolan, eds., *Myth of the Lost Cause,* 37.

42. Philip H. Sheridan, "To the Editors of the New Orleans Daily Crescent," *New Orleans Daily Crescent,* January 8, 1866, and Early, "To the Editor of the New York News," *New York News,* February 5, 1866, in "Clippings Concerning Controversy Between Sheridan and Early, January–February, 1866," Scrapbook, Early Papers, LC; Lee to JAE, March 15, 1866, George H. and Katherine M. Davis Collection, Howard-Tilton Memorial Library, Tulane University, New Orleans (hereafter cited as Davis Collection, HTML).

43. Early, *Memoir,* 141–44; Early, *Autobiographical Sketch and Narrative,* 156–68.

44. Stephen Cushman, "Walt Whitman's Real Wars," in Gary W. Gallagher and Joan Waugh, eds., *Wars within a War: Controversy and Conflict over the American Civil War* (Chapel Hill: University of North Carolina Press, 2010), 143.

45. Early, *Autobiographical Sketch and Narrative,* 170–76.

46. Ibid., 13–14.

47. Gary W. Gallagher, *Lee and His Army in Confederate History* (Chapel Hill: University of North Carolina Press, 2001), 222; Gallagher, *Lee and His Generals,* 185.

48. Early, *Memoir,* 34.

49. Stephen Berry describes southerners as liking their "leading men" to be free from apparent ambition and vanity (Berry, *All that Makes a Man: Love and Ambition in the Civil War South* [New York: Oxford University Press, 2003],18). See also Sean Wilentz, *The Rise of American Democracy: Jefferson to Lincoln* (New York: W. W. Norton, 2005), 52, which describes the interplay between elite status, character, and gentlemanly conduct, particularly regarding election campaigns.

50. Charles W. Button, *Lynchburg Daily Virginian,* January 2, 1866, p. 2.

51. JAE to Sam, August 21, 1866, Scrapbook, Early Papers, LC.

52. Krick, preface to Early, *Memoir,* vii.

53. Lee, "Farewell Address, April 10, 1865." Lee restated this purpose to Early in Lee to JAE, March 15, 1866, Davis Collection, HTML.

54. Lee to JAE, March 15, 1866, Early Family Papers, Mss1Ea765b 59, VHS.

55. For example, Lee read Early's initial letter from Havana to the *New York News* regarding numbers in the Valley campaign and was pleased with "the temper in which it was written" (Lee to JAE, March 15, 1866, Davis Collection, HTML).

56. Cheng, *Plain and Noble,* 198, explains how the most valued histories employed an objective tone, providing an account of facts without expressing opinions.

57. Lee to JAE, October 15, 1866, Davis Collection, HTML.

58. Lee to JAE, March 15, 1866, Davis Collection, HTML; JAE to Lee, November 20, 1868, Scrapbook, Early Papers, LC.

59. JAE to Edward Pollard, December 28, 1866, Scrapbook, Early Papers, LC.

60. Cooling, *Jubal Early,* 7–8.

61. Casper, *Constructing American Lives,* 5.

62. Lt. Col. George Taylor Denison, *Soldiering in Canada: Recollections and Experiences* (Toronto: George N. Morang and Co., 1900), 68, copy provided by Paul C. Culliton of Holland Landing, Ontario.

63. JAE to J. Cabell (Sam's son), August 29, 1867; JAE to Ruth (Sam's daughter), December 2, 1866; and JAE to Sam, November 3, 1868, Scrapbook, Early Papers, LC.

64. Ida Mason to My Dear Kate, August 2, 1866, Holmes Conrad Papers, MSS 1C7637a 213, VHS. See also Elizabeth A. F. Harris Diary, July 27, 1866, Early, Jubal Anderson Papers, 1846–1889, DU.

65. Early to Sam, June 19, 1867, Scrapbook, Early Papers, LC.

66. JAE to Edward Pollard, December 28, 1866, Scrapbook, Early Papers, LC. Early took serious umbrage when Pollard included him in the biography anyway (JAE to Sam, November 25, 1867, Scrapbook, Early Papers, LC).

67. Fabian, *Unvarnished Truth,* 16.

68. Early, *Autobiographical Sketch and Narrative,* xxii, xxi–xxvi.

69. Frances Clarke, *War Stories: Suffering and Sacrifice in the Civil War North* (Chicago: University of Chicago Press, 2011), 35. While Clarke focusses on northern elites, the same principle of manliness applied in the South. See Berry, *All that Makes a Man,* 191.

70. JAE to Sam, May 4, 1867, Early Family Papers, Mss1EA765b 35–36, VHS. JAE to Sam, July 15, October 28, 1867; JAE to Capt. S. H. Early, August 2, 1867, Scrapbook, Early Papers, LC. See also JAE to Sam, March 6, June 19, 1867, Scrapbook, Early Papers, LC.

71. Elizabeth A. F. Harris Diary, July 27, 1866; Early, Jubal Anderson Papers, 1846–1889, DU. See also Mrs. E. C. Wing to JAE, May 3, 1867, Jubal Early Papers, 1863–1890, 39.2 Ea5, Earl Gregg Swem Library, College of William and Mary, Williamsburg, Va. (repository hereafter cited as Swem).

72. "Sketches of Southern Generals," *Lynchburg Daily Virginian,* October 2, 1867, p.1.

73. At times the Valley was supplanted by Virginia at large. See Gary W. Gallagher, *Becoming Confederates: Paths to a New National Loyalty* (Athens: University of Georgia Press, 2013), 57–82, for more on Early's shifting loyalties to Union, Virginia, and the Confederacy.

74. *Shepherdstown* (W.Va.) *Register,* October 20, 1866; *Charles Town Spirit of Jefferson,* December 25, 1866.

75. Early, *Memoir,* 75, 119, xxi, xxiii, 120; Lee, "Farewell Address, April 10, 1865"; Early, *Autobiographical Sketch and Narrative,* 28.

76. Early, *Memoir,* 138.

77. Ibid., 71; *Shepherdstown* (W.Va.) *Register,* October 20, 1866.

78. *Charles Town Spirit of Jefferson,* December 25, 1866.

79. Ida Mason to My Dear Kate, August 2, 1866, Holmes Conrad Papers, MSS 1C7637a 213, VHS.

80. Blair, *Cities of the Dead,* 49, 53.

81. Caroline E. Janney, *Burying the Dead but Not the Past: Ladies' Memorial Associations and the Lost Cause* (Chapel Hill: University of North Carolina Press, 2008), 2.

82. Four editions of the *Memoirs* appeared in 1866–67: Toronto: Lowell & Gibson, 1866; Lynchburg, Va.: C. W. Button, 1867; New Orleans: Blelock & Co., 1867; and Augusta, Ga.: Steam Printing Presses of Chronicle & Sentinel, 1867. The best modern edition was published in 2001 by the University of South Carolina Press, bibliographical details for which are in note 1 above.

83. *Lynchburg Daily Virginian,* January 3, 1867, 3. JAE to Breckinridge, March 24, 1867, Davis Collection; Mrs. E. C. Wing to JAE, May 3, 1867, Jubal Early Papers, 1863–1890, Swem.

84. JAE to Sam, April 15, 1868, and JAE to Sam, January 22, 1867, Scrapbook, Early Papers, LC.

85. *Lynchburg Daily Virginian,* July 10, 1867, 3; JAE to Sam, January 22, 1867, Scrapbook, Early Papers, LC.

86. Fabian, *Unvarnished Truth,* 51.

87. JAE to Sam, October 28, 1867, Scrapbook, Early Papers, LC.

88. For instance, Early received $100 collected by Peyton Harrison's wife through the Southern Relief Association "as testament of Baltimore sympathy" (Peyton Harrison to JAE, November 14, 1867, Scrapbook, Early Papers, LC). In addition, while Early was in Mexico, a ship's captain had helped raise $500 in gold to ease Early's passage (JAE to John Goode Jr., June 8, 1866, Early, Jubal Anderson Papers, 1846–1889, DU).

89. *Lynchburg Daily Virginian,* July 10, 1867, 3; JAE to Lee, November 20, 1868, Lee Family Papers 1732–1892, VHS.

90. *New York Times,* August 26, 1867; *Lynchburg Daily Virginian,* August 15, 1867; *New York Times,* January 7, 1867.

91. *Lynchburg Daily Virginian,* January 18, 1867, 3; January 23, 1867, 3. "Lieutenant-General Early," *The Old Guard* (December 1866): 4, 12.

92. The first edition of *Autobiographical Sketch and Narrative of the War between the States* was published in Philadelphia by J. B. Lippincott. Three reprints of the 1912 original stand out: Indiana University Press with an introduction by Frank E. Vandiver (Bloomington, 1960); Nautical and Aviation Publishing with an introduction by Craig L. Symonds (Baltimore, 1989); and Broadfoot Publishing with an introduction by Gary W. Gallagher (Wilmington, N.C., 1989). Da Capo Press reissued the Broadfoot edition, with Gallagher's introduction, in paperback (New York, 1991).

93. JAE to Major John W. Daniel, February 17, 1867, John Warwick Daniel Papers, DU.

94. Robert Stiles, *Four Years Under Marse Robert,* 3rd ed. (New York: Neale Publishing, 1904), 190.

95. A. de Vivier, "General Jubal A. Early's 'Narrative of the War Between the States,'" *The Bookman: A Review of Books and Life* (March–August 1913): 37, 7; book review by William K.

Boyd, *Southern Atlantic Quarterly* 12 (April 1913): 180; book review by Charles W. Ramsdell, *Southwestern Historical Quarterly* 17 (July 1913): 95–96.

96. Stiles, *Four Years,* 190; JAE to Lee, November 20, 1868, Lee Family Papers 1732–1892, VHS; de Vivier, "General Early's 'Narrative,'" 37.

Charlotte Forten, ca. 1870. From Schomburg Center for
Research in Black Culture, Photographs and Prints Division,
Cartes-de-Visite Collection. Image ID DS_18SCCDV.

Considering the War from Home and the Front

Charlotte Forten's Civil War Diary Entries

BRENDA E. STEVENSON

Charlotte Forten's iconic five-volume journal chronicles her life among the South Carolina Sea Island "contrabands" during the Civil War.[1] From the time of her arrival in the "Sunny South" on the Tuesday evening of October 28, 1862, until her final entry in volume 4 on May 15, 1864, the sophisticated intellectual and inveterate abolitionist wrote of her encounters with the Fifty-Fourth Massachusetts and the First and Second South Carolina Volunteers; of the culture, living conditions, and aspirations for freedom of the Gullah people; of her interactions with "typical" Union soldiers and illustrious military figures such as Colonel Robert Gould Shaw, Colonel Thomas Wentworth Higginson, and Brigadier General Rufus Saxton; and of encounters with Harriet Tubman, who was nurse and guide to the troops. Charlotte's privately penned thoughts underscore the profound significance of the war in the imagination of African Americans, both enslaved and free. Forten's journal from her time in the South among the contraband men, women, and children; Union troops; teachers; missionaries; shopkeepers; and labor supervisors certainly was not the only one kept by a woman, or even a woman of color.[2] Nonetheless, her journal remains singularly important because of Charlotte Forten's unique status as an elite black female abolitionist and scholar. Her social status and familiarity with leading abolitionists, black and white, gave her a special entrée into the private world of her white contemporaries as they spoke to and acted on the changing status of race relations at this critical moment in the nation's history and in this hotbed of Civil War activity.

Equally significant, she allows readers to witness and benefit from her intellectual curiosity and evolving racial identity as it led her to turn ethnographic attention to the African-derived cultural and linguistic uniqueness, as well as to the social structures and experiences, of the Gullah/Geechee people located along the coasts and islands of South Carolina and Georgia. In addition, Charlotte's status as a single woman, along with her romantic and romanticist natures, fueled her Civil War writings with vignettes of an active biracial social life contextualized by the natural beauty of Low Country forests and beaches.

Charlotte Forten was an avid diarist before she turned her attention to the layered dramas of the Civil War and her part in them. Her journals give readers a comprehensive description of the personal life, education, social strivings, and activist evolution of an elite, northern female of color from adolescence through young adulthood. The journal portrayals include her extensive activist network within her African American community and across the color line among those who, like her, were dedicated to the termination of black slavery and the initiation of equality for her race. Her diary makes clear that Charlotte and many of her family, friends, and associates believed the Civil War could revolutionize the status of blacks in the United States. It really was the only reason she determined to be part of the war effort and document it in her journal. Wielding as she did this double-edged sword of black emancipation and black egalitarianism in her published poems, letters, essays, and journal entries, Forten left a formidable public, and private, record of her "sacred cause" as she pursued it through her Civil War activities. Writing on January 1, 1863, from the effusive celebration on St. Helena Island, South Carolina, to mark the issuance of President Abraham Lincoln's Emancipation Proclamation, Charlotte beamed: "Ah, what a grand, glorious day this has been. The dawn of freedom which it heralds may not break upon us at once; but it will surely come, and sooner, I believe than we had ever dared hope before. My soul is glad with an exceeding gladness."[3]

If Charlotte Forten's diary entries about the late-antebellum years and the Civil War tell us anything about their author, they vividly illustrate that issues related to race defined her life. She believed aid to her race was her singular moral duty as a woman, an African-descended person, a Christian, an elite, and an intellectual. From the time that Charlotte Louise Bridges Forten (called Lottie by her family and friends) was born to Robert Bridges Forten and Mary Virginia Woods Forten on August 17, 1837, in Philadelphia to the moment of her death on July 22, 1914, in Washington, D.C., just shy of her seventy-seventh birthday, her African-derived racial status and her resultant place in American society were constant themes in her life, in the lives of those closest to her, in the work that she pursued as a teacher, civil servant, minister's wife, literary artist, and scholar—and, of course, in her journal entries. Reading Charlotte's life through the lens of her journal entries, which she began when she was only fifteen and had just left Philadelphia to reside and attend school in Salem, one hardly could be surprised that the Civil War, in her imagination and in the activities she took on, was a struggle of liberation for four million southern black enslaved people and, more personally, a force of personal liberation for her as an activist female of color.[4]

Born just four years after the creation of the American Anti-Slavery Society[5] to a family that was centrally located on the radical side of the battle for the expulsion of slavery and the expansion of free black rights, Charlotte's destiny as a prominent "race" woman was inevitable.[6] Looking into the inner and intimate world of the young Charlotte Forten, one would find an extended family of parents, grandparents, aunts, uncles, cousins, and friends who created a home that was warm and loving, nurturing, structured, and overflowing with tireless reformers. Religion was vital to the moral and intellectual character and activities of Forten women, men, and children, and they were members of Philadelphia's venerable St. Thomas Episcopal Church. The expression of one's religious beliefs for Charlotte's family, as for many Christians of the era, especially meant service to one's community and nation. Lottie described her duty in poetic form in 1856:

In the earnest path of duty, With the high hopes and hearts sincere,
We, to useful lives aspiring, Daily meet to labor here.
Not the great and gifted only He appoints to do his will,
But each one, however lowly, Has a mission to fulfill.
Knowing this, toil we unwearied, With true hearts and purpose high;
—We would win a wreath immortal
Whose bright flowers ne'er fade and die.

Within the constructs of her time and place, that duty meant advocating the abolition of slavery and establishing black equal rights, even if that advocacy required supporting revolt, as it did in the case of her ideological backing of John Brown's 1859 insurrection in Harpers Ferry and the bloody Civil War that ripped apart the nation.[7]

It was, after all, a war whose desired consequences had been fought for by generations of her kin. Everyone in Charlotte's family, everyone she knew, admired, emulated, and loved, was in this battle for black freedom and equality. Her grandfather, the well-respected businessman James Forten, among many other abolitionist efforts publicly opposed black colonization to Africa and organized the campaign against the idea; helped to organize the first National Negro Convention; was one of the earliest and most generous supporters of William Lloyd Garrison's *Liberator*; and became the backbone, along with his sons and sons-in-law, of the American Moral Reform Society. The elder Forten, along with Charlotte's father and her uncles, commanded the core of the Philadelphia male elite helping to create, define, and sustain the antislavery movement in the City of Brotherly Love. Her brilliant father, Robert, served on the Board of Managers for the Young Men's Antislavery Society of Philadelphia and was a member of the New England Antislavery Society and the Philadelphia Vigilance Committee.[8] Charlotte's affluent, Amherst-educated uncle, Robert Purvis, not only accompanied James Forten in supporting Garrison's *Liberator* but also was known as the "godfather"/"President" of the underground railroad through his support and governance of the Philadelphia Vigilance Committee that he created in 1837.[9] Purvis also helped to found the Pennsylvania Anti-Slavery Society and the American Anti-Slavery Society in 1833 and served as president of the latter five times.[10]

Two generations of Forten men and women taught Lottie, through example and instruction, that her gender, like her race, was to have no impact on her deep commitment to and public support of black egalitarianism. The family and their close associates supported a woman's right to take up public reform efforts almost as much as they promoted abolition and racial equality. Robert Purvis was the first vice-president of the Woman's Suffrage Society, headed by Lucretia Mott.[11] All of Charlotte's female kin, moreover, were well-educated, public activists. Charlotte's mother, Virginia Woods; her grandmother Charlotte Vadine Forten; and her paternal aunts, Margaretta, Harriet, and Sarah, were all founding members of the

Philadelphia Female Anti-Slavery Society in 1833. Margaretta had helped to draft the organization's constitution and was its secretary, while Sarah served on its Board of Managers.[12] Sarah Forten Purvis also was a founding member of the Philadelphia Female Vigilance Committee, the first nonwhite vice-president of the National Women's Suffrage Association, and an active antislavery poet, sometimes publishing under the pen name "Ada."[13] Harriet Forten, Robert Purvis's spouse, was a member of the Free Produce Society, which opposed purchase of items produced by slave labor. The couple also were major activists in the American Equal Rights Association, which advocated the franchise for all men and women.[14] Indeed, the Forten sisters were so well regarded in abolitionist circles that John Greenleaf Whittier wrote the poem "To the Daughters of James Forten" in their honor.[15]

The Fortens' stately brick home on Philadelphia's Lombard Street, where Charlotte was a constant visitor and actually lived for a decade after her mother's untimely death from consumption in 1840 and her little brother's demise several weeks earlier, would have been witness to growing racial tensions, including the Lombard Street race riot of 1842, which involved black and Irish immigrant workers, and a nearby antiblack riot in 1849.[16] These violent events and the angry discussions of them by her family (Robert Purvis moved his family out of the city after the 1842 riot) would have influenced a young Lottie tremendously. Her socialization, however, was affected more by the Forten home typically being filled to the brim with radical antislavery theorists and workers, black and white. The home was also a stop on the Underground Railroad, even stocked with a trapdoor that led to a secret place for refugees from slavery to hide on their way to a more secure freedom. So too probably was the Byberry country home of Robert Purvis that served as one of Charlotte's rural retreats. William Lloyd Garrison; Charles and Sarah Remond; Lucretia Mott; Sarah Mapps Douglass and her parents, Robert and Grace; Peter Williams's family; Joseph and Amy Williams Cassey; Wendell Phillips; John Greenleaf Whittier; William Nell; Lucy Larcom; William Wells Brown; and William Still were all part of the Forten inner circle of friends and fellow reformers. Charlotte was raised for the great resistance against racial oppression, and by the time she was an adolescent, she too was publicly involved in the "family business."

Everything Charlotte did, including her own "self-improvement" efforts, was supposed to be ammunition for the struggle. Lottie had to be an exemplar of intellectual accomplishment, cultural refinement, and moral perfection in order to prove to the world that blacks were not, as was commonly believed, even among many "radical abolitionists," intellectually, socially, and culturally inferior. Black people had to demonstrate over and over again that they were naturally the equals of whites in every way and, as such, should have equal rights. Nothing, not even her health or her happiness, should have greater priority in her life. How could she, after all, be happy in a world where racism raged? Why would she even want to live in such a world that she could not hope to change? These were heady concepts and a heavy burden for the shy, introspective girl growing up in a home with a father growing more frustrated each year over the plight of his race in the United States, a frustration that eventually led Robert Forten in 1855 to emigrate to Canada and later to Great Britain with his second wife and two sons, leaving Charlotte behind to continue the fight without his financial or psychological support.[17]

It is little wonder then that Charlotte, deemed the shining star of the new generation of Forten activists and a radical woman of color, took on the mantle of immediate abolition and racial equality as her great missions in life. Her work in the Civil War as a teacher, troop supporter, war correspondent of sorts, and nurse for the Fifty-Fourth Massachusetts after its disastrous defeat at Fort Wagner, would contribute profoundly to her lifelong ambitions. But first came her intellectual and political preparations.

The Fortens were as passionate about developing their intellectual acumen as they were about abolition, temperance, women's rights, and the other social causes they embraced. Education, they believed, provided them with opportunities to know the world and the people within it. The family, like many of their free people of color friends and associates, regarded it as a basic tool of freedom for the mind, spirit, and condition—a tool, therefore, necessary for every free person and one that distinguished the free from the enslaved. Moreover, to be educated demonstrated that people of color had a natural intelligence that was equal to that of other races. Indeed, their formal education elevated the Fortens and their black associates above most white citizens at the time, given the incomplete and poor state of public education nationally, but particularly in the slaveholding South.

The Fortens had to be able not just to read and write but also to think, to analyze, to debate, and to create possible solutions to the many problems of their race. The large family spent many hours talking and debating academic, social, and political issues—discussions that had long-lasting and profound impact on the developing intellect of Lottie. James Forten Sr. attended the free primary school for black children in Philadelphia established by the famed abolitionist Anthony Benezet. His formal education ended at the age of ten when his father died and he had to go to work in order to help support his family. Still, his intellectual curiosity, the rudiments of a formal education that he had been able to get, and his continued efforts at self-education stood him well. Forten's businesses—sailmaking and real estate investments—were for a time some of the most successful and lucrative in antebellum Philadelphia, stemming in large part from his sailmaking inventions. James Forten's ability and his intellect created an expectation within his household. The family patriarch's dedication to education was matched by that of his wife. Charlotte Vadine was a teacher, and the two together socialized their children to appreciate the value of an excellent education.

James Forten supplemented his wife's teaching of their children with private tutors, trying to assure that the next generation of Forten men and women would be an intellectual force of some reckoning. The children succeeded admirably. Charlotte's father, Robert, in particular, was academically gifted. As a young man, he was known locally as a talented mathematician, poet, and orator. During his youth, he constructed a nine-foot telescope that was exhibited at Philadelphia's Franklin Institute.[18] Robert might have been considered the most intellectually accomplished—but he had stiff competition, particularly from the women in his life. His sisters Sarah and Harriet also were noted poets, Margaretta founded the Lombard School for black youth in Philadelphia, and Charlotte's mother clearly also had an impressive formal education.

Charlotte's father had especially elevated intellectual goals for his daughter. Like his father, he hired tutors for Lottie even though her Aunt Margaretta administered her school in their father's home. Robert refused, on principle, to place Charlotte in a racially segregated school. He decided to send the studious teen to board away from Philadelphia so she would have richer educational opportunities and be able to continue to evolve as an abolitionist and reformer. He chose Salem, a bustling Massachusetts city with the third largest black population in the state at the time Charlotte went to reside there.

In 1854, the year that Charlotte Forten started to keep her journal, she began to matriculate at the Higginson Grammar School in Salem, where she lived in the home of family friends—the celebrated antislavery lecturer Charles Lenox Remond, and his wife, an old Forten family friend and race activist, Amy Matilda Williams Cassey. Remond was the most important African American lecturer before Frederick Douglass arrived on the scene. His sister, Sarah Parker Remond, visited his home often. She too was a lecturer for the American Anti-Slavery Society—the first black woman to hold that distinction. Despite the close ties between the Fortens and the Casseys, however, one can only imagine Lottie's despair at being sent away from everything and everyone whom she knew intimately to a new city, a new home, and a novel and challenging intellectual world. It was, however, a sacrifice that her father and stepmother, Mary Hanscome, deemed necessary for the "cause" and Lottie's intellectual well-being.

Charlotte obliged. Although she struggled with her health—particularly through bouts of "lung fever," depression, social anxiety, and a deep longing to be reunited with her family—she thrived intellectually and became politically engaged. A year and a half after arriving in Salem, Charlotte graduated from the Higginson Grammar School with "decided éclat" and produced the winning graduation poem, which was published in the *Liberator*. It was the first of her public honors for academic merit and literary talent. In the next two years, Charlotte graduated from the Salem Normal School, ranking first in her class and again writing the best poem, which also was published in the *Liberator*. She became fluent in French and German and read Latin and Greek, voraciously exploring ancient history and philosophy, reading literary classics, and studying algebra. Forten's nightly reading schedule would cause any intellectual of the day to blush. She also played the classical piano and organ beautifully.

As was the custom for women in her family and those with whom she lived in Salem, the adolescent Lottie threw herself into the world of radical abolition soon after she arrived. She joined the biracial Salem Anti-Slavery Society in 1855 and became an active member. Along with the Remond, Purvis, and Cassey women, Charlotte routinely attended lectures, fairs, bazaars, plays, and musical recitals dedicated to the cause of abolition.

Although Lottie would not have admitted it because genteel gender conventions of the era mandated extreme modesty, and her adolescent self-doubt obscured it, she became a budding star in the antislavery movement. Many things contributed to this phenomenon, including her numerous published poems—in the *Liberator* in 1855, 1856, and 1859; in the *National*

Antislavery Standard in 1858, 1859, and 1860; and in Bishop Daniel Payne's *Anglo-African Magazine* in 1858. Her impressive antislavery pedigree and striking physical beauty also certainly played a role. By her late teens and early twenties, Charlotte was well known in most radical abolitionist quarters as a beautiful, brilliant young member of the "proscribed race," whose presence and accomplishments would put any proslavery argument linked to ideas of natural black inferiority to shame. John Greenleaf Whittier, the "Poet of Abolition" and a close friend, described Forten to Theodore Dwight Weld as "a young lady of exquisite refinement, quiet culture and ladylike and engaging manners and personal appearance. I look upon her as one of the most gifted representatives of her class."[19] A local journalist concurred, noting in 1856 that Charlotte Forten "presented in her own mental endowments and propriety of demeanor an honorable vindication of the claims of her race to the rights of mental culture and privileges of humanity."[20] By age nineteen, as the nation edged closer to division and the Civil War, Charlotte publicly lived the life of the gifted, if financially strapped, race woman.

Forten's fine education was not thought necessary just to expand her intellectual horizons, to assist in her reform efforts, or to impress those who would deem her intellectually inferior because of her race. It also was meant to provide her with a means to support herself as a single woman with no anticipated inheritance. Despite her family's earlier financial success, Robert Forten had lost most of his money, which was tied up in his father's debt-ridden sailmaking business and real estate holdings, even before Lottie moved to Salem. Her family had all been living off her stepmother's separate estate since Charlotte was a child, but most of that income had been put aside for her younger half-brothers.[21] Robert Forten's family struggled financially both at home and after he moved to Canada. By the time Lottie had completed her formal education at the Salem Normal School, it was painfully clear that she would have to be a full-time working woman in order to provide for herself. She sought help from the head of her school for a placement.

By the fall of 1859, Charlotte had acquired a position teaching at the Epes Grammar School, making her the teacher of color at a mostly white public school in Salem.[22] Within the year, however, she had to resign her position temporarily because of her poor health. She suffered terribly from "lung fever," known today as viral pneumonia. Her illness was both physically and emotionally debilitating. Charlotte, no doubt, continuously was reminded of and frightened by its deadly risks since her mother, her favorite cousins, an uncle, and two of her best friends in Salem all had died of the illness.[23] She sought treatment at a water cure in Worcester, where she met Dr. Seth Rogers, who was to become her dear friend in Massachusetts and in South Carolina when they both arrived to do service during the Civil War. One of her visits with the "excellent" doctor, she noted, "did me a world of good—spiritually as well as physically. To me he seems one of the best and noblest types of manhood I ever saw. In my heart I shall thank him always."[24] Rest and the "cure" gave Charlotte some physical ease. Nonetheless, her health problems, which grew to include poor eyesight, dragged on for the next couple of years, depriving her of much needed income and eventually driving her back to Philadelphia to reside with her grandmother, aunts, and cousins.[25] Noting her lack of funds because of illness, she wrote in 1857 after her doctor mandated that she rest instead of teach: "Shall be glad to rest if it can only be arranged so that I may have school again in the Fall. If it cannot be so, I know not what I *shall* do."[26]

Despite her popularity and intellectual acclaim in radical abolitionist circles, Lottie was terrorized by self-doubts concerning every aspect of her life—her talent, her intellectual abilities, her looks, her private relationships, her health, and even her commitment to the cause. While the abolitionist public saw her as a shining example of black feminine excellence, she saw herself as mediocre in everything she attempted, desperately trying not to fail or to be publicly exposed. Her self-doubt and criticism arose from years of enduring racist encounters in a society in which she was a numerical minority and nearly everyone thought blacks inferior, as well as from the lack of emotional and financial support from her family after she moved to Salem. Even her elite status and exceptional opportunities could not shield her from the bitter effects of racist exclusion. Writing on April 7, 1858, she noted one of the several examples of pain and humiliation: "Had a manifestation of the wicked, contemptible prejudice, which made my blood boil with indignation," she wrote. "How long, how long will this last! It is *very* hard to bear."[27]

All of her life, Charlotte strove to prove herself the equal of whites, not only to them but also to herself. Her diary revealed a pervasive sense of unworthiness and insecurity. One long entry, dated June 15, 1858, reads as a personal psalm of her deep failure. "Have been under-going a thorough self-examination," she wrote: "The result is a mingled feeling of sorrow, shame and self-contempt. Have realized more deeply and bitterly than ever in my life my own ignorance and folly. Not only am I without the gifts of Nature, Wit, beauty and talent; without the accomplishments which nearly every one of my age, whom I know, possesses; but I am not even intelligent." She could muster "not the shadow of an excuse" for these failures, which came despite her "many advantages of late years." "[I]t is entirely owing to my own want of energy, perseverance and application," she continued, "that I have not improved them. It grieves me deeply to think of this. I have read an immense quantity, and it has all amounted to nothing, because I have been too indolent and foolish to take the trouble of reflecting. I have wasted more time than I dare think of, in idle day-dreams, one of which was, how much I should know and do before I was twenty-one." Approaching twenty-one with "only a wasted life to look back upon," she confessed "to intellectual defects [and] a disposition whose despondency and fretfulness have constantly led me to look on the dark side of things, and effectually prevented me from contributing to the happiness of others; whose contrariness has often induced me to do those things which I ought not to have done, and to leave undone those things which I ought to have done, and wanted to do,—and we have as dismal a picture as one could look upon; and yet hardly dismal enough to be faithful. Of course, I want to try to reform. But how to begin!"[28]

The Civil War provided Lottie the profound opportunity to "begin again" that she desperately sought. Her desires concerning the war were, in part, the hope of many black radical abolitionists—a conflict that would bring the end to slavery in the United States. After all, the institution might have been growing in the number of enslaved and in economic importance nationally, but it already had been eliminated in most of the United States by 1861 and throughout most of the Americas—beginning in Upper Canada (Ontario) in 1793, Haiti in 1804, parts of Central America in 1824 and Mexico in 1829, gradually in the British colonies beginning in 1833, in French and Danish Caribbean colonies in 1848, and increasingly in South America (except Brazil and Surinam). In the ten years between 1813 and 1823, for example, slavery was abolished in Argentina, Columbia, and Chile. From 1831 to 1854, the institution had been outlawed in Bolivia, Uruguay, Ecuador, Peru, and Venezuela.[29] Was it such a leap, then, for many like Charlotte to hope that the Civil War would sound the death knell to slavery and open the path to free black citizenship and social equality in the United States?

War, however, was a man's domain—a white man's domain principally because black men were excluded from active service in the U.S. Army for nearly half of the Civil War. Still, Lottie longed to be part of it. She had participated in the struggle against slavery in her classrooms, as part of sewing circles, in petition drives, in her literary publications, and certainly in her private conversations and correspondence. But now was the time for a different kind of action. When John Greenleaf Whittier suggested that she apply through a northern freedmen's relief society to travel to the "Sunny South" to teach the black contrabands behind Union lines, she put aside her self-doubt and fears about her health and, for the first time, pursued a life away from her community of elite, well-educated people of color and family friends.

Although the cause of the race was her major inspiration, Charlotte also needed paid work. She wanted to be financially independent. She also yearned to make life-altering decisions, to have an experience that would build self-confidence and help her become an independent woman. At twenty-five, Charlotte was beginning to believe she might not marry or have a family. She had witnessed her Aunt Margaretta's confined life as the family spinster of her generation—taking care of aging parents and young nieces and nephews and teaching in a segregated school located in her family home. Margaretta Forten's activism in the cause had been hemmed in by her duty to family in exchange for financial dependence as a single, undercompensated teacher. Charlotte wanted more for herself. To live and work in the hated South, physically and academically to help emancipate her race, to bring support and aid to black Union soldiers and their families, permitted Charlotte to believe she was standing on the threshold of miraculous change for herself, her race, and her nation—that she was an agent of that change. This was her chance, perhaps her singular chance, she believed, to prove her Christian worth and racial equality—to rescue her race, and in so doing, to rescue herself. It also was her first chance truly to embrace her African heritage, to recognize and accept her distinction as a person of African descent. It was a profound moment in Charlotte's sense of self-realization and acceptance.

Charlotte Forten's diary detailing her life among Union soldiers and Low Country contrabands for seventeen months is, foremost, a deeply personal record of her physical, emotional, and intellectual life. Yet the Civil War started and moved quickly forward for more than a year before Lottie even mentions it in her journal. To be fair, she makes no entries between January 1, 1860, and June 22, 1862—one of the few gaps found in the first four of her five diaries that have been located. Certainly she knew of the war and its potential importance to the abolitionist cause because of her active role in radical abolitionist circles at the time. Even in the first entry once she began journal-keeping again, a summary explanation of what had occurred during the period of silence, Charlotte does not mention the Civil War. Her remarks, however, do indicate that neglect of her diary was linked to severe bouts of "lung fever" that brought her at one point "very, very near the grave." Her frail health again had curbed her financial and political ambitions, but that would not continue to be the case.[30]

Three weeks after Charlotte resumed writing in the diary, she gave her first indication of the war's relevance from her perspective. Commenting on abolitionist Wendell Phillips's famed "Address Delivered Before the Twenty-Eighth Congregational Society" at the Music Hall in Boston on July 6, 1862, she expressed complete agreement with Phillips's biting criticism of President Abraham Lincoln. Philips had used his speech to criticize Lincoln for his reluctance to use the war to force black liberation. The president's failure to do so, Philips concluded, indicated an appalling lack of leadership. "Oh dear A. let us pray to the good All Father," Forten wrote that night after returning from Phillips's speech, "to spare this noble soul [Phillips] to see the result of his life-long labors—the freedom of the slaves."[31]

Her second mention of the war came after she visited her old friend and mentor John Greenleaf Whittier and his sister Elizabeth in early August 1862.[32] Whittier, who adored Lottie and the other Forten women, whom he had met years before through their common abolitionist efforts, believed Charlotte should go to the South to try, through her teaching and example, to "uplift" the lowliest of her race—the provisionally freed contrabands in the Low Country of South Carolina. It did not take much for him to convince her to do so. On her birthday, a week after she had stayed with Whittier and his sister, Charlotte decided that, while she did not have the "accomplishments, the society, the delights of travel which I have dreamed of and longed for all my life [and] am now convinced can never be mine," the move to Port Royal could be useful. "If I can go to Port Royal, I will try to forget all these desires," she wrote: "I will pray that God in his goodness will make me noble enough to find my highest happiness in doing my duty."[33]

Whittier wrote a letter of recommendation to aid in her young friend's application for a teaching position. For the next two months, Charlotte busied herself traveling back and forth between freedmen-aid organizations in Boston and Philadelphia, chasing the opportunity to go to the heart of the Confederate States of America with Union-aligned doctors, teachers, and missionaries.

On October 22, 1862, Forten sailed from New York City for St. Helena Island, South Carolina, on one day's notice—relieved to finally be employed by the Port Royal Relief Committee as a teacher of the contrabands.[34] Her excitement was infectious. Approaching Port Royal, she exclaimed: "We were in a jubilant state of mind and sang 'John Brown' with a will. . . . [W]e soon began to feel quite at home in the very heart of Rebeldom."[35] Charlotte would be one of more than ninety persons, about one-fifth of them women, representing freedmen-relief organizations in that area. With an annual salary of about $300, Charlotte worked in the primary school that Laura Towne, a physician and teacher, and fellow instructor Ellen Murray had created on an abandoned plantation on the island.[36] She taught young children during weekdays and adults in the evenings and in Sabbath school. The needs of people there, including Union soldiers with whom she came into contact, were diverse enough to mandate that she sometimes step outside her educational role. During almost two years there, Forten labored as a missionary, nurse, music mistress, performer, seamstress, and store clerk. Her intellectual curiosity and refined manners equipped her well to take on the additional roles of explorer, keen observer, reporter, and, in addition, a much sought-after dinner companion and romantic interest. But was she as well equipped to confront "race" as manifest in the South Carolina Low Country? Unlike African Americans that Charlotte might have encountered almost anywhere else in the United States, those in the Low Country typically were Gullah, arguably the most culturally distinct, linguistically different, African Americans in North America.[37]

Her first reaction, not surprisingly, was negative: "'Twas a strange sight as our boat approached the landing at Hilton Head," she wrote upon arrival. "On the wharf was a motely assemblage,—soldiers, officers and contrabands of every hue and size. They were mostly black, however, and certainly the most dismal specimens I ever saw."[38]

For a member of Charlotte's hyperintellectual, assimilationist, multiracial, elite cadre located in the urban North, the Sea Islands and their

Gullah inhabitants proved a shock. It is not certain what she expected of the contrabands—her diary largely details expectations of herself. Race, for Charlotte, was bound up in the notion of social, political, and economic power hierarchies determined by one's skin color and phenotype, not culture. It is not clear Charlotte had considered that she would find an array of cultures among black southerners, for nothing in her formal education, or even in the lectures from former slaves she had encountered at abolitionist events in Boston, Salem, Philadelphia, or New York, really spoke to this diversity. Like most Yankee missionaries and teachers who arrived during the war, she assumed the enslaved were culturally distinct from free blacks outside of the South largely because, as slaves, they had been denied a formal education, humane treatment, and respect—not because they had managed to maintain significant attributes of ancestral western/western-central African cultures.

But Charlotte proved to be a quick study. She soon became attracted to the Low Country's Gullah people, particularly the children, whom she greatly enjoyed teaching and preparing for freedom. "We went into the school," she wrote in her diary on October 29, 1862, "and heard the children read and spell. . . . I noticed with pleasure how bright, how eager to learn many of them seem. . . . Dear children, born in slavery but free at last! . . . My heart goes out to you. I shall be glad to do all that I can to help you."[39]

Charlotte also was interested in and committed to their parents and the other adults she encountered. She searched deeply to understand the cultural context of their lives and developed an appreciation of it and its practitioners. While she was not initially comfortable with the cultural and class differences between herself and the "contraband," the predominance of the "black race" in her temporary home reassured Charlotte, and even comforted her. The coast of South Carolina—Beaufort, St. Helena, Edisto, and the other islands that Charlotte visited—with its magnificent flora and fauna, its physical warmth, the ocean and marshes, its teeming black population, military victories, and resulting "freedom" proved to be a perfect setting for new introspection and communal experiences for Charlotte. She felt serenely happy and fulfilled during most of her stay.

Forten fell in love with the Low Country Gullah people, who, she quickly realized, shared with her the burdens of their race and a desire for freedom. She often recorded in her journal small biographies of the formerly enslaved with whom she came into daily contact—lauding (sometimes romanticizing, occasionally with a patronizing tone) their heroism and survival of the physical and psychological pain they had endured under slavery. She summarized, for example, the story of the centenarian Daphne, who had been brought as an enslaved adolescent from Africa just after the American Revolution.[40] Forten wrote the story of "old Harriet," the child of Africans who lost three of her children to the domestic trade and who spoke a "very foreign tongue"; of Harriet's daughter Tillah and Tillah's husband, "a gallant looking young soldier—a member of the black regiment," and their sweet baby who died soon after birth; and of Celia, "one of the best women on the place," Charlotte explained, "a cripple" because "her feet and limbs were so badly frozen by exposure that her legs were obliged to be amputated just above her knees." "But she," Charlotte added admiringly, "manages to get about almost as actively as any of the others. Her husband, Thomas, has been a soldier, and is now quite ill with pneumonia."[41]

Forten's journal captured many other stories of these black people she met and served. Indeed, Lottie was so moved by her sense of *belonging,* in a somewhat superficial but nevertheless primal manner, to the contrabands that she even fantasized about building a family of her own by adopting one of their children—which would have meant her becoming part of their community and culture and they part of hers. Not even she could fully understand her exposed passion, her profound sense of being connected to this community of contrabands. "It is a very wild thing," she noted, "I am quite in love with one of the children here—little Amaretta. . . . She is a cunning little kittenish thing with such a gentle demure look. She is not quite black, and has pretty, close hair but delicate features. She is bright too. I love the child. Wish I c[ou]ld take her for my own."[42]

Charlotte was mesmerized by, and found beauty in, the sound of voices and linguistic difference in the Gullah people's language, the movement, rituals, clothing styles, and sense of time that recalled African cultural antecedents. The rhythm and harmony of their voices prompted her to ask the Gullah people, even the children, again and again, to sing for her. Soon after reaching Beaufort, Charlotte heard her first "concert" by boatmen hired to row the northerners to St. Helena. "As we glided along," she wrote, "the rich sonorous tones of boatmen broke upon the evening stillness. Their singing impressed me much. It was so sweet and strange and solemn. . . . It was very, very impressive. I want to hear these men sing Whittier's 'Song of the Negro Boatmen.'"[43] Once she finally arrived at her school, again it was the people's singing and dance movements that deeply affected her. "The singing delighted me most," she noted: "They sang beautifully in their rich, sweet, clear tones, and with that peculiar swaying motion which I had noticed before in the older people, and which seems to make their singing all the more effective." Charlotte often celebrated characteristic forms of Gullah movement in religious ritual, particularly the ring shout. "This evening," she wrote in May of 1863, "the people, after 'Praise,' had one of the grandest shouts, and Lizzie and I, in a dark corner of the Praise House amused ourselves with practicing a little. It is wonderful that perfect time the people keep with hands, feet and indeed with every part of the body. I enjoy these 'shouts' very much."[44]

Ritualized events among Low Country blacks, she came to understand, also meant special clothing quite distinctive from what she, as an elite free woman of color from the North, had been socialized to believe appropriate for solemn, or serious, occasions. Bright-colored handkerchiefs as symbols of celebration adorned the heads of women, who wore white for sacred rituals such as baptism and at funerals. "Clean gowns on, clean head handkerchiefs, bright colored, of course," she remarked of one church service. "I noticed that some had even reached the dignity of straw hats, with bright feathers."[45] And time, in Forten's opinion, was something simply not well kept. Both as a testament to their lives and work in an agrarian economy, as well as to different concepts of time influenced by their western/western-central African cultural origins, the Gullah did not, from Lottie's northern, industrialized perspective, either arrive or leave "on time." She attributed this tardiness to the general lack of clocks and the Gullah people's inability to tell time.[46]

Although Charlotte initially chafed at the tardiness of adults and children alike, she soon found herself loosening some of the tight controls that had defined her life before she moved among them. Similarly, female gender conventions that bound her like a tight corset in Salem, Boston, Philadelphia, and New York began to give way as she blossomed in her new freedom. She slept late, routinely rode horseback, owned and was prepared to shoot a handgun, flirted a great deal with several of the officers stationed nearby, and even fell passionately in love with one of them. Overall, her life as a Civil War teacher among the contrabands and Union army in South Carolina proved fulfilling in ways she had never allowed herself completely to anticipate.

Before long, in fact, Charlotte began to understand that, no matter what her professional and political intentions had been when she applied for her teaching position, life in a military zone prompted, indeed demanded, profound personal change. She did remain a little shy and certainly experienced moments of the self-doubt and depression that had shadowed her as a sickly adolescent and young adult. But Forten's life in South Carolina changed forever her self-perception as a woman and as a person of African descent—of what she could expect to enjoy in her life and what she had to contribute to society.

Forten's diaries document these transformations as they unfolded within herself and also as she observed them among her fellow teachers, plantation supervisors, the contrabands, and the black and white men who fought for the Union. Much of her assessment of how well individuals performed their duties to the war effort was based, not surprisingly, on her perception of how they perceived and interacted with black people—the contrabands, soldiers, and herself. They had to be, in Charlotte's estimation, "true friends" of the "People." She believed that most of the teachers were such friends. She described her supervisor, Laura Towne, for example, as "the most indispensable person on the place, and the people are devoted to her. And indeed she is quite a remarkable young lady. . . . I like her energy and decision of character." Ellen Murray, their associate, was "whole-souled warm-hearted."[47] Charlotte had noticed, however, that some of the Union officers, as well as some of the plantation supervisors sent to manage the valuable cotton crop, were racists who "should not come here." Of the supervisors' interactions with contrabands, she added, some are "strongly prejudiced against them and they have a contemptuous way of speaking of them that I do not like."[48] Having spent her public life exposed to the racist gaze in the antebellum North, Forten was keenly aware that some of the Union officers did not believe black soldiers were sufficiently courageous, disciplined, or intelligent.

Charlotte did establish close personal relationships with Union officers such as Brigadier General Rufus Saxton and, most especially, Colonel Thomas Wentworth Higginson, commander of the First South Carolina Volunteers, whom she remembered as a staunch supporter of the fugitive slave Anthony Burns. Higginson's regiment consisted of approximately seven hundred black men from Florida, Georgia, and South Carolina. Charlotte deeply admired these officers' efforts in the war, particularly their leadership of black southern soldiers. She appreciated the sustained emotional and physical burden the command and care of these troops prompted and openly worried about their health. Speaking of Colonel Higginson, she noted that "Col. H. is a perfectly delightful person in private.—So genial, so witty, so kind. But I noticed when he was silent, a care-worn almost sad expression on his earnest, noble face."[49]

Charlotte was deeply concerned with the treatment and fate of the black soldiers she encountered, particularly their physical survival, the well-being of their families, how well they demonstrated their military ability, and the ways in which white army officers treated them. Taking note of a dress parade she witnessed with the First South Carolina Volunteers—on the occasion of the grand celebration of the Emancipation Proclamation—Forten could not contain her pride and hope for the future of these men whom she believed held the destiny of their race in their hands. Conversely, she bitterly resented anyone who appraised their military skill and potential as free men with less enthusiasm. "The Dress Parade—the first I have ever seen—delighted me," she wrote. "It was a brilliant sight—the lone line of men in their brilliant uniforms, with bayonets gleaming in the sunlight," she continued. "The Col. looked splendid. The Dr. said the men went through the drill remarkably well. It seemed to me nothing could be more perfect. To me it was a grand triumph—that black regiment doing itself honor in the sight of the white officers, many of whom, doubtless 'came to scoff.' It was typical of what the race, so long down-trodden and degraded will yet achieve on this continent."[50]

Charlotte was extremely honored, as well, to meet Harriet Tubman in Beaufort. She and some of her peers spent a day with Tubman while the famed formerly enslaved woman recounted her efforts to assist fugitive slaves to freedom and to provide intelligence to, and serve in, the Union military. "She is a wonderful woman—a real heroine," Charlotte pronounced in her diary. "How exciting it was to hear her tell her story. . . . My own eyes were full as I listened to her. . . . I am glad I saw her—*very* glad."[51]

Charlotte was never more impressed than when she met Colonel Robert Gould Shaw, commander of the Fifty-Fourth Massachusetts Infantry, and his African American troops. Their first encounter occurred on July 2,

1863, when Shaw and Major Edward Needles Hallowell, the regiment's second in command, visited the home Lottie shared with Laura Towne and other teachers in order to have tea. She was immediately enthralled with the young Bostonian. "I am perfectly charmed with Col. Shaw," she gushed. "He seems to me in every way one of the most delightful persons I have ever met. There is something girlish about him, and yet I never saw anyone more manly. To me he seems a thoroughly lovable person. And there is something so exquisite about him." Although she had "seen him but once, yet I cannot help feeling a really affectionate admiration for him. We had a very pleasant talk on the moonlit piazza, and then went to the Praise House to see the shout. The Col. looked and listened with the deepest interest. And after it was over, expressed himself much gratified."[52]

A subsequent visit heightened her enthusiasm for Shaw. "What purity, what nobleness of soul," she wrote, "what exquisite gentleness in that beautiful face! As I look at it I think 'the bravest are the tenderest.' . . . May his life be spared to her! [his mother]."[53] Charlotte made a point to request his safety in the lists that comprised her daily prayers. "God bless him!" she scrawled on July 8, "God keep him in His care, and grant that his men may do nobly and prove themselves worthy of him!"[54]

Charlotte was devastated when, on July 20, she received the news of the Fifty-Fourth's disastrous defeat at Fort Wagner two days early. The report indicated that one-tenth of the regiment was lost, including Robert Shaw. Her journal captured her pain from that week: "[O]ur (*ours* especially he seems to me) noble, beautiful Colonel is killed and the regt. cut to pieces," she confessed.[55] "To-night comes news oh, so sad, so heart sickening," she confided in her diary a few hours later. "I cannot, cannot believe . . . I can scarcely write. There was an attack on Fort Wagner. The 54th put in advance; fought bravely, desperately, but was finally overpowered and driven back after getting into the Fort. Thank Heaven! They fought bravely."[56] The following day Charlotte set aside her teaching and went to Beaufort in order to nurse the soldiers of the Fifty-Fourth, which she did, as well as mending their torn and shot up uniforms, writing letters home for them, and generally trying to cheer their "brave, grateful hearts" for the next several days.[57]

Charlotte's experiences with freed people, as well as soldiers, teachers, and other Union sympathizers, included romantic encounters. Indeed, Forten's diaries from the Civil War era strongly suggest that she fell in love with one particular officer—Dr. Seth Rogers, who had been one of her personal physicians in Massachusetts. Rogers was born in 1823 and raised as a Quaker on a farm in Danby, Vermont. Like Charlotte, he was an ardent and radical abolitionist. He had left his business, as owner and resident physician of the Worcester Hydropathic Institution, to serve as surgeon alongside his longtime friend Higginson in the first organized southern black Union regiment to fight in the Civil War. Higginson and Rogers had a history as abolitionists together—the two had helped organize the Massachusetts Kansas Aid Committee to keep Kansas "free soil" in the 1850s. Rogers was married to Hannah Mitchell, and they shared a daughter, Isabel, who was eight in 1863.[58]

A married, older white man hardly was an eligible bachelor, but Rogers's marital status must have reassured Lottie that her feelings would not be realized physically, thereby avoiding a scandal that neither she nor he likely would survive. Her emotional involvement with a white man, moreover, would not have been beyond Lottie's emotional capability or even yearning. Biracial social relationships were not novel in her family. Charlotte's mother, stepmother, and uncles Robert and Joseph Purvis were all the children of biracial relationships between black women and white men—men who had made certain their children were well educated and very secure financially. At age twenty-five, with few past romantic encounters, Charlotte had a freedom during her Civil War experience that provided a ripe time to experience her first great love.

Despite their racial differences, Lottie and Seth were quite compatible. She found him to be well educated, friendly, attentive, and compassionate—and devoted to black freedom and equality. They also shared a love of nature, horseback riding, and reading. He seemed to be equally attracted to Charlotte, and with good reason. By most accounts, she was beautiful, brilliant, and had the open admiration and social acceptance of Rogers's dear friend Thomas Higginson. Rogers also was a friendly, familiar face from Charlotte's Massachusetts home. Seth would confide to his wife that Charlotte was the same for him. "But the dearest friend I found among them," he wrote regarding his first week at Camp Saxon, "was Miss [Charlotte] Forten, whom you remember. She is a teacher of the freed children on St. Helena Island."[59] Charlotte wrote more passionately in her diary of that same meeting: "Just as my foot touched the plank, on landing, a hand grabbed mine and a well known voice spoke my name. It was my dear and noble friend, Dr Seth Rogers. I cannot tell you dear Ami how delighted I was to see him; how *good* it was to see a friend from the North, and *such* a friend."[60] She later wrote of the "*unspeakable*" happiness she experienced when they met. "But I fear for his health," she confessed," I fear the exposure of a camp life. Am glad to see that he has warm robes and blankets, to keep him comfortable. I wish I c'ld do something for him."[61]

The romance flourished over the next year as Lottie and Seth continued to have regular contact and spend time with mutual friends. When Charlotte was ill, Dr. Rogers came to attend to her, as he did the week following their first meeting. Charlotte was delighted to see him on that occasion, though he could only stay a short while. During that visit, the doctor extracted a promise from Charlotte. "He said he would write to me often if I would write to him," she noted. "I shall do so gladly, for the sake of having letters from him. I don't deserve it I know."[62]

In the meantime, Rogers continued to correspond with his wife, describing his life in the South. A month after arriving, he confessed that he had tried to get Colonel Higginson to confiscate a piano they found in a warehouse and bring it to St. Helena. "I thought it would especially please Miss Forten to have it in her school," he explained. In the interim, the two had seen each other. He had written to Charlotte two more times—letting her know that he would be away on an expedition with the First South Carolina and describing how he was occupying his time. Charlotte, fearful that Seth had not received a letter she had sent, was openly anxious: "I fear he has not got my note. Not that 'twas of much importance, but I w'ld like him to know how constantly I think of him."[63]

Charlotte was elated when Dr. Rogers returned to the area with his regiment a few weeks later. Soon thereafter, he paid her a visit, sharing copious notes of what had transpired with the regiment while they were away. "It makes me so happy to see him safe back again," she wrote. "The kind, loving words he spoke to me to-night sank deep into my heart." But Rogers's words that evening were perhaps not exactly what Charlotte wanted to hear. It seemed that time away had given him an opportunity to get some emotional distance from the young teacher. He wanted her, he explained, to think of him as a brother. Charlotte complied but could not check her attraction. She noted in her diary: "He was in full uniform to-day. Makes a splendid looking officer. I looked at him and his horse with childish admiration."[64]

Dr. Rogers also seemed to have difficulty pulling back. The next day he sought Charlotte out and walked her to school while confessing that "he wished he lived nearer that he might come in and read to me sometimes."[65] Ten days later, Seth and Charlotte shared dinner and then rode alone by horseback four miles. It was, Charlotte testified, "the most delightful ride I ever had in my life." The two stopped in the beautiful coastal woods, filled with flowers and scented evergreens. Upon dismounting, Rogers gathered and then wrapped long sprays of jasmine around Lottie's body, making her feel "as grand as a queen" and prompting one eyewitness to convey a sense of surprise. Of their trip back, Charlotte wrote almost in a swoon: "The young moon [was] just a silver bow—had a singular, almost violet tinge, and all around it in the heavens was a rosy glow, deepening every moment which was wonderfully beautiful." "How wild and unreal it all seemed," she continued in her journal, "and what happiness it was as we rode slowly along. . . . There is such a magnetism about him impossible to resist. I can never be thankful enough."[66] It was that same evening that Dr. Rogers told Charlotte that Col. Higginson intended for her to travel with the First South Carolina on its next expedition.[67] The following day, Dr. Rogers returned to his camp, and a day later Charlotte arrived, bringing him some of her ginger cakes. It was not the first time she had appealed to his sweet tooth. Writing to his wife the week earlier, the doctor had observed: "Yesterday, Miss Forten sent me, from St. Helena Island, a generous box of ginger cakes. I don't know how she learned my weakness."[68]

Their next few meetings, which usually occurred on weekends, involved exchanges of gifts and intimate conversation. Charlotte even spent time alone in Dr. Rogers's tent during her visit on February 21, 1863. When apart she mended his socks and sent copies of his much-loved contraband songs; he sent her sweet notes and her favorite flowers. The two wrote often, and he even sent her a note that his eight-year-old daughter Isabel had sent to him. "Indeed, it is very kind of him to let me see this little note," she confessed. "It somehow brings me closer to him." The thought of never seeing him again, Charlotte wrote, "makes my heat ache."[69] Two months passed with the two exchanging letters frequently. On April 3, Charlotte recorded that she had received a letter from Dr. Rogers and "a very light, pretty rocking chair" he sent as a gift. "He says he will see me soon and tell me *all*," she wrote, adding wistfully: "I hope it will be very soon, indeed. I do long to see him."[70]

Dr. Rogers did return after a couple of weeks, and the two continued to meet regularly, ride and dine together, and exchange intimacies. The plan for Charlotte to accompany the First South Carolina as a teacher for the enlisted men, however, fell through. Charlotte wrote in her journal on May 18 that Seth arrived bringing her a letter from Colonel Higginson. The colonel did not mince words—he could not allow Charlotte to accompany his regiment because "there have been of late scandalous reports of some of the ladies down here."[71] It seemed as if Charlotte and Seth had been found out, or at least their behavior had raised enough eyebrows to cause their mutual friend Higginson to take matters into his own hands.

Not surprisingly, the relationship between Forten and Rogers cooled soon thereafter, although they remained close. Lottie made a conscious effort to shift her attentions elsewhere—to Edward Pierce, for one.[72] Pierce, who supervised operations in the Sea Islands for the federal government, was young, well educated (Harvard and Brown), single, and quite attentive to Charlotte. He offered just the distraction she and Seth needed to bring their relationship back within the bounds of propriety. Pierce was, she confessed, "always so kind, so full of noble sympathy, and of eager enthusiasm in the great work in which he is engaged."[73]

After her nursing stint with the Fifty-Fourth Massachusetts following the debacle at Fort Wagner, Charlotte returned to Philadelphia for much-needed rest. She traveled with other weary and depressed teachers, labor supervisors, and military personnel, including Seth Rogers and Edward Pierce. Although Seth subsequently returned to South Carolina with Charlotte on the same ship, their romantic moment seemed to have passed. The last mention of Dr. Rogers in her diary occurs on October 16, 1863, in which she describes their trip from New York to Hilton Head: "In spite of the pleasant company with me . . . had a rather dreary voyage being half sick nearly all the time."[74] Charlotte left the beautiful Sea Islands, her magnificent Gullah people, Laura Towne, Edward Pierce, and her "good" Dr. Rogers seven months later. Her father, who had returned from England to serve in the Union army, had died on April 24, 1864, of typhus in their Philadelphia home. It was time for Charlotte to bring an end to her Civil War experience. Grief-stricken and sick, she traveled back to Philadelphia to find other ways to continue her duty to her race.

The Civil War had changed Forten profoundly, as it had all those she knew at home and untold others throughout the nation. For years to come, she recalled her time in the war, having committed so much of it to her diary. She used her entries to inform letters to William Lloyd Garrison regarding the efforts of aid societies, military forces, missionaries, and the federal government to liberate the contrabands. He subsequently published them in the *Liberator* in 1862. A two-part article, which Charlotte called "Life on the Sea Islands," appeared in the *Atlantic Monthly* in 1864.[75] Her published writings helped the cause of the newly freed for material, medical, educational, and social assistance in the wake of war depredations and a hostile white southern master class that sought to maintain white supremacy.

The rich content of Charlotte Forten's diary entries from her time in the Sea Islands remained unavailable to a substantial audience until the middle of the twentieth century. The first published version, edited by Ray Allen Billington, appeared in 1953 under the title *The Journal of Charlotte L. Forten: A Free Negro in the Slave Era*. Billington included about two-thirds of the first four journals but none of the fifth in his edition, omitting a considerable amount of important information from the antebellum and war years relating to Forten's relationships and intellectual development. Thirty-five years later, as part of the Schomburg Library of Nineteenth-Century Black Women Writers, Oxford University Press published all the journals with full scholarly annotation. As editor of the new edition, I drew on several decades of scholarship that had enriched the literature since the early 1950s, which helped frame Forten's life and what she had written in her journals. In wealth of detail and historical value, the unabridged journals rank among the best and most revealing of those produced by the wartime generation. Readers seeking memorable testimony from the Civil War can turn with profit to the sections devoted to Forten's experiences in South Carolina. They convey wonderful insights into a remarkable young woman as well as providing an invaluable snapshot of the immense social, political, and military developments that unfolded in the South Carolina Low Country.[76]

NOTES

1. Charlotte Forten Grimké completed five journals, the third and fourth of which contain her Civil War entries. The dates for the five are as follows: Journal 1, 1854–56; Journal 2,

1857–58; Journal 3, 1858–63; Journal 4, 1863–64; Journal 5, 1885–92. The manuscript copies of the originals are in the Moorland-Spingarn Research Center, Howard University, Washington, D.C. All quotations in this essay are from *The Journals of Charlotte Forten Grimké*, ed. Brenda E. Stevenson (New York: Oxford University Press, 1988).

2. See, for example, other published journals of Forten's contemporaries, including: Laura Matilda Towne, *Letters and Diary of Laura M. Towne: Written from the Sea Islands of South Carolina, 1862–1884*, ed. Rupert Sargent Holland (1912; rpt., Ithaca, N.Y.: Cornell University Library, 2009); Thomas Wentworth Higginson, *Army Life in a Black Regiment and Other Writings* (1870; rpt., New York: Penguin Classics, 1997); Susie King Taylor, *Reminiscences of My Life in Camp With the 33d United States Colored Troops, Late 1st S.C. Volunteers* (1902; rpt., Laconia, N.H.: Laconia Publishers, 2016); Esther Hill Hawks, *A Woman Doctor's Civil War: Esther Hill Hawks' Diary*, ed. Gerald Schwartz (Columbia: University of South Carolina Press, 1984); and Cyrus F. Boyd, *The Civil War Diary of Cyrus F. Boyd, Fifteenth Iowa Infantry, 1861–1863*, ed. Mildred Thorne (1953; rpt., Diamond Bar, Calif.: Golden Springs Publishing, 2016).

3. Grimké, *Journals*, 434.

4. For details about Forten's early life and family, see Brenda E. Stevenson's introduction to Grimké, *Journals*, 3–55.

5. On January 6, 1832, abolitionist publisher and activist William Lloyd Garrison met in Boston with eleven other men, none of them of African descent, to form the New England Anti-Slavery Society (NEASS). The American Anti-Slavery Society (AASS), a biracial umbrella organization of men and women that encouraged the development of state and local affiliates, was formed in December 1833, with a number of members from the NEASS as well as twenty-one Quakers; three blacks, including Robert Purvis; and four women (Brenda E. Stevenson, *What Is Slavery?* [London: Polity Press, 2015], 164; Mark L. Kamrath, "American Anti-Slavery Society," in *Slavery in the United States: A Social, Political, and Historical Encyclopedia*, ed. Junius P. Rodriguez, 2 vols. [Santa Barbara, Calif.: ABC-Clio, 2007], 2:161–62).

6. Regarding the illustrious Forten and Purvis families, see, for example: Grimké, *Journals*; Julie Winch, *A Gentleman of Color: The Life of James Forten* (New York: Oxford University Press, 2003); Winch, *Philadelphia's Black Elite: Activism, Accommodation, and the Struggle for Autonomy, 1787–1848* (Philadelphia: Temple University Press, 1988); Margaret Hope Bacon, *But One Race: The Life of Robert Purvis* (Albany: State University of New York, 2007); Janice Sumler-Lewis, "The Forten-Purvis Women of Philadelphia and the Anti-Slavery Crusade," *Journal of Negro History* 6 (Winter 1981–82): 281–88.

7. Regarding John Brown, see Grimké, *Journals*, 390.

8. "Robert Bridges Forten," *The Forten Family*, Fine Ancestry Project, 2009, establisher. angelfire.com/fortens.html.

9. Margaret Hope Bacon, "The Double Curse of Sex and Color: Robert Purvis and Human Rights," *Pennsylvania Magazine of History and Biography* 121 (January–April 1997): 63.

10. Margaret Hope Bacon, "Robert Purvis: President of the Underground Railroad," hsp. org/sites/default/files/legacy_files/migrated/legaciespurvis.pdf; Joseph A. Boromé, Jacob C. White, Robert B. Ayres, and J. M. McKim, "The Philadelphia Vigilance Committee," *Pennsylvania Magazine of History and Biography* 92 (July 1968): 321.

11. Bacon, "Robert Purvis."

12. Sumler-Lewis, "Forten-Purvis Women of Philadelphia," 283–85.

13. Don Ammerman, "Purvis, Sarah Forten (c. 1811–c. 1898)," *Women in World History: A Biographical Encyclopedia,* 2002, www.encyclopedia.com/women/encyclopedias-almanacs-transcripts-and-maps/purvis-sarah-forten-c-1811-c-1898.

14. Sumler-Lewis, "Forten-Purvis Women of Philadelphia," 285.

15. Stevenson, "Introduction" to Grimké, *Journals,* 8–9.

16. Patrick Grubbs, "Riots (1830s and 1840s)," *The Encyclopedia of Greater Philadelphia,* philadelphiaencyclopedia.org/archive/riots-1830s-and-1840s/; Elizabeth M. Geffen, "Violence in Philadelphia in the 1840s and 1850s," *Pennsylvania History* 36 (October 1969): 387–88; Winch, *A Gentleman of Color* (Kindle Edition), location 5481.

17. Robert Bridges Forten remarried after the death of Charlotte's mother. He and his wife had two sons. They moved, in 1855, to Canada, staying until 1858. That year, they moved to England, where they remained until 1862 ("Robert Bridges Forten").

18. Winch, *A Gentleman of Color,* Kindle location 4771.

19. Stevenson, "Introduction" to Grimké, *Journals,* 32–33.

20. Ibid.

21. Winch, *A Gentleman of Color,* Kindle locations 5714–23.

22. Ibid., Kindle location 5937.

23. Stevenson, "Introduction" to Grimké, *Journals,* 34.

24. Grimké, *Journals,* 363.

25. Ibid., xxxii–xxxvi.

26. Stevenson, "Introduction" to Grimké, *Journals,* 35.

27. Grimké, *Journals,* 299.

28. Ibid., 315–16.

29. Stevenson, *What Is Slavery?* table 4.4, "Abolition time line (The Americas and the Caribbean)," 163.

30. Grimké, *Journals,* 362–63.

31. Ibid., 369.

32. Ibid., 372–74.

33. Ibid., 376.

34. Ibid., 380–82. On the relief efforts at Port Royal, see G. K. Eggleston, "The Work of Relief Societies During the Civil War," *Journal of Negro History* 14 (July 1929): 272–99 (regarding the number of aid workers, see 272); Willie Lee Rose, *Rehearsal for Reconstruction: The Port Royal Experiment* (1964; rpt., New York: Oxford University Press, 1976); Ruth Clark, *Strangers and Sojourners at Port Royal* (Cambridge, U.K.: Cambridge University Press, 2014).

35. Grimké, *Journals,* 390.

36. Regarding teacher's salaries, see Eggleston, "The Work of Relief Societies," 277.

37. Regarding the Gullah people, see, for example: William S. Pollitzer, *The Gullah People and Their African Heritage* (Athens: University of Georgia Press, 1999); Lorenzo Dow Turner, *Africanisms in the Gullah Dialect* (Chicago: University of Chicago Press, 1949); Michael Montgomery, ed., *The Crucible of Carolina: Essays in the Development of Gullah Language and Culture* (Athens: University of Georgia Press, 1994).

38. Grimké, *Journals,* 388.

39. Ibid., 391.

40. Ibid., 439.

41. Ibid., 412.

42. Ibid., 410.

43. Ibid., 389–90.

44. Ibid., 482.

45. Ibid., 393.

46. Ibid.

47. Ibid., 392.

48. Ibid., 419–20.

49. Ibid., 433.

50. Ibid., 432.

51. Ibid., 442.

52. Ibid., 409–10.

53. Ibid., 493.

54. Ibid., 494.

55. Ibid.

56. Ibid.

57. Ibid., 496.

58. "Wartime Letters from Seth Rogers, M.D., Surgeon of the First South Carolina, Afterwards the Thirty-Third U.S.C.T., 1862–1863," *Florida History Online,* floridahistoryonline/Projects/Rogers/index.html.

59. Dr. Seth Rogers to Hannah Rogers, January 1, 1863, "Wartime Letters from Seth Rogers, M.D."

60. Grimké, *Journals,* 428–29.

61. Ibid., 434.

62. Ibid., 436.

63. Ibid., 440.

64. Ibid., 447.

65. Ibid.

66. Ibid., 454–55.

67. Ibid., 455.

68. Dr. Seth Rogers to Hannah Rogers, February 5, 1863, "Wartime Letters from Seth Rogers, M.D."

69. Grimké, *Journals*, 461.

70. Ibid., 468.

71. Ibid., 484.

72. Regarding his work at Port Royal, South Carolina, see United States Department of the Treasury, *The Freedmen of Port Royal, South Carolina. Official Reports of Edward L. Pierce* (New York: Rebellion Records, 1863).

73. Grimké, *Journals,* 455.

74. Ibid., 508.

75. *The Liberator,* December 12, 19, 1862; *Atlantic Monthly*, May, June 1864.

76. Charlotte L. Forten, *The Journal of Charlotte L. Forten: A Free Negro in the Slave Era,* ed. Ray Allen Billington (1953; paperback ed., New York: W. W. Norton, 1981).

"Mrs. James Chesnut, Jr. From a Portrait in Oil." Frontispiece for
the first published edition of Mary Boykin Chesnut's diary. From
Mary Boykin Chesnut, *A Diary from Dixie, as written by Mary Boykin
Chesnut, wife of James Chesnut, Jr., United States Senator from South
Carolina, 1859–1861, and afterward an Aide to Jefferson Davis and
Brigadier-General in the Confederate Army,* ed. Isabella D. Martin
and Myrta Lockett Avary (New York: D. Appleton and Co., 1905).

"Forget to Weep My Dead"

Mary Chesnut's Civil War Reading

SARAH E. GARDNER

Few Civil War diaries have enjoyed the critical and popular success of Mary Chesnut's record of America at its crossroad. Three editions, two of which were reprinted decades after their initial publication, as well as a prominent place in Ken Burns's epic documentary series *The Civil War,* have secured the diary's place in the canon. Chesnut has become for many the defining voice of the Civil War. Each generation, it seems, needs its Mary Chesnut. Historian Catherine Clinton said as much in her piece for the *New York Times* "Disunion" series, itself a kind of phenomenon that captured the zeitgeist of the nation at the war's sesquicentennial. "Chesnut's writing provides a renewable energy source for those of us seeking to better understand the Confederate experience," Clinton observed for the *Times* blog, suggesting as well that part of the diary's enduring fascination rests with its resistance to genre conventions. Is it a diary or a novel, reminiscence or autobiography, memoir or history? In this sense, the diary becomes a problem to be solved, one too tempting to ignore. "In any case," Clinton concluded, "readers find her work hard to put down, as Chesnut has become the most cited eyewitness to the Civil War era."[1]

Yet the diary's hybridity was not always celebrated. Indeed, different generations have praised the diary for different reasons. Time of publication mattered. So did the ways in which the various editors pitched the diary to their readers. Chesnut's account might hold a universal appeal, but the facets of the diary that fostered interest changed with different sets of assumptions and expectations.

This essay begins with an examination of the three published editions of the diary that appeared in the twentieth century. What gets left in and what gets thrown by the wayside, what gets silently corrected, escapes the blue pencil altogether, or bears the traces of a heavy-handed academic reflects the priorities of editors and publishers whose primary concern is prospective audience. Suffice it to say that the audience does not remain constant. Like any other text, Chesnut's diary attracted unintended readers that play a part in the work's reception. Having set the stage with a consideration of the three editions, the essay then turns to its primary concern, Mary Chesnut's reading, which provides another way to understand the diary. What Chesnut read and how she read profoundly influenced her authorial decisions as well as how she understood the events of her time.

"Earthquakes as Usual"

The process by which Chesnut's diary first found its way into print is almost the stuff of legend, in part because each of the editors tells a different version of the story. As C. Vann Woodward, the last of the three editors, noted, Chesnut kept "an extensive diary intermittently during the years of the Confederacy." These diaries—or "Journal," the term Chesnut often used to refer to them—were never intended for publication. The internal evidence, Woodward demonstrates, makes that clear.[2] The introduction to the first edition, published in 1905, puts matters a bit differently: "Mrs. Chesnut wrote her Diary from day to day as the mood or occasion prompted her to do so. The fortunes of war changed the places of her abode almost as frequently as the seasons changed, but wherever she might be the Diary was continued."[3] Woodward thus complicated the diary by highlighting the significant gaps in Chesnut's writing and by pointing out that the wartime journal was for Chesnut's eyes only. The original introduction suggested to readers that Chesnut struggled heroically to maintain her diary even in the toughest of circumstances. And nowhere did it suggest that the document of the 1860s differed substantially from the published version.

All three editions, in varying degrees, acknowledged Chesnut's revisions of the diaries in the 1880s. The introduction to the 1905 edition stressed the text's authenticity: "The Diary, as it now exists in forty-eight thin volumes . . . , is entirely in Mrs. Chesnut's handwriting. She originally wrote it on what was known as 'Confederate paper,' but transcribed it afterward."[4] "Transcribe," as we shall see, is a gross understatement. Because the second editor, novelist Ben Ames Williams, took the original introduction largely at face value, the introduction to his 1949 edition hardly clarified the degree of revision. "The original . . . Diary filled some four hundred book pages," Williams explained. The 1905 edition ran to nearly 150,000 words, he told readers; "the manuscript copy of the complete Diary contains nearly 400,000. Since Mrs. Chesnut herself made the first copy for the original, the magnitude of the task suggests the vigor of her character."[5] "Made the first copy" does not suggest Chesnut's substantial revisions to the original journal.

Woodward told a different story. Between 1881 and 1884 Chesnut wrote "two full drafts of the book she now was determined to make of her Journal and her Civil War experience." Much of this material survives and suggested to Woodward that the first version was a "working draft" that Chesnut wrote alongside the second, "from day to day rather than completed in advance of it." It is equally clear that Chesnut did not consider the second version "a final and finished copy." Woodward cited an 1883 letter from Chesnut to Varina Davis explaining the process of revision. "'How I wish you could read over my journal,' Chesnut sighed. 'I have been two years overlooking it—copying—leaving myself out. You must see it—before it goes to print— but that may not be just now. I mean the printing—for I must overhaul it again—and again.'"[6] Chesnut never had the chance to overhaul her work. She died a few years later, leaving her book unfinished.

The 1905 and 1949 editions of Chesnut's work thus sought to present their readers a straightforward and unquestionable version of the diary. Woodward instead dwelled on the messiness of the text and emphasized the extent of Chensut's revisions. Note his word choice in this passage: "In exploiting material from her Journal of the sixties for her simulated diary of the eighties, Mary Chesnut took many liberties. She omitted much but usually added more than the amount omitted or condensed." In some cases, she elaborated on incidents recorded in the journal; in other cases, she invented new material. These were not minor edits. Woodward also pointed out that Chesnut never settled on an appropriate opening scene for her book. Instead, she left her editors "four alternative beginnings, three of them incomplete or mutilated drafts, which treat events in the three months before she actually began to keep her Journal, and a fourth, a retrospective introduction probably written at the time which she began the Journal." It was up to the editors to decide where to begin, a point that the 1905 and the 1949 editions fail to acknowledge. Because editorial practices had varied widely, different generations of readers had read a very different Chesnut.

Turn-of-the-century readers interested in the Civil War had much literary fare from which to choose. The first iteration of Chesnut's magnum opus joined a crowded field, a point made clear by historian William E. Dodd in his *New York Times* review of the work. "Still the civil war literature grows!" Dodd exclaimed. "Volumes of reminiscences, letters, formal treatises have made their appearance every year since the close of the great struggle." Dodd continued: "More than 300 separate works treating the events of 1860–1865 are listed as authoritative historical sources in the best bibliographies of the subject, many others have probably some claim to the students' attention." The popular success of any given work depended on how the story was told, Dodd suggested. The thirst for information about the war had not been sated, and "the story teller who can dress up the war heroes with a little romance and less historic incident are sure of his fortune and his fame."[7] For obvious reasons, then, D. Appleton had a vested interest in the diary's marketability, especially since there were, as the firm readily acknowledged, "several other similar books announced by other houses" ready for publication. *A Diary from Dixie*'s first editors, Isabella Martin, to whom Chesnut had trusted her heavily revised manuscript shortly before she died in 1886, and Myrta Lockett Avary, whose *A Virginia Girl in the Civil War* had sold well the previous year, soon found themselves engaged in protracted disputes with their publisher over how best to package the diary to this new reading audience.[8]

Among other things, Appleton's Francis W. Halsey forced Avary and Martin to purge nearly three-quarters of the revised text, claiming that publishing an unexpurgated version would be "fateful to its sale." In addition, Halsey had provided his own introduction to the diary, which Avary and Martin had found wanting. They considered his characterization of Chesnut as "the personification of the Old South," for example, simply wrong-headed. Chesnut was too cosmopolitan to be described in such provincial terms, they believed, ascribing her "breadth of vision" and her "satire" not merely to her southern heritage to but to human nature. "It is . . .

in this dual character," they explained, "that the South would accept best her criticism of persons and happenings."[9] But Appleton was unconcerned with southern readers.

Indeed, Halsey suggested the diary carry a second introduction written by a northern historian. Although Avary conceded that there are "some things which a northern man might say which Miss Martin and I do not say and can not say gracefully, but which might add to the books [*sic*] *uniqueness* and interest in the North," she did not want to "overburden" the text. "I fear, sometimes," she explained of the diary, "that its wings will be so freighted that it may not fly so swift or as far as it might have gone with a word from any of us 'explainer generals.'" Whether anyone at Appleton picked up on Avary's echo of Chesnut's oft-used descriptor of herself is unclear. Appleton's dismissal of the editors' plea, however, was obvious. "We expect the largest sale will come from the North," W. W. Appleton wrote to Martin, threatening that the diary "would fail of a proper reception unless it were authenticated by the fullest explanations." Indeed, so determined were Halsey and Appleton to cater to a northern reading audience that the former suggested dedicating the volume "to the men and women of the North who would understand."[10]

A Diary from Dixie fared well with readers and reviewers. Dodd, for his part, situated Chesnut's diary in the conciliatory culture that shaped much of the rhetoric of the war at the turn of the twentieth century. "The truth is we are all beginning to see that great crisis in American history in proper perspective," he wrote. Appealing to Confederate generals John B. Gordon and Robert E. Lee, Dodd concluded "there was not all of right on one side and all of wrong on the other." Perhaps to render Chesnut more sympathetic to a northern reading audience, Dodd made clear that she and her cohort "were not extremists; they had not been ardent nullifiers." Chesnut, Dodd told his readers, "regretted the seeming necessity of secession," realizing almost immediately the tremendous odds faced by the Confederacy. When defeat inevitably came, Dodd assured his readers, Chesnut considered slavery's demise "a relief rather than . . . an irreparable injury." Though the volume was riddled with historical inaccuracies, in large measure attributable to Chesnut's penchant for "accumulating her information and 'writing up' the happenings of some ones at a sitting," Dodd nonetheless imagined the diary would find purchase with both the general reader and the serious student of history.[11]

Dodd was correct. *A Diary from Dixie* had a kind of staying power that publishers crave. Indeed, twenty-four years after initial publication, Appleton reissued the diary, this time to a Depression-era audience, perhaps well attuned to accounts of privation and hardship. Two decades later, novelist Ben Ames Williams, who had relied heavily on *A Diary for Dixie* for his Civil War novel *House Divided* (1947), "was invited to edit a new edition" of what was well on its way to becoming a canonical text of the war. Now the diary faced a different kind of reading audience, one that had emerged victorious from World War II and experienced economic growth and financial stability that had been unknown for the past twenty years. This was an audience nursed on Civil War epics, including Stark Young's *So Red the Rose* (1934), Margaret Mitchell's *Gone with the Wind* (1936), and Hervey Allen's *Action at Aquila* (1938). Nonfiction titles enjoyed heretofore unprecedented popularity, with Douglas Southall Freeman's Pulitzer Prize–winning four-volume biography of General Robert E. Lee being the most famous. Williams's task, then, was to pitch the diary to an audience already familiar with certain tropes and conceits about the Confederacy.[12]

Williams did so with ease. "The complete Diary reveals to the present editor," he wrote in his introduction to the 1949 edition, "a hitherto undiscovered country; a southern society where remote and untouchable ladies in crinoline relish a scandalous piece of gossip or a risqué jest, and where gentlemen may share these well-spiced conversations." This is heady stuff that betrays the hand of a novelist who had subscribed fully to the notion of a chivalric South that seemed more virtuous than not. In fact, he ascribed to Chesnut a similar literary and philosophic bent. "Here are men and women of flesh and blood," he continued, "infinitely more human in their faults, their flirtations and frivolities, their sins and their sorrows, their laughter and their tears than the lay figures which march solemnly through the pages of so many books of fact and fiction dealing with the Southern scene." Chesnut's diary has something for everyone, Williams implied: "[T]he noble and the base, the cruel and the tender, the weaklings and the strong, they are all here in abounding measure." Houghton Mifflin's advertising department could hardly ask for better copy.[13]

In addition to placing Chesnut's diary in a framework that readers would likely understand, Williams had to distinguish his edition from the earlier one. He did so by noting that what made Chesnut's diary a singular achievement was precisely what Martin and Avary had edited out. Williams shared some assumptions about Martin and Avary's editorial practices, not all of them correct. "The portions which they eliminated," he explained in his introduction, "either because they might offend persons then living, or because they shocked the editors, or because they presented a picture of conditions under slavery which the editors hoped might be forgotten—proved when the whole Diary was copied to be its most interesting passages." Williams singled out the previous editors' decisions to remove almost in its entirety the courtship of General John Bell Hood and Sally "Buck" Preston, to elide letters written by Varina Davis, and to cut almost all of "the occasionally faintly off-color but deliciously amusing remarks of Mrs. Chesnut or her friends."[14]

Williams also made editorial decisions, admitting that he left out nearly a quarter of the unpublished material. He, too, elided material—in this case poems and quotations—and condensed or omitted most of the letters that Chesnut had transcribed. Finally, he "blue-penciled incidents lacking either human or historical interest." Williams claimed to be motivated by interests other than those that had animated Avary and Martin. The previous editors worried about sensitive, salacious, or offensive material, he suggested, and thus sought to protect both their historical subjects and their readers from much of the diary's content. Williams, however, merely wished to put out a truer and more interesting edition. "The attempt has been made to make the Diary easily readable without doing violence to Mrs. Chesnut's own words; so occasionally," he confessed, "a noun or a verb has been supplied, or a phrase inserted or transposed; and the dashes which were her usual form of punctuation have been replaced by more conventional marks."[15] In this way, Williams cast himself as the more benign editor, one who labored solely for the benefit of his reader.

Betty Smith, author of the best-selling novel *A Tree Grows in Brooklyn* (1943), penned the review of Williams's edition for the *New York Times*. The *Times*'s decision to choose a novelist, rather than a historian, to assess the new edition of the diary is telling. Smith seemed very much attuned to Williams's prose. Indeed, her effusive review suggests, at least in part, the influence of Williams's introduction. The similarities between the introduction and the review are striking. In describing Chesnut's treatment of antebellum southern society, for example, Smith wrote, "Fragile crinoline ladies, and gentlemen in tight-fitting pantaloons, enjoyed discussing scandal and laughed over risqué jokes. They made love as hard as they rode horses, and they hated in the same degree. They flirted and were trivial; they sinned and they philandered. They had their faults and their dreams. They had plenty of courage. And they were flesh and blood."[16] Echoes of Williams' introduction—not merely in content but also in form and tone—reverberate throughout her review.

Smith also took to heart Williams's account of his editorial practices. Without naming Martin and Avary, she indulged in an invidious comparison: "In editing another's material, most editors throw their weight around and freely delete and revise to suit their personal notions of what is dull—what is interesting. They are also prone to make numerous comments and evaluations of the material." Williams committed no such sins, according to Smith. In fact, he did the opposite. Rather than deleting, he added material, and "except for an affectionate foreword" made no intrusions in the text.[17]

Academics who penned reviews for professional journals were less taken with Williams's editorial practices. Although they appreciated a new edition from which to draw, most chastised Williams for his heavy hand. Wendell Holmes Stephenson, writing in the *American Historical Review,* predicted that Williams's editorial "liberties" would "disturb the meticulous historian, already dissatisfied with an inexact reproduction in the earlier edition." The reviewer for the *Mississippi Valley Historical Review* imagined scholars "shudder[ing]" at Williams's work. Most historians shared Henry T. Shanks's view, which appeared in the *Journal of Southern History,* that ultimately, Williams produced "not a scholarly work" but a "human and valuable document" that marks an improvement over the 1905 edition.[18] An improvement is hardly the ideal, however. Stephenson thus concluded that though historians would continue to consult *A Diary from Dixie,* sloppy editing aside, "they will also continue to hope for an accurate and definitive edition."[19]

That edition came in 1981, when Yale University Press published C. Vann Woodward's *Mary Chesnut's Civil War,* one year after Harvard University Press reissued Ben Ames Williams's edition. Interestingly, both the reissue of Williams's edition and Woodward's new one begin with a nod to literary critic Edmund Wilson, whose discussion of Chesnut in his 1962 study of Civil War literature had proven so influential to a generation of scholars. Wilson had praised Chesnut as an astute observer and as a gifted writer, a combination he considered rare among Civil War diarists.[20] The reissue of the 1949 edition of *A Diary from Dixie* merely appended the chapter in which Wilson discusses Chesnut, "Three Confederate Ladies," as a foreword to Williams's text. Wilson's commentary serves to validate continued interest in Chesnut and, by implication, yet another reprint of *A Diary from Dixie*. Chesnut's diary, Wilson had written, "is an extraordinary document—in its informal department, a masterpiece." It is worth dwelling on this passage from Wilson, for it serves as part of Woodward's opening paragraph in *Mary Chesnut's Civil War*. "Mrs. Chesnut is a very clever woman," Wilson had written, "who knows something of Europe as well as of Washington and who has read a good deal of history as well as other kinds of literature. Not only is she fully aware of the world-wide importance of the national crisis at one of the foci of which she finds herself; she has also, it would seem, a decided sense of the literary possibilities of her subject." "The very rhythm of her opening pages," he continued in another passage Woodward quoted, "puts us under the spell of a writer who is not merely jotting down her days but establishing, as a novelist does, an atmosphere, and emotional tone."[21] Although Williams never discussed the literariness of Chesnut's diary, he did acknowledge his indebtedness to Chesnut as he penned his novel *House Divided*.

Woodward, however, confronted the diary's literary qualities at the outset, in part because he did not want readers to lose sight of its value as a document of the war. Emphatic on this point, Woodward chided critics for distracting readers from the diary's central purpose. "What the critics had before them was, of course, clearly entitled a diary and was presented as such by its several editors," he lectured. "Moreover, it bore all the familiar characteristics of the genre." It proceeds chronologically, starting at one point and ending at another. The entries are dated. The narrator records her own experiences, "and they are 'real-life' experiences," Woodward added, "flesh-and-blood people, real events and crises, private and public, domestic as well as historic." Equally important, Chesnut conforms to the "style, tone, and circumstantial limitations of the diarist and conveys fully the sense of chaotic daily life." "To all appearances," he concluded, Chesnut "respects the Latin meaning of *diarium* and its denial of knowledge of the future." Chesnut managed "all this in addition to," or perhaps in spite of, her "'uncanny' anticipation and exploitation of 'the literary possibilities of her subject.'"[22]

Woodward seemed to conflate "literary" with "fiction" and thus "untrue." And that is not how he wished to read Chesnut's diary. So even though Chesnut tried her hand at writing fiction in the 1870s—and thus honed her skills at characterization and dialogue, narration, setting a scene—as well as substantially revising her diary in the 1880s, we are still left, according to Woodward, with a diary. The work remains a diary because "the integrity of the author's experience and perception is maintained in this transformation." To Woodward, that mattered more than a literal accounting of events. And the diary endures not because of the information it contains but because it endows "life and reality" to "people and events" and "evokes the chaos and complexity of a society at war."[23]

Many of Woodward's critics agreed, although he did receive some flak for his decision to work from Chesnut's revisions and not her original 1860s journal, thereby challenging "conventional editorial wisdom."[24] The most damning review came from Johns Hopkins professor Kenneth S. Lynn in the *New York Times*. Lynn conceded that Woodward had produced "not only the fullest ever published, but editorially the most careful by far," but he chastised Woodward for not calling the diary what it was: a hoax. For Lynn, the real value of Woodward's edition rested with its exposure that the diary generations of critics and readers had tripped over themselves praising was written not in the 1860s, but in the 1880s. Lynn seems to take perverse pleasure in imagining the comeuppance these critics surely must feel and credits Woodward's liberal politics for the refusal to recognize the consequences of his work. "C. Vann Woodward believes that Mrs. Chesnut's mind was illuminated by advanced ideas, and in Mr. Woodward's distinguished but rather too anxiously liberal books on southern history, the faults of forward-looking citizens are always explained away when they are not simply ignored," asserted Lynn. "In his new edition of Mrs. Chesnut's diary, Mr. Woodward hails the author as an abolitionist and a feminist—nay, as a 'militant feminist.' Should a woman with such compelling political credentials also be remembered as the perpetrator of one of the most audacious frauds in the history of American literature? Perish the thought."[25] Few of Woodward's colleagues subscribed to Lynn's position—at least in print. The reviews, even those that question Woodward's editorial decisions, acknowledge *Mary Chesnut's Civil War* as the definitive version. For that reason, Anne Frior Scott concluded, "Historians and literary scholars alike owe [Woodward] a debt of gratitude."[26]

One point that Lynn conceded to *Mary Chesnut's Civil War* was its restoration of "obscure English novels" to the diary. Woodward restored much more than that, however. Understanding Mary Chesnut's reading is essential to understanding her diary, and earlier editions had removed what the editors or publishers considered trivialities. They also tried to tame the text by erasing the confusion of genres that characterizes Chesnut's revisions. Woodward's does not. And it is only his version that allows us to read Mary Chesnut's reading, to see its importance to her understanding of the war as well as to the methods she employed to convey that understanding through the written word.

"Thackeray is dead."

So Mary Chestnut closed her journal entry for January 21, 1864. Chesnut had counted the British domestic novelist among her favorite authors, and she grieved at the news of his death. "I stumbled upon *Vanity Fair* for myself," she recalled. "I had never heard of Thackeray before. I think it was in 1850. I know I had been ill at the New York hotel. And when left alone I slipped downstairs and into a bookstore that I had noticed under the hotel for something to read. They gave me the first half. I can recall the very kind of paper it was printed on—and the illustrations as they took effect upon me. And yet when I raved of it and was wild for the other half, there were people who said it was slow!! That he was evidently a coarse, dull, sneering writer, that he stripped human nature bare, made it repulsive, &c&c&c."[27]

There is much to tease out of this one entry: the obvious and palpable delight Chesnut took in books as material objects; her acknowledgment of how the illustrations and the paper's feel influenced her experience as a reader; Chesnut's well-developed literary sensibility that had led her to Thackeray; and her independent mind that allowed her to dismiss those critics who found Thackeray either tedious, offensive, or perhaps both. Chesnut littered her diary with these sorts of comments. Some are brief. Many are enigmatic. But they are everywhere.

Not surprisingly, a number of critics and scholars have commented on Mary Chesnut's reading, including Edmund Wilson, Daniel Aaron, Elisabeth Muhlenfeld, Michael O'Brien, and, of course, C. Vann Woodward.[28] The first three, all literary critics, and the fourth, an intellectual historian of the antebellum South, were perhaps more attuned to the importance of Chesnut's reading. The last, a political historian of the postbellum South, came around more slowly. But even Woodward understood eventually that Chesnut's readerly comments were no mere trivialities. As he finished work on his edition of the diary, Woodward received a short note from Aaron, who had recently written about Chesnut in his now classic 1973 study, *The Unwritten War*. Aaron alerted Woodward to Chesnut's penchant for Thackeray, suggesting that he might spend a profitable night or two rereading the 1852 novel *Henry Esmond*. "I would swear that Mrs. C's admiration for [Thackeray]," Aaron surmised, "went further than mere pleasure in his style."[29] But Woodward had already reached that conclusion, noting for Aaron other places in the text that revealed her admiration for the British novelist.

More recently, Julia A. Stern has entered the conversation, with *Mary Chesnut's Civil War Epic,* a title which can only be read as a playful, yet deliberate, jab at both Woodward, who had failed to see "Civil War" as a modifier for the real subject, "epic," and at Aaron, who maintained that the literary masterpiece of the American Civil War had yet to be written. Stern, at least as much as O'Brien and perhaps even more so, commented on Chesnut's literary-mindedness as critical to her "creative process."[30] Yet for all that has been said about Mary Chesnut's reading, there is still more to say. Those who have written on Chesnut often appeal to her reader reports to remark on her cultivated sensibilities and her idiosyncratic and individuated literary predilections. Chesnut emerges from these discussions as extraordinarily refined, as someone who stands apart from what many considered to be an unlettered region.[31] But those reports tell us so much more.

First, Chesnut's reading influenced how she structured her diary. In this sense, she was exemplary. No other Civil War–era reader turned commentator so closely hewed to genre conventions, structure, and narrative strategies as Chesnut. As anyone who has read the diary knows, she had a lot to say. The question was, how to say it. Chesnut's reading led to her understanding that different observations, different thoughts, different stories demanded different modes of expression. Her diary thus reflects this understanding and moves seamlessly from the epigrammatic to the vignette, from dialogue to chronicle. No casual reader could have made those kinds of narrative decisions.

Second, her reading—what she read, when she read, how she read—tells us a great deal about the intersection of Chesnut's intellectual imagination and her wartime experience. In this sense, she was not exemplary but like countless other Civil War–era readers who turned to reading for myriad reasons, many of which have been underappreciated by scholars. Paying attention to Mary Chesnut's reading fundamentally changes how we read her diary as well as how we understand the importance of reading in Civil War America.

Chesnut's capacious literary tastes matter. "Somebody sent me *Denis Duval*," she noted of Thackeray's last novel, published posthumously, "and it was borne in on me sadly. You have got all you are ever to get from Thackeray."[32] The British domestic novelist certainly loomed large in Chesnut's literary imagination. Yet she admired others as well. Edmund Wilson was perhaps the briefest on this point, writing simply that Chesnut "read a good deal of history as well as of other kinds of literature."[33] Woodward said more, making "much of her Anglophile reading," noting that "few of her English contemporaries" had escaped her notice. "She read as they were published, usually, or as soon as she could get hold of them, the books of Dickens, Carlyle, Trollope, . . . Disraeli, Tennyson, the Brownings, George Eliot, Charlotte Brontë, Charles Kingsley, Charles Reade, and George Meredith," along with her beloved Thackeray.[34] To shore up his point, Woodward cited a passage from the 1870s version of the diary that did not make it into his edition: "I was always up to my ears in English novels, English reviews, English talk talk." Even if Chesnut chafed at English arrogance, Woodward noted, "English opinion and standards claimed her special attention, if not her deference."[35]

Yet Chesnut's reading was even broader than Woodward suggested. O'Brien noted that she "read the usual English authors, old and new, and one, Jane Austen, seldom read in America." She read little Russian literature; some German—Goethe, Schiller, and Richter—but not Kant or Hegel. "These were old fashioned tastes," O'Brien judged, unlike those she had in French literature, which were more contemporary: "Balzac, Sand, Dumas, Merimee, and Sue, but no Baudelaire, Rimbaud, or Flaubert." Her literary predilections ran to older French authors, too, including Montaigne, Molière, and above all, Pascal. "In all things reading," O'Brien concluded, Chesnut "seems to have preferred narratives of social interaction with a marked edge; things that flirt with cynicism."[36]

Unsurprisingly, then, Chesnut had little patience for "feminine domestic novels," finding them too much filled with "piety and pie-making." Chesnut summarized one such novel—1860's *Say and Seal*—as a tale of a "housemaid's duties made divine—when a beautiful girl does broom work—sweeping, dusting, kneading dough." "The hero is a Christian," Chesnut continued with palpable traces of contempt, and is armed head to foot with religious tracts. "He kisses close and often—calls down a blessing from heaven on every embrace—and every caress is chronicled and sanctified by a scriptural reference. The hero stands by the heroine lovingly and watches her get breakfast, dinner, and supper. He admires her butter-making, scrubbing, and making up of beds, and all the honest work she glories in."[37]

Tone matters here, and by the time readers come across this passage they know Chesnut well enough to hear the mocking disapproval of a cultivated reader who finds such obvious moralizing tiresome. No wonder, then, scholars have had much to say about Chesnut's reading, for her commentaries often reveal something about her attitude toward society and toward herself. In this same passage Chesnut cannot quite figure out why the hero disparages the housemaid's dressmaking when he admires her other "honest work."[38]

The woman who emerges from the pages of the diary is cosmopolitan. Chesnut was, as Woodward observed, "a provincial in a residential sense only." She was also heretical, at least on slavery (but not race) and on conventional gender relations, as her response to *Say and Seal* suggests. Indeed, her reader reports, although not always her tastes, often reflect a kind of critical distance—if not complete alienation—from her society, something we moderns have come to expect in our intellectuals.[39] Her wit was wry, often mordant, and sometimes quite puckish. Once, after having read Anthony Trollope's *Framley Parsonage,* Chesnut thumbed her nose at William Gilmore Simms, the South's preeminent literary critic, who had sneered at the British domestic novelist, counting among his only fans "thirteen old maids and forty or fifty fashionable ladies . . . sighing in secret." Chesnut was having none of it. "How much I owe the pleasure of my life," she wrote mischievously, "to these much reviled writers of fiction."[40] Comments such as these invite Chesnut's readers to share in the author's irreverent delight in reading across the grain.

Chesnut's capacious reading did more than amuse her. For one thing, it influenced profoundly her authorial decisions. The diary's structure, the framing of the narrative content, and the storytelling itself all owe a debt to Chesnut's reading. Put another way, she could not have written the diary the way she did had she not turned to other texts as inspiration, as a model for conveying thought. Because different genres convey different modes of thinking, Chesnut turned to particular narrative forms to fit particular circumstances. One example will suffice. Chesnut mentions Pascal only twice in the Woodward edition (not at all in the Martin/Avary or Williams editions), once to relate a religious disagreement she had with an acquaintance and later to catalogue the "traveling" library that accompanied her when she fled South Carolina in advance of Sherman's army. Yet Pascal is all over Chesnut's diary. "In a revolution shy men are run over. No one stops to pick them up." "Jealousy of the past is most of women's hell." "All comes to grief with the unlucky, the shrinking, or the daring." Flip to almost any page and something similar appears. "The possibilities of slavery the same everywhere." "Unstable as water, thou shall not excel."[41]

Chesnut does not transcribe Pascal in her journal, but without question these are her pensées. She was given to the epigrammatic, "to distilled moments of wisdom or observation, that might help to comprehend life's hurly-burly," as Michael O'Brien has explained.[42] Epigrams share a similar purpose for Pascal and Chesnut, even if the subject matter differed. "The real fascination" of the *Pensées,* one Pascal scholar has written, rests with "the frequency with which Pascal's imagination returns to certain cardinal points."[43] The same holds true for Chesnut's epigrams. For Pascal, those points centered on the religious difficulties occasioned by the confrontation between faith and doubt. Chesnut harbored entirely different concerns, of course. Hers centered on human foibles and on the demise of a civilization about which she was often ambivalent but for whose ultimate triumph she desperately yearned. Yet her intellectual indebtedness to Pascal is palpable. Read individually, her epigrams make little sense. Read as a constitutive part of a whole, however, we can better see how they contribute to the human drama that unfolds in Chesnut's diary.

Editors of the first two editions of the diary thought differently. Pascal is not everywhere in these editions. In fact, he is nowhere because the editors chose to excise Chesnut's epigrams from the text. A number of reasons might explain these editorial choices. Fransis W. Halsey had counseled Avary to include only those sections that related directly to the war and thus illustrated "the social and domestic conditions of the South." Avary resisted, declaring that there was more to Chesnut's diary than "war history— there is psychological interest, social development, the woman's personality, her keen criticism of people and things, her bon mots." "Women's talks of the war between the states are plentiful," she informed Halsey, "but such wit, such *esprit* as this, NO!" Halsey, however, remained unpersuaded.[44]

But something else is at play here. These earlier editions attempt to render Chesnut's "diary" into a coherent narrative. Williams admitted as much in his introduction. Certainly these earlier versions flow in a way that Woodward's does not. The epigrams seemingly disrupt "the story," appear disembodied from the text, and disorient the reader. Woodward understood early on that much was sacrificed for readability. He declared Williams's edition "a pretty shabby performance" in a 1964 letter to historian Avery O. Craven, for example, observing that Williams made "erratic and unaccountable omissions."[45] To be sure, Woodward did not refer here specifically or exclusively to Williams's deletions of Chesnut's epigrams; Woodward had just made his initial foray into Chesnut's manuscripts. At this point, he barely knew what he was getting himself into and was asking Craven's advice on whether he should publish a new edition of the diaries. Yet, whatever Woodward thought in 1964, he certainly understood fifteen years later the importance of these brief observations. Whether he appreciated how much Chesnut pulled from Pascal remains unclear, inasmuch as he failed to comment on the epigrams themselves or their frequent and sustained appearance in the diary.

Another and perhaps more obvious influence Chesnut's reading had on the diary's composition concerns storytelling. The recurring cast of characters and plotlines, the comings and goings of the powerbrokers and the inconsequential, the sophisticated and the boorish, of friends and foes, cosmopolitans and provincials, intimates and strangers, owes much to Honoré de Balzac, who was, according to one critic, "The Napoleon of realism"[46]—and to her beloved Thackeray. "There are scenes of all sorts: some dreadful combats, some grand and lofty horse-riding, some scenes of high life, and some very middling indeed."[47] So wrote Thackeray in his prologue to *Vanity Fair.* So, too, did Chesnut in her diary—just not in those words. In essence, she was writing at times her own *Comedie Humaine,* at others, her own *Vanity Fair.*

Through a hundred novels and stories that stage fifty years of French history, Balzac "peopled a literary empire." If Napoleon won his empire on the battlefields, Balzac "won his at his desk, writing," we are told, "through long nights alone, wearing a monk's robe, drinking black coffee as thick as soup while" Paris slept. Balzac described his writing as a struggle, a battle to be won: "Memories come up at the double bearing the standards which are to lead the troops into battle. . . . The artillery of logic thunders along with its supply wagons and shells. Brilliant notions join the combat as sharpshooters. The characters don their costumes, the paper is covered with ink, the battle has begun."[48] Chesnut peopled a civilization, if not an empire, too, and it is worth noting that both Balzac and Chesnut saw their worlds crumble to ruin in their lifetimes. "A faithful watcher have I been from my youth upward—of men and manners," Chesnut described herself. "Society has been for me only an enlarged field for character study."[49]

Still, Chesnut thought of the writing processes differently from Balzac, even if she did refer to herself as the "Explainer General."[50] At times she attempted a kind of objectivity. "These memoirs pour servir[51] may future day afford dates, facts, and prove useful to more important people than I am," she explained. "I do not wish to do any harm or to hurt anyone. If any scandalous stories creep in, they are easily burned off. It is hard, in such a hurry as things are in, to separate wheat from chaff."[52]

But Chesnut was hardly objective, and she certainly could not discern while the war waged the relevant from the irrelevant, the gratuitous or malicious from the revelatory or illuminating. And she seems to have known that. Very early on, before the shelling of Fort Sumter, Chesnut admitted: "I think this journal will be disadvantageous for me, for I spend the time now like a spider, spinning my own entrails instead of reading, as my habit was at all spare moments."[53] She could never achieve the critical distance of a Balzac or a Thackeray. Chesnut was, as she was acutely aware, quite literally a character in her own drama. Early in the diary, by way of one example, she recorded a scene, complete with lines of dialogue parceled out to various speakers, including herself—first as the "Explainer," and later as "the chorus."[54] Yet her diary is not an exercise is solipsism. She, like Balzac, peopled her world with a remarkable cast of characters. Her diary teems with voices, only one of which is hers.[55]

On occasion, Chesnut made explicit the connection between her reading and her social commentary. "Last night I sat up until one o'clock, reading a very bad book," she noted in mid-January 1862. The book that she had read the night before was *The Muse of the Department,* a story that had appeared in *Scenes of Provincial Life,* a volume in *The Human Comedy.* Chesnut often appended negative adjectives to Balzac's work—*La Cousine*

Bette she pronounced "utterly abominable," by way of example—but that is because she found the subject matter distasteful. Yet Balzac had few rivals when it came to his insights into the human condition, and she continued to consult *The Human Comedy* as she sought ways to frame her discussion of her wartime existence.

A turn to *The Muse of the Department,* which, though "bad" was nonetheless "enchanting because [of] its portraitures of the absurdities of village life," illustrates this point. "Country life is so finely illustrated to me daily, to me who suffers under it so," she noted. Chesnut then became much more specific, adding, "Think of the emptiness of life in wartimes. Mr. Hay, the reverend gentleman, tells a story nearly a month old against the Ropers. They sat by a pump and ate apples Christmas Day in the streets of Camden. Streets as desert as Sahara."[56] Here, Chesnut moved quickly and easily from stale gossip to war's hardships. How best to blend the mundane with the profound, how to document the elision between what once would have been considered tragedy with what now is ordinary—these are the kinds of questions Chesnut faced as she reworked her diary. Here, and in so many other instances, she looked to Balzac.

She also looked to Thackeray, but for other reasons. What had made the British novelist so detestable to many of Chesnut's contemporaries was his critical eye, his biting wit, and his irreverent satire, precisely those qualities Chesnut most appreciated. "My dear reader," Thackeray warned, "will please to remember that . . . Vanity Fair is a very vain, wicked, foolish place, full of all sorts of humbugs and falsenesses and pretentions. And while the moralist professes to wear neither gown nor bands"—the mark of the clergy—"yet, look you, one is bound to speak the truth as far as one knows it . . . and a deal of disagreeable matter must come out of the course of such an undertaking."[57] Thackeray's description of Vanity Fair applied equally to Camden, South Carolina, and Chesnut enjoyed deflating the puffery. Consider her evisceration of a northern "literary lady" with whom she was sucked into a drawing room conversation. The visitor had launched "a violent attack upon this mischief-making South Carolina," Chesnut recounted. "She told me she was a successful writer of the day. But when I found she used the word 'incredible' for 'incredulous,' I said not a word in defense of my native land. I left her incredible."[58]

At times, Chesnut's comments were personal. "A beautiful and deceitful minx has been to talk me over," she recorded snippily in the spring of

1862. "I found her charming while she was here. Utterly forgot my opinion of her while she was beguiling me." But the minx did more than beguile. Worse, she pinched the Goethe novel Chesnut had been reading: "Now in cold blood I think it all over. I trust her as little as ever."[59] Thackeray could hardly improve on this scene of social backbiting.

Thackeray was more than a satirist, however. He was also a historical novelist. This is essential, for historical novelists create characters that act out their lives in real places and in real times. It is worth remembering that *Vanity Fair* is set against the backdrop of the Napoleonic Wars. Like Thackeray, Chesnut "acknowledged the reality of history, of things beyond the personal," as O'Brien has observed. "The driving reality of the war that changed her life, destroyed her society, took away her ease, killed her friends, relatives, and enemies alike, was exhilarating," O'Brien concluded, "what she struggled to call 'objective.'"[60]

Yet Chesnut did not merely record her day-to-day existence. Nor did she simply chronicle the war's events. But she did not write fiction, either, a point Woodward made clear. She did not create people who did not exist, invent plotlines, or manufacture events that did not occur, even if she did script dialogue. She did not engage the reader the way mid-nineteenth-century novelists did. There are no asides to "dear reader" or summary paragraphs that explain the import of an incident she had just recounted. She did, however, turn to historical novelists, above all to Thackeray, as models for telling about a society, and not just a life.

Chesnut read for more than utilitarian reasons, however. Indeed, her diary reveals a great deal about reading's varied purposes during the Civil War. At times, reading provided a much-needed distraction from wartime anxiety. As sectional tensions mounted during the weeks leading up to the bombardment of Fort Sumter, for example, Chesnut turned to autobiography. "Trying to forget my country, woes," she noted, "I read the *Life of Lord Dondonald* today." This represented a telling choice, given Thomas Cochrane's heroic exploits during the Napoleonic Wars—the French had nicknamed him the "Wolf of the Seas." Perhaps more important, his role in organizing and leading the rebel navies of Chile, Brazil, and Greece during their respective bids for independence during the 1820s was bound to inspire. She had miscalculated. She had found the protagonist "charming" until "the cold wave comes, the shock!" Cochrane, Chesnut learned, had been convicted of stock-exchange fraud. "A hero must be like Caesar's wife!

His hands must be clean from money—or the suspicion of it. A hero who cheats?" she asked, incredulously. "On money matters!!!"[61] Chesnut ended her comments on Cochrane here, but one wonders whether her anxiety was much relieved at all by her perusal of *The Autobiography of a Seaman*.

At times, her strategy proved successful. Of recording in her journal she wrote, "It is a painful, self-imposed task. Why write when I have nothing to chronicle but disasters. So I read instead." That day she perused George Sand's 1843 novel *Consuelo,* Prosper Mérimée's 1841 novel *Columba,* and Goethe's 1809 *Elective Infinities*—in translation, she notes. "Food enough for thought in every one of this odd assortment of books."[62]

At other times, though, reading utterly failed Chesnut. "The air is so full of war news," she recorded a few weeks later. "And we are all so restless." "Tried to read Margaret Fuller Ossoli. But could not." Chesnut, like wartime readers throughout the Union and Confederacy, had succumbed to "war fever." Among its myriad effects, according to Oliver Wendell Holmes, was the abandoning of "intellectual luxuries." What once brought pleasure had become "repulsive." Indeed, Holmes confessed in the pages of *The Atlantic* that he had put down the latest work by an eminent writer for "the romance of the past grew pale before the red light of the terrible present."[63] Chesnut, as we have seen, was similarly distracted. What chance did New England transcendentalism stand against news of the times?

Like countless wartime readers, Chesnut surveyed newspapers and magazines to stay current. Also like countless others, she did not always like what she read. She found little to admire in the war dispatches of British correspondent William Howard Russell, for example, who wrote a series of special letters for *The Times* of London, later reprinted as *Pictures of Southern Life*: "Read Russell's letter written the day after the battle of Manassas. He is against us—but tries to make our success owing to the northern cowardice entirely. Gives our courage no credit." She was even less amused by his quip that Napoleon III "did not like the look of our troops. What are looks," she asked. Before finding textual justification for her retort, she snidely added: "Bull Run told who did the best fighting." She then recalled Shakespeare's *Henry V,* copying in her diary a passage from act 4 on Henry's assessment of his troops the night before Agincourt "as to the appearance of his gallant English." Though hard fighting has rendered his men "slovenry," Henry admits, "our hearts are in the trim." At the end of the transcribed passage, Chesnut wrote: "The men of Manassas."[64]

If at times war news seemed too demanding to ignore, Chesnut never abandoned completely the "romance of the past," as Holmes had feared. In late summer 1864, as Union troops laid siege to Atlanta, she "went in for the warlike," reading Sir Walter Scott's epic poem about the 1513 Battle of Flodden, *Marmion,* alongside the "stirring odes" of another Scottish poet, Thomas Campbell. Her reading that day took an unexpected turn, however. Caught up in the poems' pathos, she recorded, "Forget to weep my dead— feel exalted." Note that she used the present tense here, suggesting that, at least for a moment, Chesnut could distance patriotic sentiment from the obligation of mourning. But only for a moment. "Oh my Confederate heroes fallen in the fight!" she wrote next. "You are not to be matched in song or story." Except they were not merely matched; they were outsung. Recounting the ways in which she and her compatriots discussed the war's casualties, Chesnut acknowledged an unspoken dilemma she and her people faced: "We talk so calmly of them." The enormity of wartime losses had dulled sensibilities. Conversations had become banal and formulaic. "'Remember, now, was he not a nice fellow? He was killed at Shiloh.' Day after day," Chesnut continued, "we read the death roll. Someone holds up her hands. 'Oh, here is another one of her friends killed. He was such a good fellow.'"[65] Hardly heroic. The juxtaposition of these two entries speaks volumes. Chesnut had allowed herself to be caught up in the martial spirit expressed in Scott's and Campbell's poems, but she was unable to fulfill the other half of the bargain, namely elevating the Confederate fallen to Olympian status. We might understand, and perhaps forgive if we are so inclined, Chesnut's inability to render the Confederate dead in Scott's terms. Chesnut, however, was less understanding. Reading rekindled the patriotic fire when all seemed bleak, but it also reminded her of a duty unfulfilled.

Ralph Waldo Emerson, whom Chesnut had read and cited in her diary, described the Civil War as "a new glass to see all our old things through." Chesnut sensed something similar that day in the late summer of 1864. By the time the Confederacy gasped its last breath, she understood Emerson's sentiment in new ways. Chesnut spent these last few months of the war as a refugee, first in Lincolnton, North Carolina, and then in Chester, South Carolina. This final excerpt comes from her time in exile. In it, readers learn not just of the importance of books but of her sense that she can never read them again as she had in the past. For Chestnut, and indeed for her fellow readers in wartime, old ways of understanding had been shattered, which came as something of a shock to her. Yet we also learn that her realist sensibilities had perhaps steeled her against the reverberations. She seems prepared to stare defeat in the face. She remained unsure of her compatriots.

Here is Chesnut, in exile:

> Then they overhauled my library, which was on the floor because the only table in the room they had used for a tea table.
>
> Shakespeare—Molière—Sir Thomas Browne—*Arabian Nights* in French—Pascal's letters—folk songs.
>
> "*Lear* I read last. The tragedy of the world—it entered into my heart to understand it first—now."
>
> "Spare us Regan and Goneril and the storm and the eyeballs rolling round."
>
> "And an old king, and I am every inch a king."
>
> That is not it. It is the laying bare of the seamy side—going behind the curtain of propriety we hold up. Poor humanity morally stripped makes us shiver. Look at the judge—look at that thief. Presto—change sides—which is the judge, which is the thief? And more unmentionable horrors. He preceded Thackeray in that tearing off of shams. [Old] Mrs. Chesnut set her face resolutely to see only the pleasant things of life and shut her eyes to wrong and said it was not there. The most devoted, unremitting reader of fiction I ever knew—everything French or English came to hand—would not tolerate Thackeray. "He is a very uncomfortable, disagreeable creature."
>
> We have seen Mrs. Chesnut. She sat like a canary bird in her nest, with no care or thought of tomorrow. She lived in a physical paradise and made her atmosphere a roseate-hued mist for her own private delusion. Thackeray pulls all ostrich heads out of the sand and will make them see—will they nill they.[66]

Chesnut saw—and she saw because she read. Of others, she could not say.

The Civil War made a mockery of romanticism. Much of the scholarship on the transition from antebellum romanticism to postbellum realism has centered on writers, noting, for example, the war's influence on the New England literati. Yet the war's influence was no less profound on readers, as Mary Chesnut's diary documents so eloquently. The soul of genius mattered not a whit on the battlefield. Combat spared neither the coward nor the brave. What's more, there is nothing heroic about being picked off by a sharpshooter, about dying of dysentery or some other camp disease, or about having your bloated corpse picked clean by a hog. Romantics were not without a sense of tragedy, but that sense did not embrace cynicism or nihilism. As one of the movement's chroniclers has explained, to the romantics, tragedy "built on the experienced realization that man is radically imperfect" also "contain[ed] a recognition that man, pitiful as he may be in his finite weakness, is still capable of apprehending perfection, and of becoming transfigured by that vision."[67] The Civil War sorely tested that notion. Moreover, ideas about the heroic individual's ability to influence an event's outcome were left by the wayside in the aftermath of Shiloh, Antietam, and the Wilderness campaign. So too was romanticism's faith in historical inevitability. The Civil War's unprecedented carnage, its contingencies, and its destruction thus fundamentally challenged how wartime readers read. Readers could no longer read old and familiar texts in old and familiar ways. Nor could they read news accounts or current fiction through the "old glass." Their worldview had been upended. Many resisted, such as Chesnut's mother-in-law. Others gave in to new modes of understanding. Most continued to read.

Although extraordinary on many levels, Chesnut nonetheless shared much with her fellow wartime readers. Like others, she read to stay current, to be entertained, to be distracted, to be instructed. She read, too, for solace—for herself, surely, but also for those whom she comforted. Above all, she read to affirm her humanity. Reading connected Chesnut with people who once lived in other times and in other places. It connected her with imaginary worlds, full of fancy and dread. At its most fundamental level, reading reminded Chesnut she was human. In a war that continually tested her sense of self, that confronted her with the enormity of human suffering and loss, reading provided Chesnut's salvation.

NOTES

1. Catherine Clinton, "Queen Bee of the Confederacy," *New York Times*, May 26, 2011, opinionator.blogs.nytimes.com/2011/05/26/queen-bee-of-the-confederacy/?_r=0.

2. C. Vann Woodward, "Diary in Fact—Diary in Form," in Woodward, ed., *Mary Chesnut's Civil War* (New Haven, Conn.: Yale University Press, 1981): xvii (book cited hereafter as *MCCW*).

3. Mary Boykin Chesnut, *A Diary from Dixie, as written by Mary Boykin Chesnut, wife of James Chesnut, Jr., United States Senator from South Carolina, 1859–1861, and afterward an Aide to Jefferson Davis and Brigadier-General in the Confederate Army*, ed. Isabella D. Martin and Myrta Lockett Avary (New York: D. Appleton and Co., 1905), xv.

4. Ibid., xxi.

5. Mary Boykin Chesnut, *A Diary from Dixie*, ed. Ben Ames Williams (1949; rpt. with foreword by Edmund Wilson, Cambridge, Mass.: Harvard University Press, 1980), xxiii–xxiv.

6. Woodward, "Diary in Fact—Diary in Form," xxiv.

7. William E. Dodd, "Mary Chesnut's Diary: A Chronicle of Southern Life by the Wife of a Confederate Statesman and Soldier," *New York Times*, April 22, 1905, 22.

8. This discussion is taken from Sarah E. Gardner, *Blood and Irony: Southern White Women's Narratives of the Civil War, 1861–1937* (Chapel Hill: University of North Carolina Press, 2004), 169–70. D. Appleton published Avary's *A Virginia Girl in the Civil War, 1861–1865, Being a Record of Actual Experiences of the Wife of a Confederate Officer* in 1903.

9. Gardner, *Blood and Irony*, 171.

10. Ibid., 172. See also Woodward, "Diary in Fact—Diary in Form," xxvii.

11. Dodd, "Mary Chesnut's Diary," 22; see also Gardner, *Blood and Irony*, 172–73.

12. Williams, ed., *A Diary from Dixie* (Harvard ed., 1980), xxiii. Williams's *House Divided* (New York: Houghton Mifflin, 1947) trailed in the wake of three novels—Stark Young's *So Red the Rose* (New York: Charles Scribner's Sons, 1934), Margaret Mitchell's *Gone with the Wind* (New York: Macmillan, 1936), and Hervey Allen's *Action at Aquila* (New York: Farrar & Rinehart, 1938)—and Freeman's Pulitzer Prize–winning *R. E. Lee: A Biography*, 4 vols. (New York: Charles Scribner's Sons, 1934–35).

13. Williams, ed., *A Diary from Dixie* (Harvard ed., 1980), xxiv.

14. Ibid., xxiv.

15. Ibid., xxvi.

16. Betty Smith, "Vivacious Lady: Confederate Style," *New York Times*, October 30, 1949, 111.

17. Ibid.

18. Wendell Holmes Stephenson in *American Historical Review* 55 (April 1950): 650; John P. Dyer in *Mississippi Valley Historical Review* 37 (June 1950): 147; Henry T. Shanks in *Journal of Southern History* 16 (May 1950): 240.

19. Stephenson, *American Historical Review*, 650.

20. See Wilson, *Patriotic Gore: Studies in the Literature of the American Civil War* (New York: Oxford University Press, 1962). Chapter 8 examines Chesnut as well as two other Confederate diarists—Sarah Morgan and Kate Stone.

21. Wilson, *Patriotic Gore*, 279–80.

22. Woodward, "Diary in Fact—Diary in Form," xi–xvi.

23. Ibid., xxv. Woodward had flirted with "memoir, autobiography, fiction, chronicle, history" but finally came down on the side of diary. Michael O'Brien found each of these terms inadequate, including "diary," preferring instead "narrative journal" because that particular genre had so few rules. As he explained, "The journal had long permitted authors, publicly or privately, to use history, memoir, autobiography, and fiction." "It acknowledged only two imperatives," he continued; "the narrative must implicate self; the passage of time must be

denoted" (Michael O'Brien, "The Flight Down the Middle Walk: Mary Chesnut and the Forms of Observance," in *Haunted Bodies: Gender and Southern Texts*, ed. Anne Goodwyn Jones and Susan V. Donaldson [Charlottesville: University Press of Virginia, 1997], 123).

24. Catherine Clinton, review of Elisabeth Muhlenfeld, *Mary Boykin Chesnut: A Biography*, and C. Vann Woodward, ed., *Mary Chesnut's Civil War, Journal of American History* 68 (March 1982): 940.

25. Kenneth S. Lynn, "The Masterpiece That Became a Hoax," *New York Times*, April 26, 1981, www.nytimes.com/1981/04/26/books/the-masterpiece-that-became-a-hoax.html?pagewanted=1. See also William R. Taylor's rejoinder in letter to the editor, *New York Times*, May 27, 1981, www.nytimes.com/1981/05/17/books/1 -mary-chesnut-s-diary-124664.html.

26. Anne Frior Scott, review of Woodward, ed., *Mary Chesnut's Civil War, Civil War History* 27 (September 1981): 282. See also Carol K. Bleser, review of Elisabeth Muhlenfeld, *Mary Boykin Chesnut: A Biography,* and Woodward, ed., *Mary Chesnut's Civil War, South Carolina Historical Magazine* 83 (January 1982): 72–74; Carl N. Delger, review of Woodward, ed., *Mary Chesnut's Civil War, American Historical Review* 87 (February 1982): 262; Drew Gilpin Faust, "In Search of the Real Mary Chesnut," *Reviews in American History* 10 (March 1982): 54–59; Michael P. Johnson, "Mary Chesnut's Autobiography and Biography: A Review Essay," *Journal of Southern History* 47 (November 1981): 585–92.

27. Woodward, ed., *MCCW,* 546.

28. See Wilson, *Patriotic Gore*; Daniel Aaron, *The Unwritten War: American Writers and The Civil War* (New York: Random House, 1973); Muhlenfeld, *Mary Boykin Chesnut: A Biography*; O'Brien, "Flight Down the Middle Walk"; Woodward, ed., *MCCW.*

29. Daniel Aaron to C. Vann Woodward, June 6, 1977, C. Vann Woodward Papers, Sterling Library, Yale University, New Haven, Conn. (collection hereafter cited as Woodward Papers Yale).

30. Julia A. Stern, *Mary Chesnut's Civil War Epic* (Chicago: University of Chicago Press, 2008), 107.

31. Michael O'Brien's magisterial *Conjectures of Order: Intellectual Life and the American South, 1810–1860,* 2 vols. (Chapel Hill: University of North Carolina Press, 2004) strove mightily to lay to rest the hoary notion that the South had no mind. In a review of *Conjectures,* historian Nicholas Guyatt confronts the near insurmountable odds O'Brien faced: "Given such an unpromising landscape, who would want to read an intellectual history of the antebellum South, much less become a historian of southern intellectuals? Michael O'Brien has been working on an answer to these questions for fifteen years, and the result is a massive refutation of received wisdom. His first task is to persuade a skeptical audience of the mere existence of Southern intellectual life between 1810 and 1860, the period between Jefferson's retirement and the eve of the Civil War. To this end, O'Brien presents rich and detailed studies of approximately one hundred Southern intellectuals, organized by themes that range from immigration to European tourism, from ideas about gender to the lending habits of Southern libraries. By far the greater part of this material is fresh and interesting, though the epic proportions of this book occasionally feel like payback for the decades of derision directed at the very idea of Southern intellectual history. (If you thought that Southerners were unreflective and lazy, O'Brien is ready to punish your prejudice with a long description of, say, the relative strengths and specialties of the Parisian hospitals that

trained Southern doctors in the 1830s)" (Guyatt, "Cool Brains," *London Review of Books* 27 [June 2, 2005]: 27–28).

32. Woodward, ed., *MCCW,* 660.

33. Wilson, *Patriotic Gore,* 279.

34. Woodward, "On Heresy and Paradox," in *MCCW,* xlvii. See also O'Brien, "Flight Down the Middle Walk," 113.

35. Woodward, "Of Heresy and Paradox," xlvii note 3. See Elisa Tamarkin, *Anglophilia: Deference, Devotion, and Antebellum America* (Chicago: University of Chicago Press, 2008); Christopher Hanlon, *American's England: Literature and American Sectionalism* (New York: Oxford University Press, 2013).

36. O'Brien, "Flight Down the Middle Walk," 113–14.

37. Woodward, ed., *MCCW,* 65. *Say and Seal* was published in 1860 under the pseudonyms "Elizabeth Wertherell" and "Amy Lothrop" by two sisters, Anna Bartlett Warner and Susan Bogart Warner.

38. Woodward, ed., *MCCW,* 65.

39. Woodward, "On Heresy and Paradox," xlviii. On why Chesnut is not a modern, see O'Brien, "Flight Down the Middle Walk," 124–25.

40. Woodward, ed., *MCCW,* 10; William Gilmore Simms, "Our Literary Docket—Anthony Trollope's *The Bertrams* and *Doctor Thorne*," rpt. in James Everett Kibler Jr. and David Moltke-Hansen, eds., *William Gilmore Simms's Selected Reviews on Literature and Civilization* (Columbia: University of South Carolina Press, 2013), 153.

41. Woodward, ed., *MCCW,* 271, 449, 738, 394.

42. O'Brien, "Flight Down the Middle Walk," 113

43. Anthony Levy, "Introduction," in Blaise Pascal, *Pensées and Other Writings* (New York: Oxford University Press, 2008), viii.

44. Francis W. Halsey to Myrta Lockett Avary, September 3, 30, 1904, and Myrta Lockett Avary to Francis W. Halsey, October 19, 1904, Myrta Avary Lockett Papers, Atlanta History Center, Atlanta (qtd. in Gardner, *Blood and Irony,* 171).

45. C. Vann Woodward to Avery Craven, August 31,1964, Woodward Papers Yale.

46. Michael Lydon, "The Colossus of Paris," *Atlantic Monthly* (February 1995): 101.

47. William Makepeace Thackeray, *Vanity Fair: A Novel Without a Hero* (1848; rpt. with an introd. by John Carey, New York: Penguin Books, 2001), 6.

48. Lydon, "Colossus of Paris," 101–6.

49. Woodward, ed., *MCCW,* 690.

50. See, for example, Woodward, ed., *MCCW,* 172, 182.

51. Woodward, ed., *MCCW,* 301. Perhaps a reference to Augustin Barruel's *Memoires pour servir a l'histoire du Jacobinisme,* which appeared in London in the late eighteenth century, or to *Memoires pour servir a l'histoire de France sous Napoleon,* an 1823 text.

52. Woodward, ed., *MCCW,* 301. It is worth noting that no part of the diary Chesnut kept from 1862 to 1865 survived. As Woodward and Muhlenfeld have explained, when Chesnut worked on her "expanded version" of the diary, she "had before her at least five and probably more of the missing volumes covering this gap in the 1860s. For the period from August 1862 to October 1863 it is likely that she either kept no regular diary or had destroyed it. In her words, she 'tried to fill the gap from memory' in memoir form" (C. Vann Woodward and

Elisabeth Muhlenfeld, eds., *The Private Mary Chesnut: The Unpublished Civil War Diaries* [New York: Oxford University Press, 1984], 218).

53. The 1860s version of this sentiment read: "What nonsense I write here. However, this journal is intended to be entirely *objective*. My subjective days are over. No more *silent* eating into my own heart, making my own misery, when without these morbid fantasies I could be so happy" (Woodward, ed., *MCCW,* 172, 23). See also Stern, *Mary Chesnut's Civil War Epic*, 130.

54. Woodward, ed., *MCCW,* 181–82.

55. See O'Brien, "Flight Down the Middle Walk," 114, 117.

56. Woodward, ed., *MCCW,* 282, 288.

57. Thackeray, *Vanity Fair,* 89.

58. Woodward, ed., *MCCW,* 11.

59. Ibid., 334.

60. O'Brien, "Flight Down the Middle Walk," 116.

61. Woodward, ed., *MCCW,* 33. See Thomas Cochrane, Earl of Dundonald, *The Autobiography of a Seaman* (London: R. Bentley, 1861).

62. Woodward, ed., *MCCW,* 333.

63. Woodward, ed., *MCCW,* 43; Oliver Wendell Holmes Sr., "Bread and the Newspapers," *The Atlantic Monthly* 8 (September 1861): 346–47.

64. Woodward and Muhlenfeld, eds., *The Private Mary Chesnut*, 136, 156.

65. Woodward, ed., *MCCW,* 628.

66. Woodward, ed., *MCCW,* 761–62. For a reading of this entry, see Stern, *Mary Chesnut's Civil War Epic*, 128–29.

67. F. O. Mathiessen, *American Renaissance: Art and Expression in the Age of Emerson and Whitman* (New York: Oxford University Press, 1941), 179–80.

"General John B. Gordon. From a photograph taken at the close of the war, when he was thirty-three years of age." Frontispiece for the "Memorial Edition" of Gordon's reminiscences. From John B. Gordon, *Reminiscences of the Civil War,* Memorial Edition (New York: Charles Scribner's Sons, 1904).

The Fatal Halts

Gettysburg, the Wilderness, and Cedar Creek in
John B. Gordon's Reminiscences

KEITH S. BOHANNON

In May 1904, a review by Dr. Walter L. Fleming of John Brown Gordon's *Reminiscences of the Civil War* appeared in the *Annals of the American Academy of Political and Social Science*. Fleming, a professor at West Virginia University, echoed the praise that many reviewers had heaped on Gordon's book since its publication the previous year. *Reminiscences,* Fleming wrote, was "one of the most valuable contributions to the literature of the Civil War that has yet appeared." In Gordon's most important military operations, Fleming claimed that the general had been handicapped by "an incapable superior officer," Jubal A. Early. Fleming noted three great opportunities where Early prevented Gordon from achieving success: the battles of Gettysburg, the Wilderness, and Cedar Creek.[1]

Professor Fleming embraced the viewpoint that Gordon hoped readers would take away from *Reminiscences.* At Gettysburg, the Wilderness, and Cedar Creek, Gordon claimed in his memoir that the plans he formulated would have resulted in Confederate victories if his immediate superiors had not hesitated and halted. While some commentators argue that *Reminiscences* is flawed by having been written late in life when the author's memory was confused and faded, Gordon's interpretation of several important battles was in fact formed during and immediately after the Civil War and changed little in succeeding decades.

In November 1896, John B. Gordon approached the New York publisher Charles Scribner's Sons about publishing his memoir. At the time, Gordon was one of the best-known Confederate veterans in the United States. During the Civil War, the native Georgian had experienced a meteoric rise in rank from captain to major general in the Army of Northern Virginia and played a prominent part in numerous campaigns. He also had enjoyed a successful postbellum political career, serving two and a half terms in the U.S. Senate (1873–80 and 1891–97) and one term as governor of Georgia (1886–90). Gordon became the commander-in-chief of the United Confederate Veterans upon its organization in 1889. As biographer Ralph Lowell Eckert notes, Gordon had a central role in the success of the U.C.V. in the 1890s, using it as a vehicle to promote his goal of sectional reconciliation.[2]

Gordon told Scribner's that his memoir would be modeled in the same informal style as his lecture, "The Last Days of the Confederacy." Composed in 1893 and first delivered before an audience of five thousand in Brooklyn, New York, "The Last Days" became famous as Gordon delivered it hundreds of times throughout the United States in subsequent years, constantly reworking and modifying the speech for different audiences. In 1900, he introduced a companion lecture titled "The First Days of the Confederacy" that he also recited to audiences across the country. Gordon received widespread accolades in the southern and northern press for the lectures, with reviewers praising his dramatic speaking abilities and nationalistic message that extolled the bravery of both the Blue and Gray and claimed the Civil War had strengthened the American character.

Gordon explained to Scribner's that the purpose of his *Reminiscences,* like the companion speeches, would be to "intensify, if I can, the National patriotic and fraternal spirit and second, to make money for myself. The one I trust is a high and laudable purpose; the other is with me a stern necessity." Although Gordon had enjoyed political success in the postwar decades, numerous business failures had left him deeply in debt at the time he entered into negotiations with Scribner's.

Gordon and Scribner's reached an agreement in 1902, presumably after he had submitted a manuscript to the publisher. Gordon received an extremely generous contract, undoubtedly an acknowledgment of his fame and Scribner's belief that the book would garner huge sales. The contract specified that the ex-general would receive $3,000 as an advance, 15 percent royalty on the first ten thousand copies sold, and 20 percent on all books sold thereafter. Gordon also had the right to purchase copies of the book from Scribner's at half-price so that he could sell them on his own and would receive a personal commission on all books he helped sell for the publisher. Lastly, Scribner's acquired the right to publish articles taken from the book manuscript in *Scribner's Magazine.* Three articles appeared in the May, June, and July 1903 issues of *Scribner's* dealing with the outbreak of the Civil War and Gordon's first command, as well as the campaigns of Antietam, Chancellorsville, and Gettysburg. *Reminiscences* appeared in print in October 1903, only three months before Gordon's death in January 1904.[3]

Gordon and his friends went to great lengths in mid-1903 to publicize the forthcoming *Reminiscences,* their efforts exceeding those made to advertise most Confederate memoirs appearing in print at that time. Gordon's associates, possibly with assistance from the ex-general, organized a Bureau of Correspondence for Subscriptions based in the Century Building in Atlanta. A September 1903 letter printed on bureau stationary and addressed to a potential subscriber promised that *Reminiscences* would include the "same elevated patriotism and vivid descriptions of scenes in that great struggle" that appeared in "The Last Days of the Confederacy." Books ordered directly from Gordon, the letter explained, would yield a larger revenue to him than those bought elsewhere. The bureau claimed to have no financial interest in the sale of the book, but sought solely to promote the general's interest.[4]

Reminiscences enjoyed immediate success, and multiple printings came out within the first year. Many reviewers lauded the uplifting "patriotic and nonpartisan spirit" in Gordon's memoir. The *St. Paul Dispatch* claimed that not a page in it "bears the stamp of prejudice, not a sentiment which can offend any honest man." The *Omaha Bee* observed that the author's "abounding good will to all sections of the country unite in giving it a personal character . . . found in few of the records of the civil war."[5]

Numerous reviewers, including the editor of *Confederate Veteran* magazine, praised the "interesting and entertaining manner" in which Gordon wove "thrilling incidents" of heroism with historical facts. A Newberry, South Carolina, journalist appreciated Gordon's keen sense of humor but claimed that the old general seemed almost "afraid to portray the horrors of war too vividly" and thus "turned occasionally, and with curious abruptness, to describe the humorous aspect of an incident or person." A book review in a Grand Rapids, Michigan, newspaper opined that, because

Reminiscences was "full of anecdotes, some grave, some gay," it would be welcomed by readers "surfeited with the accounts of battle and strategy" found in other works on the Civil War.[6]

Gordon wrote only briefly in *Reminiscences* about the origins of the Civil War. While he admitted that slavery was "undoubtedly the immediate fomenting cause" of the conflict, it was not the only one. As Gordon had consistently maintained throughout the postbellum decades, "the fundamental issues which dominated and inspired all classes of the contending sections" revolved around differing interpretations of the "respective rights and powers of the States and general government." Southerners maintained that the Union formed under the Constitution was one of "consent, not force," while the North maintained that the Union formed under the Constitution was perpetual. When newly elected President Abraham Lincoln demanded the prohibition of slavery from the western territories, the southern states exercised what they believed was their right to secede.[7]

As Ralph Lowell Eckert points out, *Reminiscences* does not dwell upon constitutional differences between North and South because Gordon believed that the North's victory in the Civil War forever settled questions concerning the nature of the Union. Gordon denounced those who might "inject one-sided and jaundiced sentiments into the youth of the country in either section." Instead, he concluded his chapter on the "Outbreak of the Civil War" with the ringing, reconciliationist claim that "Truth, justice and patriotism unite in proclaiming that both sides fought and suffered for liberty as bequeathed by the Fathers—the one for liberty in the union of the states, the other for liberty in the independence of the states."[8]

Gordon's discussion of the causes of the Civil War appears in chapter 1 of *Reminiscences,* while the remaining twenty-nine chapters focus on military campaigns. Gordon's depiction of his role in these campaigns has rightfully come under scrutiny by historians in recent decades, but such analysis has not been confined to the late twentieth and early twenty-first centuries. Douglas Southall Freeman's 1939 survey of essential Confederate literature titled *The South to Posterity* offers praise and criticism of *Reminiscences*. After quoting from Gordon's description of his wife nursing the multiple wounds he sustained at the battle of Sharpsburg, Freeman notes how the passage reflects more than Gordon's admiration for his spouse. Gordon's "memory of his pain had vanished; only the pleasant aspect of his long invalidism had remained." The same spirit, Freeman claimed, pervaded

Reminiscences, which was "not free from the tricks that time plays on even so honest an intellect as his."

Despite this criticism, Freeman found that Gordon's overall character and his book's lack of rancor made *Reminiscences* "among the best-loved stories of the South." Later historians, acknowledging as Freeman did that the passage of time clouded Gordon's memory, have criticized claims made in *Reminiscences* regarding most campaigns. What Freeman and subsequent scholars did not realize fully is that most of Gordon's most controversial statements about battles originated not late in life but appeared in print as early as 1867.[9]

In late 1866 or early 1867, Edward A. Pollard, a Richmond, Virginia, newspaper editor and author of several books on the Confederacy, contacted Gordon requesting biographical information. Pollard intended to use the material in *Lee and His Lieutenants,* a book that would include biographies of the Confederacy's "most illustrious military commanders." On February 10, 1867, Gordon contacted a friend, the "Rev. Jones," claiming that he was "absolutely overwhelmed with labor" and requesting assistance in "giving the information to E. A. Pollard of N.Y. which I have promised." Gordon told Jones that he was dependent for material from "the notes furnished you by Maj. Lewis," undoubtedly a reference to John Sutherland Lewis, a former major in the Confederate army who had served on Gordon's staff. Lewis was also a devoted uncle of Gordon's wife, Fanny Haralson Gordon.[10]

In early December 1867, Gordon wrote to E. B Treat & Co. in New York, the publisher of *Lee and His Lieutenants,* that he had received a copy of the book. Gordon found the chapter devoted to him "quite correct in all important particulars" and therefore offered no suggestions, presumably for later editions of the book. The sketch of Gordon in Pollard's book, largely ignored by historians, contains significant passages on several military campaigns, including Gettysburg, the Wilderness, and Cedar Creek.[11]

Gordon's account in *Reminiscences* of the battle of Gettysburg begins with his brigade's advance on July 1, 1863, to support the hard-pressed Confederates of Major General Robert E. Rodes's division. Gordon's six Georgia infantry regiments, advancing along the Heidlersburg Road, crossed Rock Creek and "with a ringing yell" attacked the right of the Union Eleventh Corps. "Under the concentrated fire from front and flank," the Union line on Blocher's (now Barlow's) Knoll broke and retreated. As U.S. Brigadier

General Francis Channing Barlow attempted to rally men from his stricken division, he received a grievous wound.

While riding forward with his advancing lines, Gordon claimed in *Reminiscences* that he encountered the fallen Barlow. The Confederate officer quickly dismounted, lifted Barlow's head to give him water, and asked his name. "Neither of us," recounted Gordon, "had the remotest thought that he could possibly survive many hours." Gordon had soldiers place Barlow on a litter and take him to the shade. Before parting, Barlow asked Gordon to take a package of letters from Barlow's wife and destroy them.

When Gordon learned that Barlow's wife was with the Union army and near the Gettysburg battlefield, the Georgian at the close of July 1 dispatched a message to Mrs. Barlow. Gordon "assured her that if she wished to come through the lines she should have safe escort to her husband's side." Gordon wrote in his memoir that he thought no more of Barlow in the ensuing days of battle at Gettysburg, assuming the Northern general had died from his wounds.

Fifteen years after the battle of Gettysburg, during Gordon's first term in the U.S. Senate, he received a dinner invitation in Washington, D.C., from New York Congressman Clarkson N. Potter. Potter wanted Gordon to meet a Union general named Barlow. Gordon "had heard there was another Barlow in the Union army, and supposed, of course, that it was this Barlow with whom I was to dine." Barlow, having heard in 1864 of the death of a Confederate General J. B. Gordon in a battle near Richmond, believed he was meeting someone other than the Gordon he had encountered at Gettysburg. When the two former generals learned the identity of each other, Gordon recalled that "nothing short of an actual resurrection from the dead could have amazed either of us more." Thenceforth, wrote Gordon in *Reminiscences,* the friendship between the two former generals "born amidst the thunders of Gettysburg was greatly cherished by both."[12]

The Barlow-Gordon story apparently first appeared in March 1879 in a widely reprinted piece authored by an unknown Washington correspondent of the *Boston Transcript*. It significantly noted that Barlow, not Gordon, related the Gettysburg tale to the guests at Congressman Potter's table. Henry M. Field told the Barlow-Gordon story in an 1886 book titled *Blood Is Thicker Than Water: A Few Days Among Our Southern Brethren*. Field claimed that, because the incident had "been related to me by *both* the actors in the scene described, I can vouch for its literal accuracy." Like the

1879 reporter, Field noted that Barlow recounted the incident to the diners at Potter's, "at which not only the ladies, but the men round the table, found it difficult to control their emotion."[13]

At the twenty-fifth anniversary of Gettysburg, Barlow and Gordon met again on the battlefield at Barlow's Knoll. The *New York Times* claimed the meeting was "rather affecting," relating how Gordon found Barlow, took care of him, and "allowed Mrs. Barlow to come through the lines to nurse her husband." Throughout the 1890s, the story appeared in numerous publications, including Gordon's "Last Days of the Confederacy" speech where it illustrated Gordon's desire for sectional reconciliation.[14]

The Barlow-Gordon story also likely became a staple of Gettysburg battlefield tours. In 1893, when former Confederate generals James Longstreet, Edward Porter Alexander, and William Mahone accompanied Union General Oliver O. Howard and other officers of lesser rank on a tour of the field, they heard the "conventional address" of a "famous professional guide," Captain James T. Long. The Barlow-Gordon story was part of the address, which Long ended by claiming that the two generals met for the second time in 1888 on the Gettysburg battlefield. Porter Alexander, who had been "listening intently," broke in at this point, telling the group that Gordon and Barlow had actually met a second time at a dinner party in Washington. General Charles Henry Howard, a staff officer of his brother, O. O. Howard, added that he had accompanied Mrs. Arabella Barlow through Gettysburg and the Confederate lines to join her wounded husband.[15]

In recent decades, several writers contributing to popular Civil War magazines have questioned whether the battlefield meeting of Gordon and Barlow actually happened. They argue that there are inconsistencies in the accounts left by Gordon and Barlow and that the Confederate general is not mentioned in a July 7, 1863, letter Barlow wrote to his mother about his wounding. Questions also arise over whether Barlow's wife could have arrived on the battlefield as soon as Gordon claimed, primarily because General Barlow does not mention her in his July 7 letter. Gordon invented the incident, these critics claim, to promote sectional reconciliation and mutual admiration for the soldiers on both sides of the Civil War.[16]

Those who argue that the Barlow-Gordon incident did occur, including John C. Fazio, Gregory C. White, and former Gettysburg National Military Park historian Scott Hartwig, point out that the July 7, 1863, letter from Barlow is incomplete and that the Union general may have omitted mentioning his encounter with Gordon because of its brief nature. Hartwig's keen analysis concludes that there is "simply too much testimony from too many different sources" to deny that some encounter occurred between Gordon and Barlow on July 1, 1863, but concedes the Confederate general's role was likely "considerably smaller than he claimed." In reconstructing the event after the Civil War, Gordon likely took credit for the actions of other Confederate officers who moved the wounded Barlow into the shade of some woods and then into a house, later sending word of his dire condition to his wife through a flag of truce. These other officers possibly included Gordon's corps and division commanders, Lieutenant General Richard S. Ewell and Major General Jubal Early. Southern staff officers probably also assisted Barlow, including the only Confederate mentioned by name in Barlow's July 7, 1863, letter, Lieutenant Andrew L. Pitzer of Early's staff.[17]

While pursuing Barlow's retreating troops into Gettysburg, Gordon received orders to halt. In *Reminiscences,* he states that Ewell and Early were "at a distance from the field" and "could not possibly have been fully cognizant of the situation at the time." Gordon wrote that, when he stopped his brigade, "the whole of that portion of the Union army in my front was in inextricable confusion and in flight." In less than thirty minutes, Gordon claimed, his troops could have seized Cemetery Hill, "the possession of which was of such momentous importance." Gordon refused the first order to halt and "not until the third or fourth order of the most peremptory character reached me did I obey." Even then, Gordon states in his memoir that he would have risked the consequences of disobedience but that the "order to halt was accompanied with the explanation that General Lee, who was several miles away, did not wish to give battle at Gettysburg."[18]

Gordon was unable to sleep that night because of his heart being "so burdened by the fatal mistake of the afternoon." He claimed in *Reminiscences* that he spent much of the night on the picket line listening to the "busy strokes of Union picks and shovels on the hills" and the movement of enemy cannon and troops. Around 2:00 a.m. on July 2 he rode to the headquarters of Ewell and Early, urging them to launch a night attack to carry the heights rather than waiting until morning when the enemy would occupy a strong, fortified position. "There was a disposition to yield to my suggestions," Gordon wrote, "but other counsels prevailed."[19]

Gordon's account of Gettysburg in *Reminiscences* drew harsh private and public criticism from John W. Daniel, a U.S. senator from Virginia at the time of the book's publication. At Gettysburg, Daniel had served as a major and assistant adjutant general on Jubal Early's staff. Daniel wrote privately that Gordon's Gettysburg chapter demonstrated that the Georgian "either never knew the situation of the field he was on, or had forgotten it; and if he knew no more of other battles and wars than he did of Early and his division at Gettysburg, his historical reading was sadly deficient."[20]

In a letter published in the *Richmond Times-Dispatch* fifteen days after Gordon's death, Daniel wrote that he "honored and loved" the brave and charismatic Georgia general but believed the Gettysburg and Wilderness chapters of *Reminiscences* had been "full of errors." Daniel seemed particularly incensed at Gordon's contention that Ewell and Early had been "distant from the field" on July 1. Instead, Daniel claimed Early had been only one hundred yards in the left rear of Gordon's brigade when it charged on July 1 and that Ewell and Robert E. Lee had also witnessed Gordon's advance. Early and Ewell had also entered Gettysburg during the initial Confederate advance into the town, wrote Daniel, riding up Baltimore Street to examine the enemy's position on Cemetery Hill and coming under fire from Union skirmishers positioned behind fences and on rooftops.[21]

Unfortunately, neither an incomplete July 7, 1863, letter written by Gordon to his wife nor his official report offers any details of his desire to seize Cemetery Hill in the evening of July 1 or early morning hours of July 2. The official reports of Ewell and Early are likewise silent regarding Gordon's recommendations to take Cemetery Hill, although Early's report and memoir claim that he, as Gordon's division commander, also initially supported an effort to continue the advance. Several accounts written shortly after the Civil War reveal that Gordon's version of events in *Reminiscences* was not created late in life. Pollard's 1867 sketch claimed that, when the Federal line retreated on July 1, the Georgian "was anxious to continue the pursuit and seize the heights, which the enemy afterwards so strongly fortified." Instead, he was "halted by his superiors." At the close of the day, Gordon in consultation with senior officers "advised an advance at once, and expressed an opinion that the heights could be taken even at that time." Later that night, Gordon saw his superiors again and urged an advance, "offering to lead the attack with his brigade. But other counsels prevailed, and the Confederates lost the opportunity of winning what might have been the decisive victory of the war."[22]

A year after *Lee and His Lieutenants* came out, articles in Atlanta newspapers supporting Gordon's candidacy for governor wrote glowingly about his war record. One averred that at Gettysburg the Georgia general had been "earnest in his advocacy" to take Cemetery Hill, but "saw his troops recalled with grief." Another paper claimed that on the evening of July 1, 1863, Gordon withdrew in obedience to orders, "notwithstanding these orders were contrary to both his judgment and desire."[23]

Henry Kyd Douglas's famous published memoir *I Rode with Stonewall*, written shortly after the war, then rewritten in 1899, provides additional evidence that Gordon had advocated a continued advance on the evening of July 1. Douglas, serving on the staff of Major General Edward Johnson, reached a group of officers including Ewell and Gordon shortly after the latter's successful charge. Douglas reported that Johnson's division was nearing the battlefield and that its commander was ready to put it into action as soon as he arrived. Gordon seconded the request, claiming that his brigade could join Johnson in a charge on Cemetery Hill. According to Douglas, Ewell responded by saying that he did not feel like advancing without orders from Robert E. Lee, who Ewell believed was still at Cashtown. Ewell then told Douglas to ride to Johnson and tell him to halt and await further orders. Ewell's remarks "silenced all those around him," and Gordon said nothing further, according to Douglas.[24]

Although Gordon only saw action at Gettysburg on July 1, he used *Reminiscences* to criticize the performance of First Corps commander James Longstreet on the second and third days of the battle. Gordon claimed that Longstreet disobeyed orders from Lee by attacking late on July 2 and 3 and that Lee died in 1870 believing he had lost the battle because of Longstreet's tardiness. These criticisms, which became a staple of Lost Cause argument, were not original to Gordon, but had been leveled at Longstreet since the early 1870s by several ex-Confederate generals.[25]

Gordon's comments about Longstreet in *Reminiscences* did not go unnoticed. Edward Porter Alexander, Longstreet's chief of artillery during the war's last year and an outstanding historian, wrote in a private letter that Gordon's criticism of Longstreet was "*very* weak, & in *very* bad taste." Helen Dortch Longstreet, wife of James Longstreet, prepared a public response to Gordon's comments even as her husband was dying. On January 3, 1904, the day after General Longstreet's death, the *Atlanta Constitution* published his widow's lengthy response. Helen Longstreet claimed that her husband's actions at Gettysburg had been "above the suspicion of reproach" until he came under a postbellum political ban by joining the Republican Party. A conspiracy, she alleged, had made her husband the "long-desired scapegoat of Gettysburg." She accurately pointed out that Gordon "simply reiterates the old charges" made against her husband, with no new evidence to support them. She also challenged what she claimed was a widespread impression that Gordon had been a conspicuous figure at Gettysburg, noting that he had only been a brigade commander far removed from the area where Longstreet's command had fought. Editorial reactions to Helen Longstreet's defense of her husband varied; some newspapers supported her while others upheld Gordon's critique.[26]

Gordon's account in *Reminiscences* of the battle of the Wilderness, like his chapter on Gettysburg, came under scrutiny from both former Confederate officers and late-twentieth-century historians. Described in January 1864 by Robert E. Lee as "one of the best" brigadier generals in the Army of Northern Virginia, Gordon commanded the same brigade at the Wilderness that he had at Gettysburg. On May 5, 1864, the first day of the battle of the Wilderness, Gordon recounts in *Reminiscences* how his men encountered other Confederates falling back "like broken and receding waves" in the face of a Union advance.

The description in *Reminiscences* of May 5 in the Wilderness draws heavily from Pollard's sketch of Gordon in *Lee and His Lieutenants,* including passages quoted verbatim from the earlier source. A comparison of Pollard's account and Gordon's memoir reveals additional descriptive phrases in *Reminiscences,* undoubtedly added to heighten the dramatic effect. The Pollard sketch describes Ewell's riding up to Gordon as the Georgian was "quietly moving down the pike at the head of his column." Ewell said, "Gen. Gordon, they are driving us; the fate of the day depends on you." Gordon replied, "We will save it, General," and immediately wheeling into line, he told his men what was expected of them, and ordered them forward, riding in their front. After breaking the Federal line in his front and designating certain troops to guard the breech, Gordon faced the balance of his brigade to the right and left "and swept down upon the enemy's flanks in both directions, capturing many prisoners and one regiment entire."

In *Reminiscences,* Ewell rode up to Gordon "at a furious gallop" and in "rapid words . . . charged with tremendous significance" announced "General Gordon, the fate of the day depends on you sir." Gordon replied that "these men will save it sir" and, after "quickly wheeling a single regiment into line" and ordering it to countercharge, the Georgian rode back to bring up the balance of his command. Gordon subsequently exploited a gap in the Union line to advance his regiments upon the right and left flanks of "the astounded Federals." Then, in a nod to Gordon's goal in *Reminiscences* of extolling the honor of both Union and Confederate soldiers, the author admitted that the outflanked Federal line broke "as any troops that were ever marshalled would have been shattered."[27]

John W. Daniel conceded privately that Gordon's account in *Reminiscences* of the Wilderness was "all very graphic" but criticized the overly dramatic prose and self-centeredness. Daniel complained that Gordon said not a word of Brigadier General Junius Daniel, whose brigade of North Carolinians shared the honor of reclaiming the field. John W. Daniel also noted that Gordon omitted any mention of Jubal Early, who arranged for the charge "and under whose eyes and direction it was made." While *Reminiscences* depicts Ewell as being excited when giving the orders to charge, Daniel claims that Ewell and Early were "as cool and calm as if conducting a plain matter of business," both officers being mounted and surrounded by their staff near the Orange Turnpike when Gordon's brigade moved forward.

Daniel's last criticism of Gordon's account of May 5 concerned a tactical matter. Daniel claimed that none of Gordon's regiments did any "wheeling" into line, as stated in *Reminiscences*. Instead, the Georgians "simply marched down the pike right in front; filed to the right, faced to the front on the edge of the forest," and advanced. Daniel, who witnessed the maneuvering and subsequent charge, cited Gordon's own published official report of the Wilderness to challenge the description in *Reminiscences*.[28]

During the night of May 5, Gordon received orders from Jubal Early to move his brigade to the extreme left of the Confederate line. Upon reaching this destination, Gordon sent out scouts to find the Union army's opposing flank. "At early dawn" on May 6, Gordon wrote in *Reminiscences,* the scouts returned to report that the end of the Federal line rested only a short distance in front of the Southerners, "wholly unprotected, and that the Confederate lines stretched a considerable distance beyond the Union right, overlapping it." Gordon sent additional scouts who confirmed the earlier reports and added that there were no nearby supporting enemy forces.

At this point, Gordon claimed to have gone out with some of the scouts. Gordon's staff member Thomas G. Jones said that the general crawled on his hands and knees through the woods to get close enough to see the end of the Union breastworks and Federal soldiers taking breakfast with their rifles leaning against the works. Gordon quickly formulated a plan that, he immodestly claimed in *Reminiscences,* "would have resulted in the crushing defeat of General Grant's army" if "promptly adopted and vigorously followed." Gordon would move his command to a point where it was perpendicular to the Federal line. When the Confederates rushed upon the flank of the unsuspecting enemy, a simultaneous demonstration would take place against the front of the Union line. As each Federal brigade "gave way in confusion," the corresponding Confederate brigade in its front would swing to join the column of attack.[29]

When Gordon presented the plan to Jubal Early that morning between 8:00 and 9:00 a.m., the division commander "at once opposed it," claiming that the Union Ninth Corps under Major General Ambrose E. Burnside was immediately behind the Sixth Corps troops that formed the right of U.S. Grant's line. If Gordon attempted a flank movement, Early believed that the Ninth Corps Federals would assail the flanking party of Confederates and rout or capture them. Despite the findings of the scouts and Gordon that neither the Ninth Corps units nor any other Federals were behind the Union right, Early remained unmoved.

Gordon went to some length in *Reminiscences* to discredit Early's reasons for delaying a flank attack in the Wilderness. Early had originally outlined these in his 1866 *Memoir of the Last Year of the War for Independence.* Gordon revealed that for many decades he never publicly refuted Early's 1866 account of the Wilderness, but the Georgian claimed that the publication of his own memoirs made it necessary for him to speak. To prove that the Ninth Corps was not in support of the Union army's right flank on May 6, 1864, Gordon cited passages in the recently published *Official Records of the War of the Rebellion,* as well as William Swinton's 1866 *Campaigns of the Army of the Potomac* and an 1897 memoir by Grant's staff member Horace Porter, *Campaigning with Grant.*

While Gordon was correct that the Ninth Corps was not in a position on May 6 to threaten the Confederate left flank in the Wilderness, historian Gordon C. Rhea points out that Union Brigadier General Edward Ferrero's division of the Ninth Corps had been left that day at Germanna Ford on the Rapidan River to guard the crossing site. Ferrero's command, untried in battle and assuming a purely defensive disposition, "posed no serious threat" to Gordon's proposal for a flank attack, opines Rhea. At the same time, scouts from Ferrero's command exploring to the west of Germanna had undoubtedly been the Union troops spotted by Confederate cavalry on the morning of May 6. According to Early's *Memoir,* Southern cavalrymen reported to Ewell that morning that a column of the enemy's infantry was between the Confederate left and the Rapidan River.

Ewell refused throughout much of May 6 to support Gordon's desire to attack the Union flank. In *Reminiscences,* Gordon claimed that his corps commander was "naturally reluctant to take issue" with Early in a matter about which Ewell had no personal knowledge. G. Campbell Brown, Ewell's son-in-law and staff member, wrote after the war that Ewell had been in favor of allowing Gordon to attack but was "begged out of it by Early's strong personal appeals until he could go to examine the ground himself." Because of Early's opposition, Ewell delayed granting Gordon permission for the flank attack, even when Gordon said he would assume all responsibility for any disaster, should one occur. Gordon said that he urged the plan at least once more during the day after his initial morning meeting.[30]

In the *Richmond Times-Dispatch* in October 1905, John W. Daniel defended the decisions of Early and Ewell to prevent Gordon from attacking on the afternoon of May 6. "When the history of this battle is written," Daniel predicted, "it will be well understood why Ewell and Early were unwilling to send their only unengaged brigade then in hand (that of Gordon) on a flanking expedition, while they were themselves occupied." Furthermore, Daniel claimed that Ewell was under orders from Lee "to keep his troops ready to move to the right."[31]

Around 5:30 p.m. on May 6, Gordon claimed in *Reminiscences,* Robert E. Lee arrived at Ewell's headquarters. In the presence of Ewell, Early, and Gordon, Lee supposedly asked, "Cannot something be done on this flank to relieve the pressure upon our right?" Gordon listened for some time to the discussion before informing Lee of the exposed flank of the Union Sixth Corps and the Georgian's plan to attack it. Early "again promptly and vigorously protested" about the presence of the Union Ninth Corps in the woods behind the right of the Sixth Corps. Gordon then assured Lee that Early was mistaken and reiterated plans for a flank attack. According to *Reminiscences,* Lee's "words were few, but his silence and grim looks while the reasons for the long delay were being given," along with Lee's prompt orders to Gordon to attack, revealed the commanding general's thoughts "almost as plainly as words could have done."[32]

Once again, Gordon's version of events in *Reminiscences* came under fire from John W. Daniel. Daniel particularly sought to refute Gordon's claim that Lee met with Ewell, Early, and Gordon on the afternoon of May 6 and sanctioned Gordon's attack. Daniel cited testimony from five Second Corps staff officers and Colonel Thomas H. Carter of the artillery, all of whom wrote that they did not see Lee that day. Daniel also insisted that he personally witnessed Ewell giving Early permission to attack on the afternoon of May 6 and that Gordon was not there at the time. Daniel suggested that the aging Gordon's memory had caused him to conflate a May 7 meeting with Lee with events on May 6.[33]

An exchange of letters between Gordon and Robert E. Lee in 1867 and 1868 verifies portions of the Georgian's account in *Reminiscences* but reveals that the May 6 meeting at 5:30 p.m. between Lee, Ewell, Early, and Gordon probably did not happen. Instead, it seems likely that if this meeting occurred it only involved Lee, Ewell, and possibly Early. On January 8, 1867, Lee wrote Gordon, asking for copies of his official reports because the former army commander hoped to write a study of his campaigns. Lee also asked Gordon if he remembered the two men's seeing each other on the right flank in the Wilderness on May 6 and whether it was before or after Gordon's attack that evening. In response, Gordon stated that while he was "positive that I conversed with you on the morning of the 7th—Do not remember having seen you [on] that flank prior to that time. Indeed I was not aware of your desire to make a movement on that flank until after the 6th. I am glad to know that such was your wish."

The final letter in the Lee-Gordon exchange reveals Lee's confusion as to the sequence of meetings in the Wilderness. Lee explained to Gordon that he was "not certain whether I saw you before your attack on the 6th. I visited your flank, but you might have been then engaged in your reconnaissances." Lee concluded, "I may have confounded our conversation [on the morning of May 7] subsequent to your attack with my visit to Genl Ewell before it took place."[34]

The Confederate attack at dusk on May 6 involving Gordon's brigade with Robert D. Johnston's North Carolinians in support achieved some surprise and success, rolling up two Union brigades and capturing several hundred prisoners, including two generals. In the interest of promoting the bravery of men on both sides, Gordon pointed out in *Reminiscences* that the two "gallant Union leaders" made a "heroic endeavor" to rally their commands before being captured. Gordon's men were "literally reveling at the chase, when the unwelcome darkness put an end" to the Confederate advance.[35]

Jubal Early's *Memoir* presents a different assessment of Gordon's flank attack from what appears in *Reminiscences*. Early claims that, at his suggestion, Ewell "ordered the movement which Gordon proposed." Once Gordon's advance began, shortly before sunset, Early took an active role in the movement, posting his adjutant general, Major John W. Daniel, in a position to communicate with Gordon so that Early would know when to commit additional brigades to the battle. Gordon acknowledged this assistance in *Reminiscences,* noting that Ewell and Early "did all in their power to help forward the movement when once begun." Early's description of the flank attack emphasizes the confusion that plagued the Confederates as they advanced through the dense woods in the growing darkness, something not mentioned in *Reminiscences*. While Gordon's account bemoans the fading light, Early states that it was fortunate "that darkness came to close this affair, as the enemy, if he had been able to discover the disorder on our side, might have brought up fresh troops and availed himself of our condition."[36]

As Donald C. Pfanz points out in his fine biography of Richard Ewell, both Gordon and Early made valid points in their evaluation of the May 6 flank attack. The darkness that resulted in the initial Confederate success, Pfanz states, also "doomed it to failure by creating confusion in the Confederate ranks." While Robert E. Lee never publicly criticized Ewell's actions on May 6, Gordon Rhea points out how Lee privately expressed disappointment after the war in his corps commander's "want of decision." Lee stated that "he urged Ewell to make the flank attack . . . several times before it was done," but that Early had kept his superior from "pushing the matter." Lee correctly assessed that the attack "was too late in the day and . . . not supported with sufficient force to accomplish anything decisive."[37]

The last major battle in which Gordon and Early served together was Cedar Creek, during the 1864 Shenandoah Valley Campaign. Early commanded the small army charged with defending the Shenandoah Valley while Gordon led a division in Early's Second Corps. Gordon devoted more pages in *Reminiscences* to Cedar Creek than to any other battle, justifying it in part because of the absence of his official report of the battle in the

U.S. government's *Official Records.* Gordon believed it was one of his "most imperative duties" to guide future historians "to a clear apprehension of the truth in regard to the chivalrous character and conduct" of the men that served under him. At the same time, Gordon claimed credit for the initial plan of battle at Cedar Creek and blamed Early for the ultimate disaster that befell the Confederates that day.[38]

By the third week of October 1864, Early had his Valley army encamped at Fisher's Hill, recovering from costly and humiliating defeats the previous month at the battles of Third Winchester and Fisher's Hill. Facing shortages in provisions and forage and under pressure from Robert E. Lee to mount an offensive in the Valley, Early determined to attack the enemy encamped five miles to the north along the banks of Cedar Creek. Deciding that the Federals were too strongly fortified to assail their position in front, Early said in his *Memoir* that he "determined to get around one of the enemy's flanks and attack him by surprise if I could." He directed Brigadier General John Pegram to go as near as he could to Cedar Creek on the enemy's right flank to see whether it was practicable to surprise the Federals there. Early also sent Gordon on October 17, along with topographical engineer Jedediah Hotchkiss and several other officers, to a Confederate signal station atop the northern end of Massanutten Mountain to view the enemy's position.[39]

In *Reminiscences,* Gordon claims that Early had already arrived upon a plan of battle prior to sending the Georgia general and Hotchkiss to the signal station. Early's plan, Gordon stated, was to move against Sheridan's right flank. Gordon, "not entirely satisfied" with this plan, suggests in his memoir that he decided on his own to venture to the signal station on Massanutten, accompanied by several other officers. (Early's *Memoir* and the wartime diary of Hotchkiss both say that Gordon's party ventured to the signal station under orders from the army commander.) After a difficult trek to the station, the party saw "an inspiring panorama" that revealed not only every road, habitation, field, and stream, but also the entire Union position north of Cedar Creek. The Union commander, Major General Philip H. Sheridan, clearly had not anticipated a Confederate advance against his army's left flank, given that "the impassable Massanutten, with the Shenandoah River at its base, was the sufficient protecting fortress."

Gordon then claimed in his memoir to have turned to the officers at the signal station and announced that, if Early would adopt the battle plan submitted by the Georgian and "press it to its legitimate results, the destruction of Sheridan's army was inevitable." The plan involved demonstrations against Sheridan's right flank by Confederate cavalry and a movement northward of Southern infantry and artillery along the Valley Turnpike against the Union center. The "heavy and decisive blow" would be led by Gordon and the Second Corps moving around Massanutten Mountain and crossing Cedar Creek to attack the Federal left flank. Gordon gives no credit to Hotchkiss in *Reminiscences* for contributing to the plan, but the map-maker's wartime diary claimed that "General Gordon and myself fixed upon a plan of attack to suggest to General Early, which we discussed fully as we came back."[40]

On the evening of October 17, Hotchkiss and Early discussed the Union position. The following morning, Early met with both Hotchkiss and Gordon, the latter confirming the mapmaker's observations and assuring Early that an attack on the enemy's left flank would achieve success. Later that day at a conference at army headquarters, Early announced a battle plan. The plan having been explained, Gordon, Hotchkiss, and Major General Stephen D. Ramseur went to find a route that the Second Corps could take around Massanutten Mountain. The party located a "dim and narrow path-way," wrote Gordon in his memoir, "along which but one man could pass at a time." If the movement along this route began at nightfall, Gordon believed "the entire corps could be passed before daylight."[41]

In *Reminiscences,* Gordon claims that his plan of battle "was finally adopted by General Early," hinting that there had been some resistance to it. Colonel Thomas H. Carter, writing his wife two days after the battle of Cedar Creek, wrote that Gordon "suggested, planned and carried out" the attack "after the Jackson style." Several postbellum sources, especially those touting Gordon's war record as part of an endorsement for public office, also ascribe the battle plan at Cedar Creek to the Georgian. The *Atlanta Weekly Opinion* in 1868 crowed that, at Cedar Creek, Gordon "was allowed full scope of his genius" and that the "slaughter and utter route of most of Sheridan's army attest to the brilliancy of his plans." In a July 1888 visit to Gettysburg, Gordon told a reporter for a Boston newspaper that the plan of attack for October 19, 1864, had been "mine wholly, and so was the conduct of the fight up to a certain point."[42]

The Confederate attack on the morning of October 19 achieved dramatic success. "The surprise was complete," wrote Gordon in *Reminiscences*. "Two entire corps, the Eighth and Nineteenth, constituting more than two thirds of Sheridan's army, broke and fled," swarming across the fields "in utter disorganization." As Confederates from the Second Corps, temporarily under Gordon's command that morning, advanced with Southerners from Maj. Gen. Joseph B. Kershaw's division, they eventually encountered two divisions of the Union Sixth Corps in line along a series of ridges north of the valley of Meadow Brook. Hoping to drive off the Sixth Corps, Gordon wrote in his memoir, he directed his infantry brigades to attack the Federals simultaneously in front and flanks. He also ordered Colonel Thomas H. Carter, artillery chief of the Second Corps, to mass batteries along the Valley Turnpike to bombard the remaining Federals. In the 1888 interview, Gordon opined that Carter's bombardment would have "battered that federal line all to pieces, demoralized an already beaten army, and sent it in utter panic down the valley."

By the time Gordon issued these orders, General Early had crossed Cedar Creek on the Valley Turnpike, accompanying artillery batteries and an additional infantry division. Riding northward, Early encountered Gordon around 7:30 a.m. on an elevated position just east of the pike and across from a lane that led to the Belle Grove mansion. Early was "wild with joy," Gordon claimed in 1888, and the Georgian asked his commanding officer to "give me 30 pieces of artillery right here and we will destroy that army and send its fragments over the Potomac." Adding drama to his account, Gordon told the Boston reporter, "The supreme moment had come."

According to the version of this Gordon-Early meeting in *Reminiscences,* which closely resembles what the Georgian said about it in 1888, Early then exclaimed, "Well, Gordon, there is glory enough for one day." Early also pointed out that exactly a month earlier, at the battle of Third Winchester, the Confederate Army of the Valley had been routed. Gordon claimed in 1888 that he responded by saying that the Confederates needed to "finish the job. . . . We can do it in an hour, and so destroy that army that it will never show its head in the valley again." Gordon's response to Early in *Reminiscences* is slightly different but conveys the same tenor. In *Reminiscences,* Gordon says, "It is very well so far, general; but we have one more blow to strike, and then there will not be left an organized company of infantry in Sheridan's army." When Gordon pointed to the Union Sixth Corps and explained the orders he had given to drive it from the field, Early supposedly said: "No use in that; they will all go directly." Gordon then returned to his division.[43]

Early's account of this meeting in his memoir is irreconcilable with Gordon's. Early states that Gordon informed the army commander as to the condition of things and that the division of Brigadier General John Pegram had not been ordered in. While Gordon asserted that Early had no desire at that point to continue the battle, Early and several of his former staff members claimed otherwise. An 1889 article written by Early's former assistant adjutant general, Samuel J. C. Moore, states that the army commander ordered a group of artillery batteries to bombard the Federals while also instructing his infantry to continue their pursuit of a retreating foe. John W. Daniel, addressing Confederate veterans in Richmond in 1894, claimed that Early was "anxious to press forward" after the initial route of Union troops and drive the Sixth Corps from the field.[44]

Gordon's disappointment as a result of this meeting and the ensuing "fatal halt" is a recurring theme in all his postbellum accounts of Cedar Creek. In the 1867 sketch in Pollard, Gordon had "prepared to execute his plans . . . of concentrating everything upon the enemy's last corps" when Early arrived and rejected the Georgian's course of action. The following year, a newspaper sketch claimed that, if Gordon's orders had not been countermanded, Cedar Creek would have been a worthy anniversary of Yorktown, the British surrender there having taken place on the same day as the 1864 Valley battle.

In *Reminiscences,* Gordon links the hours of Confederate inactivity at Cedar Creek to earlier battles where his superiors, including Early, had shown indecision. "My heart went into my boots" after meeting with Early, the Georgian dramatically explained; "visions of the fatal halt on the first day of Gettysburg, and of the whole day's hesitation to permit an assault on Grant's exposed flank on the 6th of May in the Wilderness, rose before me." The "blow was not delivered" at Cedar Creek, Gordon claimed; "we halted, we hesitated . . . firing a few shots here, attacking with a brigade or a division there, and before such feeble assaults the superb Union corps retired at intervals and by short stages."[45]

Early justified the eventual halt in the Confederate offensive at Cedar Creek north of Middletown by pointing to the jaded and scattered condition of his troops. He also claimed that the ranks "were much thinned by the absence of men engaged in plundering the enemy's camps," a situation confirmed in many immediate post-battle letters and diary entries written by Early's men. The delays, which Early characterized as being to a degree unavoidable, allowed Sheridan to rally his troops and the Union cavalry to move into position to threaten both flanks of the Confederates' final line.

The Confederate army commander remembered the decisive role that massed Union cavalry played in his defeat at Winchester a month before and believed that any further Confederate advance on the afternoon of October 19 would be "extremely hazardous." When the Federals did attack the left flank of Early's line, held by Gordon's old division, it collapsed, and eventually the entire Confederate army was in disorderly retreat southward.[46]

Gordon's postbellum commentary on his men's plundering enemy camps at Cedar Creek changed over time. In the 1867 Pollard sketch, he admitted that by the afternoon of October 19 Confederates were "losing the spirit of the morning and being demoralized by plunder." The Federals, in contrast, had been "rallied and reassured" by the presence of Sheridan.

Three years after the publication of the Pollard sketch, Gordon told George F. Holmes, the vice-president of the University Publishing Company, that an upcoming history of the Civil War being published by the firm contained errors regarding Cedar Creek. The text explained that Confederate straggling to hunt for plunder was the major reason for the Confederate defeat. This was a great mistake, wrote Gordon. "I state with emphasis & most positively," he wrote, "that I never saw less straggling on any battlefield in the war." Gordon claimed that this was the testimony of Confederate army inspectors after the battle and that he had personally been upon the ground and remarked on the absence of straggling at the time. "The whole difficulty," he explained, "was the halting and waiting until Sheridan came up having rallied his men." In his 1888 interview with the Boston reporter, Gordon essentially repeated the claims he made in 1870 to Holmes, adding only that during the battle he had his troops "well in hand, and had issued the strictest orders that any soldier falling out for plunder should be shot instantly."[47]

The same concern Gordon voiced in the 1870s and 1880s for the reputation of his men at Cedar Creek appears emphatically in *Reminiscences*. He admitted in *Reminiscences* that there were a number of "controverted points" between him and Jubal Early regarding the battle, "but the only one in which the whole country is concerned, involving as it does the character of the Southern soldiery . . . is the question as to the responsibility for the disaster at Cedar Creek after the signal victory had been won." Early insisted that the "bad conduct" of his men caused the defeat, while Gordon believed "it was due solely to the unfortunate halting and delay after the morning victory."[48]

Gordon defended his men in *Reminiscences* against Early's charges of plundering by claiming that the army commander had been misled by reports of men leaving the ranks to "gather the tempting debris from the Federal wreck." The men reported as being in the captured camps, Gordon explained, were "without arms, and partially disabled, whom the army surgeons had pronounced scarcely strong enough for the long and rough night march and the strenuous work of the battle." The soldiers in the enemy camps, Gordon explained, were not the men who had fought and won the morning battle."[49]

Jubal Early delivered a scathing address to his army three days after its defeat at Cedar Creek. The address, printed in broadside form and reproduced in numerous southern newspapers, accused many soldiers of yielding "to a disgraceful propensity for plunder" on October 19. The men remaining in the ranks, when pressed by the enemy, had "yielded to a needless panic and fled the field in confusion." The address unsurprisingly provoked resentment in the Army of the Valley, and letters critical of Early written by Confederate soldiers appeared in southern newspapers for several weeks after Cedar Creek.[50]

A letter signed "Argus" in the October 27, 1864, issue of the *Richmond Enquirer* particularly incensed Early. The letter claimed that General Gordon had conceived the brilliant plan at Cedar Creek and that Confederates would have won a great victory had Early not engaged in "delay and hesitation" which led to disaster and defeat. Unlike Gordon's postbellum assertions regarding the absence of plundering, Argus admitted that as many as one-third of the Confederates went to the rear to scour the Union camps. Early did not know the identity of "Argus" but suspected he was Gordon's assistant adjutant general, Major Robert W. Hunter.

In a conference between Early and his division commanders nine days after Cedar Creek, the army commander confronted Gordon about the Argus letter, suggesting that the Georgian had inspired it and other similar accounts. Gordon stated in *Reminiscences* that he "could not do less than indignantly resent the injustice of such an intimation" but admitted that "the facts had been truly stated as to our unfortunate halt and delay." While few details are known about the meeting, Gordon later told his staff officer Thomas G. Jones that there was "much plain speaking on both sides."[51]

Gordon might have been sincere in telling Early that he had not directly inspired the Argus letter, but evidence suggests that at least two members of Gordon's staff communicated his views regarding Cedar Creek to the press in the days after the battle. In 1904, former Gordon staff officer Thomas G. Jones wrote his friend John W. Daniel that, while Early had suspected Robert W. Hunter as being the author of the Argus letter, Jones had learned that the real author was Lieutenant Frank Markoe Jr., a signal officer on Gordon's staff.

Even if Major Hunter was not the author of the Argus letter, he clearly sought to use the press to publicize Gordon's views on Cedar Creek. In the days immediately following the battle, Hunter corresponded with one of the best-known newspaper correspondents in the Confederacy, Peter W. Alexander. On October 27, 1864, Hunter agreed to forward a sketch of General Gordon's character and military career to Alexander. Hunter also claimed he could give Alexander facts that would "furnish an explanation of all of our late reverses, more especially that of the 19th." These remarks would "reflect very severely upon Gen Early & very creditably upon Gordon." While Hunter admitted to Alexander that he was a member of Gordon's staff, the major claimed no relation to the general and was under "no obligation to him & will tell you nothing but the exact truth."[52]

Thomas G. Jones wrote many years after Cedar Creek that Early eventually sought a détente with Gordon, the army commander claiming that "there were no differences between them which effected the honor of either" despite holding "different views" about the battle. Early undoubtedly remained sore about Gordon's charges, however, and in 1888, when Early read Gordon's interview with the *Boston Herald* reporter about Cedar Creek, he wrote the Georgian asking about it. Early claimed he did not believe Gordon had made the statements attributed to him but wanted assurance that this was truly the case. Gordon never responded, instead "preserving a profound silence on the subject," according to Early's former staff member, Samuel J. C. Moore.[53]

Early's death in 1894 allowed Gordon's version of Cedar Creek in *Reminiscences* to go largely, but not completely, unchallenged in the public realm. John W. Daniel, likely the most vocal critic of *Reminiscences* in the years immediately following its publication, used his platform as editor of the weekly "Confederate Column" in the *Richmond Times Dispatch* to challenge much of what Gordon's memoir said about Cedar Creek and other battles. While Daniel praised Gordon's personal bravery and leadership abilities, the Virginian admitted to *Times-Dispatch* readers that he could not "follow General Gordon in the description given by him of the battles in which he was engaged." In private correspondence with ex-Confederate General Robert D. Johnston, Daniel asserted that Gordon "befogged and confused" every battle he wrote about.[54]

Late-twentieth-century scholars writing of the battles in which Gordon fought have echoed the criticism of Daniel. Harry W. Pfanz asserts in his study of the first day of Gettysburg that Gordon's "credibility is often in doubt." Gary W. Gallagher opines that "few witnesses matched Gordon in his egocentrism or his willingness to play loose with the truth." Gordon's *Reminiscences,* Gallagher observes, leaves unwary readers "with a distinct impression that the South would have triumphed if only misguided superiors such as Ewell and Early had acted on his advice." Although neither Pfanz nor Gallagher specifically mentions it as a factor, there is little if any of the "fog of war" in Gordon's battle accounts; the complex factors that led his superiors to hesitate or delay on the field of battle are often ignored or barely mentioned. Gordon, in contrast, depicts himself in *Reminiscences* as having the ability to see developments and opportunities on the battlefield with perfect clarity.[55]

Gallagher and other historians situate *Reminiscences* within a body of Confederate literature that reflects the mythology of the Lost Cause, particularly in its efforts to canonize Robert E. Lee. While Gordon's *Reminiscences* certainly illustrate key Lost Cause tenets, his viewpoints on battles such as Gettysburg, the Wilderness, and Cedar Creek were not solely a product of beliefs popularized at the end of the nineteenth and the beginning of the twentieth centuries. Gordon's battle narratives, formed in the immediate aftermath of the engagements and repeated on occasion in the postbellum decades, sought to discredit critics, especially Jubal Early, and protect and enhance the Georgian's substantial reputation in the pantheon of Confederate military heroes.

NOTES

The author thanks the following individuals for their assistance with this essay: Randy Allen, Gary W. Gallagher, Clark Johnson, Robert E. L. Krick, Robert K. Krick, Alex Kuhn, Eric Mink, and Greg White.

1. Walter L. Fleming, review of John B. Gordon, *Reminiscences of the Civil War*, in *Annals of the American Academy of Political and Social Science* 23 (May 1904): 135–36.

2. William C. Davis, ed., *The Confederate General*, 6 vols. ([Harrisburg, Pa.]: National Historical Society, 1991), 3:12; Ralph L. Eckert, *John Brown Gordon, Soldier, Southerner, American* (Baton Rouge: Louisiana State University Press, 1989), 293.

3. Eckert, *John Brown Gordon*, 315–21, 332–33; "Gen. Gordon Tells of Great War Drama," *Atlanta Constitution*, April 13, 1901; "Gen. John B. Gordon To-night, Tuesday, Nov. 10. Clement Opera House" (n.p., ca. 1904), copy of original flyer in possession of Robert K. Krick, Fredericksburg, Va.

4. C. E. Gibbs to Mr. E. A. Brown, September 21, 1903, letter in possession of Robert K. Krick, Fredericksburg, Va. Krick asserts that the marketing efforts involved in creating a Bureau of Correspondence for Subscriptions to promote a Confederate memoir in the early twentieth century is highly unusual (Robert K. Krick email to author, May 3, 2016).

5. *Confederate Veteran* 12 (February 1904): 52.

6. Ibid., 41; "A Reminiscence," *Herald and News* (Newberry, S.C.), February 3, 1905; "The Great Struggle," *Evening Press* (Grand Rapids, Mich.), November 21, 1903.

7. John B. Gordon, *Reminiscences of the Civil War* (1903; rpt., Baton Rouge: Louisiana State University Press, 1993), 14, 15, 19, 20; Eckert, *John Brown Gordon*, 334–35.

8. Eckert, *John Brown Gordon*, 335; Gordon, *Reminiscences*, 24–25.

9. Douglas Southall Freeman, *The South to Posterity: An Introduction to the Writing of Confederate History* (New York: Charles Scribner's Sons, 1939), 174–75.

10. Edward A. Pollard, *Lee and His Lieutenants* (New York: E. B. Treat & Co., 1867), iii; John B. Gordon to Rev. Jones, Brunswick, Ga., February 10, 1867, Item 86, Alexander Autographs, Inc., Catalog for October 21, 2000, live sale; "Burial of a Distinguished Citizen," *LaGrange* (Ga.) *Reporter*, May 2, 1890.

11. John B. Gordon to E. B. Teatt & Co., December 12, 1867, Item 74, Alexander Autographs, Inc., Catalog for June 4, 2005. (Treat is misspelled in this letter.)

12. Gordon, *Reminiscences*, 151–53.

13. Greg White to editor, *Blue and Gray Magazine* 19 (February 2002): 7; Henry M. Field, *Blood Is Thicker Than Water: A Few Days Among Our Southern Brethren* (New York: George Munro, 1886), 34–35.

14. Greg White to editor, *Blue and Gray Magazine* 19 (February 2002): 9.

15. "Again at Gettysburg," *Newnan* (Ga.) *Herald and Advertiser*, May 12, 1893.

16. William F. Hanna, "A Gettysburg Myth Exploded," *Civil War Times Illustrated* 24 (May 1985): 42–47; Gary M. Kross, "The Barlow-Gordon Incident," *Blue and Gray Magazine* 18 (December 2001): 51; Gordon, *Reminiscences*, xii.

17. D. Scott Hartwig, "Romances of Gettysburg—The Barlow-Gordon Incident," Parts 1, 2, and 3, *From the Fields of Gettysburg, The Blog of Gettysburg National Military Park*, npsgnmp. wordpress.com (accessed July 22, 2017); John C. Fazio, "The Barlow-Gordon Controversy:

Rest In Peace," *Gettysburg Magazine* 41 (July 2009): 33–54; Greg White to editor, *Blue and Gray Magazine* 19 (February 2002): 9.

18. Gordon, *Reminiscences,* 153–54.

19. Ibid., 156–57; Donald C. Pfanz, *Richard S. Ewell, A Soldier's Life* (Chapel Hill: University of North Carolina Press, 1998), 582. Pfanz questions the veracity of Gordon's claim that he had a 2:00 a.m. meeting with Ewell and Early on July 2. Pfanz also notes that it would not have been possible for Gordon to hear Union troops moving and building breastworks from his brigade's distant position on the York Pike on the evening of July 1.

20. John W. Daniel, "Misc. Notes Concerning Gordon's Brigade," copy in box B-8, Gettysburg National Military Park Library, Gettysburg, Pa.

21. John W. Daniel, "Pickett's Losses," *Richmond Times-Dispatch,* January 24, 1904; Jubal A. Early, *Autobiographical Sketch and Narrative of the War Between the States* (Philadelphia: J. B. Lippincott, 1912), 270–71. Early's official report and memoir both claim that before he found Ewell in Gettysburg he sent Gordon to take command of his brigade and that of Brigadier General William Smith on the York Road to watch for an enemy advance. Gordon does not mention this in either his official report or *Reminiscences.*

22. John B. Gordon to wife, July 7, 1863, Gordon Family Papers, Ms. 1637, University of Georgia Special Collections, Athens; U.S. War Department, *The War of the Rebellion: A Compilation of the Official Records of the Union and Confederate Armies,* 128 vols. (Washington, D.C.: Government Printing Office, 1880–1901), ser. 1, vol. 47, pt. 2: 445–46, 469–70, 493–94 (hereafter cited as *OR,* all citations to series 1); Pollard, *Lee and His Lieutenants,* 542. Gordon's use of the phrase "other counsels prevailed" in both the Pollard sketch and *Reminiscences* to describe his superiors' opposition to an attack on Cemetery Hill suggests that he likely utilized the former piece when writing his memoirs.

23. "General John B. Gordon," *Atlanta Weekly Opinion,* April 14, 1868; "John B. Gordon," Atlanta *Weekly Intelligencer,* April 22, 1868. Isaac W. Avery, writing in 1878, recounted the same Gettysburg narrative that appeared in Pollard and the 1868 Atlanta newspapers, but added that, although Gordon's judgment was overruled, "from this time his reputation for military capacity of the highest order was fixed" (Isaac W. Avery, "Senator Gordon," *Newnan* [Ga.] *Herald,* January 24, 1878).

24. Henry Kyd Douglas, *I Rode With Stonewall* (1940; rpt., St. Simons Island, Ga.: Mockingbird Books, 1979), 239.

25. Gordon, *Reminiscences,* 160–61. Gordon and Longstreet apparently maintained a cordial public relationship but privately disliked each other. For an example of public affection between the two, see "Gordon and Longstreet," *New York Times,* September 1, 1889. For an 1894 letter that reveals Longstreet's disdain for Gordon, see Thomas J. Goree, *Longstreet's Aide: The Civil War Letters of Major Thomas J. Goree,* ed. Thomas W. Cutrer (Charlottesville: University Press of Virginia, 1995), 177.

26. Edward Porter Alexander to Frederick Colston, February 9, 1904, Campbell Family Papers, Mss. 135, Southern Historical Collection, University of North Carolina, Chapel Hill; Helen D. Longstreet, "Longstreet's Gettysburg Movements Reviewed," *Atlanta Constitution,* January 3, 1904; "Mrs. Longstreet Defends Husband," *Richmond Times-Dispatch,* January 5, 1904; "Gordon and Longstreet," *Richmond Times-Dispatch,* January 6, 1904; "Lee and Longstreet," *New York Daily Tribune,* January 10, 1904.

27. Robert E. Lee, *The Wartime Papers of R. E. Lee,* ed. Cifford Dowdey and Louis H. Manarin (Boston: Little, Brown, 1961), 662; Pollard, *Lee and His Lieutenants,* 542–43; Gordon, *Reminiscences,* 238–41.

28. John W. Daniel, "My account, May 5th [1864]," John W. Daniel Papers, box 24, University of Virginia Special Collections, Charlottesville (repository hereafter cited as UVA). On Daniel's Brigade, see Gordon C. Rhea, *The Battle of the Wilderness, May 5–6, 1864* (Baton Rouge: Louisiana State University Press, 1994), 164–65.

29. Gordon, *Reminiscences,* 243–48; Thomas G. Jones to John W. Daniel, July 3, 1904, box marked "1849–1904," John W. Daniel Papers, UVA.

30. Gordon, *Reminiscences,* 255, 259–60; Campbell Brown, "Memorandum—Campaign of 1864," Ewell-Stewart-Brown Collection, folder 2, box 2, Tennessee State Library, Nashville; Rhea, *Battle of the Wilderness,* 409–10. Thomas G. Jones claimed that Gordon sent him in the morning to meet with Early and Ewell and convey information about the scouting expedition. After listening to Jones, Early voiced his concerns about a flank movement and, according to Jones, instructed him to tell Gordon "to hold still, and later, they would come over to the left and see what could be done." Gordon met with his corps and division commander not long after Jones left them (Thomas G. Jones to John W. Daniel, July 3, 1904, John W. Daniel Papers, UVA).

31. "Pegram's Grade [*sic*] Early's Division," *Richmond Times-Dispatch,* October 8, 1905.

32. Gordon, *Reminiscences,* 255–58.

33. Rhea, *Battle of the Wilderness,* 413–14. Gordon mentions in *Reminiscences* a ride with Lee on the morning of May 7 over part of the ground where the flank attack had taken place the previous evening. This passage might reflect an effort on Gordon's part to reconcile his correspondence with Lee in 1867–68 in which Lee claimed to have seen Gordon on May 7 (Gordon, *Reminiscences,* 267).

34. Robert E. Lee to John B. Gordon, January 8, 1867; February 22, 1868, John B. Gordon Papers, box 5, University of Georgia Special Collections, Athens. John B. Gordon to Robert E. Lee, February 6, 1868, Robert E. Lee Headquarters Papers, Mss 3 L515a 603, Virginia Historical Society, Richmond. Evidence of Lee's visit to Ewell on the afternoon of May 5, including Lee's desire to launch a flank attack against the Federal right that day, appears in notes taken in 1868 by William Allan of a conversation with Lee (Gary W. Gallagher, ed., *Lee The Soldier* [Lincoln: University of Nebraska Press, 1996], 11).

35. Gordon, *Reminiscences,* 250; *OR* 36(1): 1078.

36. Jubal A. Early, *A Memoir of the Last Year of the War for Independence* (Toronto: Lovell and Gibson, 1866), 18, 19; Gordon, *Reminiscences,* 250.

37. Pfanz, *Richard S. Ewell,* 374; Rhea, *Battle of the Wilderness,* 428–29; Gallagher, ed., *Lee the Soldier,* 11.

38. Gordon, *Reminiscences,* 332–33, 371–72.

39. Early, *Memoir of the Last Year,* 107.

40. Gordon, *Reminiscences,* 333–36; Early, *Memoir of the Last Year,* 107; Jedediah Hotchkiss, *Make Me a Map of the Valley: The Civil War Journal of Stonewall Jackson's Topographer,* ed. Archie P. McDonald (Dallas: Southern Methodist University Press, 1973), 237. Gordon told a reporter in 1888 that while at the signal station members of Early's staff were "utterly incredulous" of his plan to attack the Federals. The wartime diary of Jedediah Hotchkiss

contradicts Gordon's 1888 account ("Flanking 'Little Phil.' The Man Who Almost Spoiled Sheridan's Ride. Old 'Glory Enough' Saved the Union Army. Gen. John B. Gordon Sets History Right," *Boston Herald*, August 19, 1888).

41. Gordon, *Reminiscences,* 336; Hotchkiss, *Make Me a Map,* 238. Gordon's memoir suggests that the initial trip to the signal station and the discovery of the path around the base of Massanutten Mountain took place on the same day, but the Hotchkiss diary suggests otherwise. The timeline presented by Hotchkiss is used here.

42. Gordon, *Reminiscences,* 336; Thomas Henry Carter, *A Gunner in Lee's Army: The Civil War Letters of Thomas Henry Carter,* ed. Graham T. Dozier (Chapel Hill: University of North Carolina Press, 2014), 259; "General John B. Gordon," *Atlanta Weekly Opinion,* April 14, 1868; "Flanking 'Little Phil.'"

43. Gordon, *Reminiscences,* 339–41; "Flanking 'Little Phil.'"

44. Early, *Memoir of the Last Year,* 112; Samuel J. C. Moore, "In Defence of General Early," *Clarke* (Berryville, Va.) *Courier,* October 17, 1889; John W. Daniel, *Speeches and Orations of John Warwick Daniel* (Lynchburg, Va.: J. B. Bell, 1911), 554. Moore's defense of Early, written in response to Gordon's 1888 interview, claims that the account of Cedar Creek told by Gordon to the Boston reporter had been related earlier by the Georgian in private conversations "with gentlemen not familiar with the facts." Moore believed that Gordon's interview with the reporter was the first time the Georgian had made public his views on Cedar Creek.

45. Pollard, *Lee and His Lieutenants,* 546; "General John B. Gordon," *Atlanta Weekly Opinion,* April 14, 1868; Gordon, *Reminiscences,* 341–42, 344.

46. For immediate post-battle Confederate accounts that verify widespread plundering, see Theodore C. Mahr, *The Battle of Cedar Creek* (Lynchburg, Va.: H. E. Howard, 1992), 249–52, and Gary W. Gallagher, ed., *The Shenandoah Valley Campaign of 1864* (Chapel Hill: University of North Carolina Press, 2006), 66–67, 69; Early, *Memoir of the Last Year,* 116.

47. Pollard, *Lee and His Lieutenants,* 546; John B. Gordon to George F. Holmes, December 29, 1870, George F. Holmes Papers, Library of Congress, Washington, D.C. (repository cited hereafter as LC); "Flanking 'Little Phil.'"

48. John B. Gordon to George F. Holmes, December 29, 1870, George F. Holmes Papers, LC; Gordon, *Reminiscences,* 355.

49. Gordon, *Reminiscences,* 368–70.

50. Jubal Early, "Soldiers of the Army of the Valley" (n.p., 1864); Robert G. Stephens, *Intrepid Warrior: Clement Anselm Evans* (Dayton, Ohio: Morningside Press, 1992), 490, 493. For a discussion of the correspondence in the southern press about Cedar Creek, see Gallagher, ed., *Shenandoah Valley Campaign of 1864,* 71–72.

51. "Argus" letter of October 21, 1864, *Richmond Daily Enquirer,* October 27, 1864.

52. Thomas G. Jones to John W. Daniel, Thomas G. Jones Papers, Alabama Department of Archives and History, Montgomery; Robert W. Hunter to Peter W. Alexander, October 27, 1864, Peter W. Alexander Papers, Rare Books and Manuscripts Department, Columbia University, New York.

53. Thomas G. Jones to John W. Daniel, December 25, 1904, Thomas G. Jones Papers, Alabama Department of Archives and History; Moore, "In Defense of General Early," *Clarke Courier,* October 17, 1889.

54. John W. Daniel, "The Famous Fight at Cedar Creek," *Richmond Times Dispatch,* May 21, 1905; John W. Daniel, "General J. B. Gordon," *Richmond Times Dispatch,* December 6, 1903; John W. Daniel to Robert D. Johnston, July 22, 1905, copy of original in possession of Gary W. Gallagher.

55. Harry W. Pfanz, *Gettysburg—The First Day* (Chapel Hill: University of North Carolina Press, 2001), 418; Gary W. Gallagher, ed., *The First Day at Gettysburg* (Kent, Ohio: Kent State University Press, 1992), 37, 39.

Edward Porter Alexander, *second from right in back row,* with his brothers and sisters in the early 1890s. He corresponded with his sister Louisa Alexander Gilmer, *center of the middle row,* about progress on his first memoir. From the editor's collection.

The Best Confederate Memoirist

Edward Porter Alexander's Unrivaled Military Accounts

GARY W. GALLAGHER

Edward Porter Alexander's two memoirs stand unrivaled among all accounts published by Confederate soldiers. Written over the course of a decade, beginning in the late 1890s, they appeared in print more than eighty years apart as *Military Memoirs of a Confederate: A Critical Narrative* (1907) and *Fighting for the Confederacy: The Personal Recollections of General Edward Porter Alexander* (1989). This essay will explain the unusual gap between publication dates for the two books—as well as my role in identifying and editing the second one. For now, it is more important to note that Alexander brought to both of his books analytical acuity, a gift for describing key scenes in dramatic and memorable fashion, and the perspective of one who literally had been at the center of operations in the Eastern Theater from First Bull Run to Appomattox. He served on the staffs of generals P. G. T. Beauregard, Joseph E. Johnston, and Robert E. Lee before distinguishing himself as the Confederacy's preeminent artillerist. Although an ardent Confederate during the war, he wrote with almost none of the Lost Cause special pleading evident in the writings of most of his former comrades. He did embrace a form of sectional reconciliation by the time he wrote his recollections but never apologized for his military service in support of the breakaway slaveholding republic.[1]

Explaining why the two books are so remarkable requires several elements. Some biographical information about Alexander will establish his place in Civil War military history and set the stage for exploring how and why he wrote the books and what audience he envisioned for each. Passages from the books will then illustrate four notable attributes: (1) Alexander's narrative skill—with examples of memorable descriptive passages that also yield insights into the history and character of the Army of Northern Virginia; (2) his willingness to present the hard, or, in the current fashion, the dark side of the war; (3) his unblinking critique of Lost Cause icons Robert E. Lee and Thomas J. "Stonewall" Jackson at a time when most former Confederates treated those two figures as demigods; and (4) other ways in which he deviated from conventions almost universally observed by former Confederates writing about the conflict.

I. The Soldier

Alexander was born into a prominent slaveholding family in Washington, Georgia, on May 26, 1835, and received his early education from private tutors. He entered the U.S. Military Academy in 1853, graduating third of thirty-eight cadets in the class of 1857. Superiors predicted success for him from the outset. Over the three years following graduation, he taught at the academy, participated in the final stage of the Mormon War, and assisted Surgeon Albert J. Meyer in developing the "wig-wag" system of motion telegraphy. Alexander left the U.S. Army upon hearing in February 1861, while stationed at Fort Steilacoom in Washington Territory, that Georgia had seceded. The preceding November, he had written his sister about the political situation and Abraham Lincoln's candidacy: "If he is elected I believe the interests of humanity, civilization, and self-preservation call on the South to secede, and I'll go my arm, leg, or death on it." Alexander's choice of language—especially the use of "civilization," a word often deployed by white southerners in discussing perceived Republican or abolitionist threats to sectional harmony—affirmed his feeling that Lincoln's success would place in jeopardy the South's slaveholding social structure. After a long journey from the West Coast, Alexander arrived in Richmond, Virginia, on June 1, 1861, and learned that he had been commissioned a captain of engineers in the Confederacy's fledgling army.[2]

No other Confederate officer played more varied roles or worked closely with a larger number of famous figures. Alexander joined Beauregard's staff as chief signal officer in late June 1861 and subsequently added responsibilities as chief of ordnance for the army defending northern Virginia. From the summer of 1861 through the close of the Maryland campaign in 1862, he held the posts of chief signal officer and head of ordnance under Beauregard, Joseph E. Johnston, and Robert E. Lee. He kept arms and ammunition flowing to the army under difficult circumstances during the Peninsula campaign, the Seven Days, Second Bull Run, and operations that climaxed at Antietam. Somehow, he also found time to offer a plan for reorganizing the army's artillery, coordinated intelligence activities, supervised the use of a balloon during the Seven Days (he was aloft for part of the battle of Gaines's Mill), performed reconnaissance, and carried out engineering tasks. Lee and others appreciated Alexander's manifold talents but discerned a special aptitude for artillery. "We have no more accomplished officer," wrote chief of artillery William Nelson Pendleton in recommending that Alexander be promoted to lieutenant colonel and given a battalion of guns in James Longstreet's First Corps. Lee agreed, and Alexander, promoted to full colonel in early March 1863, found a place in the branch where he would earn a dazzling reputation. "He was far and away the superior of all others in his arm," observed the leading student of artillery in Lee's army in assessing the young Georgian fifty years after the war.[3]

Alexander immediately excelled in his new position. He arranged the Rebel batteries at Fredericksburg that helped decimate Union attackers on the plain below Marye's Heights on December 13, 1862. At Chancellorsville on May 3, 1863, he directed the movement of Confederate artillery to Hazel Grove, a plateau from which southern guns overwhelmed Union artillery at Fairview Cemetery and helped Lee to reunite the two wings of his army. Alexander handled Longstreet's artillery on July 2–3 at Gettysburg, rendering his most famous service in overseeing the barrage that preceded the Pickett-Pettigrew assault. Accompanying Longstreet's corps to northern Georgia in September 1863, he just missed the battle of Chickamauga but fought at Chattanooga and Knoxville later that year.

On all these fields, Alexander functioned as Longstreet's tactical chief of artillery. It made sense for the best gunner in the army to control as many batteries as possible in combat; however, Colonel John B. Walton, a friend of Longstreet's, remained titular head of the First Corps artillery. A situation frustrating to all concerned ended in March 1864 when Alexander replaced Walton. Joseph E. Johnston, whom Alexander admired a great deal, had forced a resolution by requesting his former staff officer's promotion to brigadier general and transfer to the Army of Tennessee. Jefferson Davis discussed Johnston's proposal with Lee, who refused to let Alexander go but approved his promotion to brigadier general. "General Lee objects that he is too valuable in his present position to be taken from it," Johnston noted somewhat sourly. "His value to the country would be more than doubled, I think, by the promotion and assignment I recommend." Davis later told one of Alexander's sisters that her brother was one of a very few officers "whom Gen. Lee would not give to anybody."[4]

Alexander maintained his high reputation through the Overland campaign of 1864, the siege of Petersburg, and the retreat to Appomattox. Drawing on his engineering expertise, he helped lay out part of the defensive line outside Richmond, and Lee eventually expanded Alexander's authority to embrace all the artillery between the James and Appomattox rivers. On April 9, 1865, at Appomattox, when U. S. Grant's forces blocked Lee's effort to break free of the Union pursuit, Alexander formed the last battle line of the Army of Northern Virginia. He surrendered with the rest of Lee's army. Thus ended the memorable military career of the Confederacy's ablest practitioner of the "long arm."

II. The Memoirist and Historian

Alexander achieved considerable success throughout the postwar years. He first thought of pursuing a military career abroad. "Our cause has been lost, for the present at least, but my faith in its righteousness is not for one moment shaken . . . ," he wrote two weeks after Appomattox from New York City. "I sail to-morrow for Georgia, having come North only to see if I could arrange any way of getting in the Brazilian Army, having to seek a support for my family from my only profession—that of arms." Nothing came of his plans to remain a soldier, and Alexander's search for a career took him first to higher education, where he taught mathematics and engineering at the University of South Carolina, and eventually into the railroad business as an executive. A staunch Democrat with a wide circle of friends that included President Grover Cleveland, Alexander remained cordial with James Longstreet, whose embrace of the Republican

Party rendered him a pariah across much of the old Confederacy. In 1902, forty-five years after his graduation, he delivered a lecture on Alumni Day at West Point during the academy's centennial commemoration. The *New York Times* reported that Alexander's speech "was continually applauded, especially his reference to General Longstreet, who occupied a seat on the platform near the speaker." The address made no apology for secession but insisted, in a strong reconciliationist tone, that former Confederates and their children acknowledged "that it was best for the South that the cause was 'lost.'" Mary Lee, the general's daughter, sent Alexander "quite a severe reproof" for speaking "in the presence of Longstreet who had abused her father"—while also admitting that "others may well agree that the Nation is better than any Confederacy."[5]

Despite the demands of his postwar careers, Alexander found opportunity to study and write about the war. He initially embarked on a history of Longstreet's First Corps. "Gen. Longstreet begged me to do it & I thought I could finish it in a three-month vacation," Alexander explained to a former member of "Old Pete's" staff in the spring of 1868. But after "nearly two years . . . I have hardly made a beginning. What I want is not the general facts that everybody knows but the details & they only exist in the memories of survivors." The prospect of obtaining sufficient material seemed "utterly hopeless" because "[f]or every one hundred letters and circulars I send, I get about ten replies, & of these ten, about six simply say that they have lost all records & can't remember anything they think important enough to write." Former Confederate major general Cadmus M. Wilcox was among those who did respond, wishing Alexander "all success" and expressing faith that "you will have no other motive but to present impartially & truthfully as far as you can the history of Longstreet's Corps." Alexander eventually abandoned the project because of the press of business and the difficulty of procuring sufficient information from former comrades. He did so reluctantly and shared his frustration with a visitor at the University of South Carolina. "Confederate officers who could have furnished the necessary materials are almost all engaged now in other employments," recorded the visitor, "and so driven, many of them, by the necessities of daily life, that they have no time to spend on history." As a result, Alexander feared posterity would be left "with little more than one side of the question."[6]

A short while after abandoning his initial project, Alexander returned to historical endeavors in the mid-1870s. Over the ensuing decade, he published seven pieces in the *Southern Historical Society Papers,* in whose pages former Confederates revisited and argued about many war-related topics, and two in *The Century*'s hugely successful *Battles and Leaders of the Civil War.* All of these articles exhibited scrupulous attention to detail and an absence of the type of self-interested argument common among writings by participants. Robert Underwood Johnson, a coeditor of *Battles and Leaders,* considered Alexander one of "the two most lovable men I met in the long course of our relations to the War Series"—a man of "genial and winning personality, and of such integrity and candor" that anything he wrote could be relied upon.[7]

Alexander undertook a full-scale memoir of the war in the late 1890s. Sent by President Cleveland to Greytown, Nicaragua, in early 1897 to help arbitrate a boundary dispute, he acceded to his daughter Bessie Alexander Ficklen's request that he write his Confederate recollections. He began slowly but soon warmed to the task. Relying on a small library that included the one-volume popular edition of *Battles and Leaders* and William Swinton's *Campaigns of the Army of the Potomac,* his own brief diaries and journals that covered part of the war, and correspondence with former officers similar to that he had pursued when working on his history of the First Corps, Alexander traced his activities during the campaigns of the Army of Northern Virginia. He intended to let no one but his family and a few close friends see the finished work. As he explained to one of his sisters, the recollections were not "to publish, but only for my children, so of course they are very personal." "But partly to tell them the *real* story of the war, & partly because I was often concerned in important affairs which they will be interested to understand," he added in a passage describing the purpose and scope of the recollections, "I have written, along with my own little doings, a sort of critical narrative of the military game wh[ich] was being played, & I have not hesitated to criticise our moves as I would moves in chess—no matter what general made them." Restricting his audience to a small group of intimates freed him to write in a way that would have been impossible had he planned to publish for commercial distribution. "I doubt whether our people . . . are yet prepared," he averred, "to have it said that either Lee or Jackson ever made a military mistake."[8]

Although Alexander considered his manuscript penned in Greytown only a first draft, he fretted about the possibility of getting details wrong. In August 1899, he shared this fear, which arose from an engineer's love of precision, with Frederick M. Colston, who had served as a subordinate officer in Alexander's artillery battalion. "I am writing only for my children & intimate friends," he related, "yet I am as anxious to eliminate all mistakes as if it were for publication. I know how easily mistakes can creep into any narrative, & particularly into one written so far from books of reference as I am here." Throughout the Greytown manuscript, Alexander left blank spaces where he lacked firm knowledge of specific strengths, distances, names, or other details. Those could be filled in later. Once back in the United States, he assured Colston, "I expect to revise at home with the 'War Records' of the Govt by me. Then I am going to have it typewritten & leave to my children." Two months later, Alexander similarly informed his sister Louisa that when home he would "go over it all at leisure, with all my military library at hand to put on finishing touches, & fill some few gaps." That process, he estimated, might consume "a year or two—maybe more."[9]

The letter to Colston in August 1899 also betrayed impatience with Lost Cause hagiography of Robert E. Lee. Colston apparently had mentioned possible pitfalls in writing about the Confederate hero, which elicited a strong response: "As to what I write being considered an attack on Gen Lee, I am afraid that there are but too many people who will insist upon regarding as an attack upon him anything wh[ich] admits or implies that he ever did make the slightest mistake in the world." That attitude toward Lee, Alexander continued, "robs of any real value every Confederate Life of Gen Lee which I have yet seen, and Gen Fitz's as much as any." "Gen. Fitz" was Fitzhugh Lee, Robert E. Lee's nephew, former governor of Virginia, and a major figure in the Army of Northern Virginia's cavalry. His *General Lee,* first published in 1894 as part of New York publisher D. Appleton's "Great Commanders" series, had gone through four printings by the time Alexander wrote to Colston. In correspondence with Fitzhugh Lee, Alexander had taken issue with his assignment of blame for defeat at Gettysburg to James Longstreet—a staple of Lost Cause argument. "I don't undertake to defend Longstreet because he is Longstreet at all," insisted Alexander, who never had "been able to understand how anyone could maintain that at Gettysburg he acted without Gen. Lee's knowledge & implied approval." What Alexander told Colston he wished to see—and what he would provide in both of his own memoirs—was "a really *fine* military criticism *as severe as possible,* of every one of our campaigns."[10]

Alexander completed a full draft of his recollections just before leaving

Greytown in October 1899. The narrative, which he titled "Fighting for the Confederacy,"[11] totaled more than twelve hundred pages and offered innumerable insights into Lee's campaigns as well as a bountiful supply of anecdotes about Alexander's activities. Bluntly honest in a text he believed few people would see, Alexander dissected campaigns with an impartial eye, criticized Lee and others in the Confederate pantheon, quoted profane comments from various comrades, and shunned the romanticism and partisan agenda that tainted many Rebel reminiscences. Once home in South Carolina, he neither followed through on his intention to have copies of the manuscript typed nor distributed the bulky text to his children or select friends—though he eventually presented at least portions of it to his daughter Bessie, whose urgings had gotten him started on the project soon after he reached Greytown. In fact, after Alexander's death at the age of seventy-four on April 28, 1910, the Greytown reminiscences, for all practical purposes, disappeared.[12]

Military Memoirs of a Confederate: A Critical Narrative grew out of the twelve-hundred-page manuscript completed in Greytown. The deaths of his wife in November 1899 and a daughter five months later staggered Alexander, who grieved for several months on his plantation on South Island off the coast of Georgetown, South Carolina. Determination to revise his Greytown memoirs helped pull him out of mourning. "I've actually *begun* in rewriting my Recollections," he reported to his son Will in September 1900, "& that puts an end to every idle moment—for I try to write a little bit every day." Despite being alone and missing his family, he assured Will, he was "not lonesome—for I am so busy." At first intending only to correct errors and fill gaps in the existing narrative, he had decided by the summer of 1901 to make significant changes. "I want to tell the story *professionally,*" he wrote that August, "& to comment *freely* on every professional feature as one w[oul]d comment on moves of chess, even tho[ugh] it may seem to reflect on Lee or Jackson or anybody else."[13]

Alexander envisioned an audience well beyond family and friends for his revised memoirs and increasingly assumed a historian's, rather than a participant's, perspective. An early letter to Bessie from Greytown had described the personal, even emotional, nature of his initial effort: "I am *delighted* if you like my poor little 'recollections,'" he told her in the summer of 1896, "but lots of them bring my eyes full of tears as I write." Five years later, he had far more interest in presenting a detached, analytical treatment of the Army of Northern Virginia's operations and leaders. To that end, he concluded that much of the text relating to his own activities should go, a decision abetted by discussions with prominent historians William A. Dunning and J. Franklin Jameson, both active with the American Historical Association, and Frederic Bancroft, whose work focused on the nineteenth-century South. Alexander shared revised drafts of chapters with Bancroft and took him on tours of battlefields, and in 1908 he published an essay on U. S. Grant in the Wilderness campaign in the AHA's *Annual Report.*[14]

As he labored on revisions, Alexander corresponded with old comrades and mined a growing body of published primary materials. Foremost among the latter was the 128-volume *The War of the Rebellion: The Official Records of the Union and Confederate Armies,* which had been published by the U.S. Department of War between 1880 and 1901. In September 1902, he wrote to James Longstreet, assuring his old chief that "of course I have read your book & will have the benefit of all you have said therein." But surely, ventured Alexander, Longstreet had omitted, or only partially touched upon, "many points of interest" in *From Manassas to Appomattox: Memoirs of the Civil War in America* (1896). Should examples of such omissions occur to Longstreet, "[W]ill you not kindly make informal notes upon them at your leisure & let me have the benefit of them." In the meantime, Alexander stated, "I am going slow & studying the official reports carefully, & if you can kindly give me any points of interest they will be gratefully received." Longstreet likely approved of Alexander's assurance that he planned a full critique of "Jackson's conduct thro[ugh]out the Seven Days—I have written more fully & explicitly than has ever before been done showing that on June 29 he excused himself & command from battle on the grounds of 'other important duties,' by wh[ich] he meant having religious services."[15]

Six years passed before Alexander completed his task. The text for *Military Memoirs* differed from the Greytown recollections in several important ways. Somewhat more polished, it lacked the earlier version's raw power. Most of the personal anecdotes disappeared, though a few wonderful vignettes, such as an exchange with James Longstreet on the afternoon of July 3 at Gettysburg, remained to enliven the narrative. Alexander also softened or cut some harsh estimates of friends and foes and removed profanity he had quoted. Yet he still evaluated Lee, whom he admired greatly, far more rigorously than had almost any other ex-Confederate. The proportions of coverage also changed: the Greytown version allocated 6 percent of its text to the prewar years, 33 percent to wartime events before Gettysburg, almost 12 percent to Gettysburg, and 49 percent to campaigns after Gettysburg. For *Military Memoirs,* the percentages were less than 2 percent to the prewar period, 56 percent to military operations before Gettysburg, approximately 13 percent to Gettysburg, and roughly 28 percent to post-Gettysburg action. Finally, in line with his intention to provide a comprehensive history of Confederate military operations in the Eastern Theater, Alexander added a chapter on the 1862 Shenandoah Valley campaign, an operation in which he had played no role, as well as more material on John Bell Hood's 1864 Tennessee campaign, William Tecumseh Sherman's activities in Georgia, and other events he had not witnessed.

Published by Charles Scribner's Sons in 1907, *Military Memoirs of a Confederate* quickly gained the status of a classic.[16] Reflecting Alexander's aspiration to create a piece of serious historical scholarship, Scribner's marketed the book as "devoted primarily to criticism of the strategy of the war on both sides"—while also noting "Gen. Alexander's keen and alert personality, his delightful personal reminiscences and anecdotes, . . . [and] the rare literary quality of the style." Readers and reviewers responded quite enthusiastically. "One of the most valuable of all the books on the war," trumpeted the *Army and Navy Journal.* William A. Dunning read it several times and, in a letter to Frederic Bancroft, pronounced it "fascinating." "It professes to be written particularly for military students," wrote Ezra A. Carman in the *American Historical Review,* "but will be found of great interest to the general reader. The narrative is clear and concise, praise is worthily bestowed and criticism generally well taken and temperate." One notable non-specialist wrote to Alexander very shortly after the book came out. "I have so thoro[ugh]ly enjoyed your 'Military Memoirs,'" President Theodore Roosevelt gushed, "that I must write to tell you so." The president also issued an invitation for dinner at the White House so he and Alexander could discuss the book.[17]

Although a number of former Confederates complained about Alexander's sometimes pointed evaluation of Lee or took exception to his lack of regret over the demise of the Confederacy, they generally admitted to considerable admiration for the book. Typical of these individuals was William Gordon McCabe, who had served as a staff officer in William R. J. Pegram's battalion of artillery. Disappointed in Alexander's statement that

Confederate independence would have proved a curse in the long run, McCabe nonetheless believed it "no exaggeration to call this a great book . . . by one of the most high-minded, resolute, and resourceful officers" in Lee's army. Overall, thought Douglas Southall Freeman in evaluating reaction among white southerners, early "mutterings because General Alexander was thought by some veterans to have been unduly critical of General Lee" dissipated and allowed *Military Memoirs,* by the 1930s, to become "one of the most frequently quoted of Confederate authorities."[18]

Historians throughout the twentieth century eagerly embraced the book. None was more influential than Freeman, the most famous student of Lee's army from the mid-1930s through the centennial years and beyond. He leaned heavily on Alexander's account, judging it to be "the most valuable single commentary on the operations of the Army of Northern Virginia." Another careful student of Confederate literature called the book a "hard-hitting, authoritative narrative by one of Lee's finest young officers" that contains "assessments of the military operations of the Army of Northern Virginia [that] are honest, fair, and sound." T. Harry Williams, one of the most respected mid-twentieth-century historians of the war, contributed a long introduction to a reprint published by Indiana University Press in 1962. "Probably no book by a participant in the war has done so much to shape the historical image of that conflict," commented Williams: "As Alexander drew lessons from the battles, so a lesson can be drawn from his book—that the finest military history may be written by a soldier who is also a scholar." Another reprint, by the Press of Morningside Bookshop in 1977, offered an introduction by Maury Klein, Alexander's biographer. Conceding that the book "is not without errors," Klein characterized it as "a brilliant and incisive piece of military history . . . which no student of the war can afford to neglect."[19]

The principal criticism of *Military Memoirs* registered by modern historians concerned Alexander's decision to restrict the amount of personal material. They knew how close to the center of operations he had been and could detect places in the narrative where he clearly stopped short of relating everything he must have seen and known. "One could wish that he had written two books," mused T. Harry Williams, "a general history and a more personal narrative." Douglas Southall Freeman also lamented Alexander's reticence, positing that much "he could have said for the instruction of soldiers and to the enlightenment of students, he felt it improper to put in print." James I. Robertson Jr. offered a novel explanation for the tone of the book. "Perhaps the Scribner's editors recoiled at the directness and/or bluntness of some of Alexander's original statements," he speculated, "or possibly the manuscript was too long and descriptive in the opinion of the publisher. In any event, someone other than Alexander wrote much of the finished narrative."[20]

All confusion would have evaporated had anyone been aware of the full Greytown manuscript. When Alexander's papers arrived at the Southern Historical Collection at the University of North Carolina, the staff sought to make sense of what they described as drafts of "a volume of Civil War recollections, published in 1907 as *Military Memoirs of a Confederate.*" Written in two blank books, on foolscap, and on other kinds of paper, the apparent drafts were repetitive and "confusing to organize and use." Most of the text, concluded the librarians, seemed to have been composed "in the period 1900–1907, and some of it was extensively revised before publication." Unaware that Alexander had completed a full reminiscence before beginning to revise, and hampered because the family did not treat the Greytown manuscript as a separate entity, the staff intermingled chapters from the original recollections with drafts of chapters from *Military Memoirs* in chronological files corresponding to major military campaigns. This logical solution to a processing nightmare consigned the Greytown narrative to oblivion, submerging it in a confusing mass of material assumed to be parts of *Military Memoirs.*[21]

None of the scholars who used the Alexander Papers through the early 1980s discovered the presence of the entire Greytown manuscript. Maury Klein came closest to doing so. "When his daughter Bessie pointedly dispatched some large ledgerbooks to Greytown," observed Klein, "Alexander agreed to fill them with his reminiscences. . . . Those now faded ledgers comprise Alexander's personal memoir of the war. Regarding them as a private legacy for his family, he included a rich stock of personal anecdotes about himself and his comrades."[22] But Bessie Alexander Ficklen's two light-brown ledgers hold just a quarter of the Greytown manuscript—the portion covering the period through the early stages of the Second Bull Run campaign. Alexander wrote the rest on foolscap and other paper, and these sections are far harder to distinguish from drafts of chapters of *Military Memoirs.* The key to disentangling the Greytown material, I learned while working on the manuscript for *Fighting for the Confederacy,* lies in Alexander's correspondence from Nicaragua. As he proceeded with his writing, he reported to members of his family and a few friends how many pages he had written on various episodes during the war. For example, on February 6, 1899, he noted, "I've just finished Gettysburg *115 pages* & 2 maps, & I'll soon go on with East Tennessee campaign." A careful search of Alexander's papers for chapters corresponding in length to those mentioned in the letters reveals the entire manuscript for *Fighting for the Confederacy*.[23]

Reaction to *Fighting for the Confederacy* exceeded in enthusiasm what had greeted *Military Memoirs*. This response stemmed in part from the excitement of finding new testimony from Alexander, a participant whose observations already had done so much to shape understanding of Lee, his army, and the war in the Eastern Theater. Writing in the *New Republic,* literary critic Alfred Kazin deemed the book "a treasure of Civil War 'personal memoirs' . . . altogether livelier and more irreverent than anything in Grant's and Sherman's books." Geoffrey C. Ward, the principal writer for Ken Burns's PBS documentary *The Civil War,* found *Fighting for the Confederacy* "in at least two ways an astonishment. First, it is not a reprint but a brand-new book by one of the South's ablest soldiers, 124 years after Appomattox. . . . More surprising still is the compelling, intensely personal style in which it is written."[24]

Professional scholars echoed Kazin and Ward. William J. Cooper, a leading historian of the nineteenth-century South, exhibited unabashed scholarly excitement: "What a marvelous book! . . . [I]t is amazing that this remarkable and significant account has never before been published. Now . . . everyone interested in the Confederacy has ready access to what may very well be the most outstanding Confederate military memoir." James I. Robertson Jr. welcomed "a book that every serious student of the Army of Northern Virginia should have," adding, with more than a touch of hyperbole, that it "is so outstanding that it renders obsolete the later and long-respected memoirs Alexander released for publication." Another reviewer asserted that "the more critical approach taken in *Fighting for the Confederacy,* together with its more pungent language and wealth of entertaining anecdotes, combine to make it an even greater work than its famous predecessor." Near the end of the 1990s, a prominent bibliographer dealt with both of Alexander's books: "The two works complement each other very well. *Military Memoirs* is a superb history of Lee's army with some of Alexander's own actions in it. *Fighting for the Confederacy* . . . constitutes a superb personal narrative with a good deal of analysis of Lee's operations thrown in. Hence, this version of Alexander's recollections is dramatic and revealing, an important source on the general, his fellow officers, and the Army of Northern Virginia."[25]

III. The Books

Excerpts from Alexander's two books will convey why the pair constitutes a matchless contribution to the literature on the military side of the war and why they have been so frequently cited by historians and other writers. A few passages exceed the ideal length for quotations, but condensing them would prevent a full appreciation of Alexander's ability to evoke a dramatic moment while simultaneously giving readers information that illuminates a larger point. As a group, these quotations touch on only a few of the major themes and strengths of the books—constraints of space prevent a more exhaustive sampling. For an appreciation of Alexander's use of humor, his ability to capture salient elements of personalities in a few words, and his meticulous analysis of very complicated tactical maneuverings (most notably at Gettysburg), readers will have to go to the texts.

Three superb narrative set pieces, one at the outset and two at the end, will open and close my consideration of the books. The description in *Military Memoirs* of the scene on December 11, 1862, at Fredericksburg provides an excellent beginning point. It places readers with Confederates who watched Union engineers build pontoon bridges across the Rappahannock River under fire. Alexander and his comrades took in a vast amphitheatrical landscape, bounded by high ground occupied by Federals east of the river and by a string of hills held by Confederates west of the river, with open ground leading down to the Rappahannock and more soldiers visible in one place than at any other time in the war. The Army of the Potomac, the largest and most important military expression of the American republic, was moving into positions from which it would assail the Rebel position two days later. Alexander's prose, which in another context could be attributed to a cinematographer's eye, conjures a vivid mental image:

> The city, except its steeples, was still veiled in the mist which had settled in the valleys. Above it and in it incessantly showed the round white clouds

of bursting shells, and out of its midst there soon rose three or four columns of dense black smoke from houses set on fire by the explosions. The atmosphere was so perfectly calm and still that the smoke rose vertically in great pillars for several hundred feet before spreading outward in black sheets. The opposite bank of the river, for two miles to the right and left, was crowned at frequent intervals with blazing batteries, canopied in clouds of white smoke.

Beyond these, the dark blue masses of over 100,000 infantry in compact columns, and numberless parks of white-topped wagons and ambulances massed in orderly ranks, all awaited the completion of the bridges. The earth shook with the thunder of the guns, and, high above all, a thousand feet in the air, hung two immense balloons. The scene gave impressive ideas of the disciplined power of a great army, and of the vast resources of the nation which sent it forth.[26]

Alexander did not shy away from the brutal aspects of the conflict now often labeled the "dark war." Indeed, he revealed his own willingness to embrace a bloodthirsty approach to waging war against the Federals and to describe passions, usually released in the heat of combat, that often overtook combatants on both sides. Examples from *Fighting for the Confederacy* illustrate this dimension of his work. The first relates to action on May 3 at Chancellorsville, the costliest day by far in the battle waged between Lee's and Joseph Hooker's forces in early May 1863. As Confederate artillery moved from Hazel Grove toward Fairview Cemetery that morning, Alexander found himself in position for his batteries to wreak havoc on retreating Union troops. "[W]e deployed on the plateau," he recalled, "& opened on the fugitives, infantry, artillery, wagons—everything—swarming about the Chancellorsville house, & down the broad road leading thence to the river. That is the part of artillery service that may be denominated 'pie'—to fire into swarming fugitives, who can't answer back." Deploying a reference to the British romantic poet Robert Southey, he continued: "One has usually had to pay for this pie before he gets it, so he has no compunctions of conscience or chivalry, but feels like the women in Southey's poem, who 'all agreed that revenge was sweet, and young prince Crocodiles delicate meat.' Some of our shells soon set fire to the big Chancellorsville house itself, & the conflagration made a striking scene with our shells bursting all about it." As he rode forward to the house, Alexander saw numerous wounded

Federal officers and "a beautiful Newfoundland dog which had been killed, also lying in the yard."[27]

More than two years later, Lee's army first encountered large numbers of black Union soldiers on July 30, 1864, in the battle of the Crater at Petersburg. Alexander matter-of-factly recounted the fury unleashed in Confederate ranks by the thought of facing African Americans in combat. "[T]here were, comparatively, very few Negro prisoners taken that day," he noted: "It was the first occasion on which any of the Army of Northern Virginia came in contact with Negro troops, & the general feeling of the men toward their employment was very bitter." The United States Colored Troops summoned memories of "sympathy of the North for John Brown's memory" and gave "proof of a desire that our slaves should rise in servile insurrection & massacre throughout the South." Such sentiment "made the fighting on this occasion exceedingly fierce & bitter on the part of our men," concluded Alexander, "not only toward the Negroes themselves, but sometimes even to the whites along with them. . . . Some of the Negro prisoners, who were originally allowed to surrender by some soldiers, were afterward shot by others, & there was, without doubt, a great deal of unnecessary killing of them."[28]

A final example of Alexander's relating darker scenes from battlefields comes near the end of his chapter on First Bull Run. As combat wound down on July 21, 1861, he witnessed a scene between Ellerbe B. C. Cash, colonel of the Eighth South Carolina Infantry, and Congressman Alfred Ely of New York, who had ventured out from Washington to see the fighting and been captured by some of Cash's men. The colonel was threatening Ely with a pistol, and Alexander, then on Beauregard's staff, asked, "What are you trying to shoot that man for?" "He's a member of Congress, God damn him," replied Cash, "Came out here to see us whipped & killed! God Damn him! If it was not for such as he there would be no war. They've made it & then come to gloat over it! God damn him. I'll show him." Alexander managed to calm Cash down, and Ely soon made his way to the rear under guard. But Cash, who evidently had heard that Senator Lafayette Sabine Foster of Connecticut was on the field, engaged in a final outburst, ordering a sergeant to "go & hunt the woods for Senator Foster. He is hiding here somewhere. Go & find him, & God damn you, if you bring him in alive I'll cut your ears off."[29]

Much as he proved willing to reveal war at its most unromantic, so also did Alexander approach Robert E. Lee and Stonewall Jackson with an unblinkingly dispassionate eye. Opportunities to see Lee up close over a long period allowed him to relate stories that revealed many facets of the army commander's public and private personality—including his sense of humor, occasional pettiness and stubbornness, strategic and tactical aggressiveness, and willingness to take breathtaking risks. Alexander knew, as his letters from Greytown suggest, how far his unsparing assessment of Lee removed him from the Lost Cause mainstream. Nowhere did he depart more strikingly from most ex-Confederates than in his handling of Gettysburg. A virtual cottage industry focused on absolving Lee of any responsibility for the defeat had taken root in the early 1870s and flourished thereafter, casting blame on Jeb Stuart, on Richard S. Ewell, and, most often and most stridently, on James Longstreet. Alexander would have none of it. He read the official reports, pondered what he had seen as a participant in the battle, and rigorously evaluated available options and crucial decisions.[30]

His summary findings in *Fighting for the Confederacy* laid significant responsibility for the battle's outcome on Lee's shoulders. Lee's official report suggested that he maintained the tactical offensive on the second day because circumstances, in part, forced him to do so. Alexander demurred: "I think it must be frankly admitted that there was no real difficulty, whatever, in our taking the defensive the next day; & in our so manouvring afterward as to have finally forced Meade to attack." He thought "it a reasonable estimate to say that 60 per cent of our chances for a great victory were lost by our continuing the aggressive." Success on July 1 had left Lee with "an utter disregard of all physical disadvantages" on a field where the Army of the Potomac held superior ground. "I am impressed," Alexander said in language scarcely calculated to win approbation south of the Potomac, "by the fact that the strength of the enemy's position seems to have cut no figure in the consideration [of] the question of the aggressive." He also criticized "the very great mistake made, in my judgment, in the selection of the point of attack" for the Pickett-Pettigrew assault on July 3, a second instance where Lee manifested "a lack of appreciation of the immense figure which the character of the ground may cut in the results of an aggressive fight."[31]

Stonewall Jackson came in for similarly unvarnished criticism from Alexander. "Old Jack" stood just behind Lee as a Confederate icon, a Christian hero martyred at Chancellorsville at the height of the two men's fabled collaboration. "If only Jackson had been at Gettysburg," speculated former Confederates who saw Longstreet, in their minds a turncoat Republican and ungenerous critic of Lee after the war, as a prime villain. In fact, Long-street always had been Lee's senior corps commander and enjoyed his su-perior's affection and trust—something Lost Cause authors and speakers almost always ignored. Moreover, Jackson's record included a number of fumbling tactical performances, though he excelled at semi-independent operational movement in the Shenandoah Valley in 1862 and during the campaign of Second Bull Run.[32]

In *Military Memoirs,* Alexander attested to Jackson's "increasing bril-liancy on the fields of Cedar Mountain, Second Manassas, Harper's Ferry, Sharpsburg, and Fredericksburg" but took him severely to task for "the disappointments felt during the Seven Days." He especially focused on June 29–30, a critical period when Lee sought to deliver a telling blow against George B. McClellan as the Army of the Potomac retreated toward the James River. "Lee's instructions to him were very brief and general," began Alexander, "in supreme confidence that the Jackson of the Valley would win even brighter laurels on the Chickahominy." Once Jackson had his instructions, "Lee then took himself off to the farthest flank, as if gen-erously to leave to Jackson the opportunity of the most brilliant victory of the war." Stonewall's ensuing failure was "not so much a military as a psychological phenomenon. He did not try and fail. He simply made no effort." More than four decades after the events, Alexander's disapproba-tion of Jackson showed clearly: "He spent the 29th in camp in disregard of Lee's instructions, and he spent the 30th in equal idleness at White Oak Swamp. His 25,000 infantry practically did not fire a shot in the two days." In *Fighting for the Confederacy,* Alexander chose even stronger language, highlighting the "incredible slackness, & delay & hanging back, which char-acterized Gen. Jackson's performance of his part of the work."[33]

Alexander also departed from Lost Cause orthodoxy in discussing U. S. Grant. For most former Confederate authors, the Union general-in-chief served as a minimally gifted foil for the noble Lee—a general whose vast superiority in men and materiel, rather than his own skill, explained even-tual U.S. triumph. In *Fighting for the Confederacy,* Alexander's handling of the Union movement from Cold Harbor to Petersburg during the second week of June 1864 underscores the degree to which he avoided many Lost Cause clichés. "Grant had devised a piece of strategy all his own," noted the admiring passage, "which seems to me the most brilliant stroke in all the Federal campaigns of the whole war. . . . Not only was this strategy brilliant in conception, for which all the credit, I believe, belongs to Gen. Grant, but the orders & the details of such a rapid movement of so mighty an army . . . make it also the most brilliant piece of logistics of the war." *Military Memoirs* toned down the praise but nonetheless applauded Grant's bold plan and "the performance of a feat in transportation which had never been equaled, and might well be considered impossible, without days of delay."[34]

The emphasis on Grant's application of overwhelming numbers supported the premise, almost universally held among ex-Confederates but shunned by Alexander, that Union victory was inevitable. This fixation on relative numerical strength allowed vanquished Rebels to assert no loss of honor in waging a hopeless military resistance in support of high constitutional principle. Indeed, Lost Cause memorials often boasted inscriptions with some variation of a standard declaration absolving Confederate politicians and soldiers of responsibility for defeat: "Fate Denied Them Victory But Gave Them a Glorious Immortality." If Fate conspired against the Confederates, how could they possibly have won?[35] Once again, Alexander would have none of it. "It is customary to say that 'Providence did not intend that we should win,'" he wrote somewhat sarcastically in *Fighting for the Confederacy,* "but I do not subscribe in the least to that doctrine. Providence did not care a row of pins about it. If it did it was a very unintelligent Providence not to bring the business to a close—the close it wanted—in less than four years of most terrible & bloody war."[36]

Whereas most former Confederates celebrated the Christian faith of Lee, Jackson, and others who detected God's hand in all events, Alexander thought such an attitude counterproductive. "I will say here that I think it was a serious incubus upon us," he continued in his discussion of Providence, "that during the whole war our president & many of our generals really & actually believed there *was* this mysterious Providence always hovering over the field & ready to interfere on one side or the other, & that prayers and piety might win its favor from day to day." For example, during the Seven Days, "our great & glorious Gen. Jackson for once seemed to put all of his reliance on Providence & very decidedly slackened his own exertions, with the result that Gen. Lee's victory was shorn of the capture of McClellan's entire army." Whether that kind of decisive result had been possible in late June 1862, whatever Jackson's behavior, certainly is open to debate. Alexander's opinion about what explained outcomes was not:

"[I]t was a weakness to imagine that victory could ever come in even the slightest degree from anything except our own exertions."[37]

Alexander did embrace the foundational Lost Cause argument about secession's origins and Confederate motivation. "We were going to fight for our 'liberty,'" he insisted in *Fighting for the Confederacy*: "That was the view the whole South took of it. It was not for slavery but the *sovereignty of the states,* which is practically the right to resume self government or to secede." Agitation about slavery, he allowed, did provoke discussion "of the right in Congress & in the press, but the South would never have united as it did in secession & in war had it not been generally denied at the North & particularly by the Republican party." *Military Memoirs* echoed this line of thinking, suggesting that readers would know "every former Confederate repudiates all accusations of treason or rebellion in the war, and even of fighting to preserve the institution of slavery." Only a struggle for self-government could have produced the "unanimity and the desperation of our resistance." The link between claiming the right of self-government and the desire to protect a slave-based society goes unexplored in both books.[38]

Unsurprisingly for someone whose family owned two plantations in Georgia, Alexander made no apology for the institution of slavery. Overall, he presented it as benign and slaves as generally well treated, which fit very comfortably within turn-of-the-century white southern interpretive conventions. "My father had two plantations," he explained, "one in Liberty Co., Geo. ('Hopewell'), a rice & Sea Island Cotton place, near Riceboro; & the home place in Washington. There were about forty to 50 Negroes—little & big on each place. They were all looked after by him & my mother as if they were children." *Fighting for the Confederacy* includes many mentions of a slave named Charley, "a 15 year old darkey" hired from his owner near Aldie, Virginia, as "an ostler & servant." "In all the 3 ½ years I had him," Alexander commented dryly, "I had to give him a little licking but twice." A second leased slave, "a most faithful old fellow named Abram, small and pure black from King William County, Va.," worked as a driver, and the pair remained with Alexander through many campaigns. *Military Memoirs* includes one passage that hints at Alexander's complete acceptance of slavery. "The effort of the enemy to destroy it without compensation," he observed, "was practical robbery, which, of course, we resisted."[39]

Two final quotations, both from *Fighting for the Confederacy,* will demonstrate how effectively Alexander could describe a moment while also imparting information about important themes. The first captures the emotional reunion between Lee and soldiers of Longstreet's corps in late April 1864. Recently returned to Virginia after many months in Tennessee, the veterans welcomed the chance to see their old commander. Alexander's passage, better than anything else in the literature, helps readers grasp the depth of connection between Lee and his men that yielded impressive results on many battlefields. Alexander's artillery batteries, on that spring day not far from Gordonsville, played a prominent role in the review:

> I can see now the large square gate posts, without gate or fence, marking where a broad country road lead [*sic*] out of a tall oak wood upon an open knoll, in front of the centre of our long grey lines. And as the well-remembered figure of Lee upon Traveller—at the head of his staff, rides between the posts, & comes out upon the knoll, my bugle sounds a signal, & my old battalion thunders out a salute, & the general reins up his horse, & bares his good gray head, & looks at us & we shout & cry & wave our battleflags & look at him again. For sudden as a wind, a wave of sentiment, such as can only come to large crowds in full sympathy, something alike what came a year later at Appomattox, seemed to sweep over the field. Each man seemed to feel the bond which held us all to Lee. There was no speaking, but the effect was that of a military sacrament, in which we pledged anew our lives. Dr. Boggs, a chaplain in [Micah] Jenkins's brigade, said to Col. [Charles S.] Venable, Lee['s] aid, "Does it not make the general proud to see how these men love him?" Venable answered, "Not proud, it awes him."[40]

Just short of a year later, the war in Virginia had entered its final phase. Lee had decided to abandon Petersburg and Richmond, and Alexander found himself on April 3, 1865, coordinating the withdrawal of some of the last Confederates to leave the capital. As first light broke, he crossed the James River on Mayo's Bridge while fires spread along the riverfront in the chaos surrounding the evacuation of the city. When his last battery had traversed the bridge, he stopped briefly to contemplate what he saw and what it meant. No other Confederate present that day left an account that conveys so well the impact of marching away from the city that had been the symbol of Confederate nationhood and the focus of military operations that had extracted a fearful toll on the Army of Northern Virginia:

It was after sunrise of a bright morning when from the Manchester high grounds we turned to take our last look at the old city for which we had fought so long and so hard. It was a sad, a terrible & a solemn sight. I don't know that any moment in the whole war impressed me more deeply with all its stern realities than this. The whole river front seemed to be in flames, amid which occasional heavy explosions were heard, & the black smoke spreading & hanging over the city seemed to be full of dreadful portents. I rode on with a distinctly heavy heart & with a peculiar sort of feeling of orphanage.[41]

In early March 1898, Alexander informed his daughter about progress on the memoirs. He had filled the second ledger book and switched to paper and pencil, which would allow much easier revision when he returned to the United States. "It encourages me so much," he assured Bessie, "to have you like it."[42] Untold others, who subsequently expressed appreciation for Alexander's writings, owed a debt to Bessie Alexander Ficklen for prodding her father into action. The conjunction of scholarship and narrative prowess in *Military Memoirs* and *Fighting for the Confederacy* ensures that additional readers will be both enlightened and entertained. They also will come away with a feeling of Alexander as a perceptive conversationalist, whose access to leading figures and presence at so many storied moments allows him to pull us back into another century better to understand the nation's transformative event.

NOTES

1. For the only full biography, see Maury Klein, *Edward Porter Alexander* (Athens: University of Georgia Press, 1971). Klein devotes approximately equal attention to Alexander's Confederate career and his pre- and post–Civil War years. See also Michael Golay, *To Gettysburg and Beyond: The Parallel Lives of Joshua Lawrence Chamberlain and Edward Porter Alexander* (New York: Crown, 1994), and Charles L. Dufour, *Nine Men in Gray* (Garden City, N.Y.: Doubleday, 1963), 299–339. Publication data for both memoirs and some details about my part in the publication of *Fighting for the Confederacy* appear below.

2. Edward Porter Alexander (hereafter EPA) to Mary Clifford Alexander Hull, November 11, 1860, in Marion Alexander Boggs, ed., *The Alexander Letters, 1787–1900* (1910; rpt., Athens: University of Georgia Press, 1980), 220. For information about all phases of Alexander's life, see Klein's *Edward Porter Alexander*. For dates and other details about Alexander's various ranks during his U.S. and Confederate military service, see Gary W. Gallagher, "Ed-

ward Porter Alexander," in William C. Davis, ed., *The Confederate General*, 6 vols. ([Harrisburg, Pa.]: National Historical Society, 1991), 1:11–12.

3. U.S. War Department, *The War of the Rebellion: The Official Records of the Union and Confederate Armies*, 128 vols. (Washington: GPO, 1880–1901), ser. 1, vol. 25, pt. 2:616; Jennings C. Wise, *The Long Arm of Lee, or, The History of the Artillery of the Army of Northern Virginia, With a Brief Account of the Confederate Bureau of Ordnance*, 2 vols. (1915; rpt., Richmond, Va.: Owens Publishing Co., 1988), 2:758.

4. Joseph E. Johnston, *Narrative of Military Operations, Directed, during the Late War between the States, by Joseph E. Johnston, General, C.S.A.* (New York: Appleton, 1874), 288; Edward Porter Alexander, *Fighting for the Confederacy: The Personal Recollections of General Edward Porter Alexander*, ed. Gary W. Gallagher (Chapel Hill: University of North Carolina Press, 1989), 336. Alexander observed that Johnston considered himself "badly used" by Davis in this episode.

5. EPA to Josiah Colston, April 22, 1865, copy provided by Robert E. L. Krick (the original resides in the Maryland Historical Society in a bound collection of notes and miscellany); *The Confederate Veteran: Address of Gen. E. Porter Alexander, on Alumni Day, West Point Centennial, June 9, 1902* (n.p., [1902]), 5 (quotation from *New York Times* printed opposite page 1); EPA note dated June [?] 1902, folder 53, Edward Porter Alexander Papers, Southern Historical Collection, Wilson Library, University of North Carolina, Chapel Hill (hereafter cited as Alexander Papers SHC). The front cover of this pamphlet states, "Twenty-five thousand copies have been printed for free distribution." On the topic of railroads, Alexander published *Railway Practice* (New York: G. P. Putnam's Sons, 1887) and *Reply to Questions of the Special Committee on Railroad Transportation of the New York Chamber of Commerce* (Louisville, Ky.: Bradley, Gilbert & Mallory, 1881).

6. EPA to Thomas Jewett Goree, April 24, 1868, in Thomas W. Cutrer, ed., *Longstreet's Aide: The Civil War Letters of Major Thomas J. Goree* (Charlottesville: University Press of Virginia, 1995), 156; Cadmus M. Wilcox to EPA, March 10, 1869, folder 25a, Alexander Papers SHC; David Macrae, *The Americans at Home* (1870; rpt., New York: E. P. Dutton, 1952), 264.

7. Robert Underwood Johnson, *Remembered Yesterdays* (Boston: Little, Brown, 1923), 197 (the second "lovable" and reliable man was Union artillery chief Henry J. Hunt). See J. William Jones and others, eds., *Southern Historical Society Papers*, 52 vols. (1876–1959; rpt., Wilmington, N.C.: Broadfoot, 1990–92), for EPA's "The 'Seven Days Battles'" (1:61–76); "Letter from General E. P. Alexander, late Chief of Artillery First Corps, A.N.V." (4:97–111); "Sketch of Longstreet's Division. Winter of 1861–62" (9:512–18); "Sketch of Longstreet's Division—Yorktown and Williamsburg" (10:32–45); "The Battle of Fredericksburg. Paper No. I" (10:382–92); "The Battle of Fredericksburg. Paper № 2—(Conclusion.)" (10:445–64); and "Confederate Artillery Service" (11:98–113). See also Robert Underwood Johnson and Clarence Clough Buel, eds., *Battles and Leaders of the Civil War*, 4 vols. (New York: Century, 1887), for EPA's "The Great Charge and Artillery Fighting at Gettysburg" and "Longstreet at Knoxville" (3:557–68, 745–51).

8. EPA to Louisa Alexander Gilmer, July 2, October 2, 1899, folder 4 titled "1898–1904," box 1, Minis Family Papers, SHC; EPA to Frederick M. Colston, April 26, June 13, 1899, folder 16, Campbell-Colston Papers, #135, SHC. Alexander later commented about the reaction to

James Longstreet's "awkward and apparently bitter criticisms of Gen Lee" in his memoirs, which were published in 1896. "Many an old soldier will *never forgive* Longstreet such a sentiment," he stated, "& yet I do not believe he ever knew how it reads to a lover of Lee" (EPA to Frederic Bancroft, October 20, 1907, copy supplied by Robert K. Krick from manuscript collections at Kennesaw Mountain National Battlefield Park).

9. EPA to Frederick M. Colston, August 8, 1899, Campbell-Colston Papers, #135, SHC; EPA to Louisa Alexander Gilmer, October 2, 1899, folder 4 titled "1898–1904," box 1, Minis Family Papers, SHC. On how he envisioned finishing the manuscript after returning from Greytown, see also EPA to Bettie Mason Alexander (his wife), February 13, 1898, folder 43, Alexander Papers SHC.

10. EPA to Frederick M. Colston, August 8, 1899, Campbell-Colston Papers, #135, SHC; EPA to Fitzhugh Lee, July 26, 1894, Fitzhugh Lee Papers in the possession of Fitzhugh Lee Opie (the general's grandson), who kindly granted permission to publish quotations from them when I was writing an introduction to a reprint of *General Lee* (Wilmington, N.C.: Broadfoot, 1989).

11. Volume 26 of the Alexander Papers SHC includes a list of eight potential titles: "Fighting for the Lost Cause," "Fighting for the Confederacy" (the one EPA finally chose), "Fighting under the Conquered Banner," "How the Cause Was Lost," "What Became of the Lost Cause," "Fighting under Lee & Longstreet," "Personal Recollections of the Civil War," and "Military Experiences in the Civil War." Interestingly, none of the eight includes "War between the States," the term most former Confederates preferred in discussing the conflict.

12. Two ledger books Bessie sent to her father, in which he wrote the first part of the Greytown manuscript, contain notes indicating he gave them to her many years after returning from Nicaragua. The first note reads: "Presented to Bessie A. Ficklen by E. P. Alexander when he wrote his last version—called by him 'Memoirs by a Confederate.'" The second note reads: "Presented to B. A. Ficklen by E. P. Alexander" (vols. 27 and 28, Alexander Papers SHC).

13. EPA to William Mason Alexander, September 26, 1900, folder 49, Alexander Papers SHC; EPA to "My Dear Hal," August 20, 1901, folder 50, Alexander Papers SHC.

14. EPA to Bessie Alexander Ficklen, June 13, 1898, folder 2, titled "1894–1898," John Rose Ficklen Papers, SHC; Klein, *Edward Porter Alexander,* 220–22. For the essay on Grant, see Alexander, "Grant's Conduct of the Wilderness Campaign," in *Annual Report of the American Historical Association for the Year 1908,* 2 vols. (Washington: GPO, 1908), 1:225–34.

15. EPA to James Longstreet, September 10, 29, 1902, copies of originals and typescripts made available by Daniel Weinberg, owner of the Abraham Lincoln Book Shop in Chicago, on May 11, 1991. For an example of Alexander's correspondence relating to Jackson during the Seven Days, see Wade Hampton to EPA, no date (received on March 14, 1901), folder 48, Alexander Papers SHC.

16. The book has been widely available since 1907. Scribner's, a prominent New York publisher, reprinted it in 1908, 1910, 1912, 1914, and 1918, and there was a British edition in 1908 titled *The American Civil War: A Critical Narrative* (London: Siegle, Hill, & Co.). Notable later reprints include those by Indiana University Press (Bloomington, 1962, as part of the Civil War Centennial series, introduction by T. Harry Williams); Morningside (Dayton, Ohio, 1977, introd. by Maury Klein); and Da Capo (New York, 1993, introd. by Gary W. Gallagher). A personal aside will be of interest to confirmed bibliophiles. I have owned many copies of

Military Memoirs of a Confederate—including the only first edition in a dust jacket I have seen or heard about; even the incredible John Page Nicholson Collection at the Henry E. Huntington Library, which contains innumerable rarities, does not have a copy with a jacket.

17. Scribner's description and excerpts from the review in *Army and Navy Journal* qtd. in an advertisement for *Military Memoirs* in *Confederate Veteran* 15 (June 1907): third page of advertisements inside the front cover; *American Historical Review* 13 (October 1907): 166; Klein, *Edward Porter Alexander*, 226–27; Theodore Roosevelt to EPA, July 16, 1907, folder 67, Alexander Papers SHC. Carman was a Union veteran who, as the historical "expert" on the Antietam Battlefield Board in the 1890s, gathered an immense body of testimony about the 1862 Maryland campaign.

18. *Confederate Veteran* 23 (June 1915): 252; Douglas Southall Freeman, *The South to Posterity: An Introduction to the Writing of Confederate History* (1939; rpt., Baton Rouge: Louisiana State University Press, 1998), 177–78.

19. Douglas Southall Freeman, *R. E. Lee: A Biography*, 4 vols. (New York: Charles Scribner's Sons, 1934–35), 4:566; Richard Barksdale Harwell, *In Tall Cotton: The 200 Most Important Confederate Books for the Reader, Researcher and Collector* (Austin, Tex.: Jenkins Publishing Co., 1978), 1; T. Harry Williams, introduction to Indiana University Press reprint of *Military Memoirs*, xxxv; Maury Klein, introduction to Morningside reprint of *Military Memoirs*, 1.

20. T. Harry Williams, introd., Indiana University Press rpt. of *Military Memoirs*, xxxiv; Freeman, *South to Posterity*, 178; James I. Robertson Jr., "The War in Words," *Civil War Times Illustrated* 14 (October 1975): 44.

21. Quotations in this paragraph are from the printed description for the Edward Porter Alexander Papers, Collection #7, prepared by Dr. Carolyn Wallace and dated January 13, 1960.

22. Klein, introduction to Morningside reprint of *Military Memoirs*, 8–9.

23. EPA to "Well dem dear little daughters," February 6, 1899, folder 45, Alexander Papers SHC. For additional details about the identification and editing of the Greytown reminiscences, which took four years, see my introduction and editor's note in *Fighting for the Confederacy*, xiii–xxviii.

24. *New Republic*, February 18, 1991, 65; Geoffrey C. Ward, "The Life and Times," *American Heritage* 41 (March 1990): 14.

25. *Virginia Magazine of History and Biography* 98 (April 1990): 319 (Cooper's review); *Richmond News Leader*, September 13, 1989, 17 (Robertson's review); *Georgia Historical Quarterly* 74 (Summer 1990): 327 (Donald E. Reynolds's review); David J. Eicher, *The Civil War in Books: An Analytical Bibliography* (Urbana: University of Illinois Press, 1997), 63.

26. Alexander, *Military Memoirs of a Confederate*, 291 (all citations are to the Da Capo edition).

27. Alexander, *Fighting for the Confederacy*, 210. Alexander included none of this in *Military Memoirs*. The poetical lines are the last two of the final quatrain of Part II of Southey's "The King of the Crocodiles." EPA probably read the poem in *The Poetical Works of Robert Southey* (New York: D. Appleton and Co., 1839), 457. For an example of the literature on the dark war, see Michael C. C. Adams, *Living Hell: The Dark Side of the Civil War* (Baltimore: Johns Hopkins University Press, 2014).

28. Alexander, *Fighting for the Confederacy*, 462. Alexander deleted all mention of this episode from *Military Memoirs*.

29. Alexander, *Fighting for the Confederacy*, 55. The profane Ellerbe B. C. Cash makes no appearance in *Military Memoirs*, in which Alexander reduced this story to a single sentence: "A mile beyond the Stone Bridge a member of Congress, Mr. Ely of N.Y., was brought out of the woods a prisoner, as I passed, and turned over to the guard" (*Military Memoirs*, 45).

30. For examples of influential writings that treated Lee as an almost perfect commander, see Jubal A. Early, *The Campaigns of Gen. Robert E. Lee: An Address by Lieut. General Jubal A. Early, before Washington and Lee University, January 19th, 1872* (Baltimore: John Murphy, 1872), and John B. Gordon, *Reminiscences of the Civil War* (New York: Charles Scribner's Sons, 1903).

31. Alexander, *Fighting for the Confederacy*, 377–78.

32. For examples of speculation about what Jackson would have done at Gettysburg, see Henry Kyd Douglas, *I Rode with Stonewall* (Chapel Hill: University of North Carolina Press, 1940), 246–47, and Gordon, *Reminiscences*, 154. On Jackson's reputation, see chapter 5 of Gary W. Gallagher, *Lee and His Generals in War and Memory* (Baton Rouge: Louisiana State University Press, 1998).

33. Alexander, *Military Memoirs*, 143–44; Alexander, *Fighting for the Confederacy*, 96.

34. Alexander, *Fighting for the Confederacy*, 419; Alexander, *Military Memoirs*, 547. For the most detailed argument regarding Grant's superior numbers as a major factor, see Walter H. Taylor (a member of Lee's staff), *Four Years with General Lee: Being a Summary of the More Important Events Touching on the Career of General Robert E. Lee, in the War between the States; Together with an Authoritative Statement of the Strength of the Army which he Commanded in the Field* (New York: D. Appleton, 1877).

35. Two examples of this inscription are on Confederate monuments in Hollywood Cemetery in Richmond, situated a few yards from George E. Pickett's grave, and near the main entrance to the University of Virginia's cemetery in Charlottesville.

36. Alexander, *Fighting for the Confederacy*, 58–59.

37. Ibid., 59.

38. Ibid., 25; Alexander, *Military Memoirs*, vii–viii.

39. Alexander, *Fighting for the Confederacy*, 5–6 (EPA listed many of the slaves he remembered from his boyhood, together with their duties on the plantations), 76–77, 127, 229; Alexander, *Military Memoirs*, viii.

40. Alexander, *Fighting for the Confederacy*, 346.

41. Ibid., 519.

42. EPA to Bessie Alexander Ficklen, March 2, 1898, folder 43, Alexander Papers SHC.

CONTRIBUTORS

KEITH S. BOHANNON is professor of history at the University of West Georgia.

STEPHEN CUSHMAN is Robert C. Taylor Professor of English at the University of Virginia.

WILLIAM C. DAVIS is professor of history emeritus at Virginia Tech.

GARY W. GALLAGHER is John L. Nau III Professor of History Emeritus at the University of Virginia.

J. MATTHEW GALLMAN is professor of history at the University of Florida.

SARAH E. GARDNER is professor of history and director of southern studies at Mercer University.

KATHRYN SHIVELY is associate professor of history at Virginia Commonwealth University.

BRENDA E. STEVENSON holds the Nickoll Family Endowed Chair in History at the University of California, Los Angeles.

ELIZABETH R. VARON is Langbourne M. Williams Professor of History at the University of Virginia.

INDEX

Aaron, Daniel, 4, 211–12

Abolition, 9, 21, 28, 35, 123, 129, 171, 210; radical, 173–76, 181, 191; women in movement, 178–81; and the Civil War, 182–83

African Americans, 20, 22, 23, 24–26, 29, 171, 184, 274; military service of, 13; and literary culture, 14; and historical writing, 14; postbellum political involvement of, 15–16; and postwar institutions, 16; and voting, 16–18, 36; racial passing among, 25; and theories of black inferiority, 25; disfranchisement, 36; activist networks among, 172; and fight for equality, 176, 180–81. *See also* Contrabands (black refugees)

Alcott, Louisa May, 7–8, 109–35; *Little Women,* 8, 109–35; *Hospital Sketches,* 8, 116, 123–25; experience as a nurse, 110, 118–19, 123; *Little Men,* 111; *Jo's Boys,* 111; as historian, 112; employs military language, 115; as children's author, 120, 125–26; does not discuss emancipation, 129; film adaptations, 131–35

Alemán, Jesse, 69–71

Alexander, Edward Porter, 6, 10, 85, 235, 238, 259–80; *Military Memoirs of a Confederate,* 6, 10, 259, 266–70, 272; *Personal Recollections,* 6, 10–11, 259, 270–71, 273, 276–78; and absence of Lost Cause sentiment, 259–60, 265–66; campaigns taken part in, 261; contemplates writing memoir, 263–64; writes for his children, 264; writes in Greytown, Nicaragua, 264–68; loses wife and daughter, 266; leaves personal stories out of *Memoirs,* 266; evaluates Lee, 267–69; manuscript differences, 268, 272; reviewed, 269–72; opinion of USCT soldiers, 274; evaluates Longstreet at Gettysburg, 275; evaluates Stonewall Jackson, 276–77; plantations of, 278; states' rights views, 278; accession of papers, 282n11

Alexander, Peter W., 251

Allen, Hervey, 206

American Anti-Slavery Society, 173–74, 178, 196n5

American Equal Rights Association, 175

American Historical Association, 3, 267

American Moral Reform Society, 174

American Publishing Company, 13–14,

American Revolution, black military service in, 21

American Studies Association, 3

Antebellum education, 46

Antietam, battle of, 145–46, 148, 223, 231–32, 261, 276

Appleton, W. W., 205

Appomattox Court House, Va., 143, 259; Lee surrenders to Grant at, 16, 81–85, 89–90, 93, 95–97, 101, 103, 110, 262; dominates memory of surrenders, 89